CONSTRUCTING THE AMERICAN PAST

A SOURCE BOOK OF A PEOPLE'S HISTORY

VOLUME I

Fourth Edition

ELLIOTT J. GORN
Purdue University

RANDY ROBERTS
Purdue University

TERRY D. BILHARTZ
Sam Houston State University

Longman

New York   San Francisco   Boston
London   Toronto   Sydney   Tokyo   Singapore   Madrid
Mexico City   Munich   Paris   Cape Town   Hong Kong   Montreal

Vice President and Publisher: Priscilla McGeehon
Executive Marketing Manager: Sue Westmoreland
Supplements Editor: Kelly Villella
Media Supplements Editor: Pat McCarthy
Production Manager: Joseph Vella
Project Coordination, Text Design, and Electronic Page Makeup: Shepherd, Inc.
Photo Research: Photosearch, Inc.
Cover Designer/Manager: Wendy Fredericks
Cover Illustration: *The Skating Pond, 1862*, Charles Parsons. © Museum of the City of New
    York, USA/Bridgeman Art Library.
Senior Manufacturing Buyer: Dennis J. Para
Printer and Binder: The Maple-Vail Book Manufacturing Group
Cover Printer: John P. Pow

For permission to use copyrighted material, grateful acknowledgment is made to the copyright holders on pp. 273–277, which are hereby made part of this copyright page.

Library of Congress Cataloging-in-Publication Data

Constructing the American past: a source book of a people's history/[edited by] Elliott
J. Gorn, Randy Roberts, Terry D. Bilhartz.—4th ed.
    p. cm.
  Includes bibliographical references and index.
  ISBN 0-321-09342-9 (v. 1)—ISBN 0-321-09340-2 (v. 2)
  1. United States—History—Sources. I. Gorn, Elliott J., 1951- II. Roberts, Randy, 1951-
III. Bilhartz, Terry D.

E173.C69 2001
973—dc21   2001038425

Please visit our website at http://www.ablongman.com

ISBN 0-321-09342-9

  2 3 4 5 6 7 8 9 10—MA—04 03 02

For our children
Jade Rachel Yee-Gorn
Alison Mackenzie Roberts
Kelly Rankin Roberts
Teri Noel Bilhartz
Rocky Bilhartz and Lindsey Lee Barton

Contents

Preface

Every historian knows the feeling. You're working in an archive, sleepy and bored, when something jumps out at you. Maybe a letter written by someone who has been dead a hundred years boldly states an idea that was just a glimmer in your mind; or a diary turns up and unexpectedly takes you into the inner life of someone who seemed so unknowable; or an eyewitness account of clashing armies makes you see and hear and smell the battlefield. Doing history can be as exciting as any act of discovery and exploration.

We developed this anthology to communicate some of that excitement to students. All three of us take pride in our work as teachers and writers of history. Sometimes, however, those two sides of the historian's job seem terribly distant from each other. Bridging that gap is our task here. We have tried to put some of our best teaching between these covers. We hope students will learn the challenges, the rigors, and the joys of hands-on history. Our goal is to present students with exciting documents on a series of topics that will help them learn to think critically.

Each chapter centers on a particular problem in American history. The introductions, documents, and study questions direct students to participate in the past. What was it like, for example, to be at a religious revival at the beginning of the nineteenth century? Who attended them and why? Our chapter on camp meetings offers eyewitness accounts. To give another example, what really happened at Wounded Knee, South Dakota, in 1890? Students read descriptions of the clash between the Sioux and the U.S. cavalry from a variety of vantage points: the voices of the Sioux, the letters of military officers, and the statements of government officials.

The fourth edition of *Constructing the American Past* contains major changes, including cuts and revisions in most chapters, as well as new chapters on the Constitution of 1787, the Cold War, and the Vietnam War, and an epilogue on the Election of 2000. The changes in this edition were specifically designed to sharpen the work, to improve its classroom usefulness, and to incorporate a still wider range of American experiences across ethnic, class, and gender lines. Almost every chapter in this fourth edition includes both male and female voices, as well as voices from diverse social and ethnic populations.

As we compiled these volumes, we also compiled numerous debts. We want to thank the library staffs at Purdue, Miami, Stanford, and Sam Houston State Universities; at the Museum of the City of New York; the Western College Archives; the archives of the Southern Regional Council, Atlanta; the Library of Congress; the New York Public Library; the Newberry Library; the American Antiquarian Society; the Huntington Library; and the Wisconsin Center for Film and Theater Research.

Many colleagues and graduate students have made suggestions and corrected us when we went astray. We especially acknowledge the assistance of Arthur Casciato, Allan Winkler, Jack Kirby, Mary Frederickson, James Hamill, Lynn Depew, Linnea Dietrich, Joshua Brown, Margo Horn, Timothy Gilfoyle, Paul Hutton, Howard Shorr, Gary Bell, Greg Cantrell, James Olson, Roseanne Barker, Ken Hendrickson, Caroline Crimm, Ty Cashion, Joseph Rowe, and Robert Shadle.

Terry Bilhartz still remembers with appreciation the following teachers and colleagues in a 1987 National Endowment for the Humanities Summer Institute on Classic Texts in Early American History who gave inspiration for the first edition of this work: Richard D. Brown, Karen O. Kupperman, Harry S. Stout, John P. Demos, Robert A. Gross, Stephen Nissenbaum, R. Kent Newmyer, Philip Boucher, Alan V. Briceland, Jerald Combs, Donald R. Hickey, Richard L. Hillard, Graham Hodges, John Ifovic, Thomas W. Jodziewicz, Lawrence Kazura, Patricia O'Malley, Jacqueline Peterson, Bruce Stuart, William Swagerty, Alan S. Thompson, Louis P. Towles, Kerry A. Trask, James A. Trask, and Daniel E. Williams.

Several outside readers have strengthened our work. We acknowledge with gratitude the comments we received from James R. Sweeney, Old Dominion University; Brian Dirck, Anderson University; Margaret A. Lowe, Bridgewater State College; Michael Krenn, University of Miami; Lisa Tolbert, The University at North Carolina at Greensboro; Vernon Burton, University of Illinois at Urbana-Champaign; and Juliana Barr, Rutgers University.

Many of the events and documents in this collection were first used in our own classrooms. We thank all of our students over the years who have helped teach us about teaching. We dedicate this work to our children, our representatives in the next generation, who will construct their own pasts in order to understand themselves and their future. To this illustrious list, which includes Jade Rachel Yee-Gorn, Alison MacKenzie Roberts, Kelly Rankin Roberts, Rocky Bilhartz, and Teri Noel Bilhartz, we add for this fourth edition the name of Rocky's adorable fiancée, Lindsey Lee Barton.

Introduction
Doing History

PREREQUISITES—CURIOSITY AND IMAGINATION

What was it like back then? What did people think and believe? What motivated them to laugh and cry, fight and die? How did people live? Were their homes comfortable? Were their workdays long? Were their diets sufficient? These questions—and hundreds more—surface instantly when historians and students ponder the past. Indeed, the question "What was it like back then?" is fundamental to any person with a sense of curiosity. It also lies at the core of the historical profession. Using a wide range of sources, historians try to "construct" what life was like in the past.

The process of construction is challenging. Since the sources needed to answer any important historical question are frequently incomplete, contradictory, or evasive, the writing of history can never be as precise as we would like. Imagine putting together a picture puzzle that is supposed to contain 1000 pieces, but half of the pieces have been lost. Still, with much effort and imagination, you might be able to reconstruct the general outlines of the picture. The process is roughly akin to historical inquiry. Hard work, analytical ability, and imagination—these come into play in both ventures.

IN SEARCH OF EVIDENCE

While sources are often fragmentary, the kinds of documents historians may use exist in abundance. Let us take, for example, the following Christmas staple, which was written in 1822 by Clement Clarke Moore, a professor of divinity in a New York City Episcopal seminary:

> 'Twas the night before Christmas, when all through the house,
> Not a creature was stirring, not even a mouse.
> The stockings were hung by the chimney with care,
> In hopes that Saint Nicholas soon would be there.
> The children were nestled all snug in their beds,
> While visions of sugarplums danced on their heads;
> And Mama in her kerchief, and I in my cap,
> Had just settled our brains for a long winter's nap,

When out on the lawn there arose such a clatter,
I sprang from my bed to see what was the matter.
Away to the window I flew like a flash,
Tore open the shutters and threw up the sash.
The moon on the breast of the new-fallen snow
Gave a luster of midday to the objects below;
When what to my wondering eyes should appear
But a miniature sleigh and eight tiny reindeer,
With a little old driver, so lively and quick,
I knew in a moment it must be Saint Nick!
More rapid than eagles his coursers they came,
And he whistled and shouted and called them by name:
"Now, Dasher! now, Dancer! now, Prancer and Vixen!
On, Comet! on, Cupid! on, Donner and Blitzen!
To the top of the porch! to the top of the wall!
Now dash away! dash away! dash away, all."
As the dry leaves that before the wild hurricane fly,
When they meet with an obstacle, mount up to the sky,
So up to the housetop, the coursers they flew,
With a sleigh full of toys—and Saint Nicholas too.
And then, in a twinkling, I heard on the roof
The prancing and pawing of each little hoof.
As I drew in my head and was turning around,
Down the chimney Saint Nicholas came with a bound.
He was dressed all in fur, from his head to his foot,
And his clothes were all tarnished with ashes and soot;
A bundle of toys he had flung on his back,
And he looked like a peddler just opening his pack.
His eyes, how they twinkled! his dimples, how merry!
His cheeks were like roses, his nose like a cherry!
His droll little mouth was drawn up like a bow,
And the beard on his chin was as white as the snow.
The stump of a pipe he held tight in his teeth,
And the smoke, it encircled his head like a wreath.
He had a broad face and a little round belly
That shook, when he laughed, like a bowl full of jelly.
He was chubby and plump, a right jolly old elf,
And I laughed when I saw him, in spite of myself.
A wink of his eye and a twist of his head
Soon gave me to know I had nothing to dread.
He spoke not a word, but went straight to his work,
And filled all the stockings, then turned with a jerk,
And laying a finger aside of his nose,
And giving a nod, up the chimney he rose.
He sprang to his sleigh, to his team gave a whistle,
And away they all flew like the down of a thistle.
But I heard him exclaim, ere he drove out of sight,
"Happy Christmas to all, and to all a good night!"

For the historian interested in reconstructing the past, Moore's "'Twas the Night Before Christmas" (published in 1823 under the title "A Visit from Saint Nicholas") is a wonderful source. To be sure, it cannot be used to verify the existence of Saint Nicholas. But it does contain plenty of information about American life in the early nineteenth century. Let us ask one question of the poem. What was it like at night in an early-nineteenth-century home? Moore clearly tells us that it was cold. People wore kerchiefs and caps to bed; shutters and sashed windows obviously did little to diminish the bitter cold. But why was it so cold indoors? The poem mentions chimneys several times, and anyone who has stood or sat beside a hearth on a winter's night knows the amount of heat a fireplace can generate. Why then was it necessary for a person to dress for bed as if he or she were preparing for an Arctic expedition? But wait! Moore informs us that the fireplaces were unused at night. Or at least he indirectly informs us. Saint Nicholas comes down the chimney in the beginning of the poem and goes back up it in the end. As a result, he is covered with ashes and soot, but he is not on fire, as he surely would be if he entered and left a house via a blazing fireplace. So why was the fireplace unlighted? Was it because the family lacked the funds for fuel? This is not implied in the poem. In fact, the described household had a lawn, windows, shutters, multiple beds for the children, and a porch—features suggesting, at the very least, a comfortable middle-class dwelling. Did these Americans like to sleep in stone cold houses? Did they enjoy awakening to the sight of their own breath and shivering as they prepared to meet a new day? Of course not. But apparently they enjoyed even less the prospect of their homes burning down as they slept. And the simple fact of the matter was that fires were a constant problem in nineteenth-century houses, and that malfunctioning fireplaces were the primary causes of fires.

Other nuggets of historical information also lie buried in this well-known children's poem. For instance, the verses hint that it was customary for some early American families to hang stockings and give gifts to children at Christmas and that celebrating the religious holiday in this manner was not offensive to the divinity professor who wrote the tale. Moreover, the author's description of the hero Saint Nicholas suggests that at least this Episcopalian saw nothing objectionable in wearing fur clothing or smoking a pipe—characteristics that, in other times and places, have carried negative connotations. Note also that Moore uses not the name Santa Claus, but the Anglicized version, Saint Nicholas, a reminder that in 1822, Americans remained predominantly English in origin. And the author compares Saint Nick to a peddler, a traveling salesperson or trader, with his pack of goods; before the twentieth century, peddlers were ubiquitous in American towns. Although Moore obviously wrote the poem to entertain rather than to inform, he unwittingly provided us with a glimpse of life in the early nineteenth century. His words testify to the houses, rituals, and values of many Americans.

Like most historical sources, however, this document is more suggestive than authoritative. It offers us many clues, but few definitive answers. How representative was the kind of dwelling place described by Moore? Surely not all Americans lived in houses with lawns, windows, shutters, porches, and chimneys. For what regions, social classes, and ethnic groupings is Moore's commentary valid? How many and what types of Americans observed the religious holiday in the way Moore depicted? Were the values Moore embraced shared by those in other social and religious circles? Answers to these questions cannot be found within the poem. Further investigation into other documents of the era will be necessary before the historian can speak with confidence about such details of early-nineteenth-century American life.

Nonetheless, Moore's popular children's fantasy illustrates how readers with a quick eye and an imaginative mind can extract historical understanding from materials originally written for largely different purposes. The activity also suggests how information gained from one source often leads historians to ask additional questions and to search for clues from other sources. Reconstructing the past—trying to make history knowable, to give it shape and meaning—is rarely a simple process that leads to indisputable and easy conclusions. But by raising questions, interrogating sources, revising hypotheses, and returning to the primary sources for additional data, historians slowly move closer to the goal of satisfying their curiosity about what life was like back then and why things happened as they did.

THE PROBLEM OF CONFLICTING EVIDENCE

But it is not always lack of evidence about the past that obstructs our understanding of it. Sometimes we have ample information about an event, but the historic witnesses offer conflicting testimonies. One classic example of the problem of conflicting evidence involves the circumstances surrounding a duel between two notable American politicians, Aaron Burr and Alexander Hamilton. While certain facts regarding this famous duel are well established, historians disagree on one important detail: Did Hamilton try to kill Burr and fail, or did he intentionally fire his shot in the air, thereby leaving his fate solely in Burr's hands?

How is one to arrive at a verdict on this question? Before offering an opinion on the matter, the serious student must first study all the available evidence at hand. This study involves learning as much as possible about the character and background of the principal combatants, the circumstances that led up to the duel, and the testimonies of the eye-witnesses who observed the event. After amassing the "facts" and carefully weighing the evidence, the historian renders a verdict. How one decides the case depends ultimately on how one determines which witnesses came closest to getting the story right.

Try your hand at "doing history" rather than simply "reading" it. Consider the introductory essay and documents presented below, and attempt to solve the mystery. Be imaginative. Read the sources carefully, and interrogate the witnesses. You be the judge. Did Hamilton attempt to kill Burr, or did he throw his shot away? What evidence supports your decision?

SETTLING DISPUTES THE HONORABLE WAY
The Setting

Shortly after dawn on Monday, July 11, 1804, Burr, Hamilton, and a few friends gathered outside Weehawken, New Jersey, to settle a personal dispute the "gentlemanly way"—with pistols at ten paces. Although dueling was illegal in most states, including New Jersey, early-nineteenth-century "gentlemen" commonly resorted to this custom to vindicate their sacred honor. After all, for those reared according to the *code duello*, defending one's name often took priority over obeying the law, preserving one's life, and protecting one's fortune. Consequently, although both of the combatants at Weehawken were healthy and prosperous grandfathers who had achieved in their forty-eight or forty-nine years considerable fame as attorneys and statesmen, their willingness to participate in an illegal duel would not have been regarded by many of their peers as deviant behavior. This particular duel, however, was highly irregular because at that time Burr was vice president of the United States and Hamilton was the distinguished leader of the opposition party.

The Personalities

An overview of the lives of the two combatants reveals that the duel itself was the climax of a long-standing personal rivalry that had been brewing for three decades. In some ways, Burr and Hamilton were much alike: ambitious, talented, and driven. In other ways, their backgrounds were very different.

Aaron Burr, a grandson of the brilliant American theologian Jonathan Edwards, lost both of his parents at an early age and became a ward of his uncle. Despite the tragic circumstances of his childhood, Burr received an excellent education at the College of New Jersey (now Princeton University). During the Revolutionary War, he served as a gentleman volunteer but never received the recognition he felt he deserved. When ill health forced his retirement in 1779, Burr left the army as a physically exhausted and embittered lieutenant colonel. Finding comfort in a friendship with a married female nurse ten years his senior, Burr gradually regained his health. Burr, however, never lost his resentment toward General George Washington, the man he blamed most for frustrating his military aspirations. In 1782, after securing a New York law license, Burr married his friend and nurse, Theodosia Prevost, now a widow and the mother of five children. As a devoted husband and father, Burr took a strong interest in directing the studies of his five stepchildren and later became passionately attached to his own daughter, also named Theodosia, who was born in 1783.

Unlike Burr, Alexander Hamilton had not enjoyed the benefits of a privileged birth. An illegitimate child born in the West Indies, Hamilton received a rudimentary education from his mother and, at age twelve, went to work as a clerk in a general store. Intensely ambitious for a college education, Hamilton was rescued from his lowly position by the generosity of affluent friends who recognized his intellect and drive. In 1773, he sailed to the middle colonies, secured some preliminary training in a grammar school, and entered King's College (now Columbia University). When hostilities with England began, Hamilton formed an artillery company and so distinguished himself in battle around New York City that he was invited to join George Washington's staff. For four years Hamilton worked closely with Washington as his secretary and confidential aide. Hamilton emerged from the war as a decorated soldier and a personal friend of General Washington. In 1780, Hamilton permanently secured his position in society when he married Elizabeth Schuyler, the daughter of the wealthy and influential General Philip Schuyler of New York. Early in 1782, Elizabeth gave birth to Philip, the first of the Hamilton's eight children.

The Rivalry

The 1780s were prosperous times for both Burr (the colonial aristocrat who had married down) and Hamilton (the self-made immigrant who had married up). Both men were highly esteemed attorneys, considered by many the most able lawyers in New York State. When they faced each other in court, Burr, the more eloquent courtroom speaker, generally won the upper hand. In business and politics, how-ever, Hamilton rose more rapidly. The attorney for many of New York's wealthy merchants, Hamilton drew up the charter for the Bank of New York and became one of its directors. He was also elected as a delegate to represent New York at the Continental Congress (1782–1783), the Annapolis Convention (1786), and the Philadelphia Constitutional Convention (1787). In 1789, President Washington appointed Hamilton as the nation's first secretary of the treasury, a position he held until 1795, when he returned to his more lucrative private law practice. Although Hamilton never again held public office, he remained until his death a preeminent leader of the Federalist party.

Hamilton's role as architect of the Federalist party made him a natural political enemy of the independently minded Burr. Although somewhat of a latecomer to pol-itics, Burr rapidly gained ascendancy within Republican party ranks, serving as New York's attorney general (1789–1791), U.S. senator (1791–1797), and state assemblyman (in 1797, 1798, and 1800). On several occasions, Hamilton cam-paigned against his rival New Yorker, opposing Burr's candidacy for the vice pres-idency in 1792, his reelection to the U.S. Senate in 1796, and his candidacy for the presidency in 1800. In fact, Thomas Jefferson's election to the presidency was largely a consequence of Hamilton's decision to support Jefferson over Burr. Four years later, when Vice President Burr sought the governorship of New York, Hamilton again successfully foiled his ambition. Not long after this defeat, Burr challenged Hamilton, a challenge that led to the fight at Weehawken.

DOCUMENTS: SELECTED EVIDENCE ON THE BURR-HAMILTON DUEL

In June 1804, Burr received word that Hamilton had made some derogatory remarks about his character. The alleged remarks about Burr were contained in a published letter by Dr. Charles Cooper, who had reportedly heard Hamilton's com-ments at a dinner party at his father-in-law's house in Albany. On reading Cooper's account of Hamilton's conversation, Burr sent Hamilton a letter demanding an explanation. Hamilton responded in writing to Burr, but Burr found his answer to be unsatisfactory. Printed below are Burr's initial letter to Hamilton; excerpts from Cooper's published letter, which discussed Hamilton's opinion of Burr; and extracts from the subsequent Hamilton-Burr correspondence.

[Aaron Burr to Alexander Hamilton.]

N York 18 June 1804

Sir

I send for your perusal a letter signed Ch. D. Cooper which, though apparently published some time ago, has but very recently come to my knowledge. Mr Van Ness, who does me the favor to deliver this, will point out to you that clause of the letter to which I particularly request your attention.

You must perceive, Sir, the Necessity of a prompt and unqualified acknowledgment or denial of the use of any expressions which could warrant the assertions of Dr. Cooper.

I have the honor to be
Your Obdt s[t]
A. Burr

[Burr enclosed a copy of Cooper's letter, which had been written to Philip Schuyler, Hamilton's father-in-law, on April 23, 1804. The offending passage read as follows.]

> I assert, that Gen. Hamilton and Judge Kent have declared, in substance, that they looked upon Mr. Burr to be a dangerous man, and one who ought not to be trusted with the reins of government. If, Sir, you attended a meeting of federalists, at the city tavern, where Gen. Hamilton made a speech on the pending election, I might appeal to you for the truth of so much of this assertion as relates to him. . . . For really sir, I could detail you a still more despicable opinion which General Hamilton has expressed of Mr. Burr.

[For the next few days, letters between Burr and Hamilton went back and forth. The following one is from Alexander Hamilton to Aaron Burr.]

New York June 20, 1804

Sir

I have maturely reflected on the subject of your letter of the 18th instant; and the more I have reflected the more I have become convinced, that I could not, without manifest impropriety, make the avowal or disavowal which you seem to think necessary.

The clause pointed out by Mr Van Ness is in these terms, "I could detail to you a *still more despicable opinion*, which General Hamilton has expressed of Mr Burr." To endeavour to discover the meaning of this declaration, I was obliged to seek in the antecedent part of the letter for the opinion to which it referred, as having been already disclosed. I found it in these words "General Hamilton and Judge Kent have declared, *in substance*, that they looked upon Mr Burr to be a *dangerous man*, and one *who ought not to be trusted with the reins of Government.*" The language of Doctor Cooper plainly implies, that he considered this opinion of you, which he attributes to me, as a *despicable* one; but he affirms that I have expressed some other *still more despicable*; without however mentioning to whom, when, or where. 'Tis evident, that the phrase "still more despicable" admits of infinite shades, from very light to very dark. How am I to judge of the degree intended? Or how shall I annex any precise idea to language so indefinite? . . .

I stand ready to avow or disavow promptly and explicitly any precise or definite opinion, which I may be charged with having declared of any Gentleman. More than this cannot fitly be expected from me; and especially it cannot reasonably be expected, that I shall enter into an explanation upon a basis so vague as that which you have adopted. I trust, on more reflection, you will see the matter in the same light with me. If not, *I* can only regret the circumstance, and must abide the consequences.

The publication of Doctor Cooper was never seen by me till after the receipt of your letter.

I have the honor to be
Sir
Your obed. servt
A. Hamilton

[Aaron Burr to Alexander Hamilton.]

N York 21 June 1804

Sir

Your letter of the 20th inst. has been this day received. Having Considered it attentively I regret to find in it nothing of that sincerity and delicacy which you profess to Value.

Political opposition can never absolve Gentlemen from the Necessity of a rigid adherence to the laws of honor and the rules of decorum. I neither claim such priviledge nor indulge it in others.

The Common sense of Mankind affixes to the epithet adopted by Dr Cooper the idea of dishonor: it has been publicly applied to me under the sanction of your Name. The question is not whether he has understood the Meaning of the word or has used it according to syntax and with grammatical accuracy, but whether you have authorised their application either directly or by uttering expressions or opinions derogatory to my honor. The time "when" is in your own knowledge, but no way material to me, as the Calumny has now first been disclosed so as to become the subject of my Notice, and as the effect is present and palpable.

Your letter has furnished me with new reasons for requiring a definite reply.

I have the honor to be
Sir
Your Obd^t St
A. Burr

[Aaron Burr to Alexander Hamilton.]

N York June 22^d 1804

Sir

M^r V Ness has this evening reported to me verbally that you refuse to answer my last letter, that you consider the course I have taken as intemperate and unnecessary and some other conversation which it is improper that I should notice.

My request to you was in the first instance prepared in a form the most simple in order that you might give to the affair that course to which you might be induced by your temper and your knowledge of facts. I relied with unsuspecting faith that from the frankness of a soldier and the Candor of a gentleman I might expect an ingenuous declaration; that if, as I had reason to believe, you had used expressions derogatory to my honor, you would have had the Spirit to Maintain or the Magnanimity to retract them, and, that if from your language injurious inferences had been improperly drawn, Sincerity and decency would have pointed out to you the propriety of correcting errors which might thus have been widely diffused.

With these impressions, I was greatly disappointed in receiving from you a letter which I could only consider as evasive and which in manner, is not altogether decorous. In one expectation however, I was not wholly deceived, for at the close of your letter I find an intimation, that if I should dislike your refusal to acknowledge or deny the charge, you were ready to meet the consequences. This I deemed a sort of defiance, and I should have been justified if I had chosen to make it the basis of an immediate Message: Yet, as you had also said something (though in my opinion unfounded) of the indefiniteness of my request; as I believed that your communication was the offspring, rather of false pride than of reflection, and, as I felt the utmost reluctance to proceed to extremities while any other hope remained, my request was repeated in terms more definite. To this you refuse all reply, reposing, as I am bound to presume on the tender of an alternative insinuated in your letter.

Thus, Sir, you have invited the course I am about [to] pursue, and now by your silence impose it upon me. [If] therefore your determinations are final, of which I am not permitted to doubt Mr Van Ness is authorised to communicate my further expectations either to yourself or to such friend as you may be pleased to indicate.

I have the honor to be
Your Ob st
A. Burr

[Alexander Hamilton to Aaron Burr.]

New York June 22ᵈ 1804

Sir

Your first letter, in a style too peremptory, made a demand, in my opinion, unprecedented and unwarrantable. My answer, pointing out the embarrassment, gave you an opportunity to take a less exceptionable course. You have not chosen to do it, but by your last letter, received this day, containing expressions indecorous and improper, you have increased the difficulties to explanation, intrinsically incident to the nature of your application.

If by a "definite reply" you mean the direct avowal or disavowal required in your first letter, I have no other answer to give than that which has already been given. If you mean any thing different admitting of greater latitude, it is requisite you should explain.

I have the honor to be
Sir Your obed Servᵗ
A. Hamilton

[Once the two men reached this impasse, a duel was likely, given the rules of etiquette and of honor that they both accepted. Hamilton wrote the following remarks in a sealed letter to his friend, Nathaniel Pendleton.]

[New York, June 27–July 4, 1804]

On my expected interview [duel] with Col Burr, I think it proper to make some remarks explanatory of my conduct, motives and views.

I was certainly desirous of avoiding this interview, for the most cogent reasons—

1. My religious and moral principles are strongly opposed to the practice of Duelling and it would ever give me pain to be obliged to shed the blood of a fellow creature in a private combat forbidden by the laws.
2. My wife and Children are extremely dear to me, and my life is of the utmost importance to them, in various views.
3. I feel a sense of obligation towards my creditors; who in case of accident to me, by the forced sale of my property, may be in some degree sufferers. I did not think myself at liberty as a man of probity, lightly to expose them to this hazard.
4. I am conscious of no *ill-will* to Col Burr, distinct from political opposition, which, as I trust, has proceeded from pure and upright motives.

Lastly, I shall hazard much, and can possibly gain nothing by the issue of the interview. But it was, as I conceive, impossible for me to avoid it. . . .

I trust at the same time, that the world will do me the Justice to believe, that I have not answered him on light grounds, or from unworthy inducements. I certainly have had strong reasons for what I may have said, though it is possible that in some particulars, I may have been influenced by misconstruction or misinformation. It is also my ardent wish that I may have been more mistaken than I think I have been, and that he by his future conduct may shew himself worthy of all confidence and esteem, and prove an ornament and blessing to his Country.

As well because it is possible that I may have injured Col Burr, however convinced myself that my opinions and declarations have been well founded, as from my general principles and temper in relation to similar affairs—I have resolved, if our interview is conducted in the usual manner, and it pleases God to give me the opportunity, to *reserve* and *throw away* my first fire, and I *have thoughts* even of *reserving* my second fire—and thus giving a double opportunity to Col Burr to pause and to reflect.

It is not however my intention to enter into any explanations on the ground. Apology, from principle I hope, rather than Pride, is out of the question.

To those, who with me abhorring the practice of Duelling may think that I ought on no account to have added to the number of bad examples, I answer that my *relative* situation, as well in public as private appeals, inforcing all the considerations which constitute what men of the world denominate honor, impressed on me (as I thought) a peculiar necessity not to decline the call. The ability to be in future useful, whether in resisting mischief or effecting good, in those crises of our public affairs, which seem likely to happen, would probably be inseparable from a conformity with public prejudice in this particular.

A. H.

[One week before this duel, Hamilton wrote the following to his wife, Elizabeth.]

[New York, July 4, 1804]

This letter, my very dear Eliza, will not be delivered to you, unless I shall first have terminated my earthly career; to begin, as I humbly hope from redeeming grace and divine mercy, a happy immortality.

If it had been possible for me to have avoided the interview, my love for you and my precious children would have been alone a decisive motive. But it was not possible, without sacrifices which would have rendered me unworthy of your esteem. I need not tell you of the pangs I feel, from the idea of quitting you and exposing you to the anguish which I know you would feel. Nor could I dwell on the topic lest it should unman me.

The consolations of Religion, my beloved, can alone support you; and these you have a right to enjoy. Fly to the bosom of your God and be comforted. With my last idea, I shall cherish the sweet hope of meeting you in a better world.

Adieu best of wives and best of Women. Embrace all my darling Children for me.

Ever yours
A. H.

[The code *duello* specified that each combatant name a "second," or friend, to help negotiate a reconciliation or to assist on the "field of honor." By June 22, Burr and Hamilton had ceased writing to each other. Hamilton's second, Nathaniel Pendleton, and Burr's friend and political protégé, William Van Ness, tried to patch things up between the principals. That failing, they arranged the duel. The following is Pendleton's statement of the rules the two men would follow.]

1. The parties will leave town tomorrow morning about five oClock, and meet at the place agreed on. The party arriving first shall wait for the other.
2. The weapons shall be pistols not exceeding Eleven inches in the barrel. The distance ten paces.
3. The Choice of positions to be determined by lot.
4. The parties having taken their positions one of the seconds to be determined by lot (after having ascertained that both parties are ready) shall loudly and distinctly give the word "present"—If one of the parties fires, and the other hath not fired, the opposite second shall say one, two, three, fire, and he shall then fire or lose his shot. A snap or flash is a fire.

[The etiquette of dueling demanded privacy, and the illegality of the practice enforced it. We have testimony by three individuals who witnessed the events in Weehawken on the morning of July 11, 1804. A few hours after the duel, Pendleton and Van Ness wrote a joint statement that became the basis of the first newspaper reports.]

[New York, July 11, 1804]

Col: Burr arrived first on the ground as had been previously agreed. When Gen¹ Hamilton arrived the parties exchanged salutations and the Seconds proceeded to make their arrangements. They measured the distance, ten full paces, and cast lots for the choice of position as also to determine by whom the word should be given, both of which fell to the Second of Gen¹ Hamilton. They then proceeded to load the pistols in each others presence, after which the parties took their stations. The Gentleman who was to give the word, then explained to the parties the rules which were to govern them in firing which were as follows:

The parties being placed at their stations—The Second who gives the word shall ask them whether they are ready—being answered in the affirmative, he shall say *"present"* after which the parties shall present & fire when they please. If one fires before the opposite second shall say one two, three, fire, and he shall fire or lose his fire.

And asked if they were prepared, being answered in the affirmative he gave the word *present* as had been agreed on, and both of the parties took aim & fired in succession. The intervening time is not expressed as the seconds do not precisely agree on that point. The pistols were discharged within a few seconds of each other and the fire of Col: Burr took effect; Gen¹ Hamilton almost instantly fell, Col: Burr then advanced toward Gen¹ H—n with a manner and gesture that appeared to Gen¹ Hamilton's friend to be expressive of regret, but without Speaking turned about & withdrew—Being urged from the field by his friend as has been subsequently stated, with a view to prevent his being recognised by the Surgeon and Bargemen who were then approaching. No farther communication took place between the principals and the Barge that carried Col: Burr immediately returned to the City. We conceive it proper to add that the conduct of the parties in that interview was perfectly proper as suited the occasion.

[A week later, Nathaniel Pendleton felt the need to elaborate on the events of July 11. He cited evidence to prove that Hamilton had not fired at Burr: Hamilton's private letter, his personal statements to Bishop Moore and to his second, and many other details. Note that Pendleton referred to himself in the third person as "Mr. P." Dueling's illegality made such grammatical gymnastics necessary.]

[New York, July 19, 1804]

. . . Mr. P. expressed a confident opinion that General Hamilton did not fire first—and that he did not fire at all *at Col. Burr.* Mr. V. N. seemed equally confident in the opinion that Gen. H. did fire first—and of course that it must have been *at* his antagonist.

General Hamilton's friend thinks it to be a sacred duty he owes to the memory of that exalted man, to his country, and his friends, to publish to the world such facts and circumstances as have produced a decisive conviction in his own mind, that he cannot have been mistaken in the belief he has formed on these points—

1st. Besides the testimonies of Bishop Moore, and the paper containing an express declaration, under General Hamilton's own hand, enclosed to his friend in a packet, not to be delivered but in the event of his death, and which have already been published, General Hamilton informed Mr. P. at least ten days previous to the affair, that he had doubts whether he would not receive and not return Mr. Burr's first fire. Mr. P. remonstrated against this determination, and urged many considerations against it, as dangerous to himself and not necessary in the particular case, when every ground of accommodation, not humiliating, had been proposed and rejected. He said he would not decide lightly, but take time to deliberate fully. It was incidentally mentioned again at their occasional subsequent conversations, and on the evening preceding the time of the appointed interview, he informed Mr. P. he had made up his mind *not to fire at Col. Burr the first time, but to receive his fire, and fire in the air.* Mr. P. again urged him upon this subject, and repeated his former arguments. His final answer was in terms that made an impression on Mr. P's mind which can never be effaced. "My friend, it is the effect of a RELIGIOUS SCRUPLE, and does not admit of reasoning, it is useless to say more on the subject, as my purpose is definitely fixed."

2d. His last words before he was wounded afford a proof that this purpose had not changed. When he received his pistol, after having taken his position, he was asked if he would have the hair spring set?—His answer was, *"Not this time."*

3d. After he was wounded, and laid in the boat, the first words he uttered after recovering the power of speech, were (addressing himself to a gentleman present, who perfectly well remembers it) *"Pendleton knows I did not mean to fire at Col. Burr the first time."*

4th. This determination had been communicated by Mr. P. to that gentleman that morning, before they left the city.

5th. The pistol that had been used by General Hamilton, lying loose over the other apparatus in the case which was open; after having been some time in the boat, one of the boatmen took hold of it to put it into the case. General Hamilton observing this, said *"Take care of that pistol—it is cocked. It may go off and do mischief."* This is also remembered by the Gentleman alluded to.

This shews that he was not sensible of having fired at all. If he had fired *previous* to receiving the wound, he would have remembered it, and therefore have known that the pistol could not go off; but if *afterwards* it must have been the effect of an involuntary exertion of the muscles produced by a mortal wound, in which case, he could not have been conscious of having fired.

6th. Mr. P. having so strong a conviction that if General Hamilton had fired first, it could not have escaped his attention (all his anxiety being alive for the effect of the first fire, and having no reason to believe the friend of Col. Burr was not sincere in the contrary opinion) he determined to go to the spot where the affair took place, to see if he could not discover some traces of the course of the ball from Gen. Hamilton's pistol. He took a friend with him the day after General Hamilton died, and after some examination they fortunately found what they were in search of. They ascertained that the ball passed through the limb of a cedar tree, at an elevation of about twelve feet and a half, perpendicularly from the ground, between thirteen and fourteen feet from the mark on which General Hamilton stood, and about four feet wide of the direct line between him and Col. Burr, on the right side; he having fallen on the left. The part of the limb through which the ball passed was cut off and brought to this city, and is now in Mr. Church's possession.

No inferences are pointed out as resulting from these facts, nor will any comments be made. They are left to the candid judgment and feelings of the public.

[William Van Ness, Burr's second, responded as follows to Pendleton's denial that Hamilton shot at Burr.]

The second of G H having considered it proper to subjoin an explanatory note to the statement mutually furnished, it becomes proper for the gentleman who attended Col Burr to state also his impressions with respect to those points on which there exists a variance of opinion. In doing this he pointedly disclaims any idea disrespectful to the memory of G H, or any intention to ascribe any conduct to him that is not in his opinion perfectly honorable & correct.

The parties met as has been above related & took their respective stations as directed: the pistols were then handed to them by the seconds. Gen Hamilton elevated his, as if to try the light, & lowering it said I beg pardon for delaying you but the direction of the line renders it necessary, at the same time feeling his pockets with his left hand, & drawing forth his spectacles put them on. The second then asked if they were prepared which was replied to in the affirmative. The word *present* was then given, on which both parties took aim, the pistol of General Hamilton was first discharged and Col Burr fired immediately after, only five or six seconds of time intervening. On this point the second of Col Burr has full & perfect recollection, he noticed particularly the discharge of G H's pistol, & looked to his principal to ascertain whether he was hurt, he then clearly saw Col B's pistol discharged. At the moment of looking at Col B on the discharge of G H's pistol he perceived a slight motion in his person, which induced the idea of his being struck, on this point he conversed with his principal on their return, who ascribed that circumstance to a small stone under his foot, & observed that the smoke of G H's pistol obscured him for a moment previous to his firing.

When G H fell Col B advanced toward him as stated & was checked by his second who urged the importance of his immediately repairing to the barge, conceiving that G H was mortally wounded, & being desirous to secure his principal from the sight of the surgeon & bargemen who might be called in evidence. Col B complied with his request.

He shortly followed him to the boat, and Col B again expressed a wish to return, saying with an expression of much concern, I must go & speak to him. I again urged the obvious impropriety stating that the G was surrounded by the Surgeon & Bargemen by whom he must not be seen & insisted on immediate departure.

[Five weeks after the duel, Dr. David Hosack—who did not see the fight, but who tended Hamilton's wounds afterward—commented on the fateful day in a letter to William Coleman. His remarks were in substantial agreement with Pendleton's description of events.]

[New York] *August 17th, 1804.*

Dear Sir,

To comply with your request is a painful task; but I will repress my feelings while I endeavour to furnish you with an enumeration of such particulars relative to the melancholy end of our beloved friend Hamilton, as dwell most forcibly on my recollection.

When called to him, upon his receiving the fatal wound I found him half sitting on the ground, supported in the arms of Mr. Pendleton. His countenance of death I shall never forget—He had at that instant just strength to say, "This is a mortal wound, Doctor"; when he sunk away and became to all appearance lifeless. I immediately stripped up his clothes, and soon, alas! ascertained that the direction of the ball must have been through some vital part. His pulses were not to be felt; his respiration was entirely suspended; and upon laying my hand on his heart and perceiving no motion there, I considered him as irrecoverably gone. I however observed to Mr. Pendleton that the only chance for his reviving was immediately to get him upon the water. We therefore lifted him up, and carried him out of the wood, to the margin of the bank where the bargemen aided us in conveying him into the boat, which immediately put off. . . . When we had got, as I should judge about 50 yards from the shore, some imperfect efforts to breathe were for the first time manifest: in a few minutes he sighed, and became sensible to the impression of the hartshorne, or the fresh air of the water. He breathed; his eyes, hardly opened, wandered, without fixing upon any objects; to our great joy he at length spoke: "My vision is indistinct," were his first words. His pulse became more perceptible; his respiration more regular; his sight returned. I then examined the wound to know if there was any dangerous discharge of blood; upon slightly pressing his side it gave him pain; on which I desisted. Soon after recovering his sight, he happened to cast his eye upon the case of pistols, and observing the one that he had had in his hand lying on the outside, he said, "Take care of that pistol; it is undischarged, and still cocked; it may go off and do harm;—Pendleton knows, (attempting to turn his head towards him) that I did not intend to fire at him." "Yes," said Mr. Pendleton, understanding his wish, "I have already made Dr. Hosack acquainted with your determination as to that." He then closed his eyes, and remained calm, without any disposition to speak; nor did he say much afterwards, excepting in reply to my questions as to his feelings. He asked me once or twice, how I found his pulse; and he informed me that his lower extremities had lost all feeling; manifesting to me that he entertained no hopes that he should long survive. I changed the posture of his limbs, but to no purpose; they had totally lost their sensibility. Perceiving that we approached the shore, he said, "Let Mrs. Hamilton be immediately sent for—let the event be gradually broken to her; but give her hopes." . . .

During the night, he had some imperfect sleep; but the succeeding morning his symptoms were aggravated, attended however with a diminution of pain. His mind retained all its usual strength and composure. The great source of his anxiety seemed to be in his sympathy with his half distracted wife and children. He spoke to me frequently of them—"My beloved wife and children," were always his expressions. But his fortitude triumphed over his situation, dreadful as it was; once, indeed, at the sight of his children brought to the bed-side together, seven in number, his utterance forsook him; he opened his eyes, gave them one look, and closed them again, till they were taken away. As a proof of his extraordinary composure of mind, let me add, that he alone could calm the frantic grief of their mother. "*Remember, my Eliza, you are a Christian,*" were the expressions with which he frequently, with a firm voice, but in pathetic and impressive manner, addressed her. His words, and the tone in which they were uttered, will never be effaced from my memory. At about two o'clock, as the public well knows, he expired.

I am, Sir,
Your friend and humble serv't,
David Hosack

ASSESSING YOUR VERDICT

How did you decide the case? Did Hamilton try to kill Burr, or did he intentionally throw his shot away? What evidence supports your conclusion? What evidence did you have to disregard in order to accept your hypothesis? What biases did you find in the documents? How did you decide which sources to believe?

To compare your answer with those of other college students, consider the following data. For three decades, Professor Jerry Combs of San Francisco State University has discussed the Burr-Hamilton documents with his students and asked them to vote on whether they believed Hamilton threw his shot away or plotted to kill Burr and failed. The majority of the students in most years accepted Hamilton's testimony that he threw away the shot, but the margin of support for Hamilton has varied significantly over the years. During the late 1950s and early 1960s, students believed Hamilton by overwhelming margins, but during the late 1960s and early 1970s, Hamilton's supporters dropped to only about six in ten. Students again gave large majorities to Hamilton during the late 1970s and early 1980s, but Burr's advocates have staged another comeback after that. How do you explain these trends? What factors other than the content of historical documents influence how students interpret the past? Do influences such as the political climate of the nation, the relative plausibility of conspiracy theories at different times in our history, or the state of the nation's economy affect the historical judgment of students? Are professional historians also influenced by such factors?

We have deliberately focused here on the simple question of how Hamilton acted on the dueling ground. But think back on the documents you just read, and consider all of the interesting issues they raise. People sometimes fight today, but that is very different from killing each other according to strict rules of etiquette. Why did individuals in the late eighteenth and early nineteenth centuries shoot at each other in this manner?

Who was ethically right or wrong in any dispute could not be determined by proving who was the better marksman. Rather, dueling, as Hamilton's letters make clear, was about honor. The willingness to risk one's life was meant to disprove the allegations that had led to the duel. A man with the courage to fight, and to do so according to strict rules of decorum and self-control, was a man worthy of respect. Honor among peers—and note that the peers of the likes of Hamilton and Burr were the most powerful men in the land—secured an individual's wealth, status, and social position. Honor was closely tied to particular ideals of manhood. The cult of honor was a way for powerful *men* to define the social circles in which they moved and to exclude others from those charmed circles. Slaves did not have honor; women did not have honor; the poor did not have honor. To be esteemed an honorable man by one's peers marked one as socially significant. Most men who accepted the code of honor, contemporaries of Burr and Hamilton, never fought a duel. But if the occasion arose, they knew that their social position hinged on proving their claims to honor.

CONSTRUCTING YOUR OWN PAST

This volume is a series of "case studies" of particular episodes or events in American history, much like the Burr-Hamilton duel. The "Historical Context" essay that introduces each chapter sets the stage for the issue at hand. The essay is followed by a selection of primary documents, including maps, figures, diaries, letters, newspaper articles, trial records, and memoirs, and political pamphlets—the basic stuff that historians use to construct the past. The documents are followed by sets of questions. The "Defining Terms" section invites readers to review the chapter's key figures, events, and ideas; "Probing the Sources" questions raise specific points about the sources; "Interpreting the Sources" questions seek more speculative responses about the meaning and importance of that chapter's subject. "Additional Reading" provides suggestions for other sources and readings on the subject.

Constructing the American Past asks you to become your own historian. As in the case of the Burr-Hamilton duel, the documents in a given chapter may contradict one another. All historical sources have biases, but some sources are more reliable than others. The historian's task—your task—is to construct a plausible version of an episode from contradictory evidence. But equally important, documents come from people, and people disagree in their fundamental values and beliefs. You want to get "underneath" the sources, to think about what sorts of assumptions their authors made, to consider why people believed and acted as they did, to ponder why history is so frequently contested ground. Remember above all that constructing the past is interpretive work; history is more an art than a science.

A final point. Several of the chapters include a postscript section. The purpose of this section is *not* to provide the "correct" answer to questions raised by the documents. Rather than lead you toward a given verdict, the postscript section—like the P.S. we occasionally pen in private letters—is intended to provide additional information about secondary issues raised in the original document. The concluding remarks offer abbreviated responses to questions that students commonly ask after they have studied the materials presented in the chapter. For instance, after reading the Burr-Hamilton documents, many students still ponder two questions: What happened to Burr after the duel, and how long did the custom of dueling survive? The postscript section presented below will partially satisfy the curiosity of those serious students who have found that "doing history" can become addictive.

POSTSCRIPT

Hamilton's death shocked the nation. Overnight he was a hero, and Vice President Burr, a villain. Charged with murder in both New York and New Jersey, Burr fled the region, first to Philadelphia and later to asylum in the South. While he never stood trial for murder, his political career was ruined. Dropped from Jefferson's presidential ticket in 1804, Burr traveled to the West, where he entered into a scheme with James Wilkinson, the military governor of Louisiana. Apparently, his plan was to seize Spanish territory in Texas and California, to separate from the United States the land west of the Mississippi, and to create an empire from this territory with himself as its head. The conspiracy was foiled, however, when Wilkinson, betraying Burr and warned Jefferson of the plot. In 1807, Burr was tried for treason but, much to Jefferson's dismay, was acquitted. Besieged by creditors, Burr left for Europe, where he fell into debt and opium addiction. Later in life he returned to New York and practiced law in relative obscurity until his death in 1833.

Although the publicity surrounding Hamilton's death provoked loud protests against the practice of dueling, it did not bring an end to the bloody custom. In 1806, for instance, Andrew Jackson shot and killed Charles Dickinson and took a bullet that broke several of his own ribs. In 1820, naval hero Commodore Stephen Decatur fell to fellow officer Captain James Barron. The John Randolph–Henry Clay duel of 1826, fortunately, harmed neither man. Twelve years later, however, Congressman William Graves of Kentucky killed his longtime friend Congressman Jonathan Cilley of Maine in a duel that neither wanted, but neither dared to stop.

Still, within a few decades dueling was dead. Here, very briefly, is what many historians regard as a plausible explanation of the decline of the code of honor.

Dueling in the nineteenth century gradually became confined to the South and became part of the hierarchical culture of slavery. Increasingly, humanitarian reformers condemned the practice as savage. In the heady optimism of the antebellum North, where progress, even social perfection, seemed possible to so many Americans, customs that smacked of Old World corruption came under attack. Gunplay certainly did not end. On the contrary, mass-produced repeating weapons, manufactured by companies like Colt around mid-century, facilitated murderous informal battles.

But the notion that a gentleman could defend his honor—his reputation among other men on whose good opinion his influence and social position rested—only by displays of valor came to seem absurd in the individualistic spirit of nineteenth-century America. When young Abraham Lincoln responded to a challenge by naming cow flops at ten paces as the weapons to be used, it was a sign that the code *duello* had outlived the social and cultural environment that had given it birth. Dueling had been rooted in social ideals of deference, paternalism, and hierarchy;

only men of equal social status could duel with each other, and that code explicitly excluded those clearly above or below oneself. In the North, those old social ideals gave way to the ideology of equality, which made dueling seem at best obsolete, at worst barbaric. And in the South, Northern armies, carrying those new repeating weapons, finally destroyed the social hierarchy—based on slavery—that had been the last bastion in America of the code of honor.

ADDITIONAL READING

A detailed introduction to the Burr-Hamilton duel is found in Harold C. Syrett and Jean G. Cooke, eds., *Interview in Weehawken: The Burr-Hamilton Duel as Told in the Original Documents* (1960). Recent biographies of the combatants include Jacob E. Cooke, *Alexander Hamilton* (1982) and Milton Lomask, *Aaron Burr*, 2 vols. (1979, 1983). Older but still useful studies include John C. Miller, *Alexander Hamilton: Portrait in Paradox* (1958) and Nathan Schachner, *Aaron Burr* (1937). For an intriguing discussion of the practice of dueling, see V. G. Kiernan, *The Duel in European History: Honour and the Reign of Aristocracy* (1990).

Contact and Conquest
The Meeting of the Old and New Worlds

HISTORICAL CONTEXT

On "Discovery Day" 1892, the citizens of the United States were in a festive mood. Along parade routes, at neighborhood picnics, and in town square rallies, flag-waving Americans celebrated the four hundredth anniversary of Columbus's voyage by eating hot dogs, swaying to the music of brass bands, and applauding local celebrities who touted the exploits of the "Admiral of the Ocean Sea."

In large cities, the festivities were more elaborate. In New York, for example, the editors of the *New York Times* used hyperbole to describe the opening of the Columbian Celebration: "YOUNG AMERICA LEADS OFF—FIRST OF THE GREAT PARADES OF COLUMBUS WEEK—SOLID MASSES OF HUMANITY LINE THE ROUTE—THE CITY HIDDEN UNDER FLAGS AND BUNTING." The next day, it wrote, "BEFORE TWO MILLION EYES—THE GREAT PARADE OF WAR SHIPS AND RIVER CRAFT—SPECTATORS HIDE THE WATER FRONT FROM SIGHT." On the third day, the headlines screamed, "THE CLIMAX OF THE WEEK—ALL PAST PARADE RECORDS SENT TO THE REAR—CASCADES OF GAY COLORS EVERYWHERE— THE AVENUES PACKED WITH VAST THRONGS BY SUNRISE AND FILLED TO THEIR UTMOST CAPACITY ALL DAY AND NIGHT—MODEL WORK BY THE POLICE IN HANDLING THE GREATEST CROWD NEW-YORK EVER HELD."

The quadricentennial parties in New York City, as spectacular as they were, could not match the size or duration of the festivities in Chicago. On October 21, 1892, Chicago's World Columbian Exposition—an event destined to attract about 40 percent of the U.S. population!—held its opening-day ceremonies. Cardinal James Gibbons declared:

> Four hundred years ago Columbus discovered this American continent, and therefore, we are primarily indebted to him for the land which we enjoy in peace and security. Columbus united the skill and daring of a navigator with the zeal of an apostle, and in his voyage of exploration he was not only impelled by the desire of enriching his sovereign with the wealth of new dominions, but he was also inspired by the lofty ambition of carrying the light of the Gospel to a people that were buried in the darkness of idolatry. . . . Fervent should be our gratitude since we possess the fruits of his labors and of his victory. But not for this earthly possession only should we be thankful, more for the precious boon of constitutional liberty which we inherit.

Gibbons's words resonated with themes common to most 1892 Columbus obser-
vances. For millions of late-nineteenth-century Americans, hailing Columbus was
synonymous with celebrating the progress of humanity, the opening of the American frontier, the triumph of Western technology, the advance of the Christian religion, and the spread of democratic institutions.

One hundred years later, Americans prepared for the five hundredth anniversary
of the Columbus voyage. This time, however, reflections on the era of Old and New
World contact evoked different reactions. There were plenty of parades and patriotic speeches. But there were also some discordant notes. In Denver, Colorado, a
scheduled Columbus Day parade was called off to prevent a clash between the
marchers and Native American protesters. In Berkeley, California, the city council
renamed October 12 Indigenous People's Day and dedicated the site of a planned
Turtle Island Monument, which was to commemorate a Native American story of
creation. In Columbus, Ohio (the world's largest city named for Columbus), groups
of Native Americans held a memorial service in a park about two blocks from a full-
scale model of the *Santa Maria*. In New York, the National Council of Churches announced that 1992 should be a time, not of celebration, but of repentance for an
"invasion and colonization with legalized occupation, genocide, economic exploitation, and a deep level of institutional racism and moral decadence."

Contemporary Americans remember an unpopular war in Vietnam, a civil rights
movement, and the ugly stain of numerous "ethnic cleansings" around the world.
We look at the past differently from U.S. citizens of 1892. The past itself has not
changed, but assessments of the consequences of past events have undergone dramatic alterations. With a greater sensitivity to Native American perceptions and to
environmental concerns, recent interpretations of history often emphasize the negative side of the Columbian exchange. Contact brought not "progress," but disease,
starvation, and enslavement. It wrought havoc on the cultures and environment of
the Western Hemisphere, and it resulted in the death of tens of millions of people.
Indeed, according to the interpretation offered by David E. Stannard in *American
Holocaust: Columbus and the Conquest of the New World* (1992), the "European
and white American destruction of the native peoples of the Americas was the most
massive act of genocide in the history of the world."

This chapter focuses on the era of initial contact between the peoples of Europe
and the Americas. It was a period of discovery and disease, of exploration and exploitation, of colonization and conquest. The chapter includes excerpts from Columbus's narrative of his first voyage; from the works of Bartolomé de Las Casas, the
controversial "Protector of the Indians"; and from Aztec accounts of the coming of
the Spanish. The first two sources, although among the most significant texts describing the period of encounter, are both products of European minds, and they tell
us as much about Old World perceptions and ambitions as they do about New
World realities. Consequently, do not be too quick to accept at face value the assertions stated in the texts. Rather, interrogate the sources thoroughly, always asking
why these words were written and how much of the testimony is trustworthy. While
no full narratives exist that reveal how the indigenous peoples of the Caribbean reacted to those early days of contact, other voices give us hints of how they experienced the coming of Europeans. The Aztec chroniclers left moving accounts of the
clash between the two peoples.

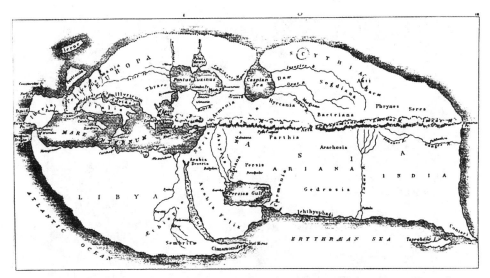

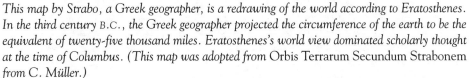

This map by Strabo, a Greek geographer, is a redrawing of the world according to Eratosthenes. In the third century B.C., *the Greek geographer projected the circumference of the earth to be the equivalent of twenty-five thousand miles. Eratosthenes's world view dominated scholarly thought at the time of Columbus. (This map was adopted from Orbis Terrarum Secundum Strabonem from C. Müller.)*

Columbus had a simple but expensive idea: to reach the Eastern world by sailing west. While European monarchs coveted the profits that could be made from finding a waterway to the Orient, most gave little consideration to Columbus's plan. They rejected Columbus's scheme, not because they believed the earth to be flat, but because their advisers told them that the earth was quite large, and that to reach the East by sailing west, one would have to travel some ten thousand miles across dangerous Atlantic waters. Columbus, however, believing the earth to be much smaller than scholars estimated, insisted that Japan was only about twenty-four hundred miles from the Canary Islands. If given the opportunity, Columbus promised not only to prove the calculations of the scholars wrong, but also to find a waterway to the riches of Asia.

Several developments worked to Columbus's advantage. In searching for a southern sea-lane to India in 1488, the Portuguese sailed five thousand miles down the African coastline to the tip of the continent. These explorations—while confirming the possibility of reaching the East by sailing south—also demonstrated that such a trip would be longer and more costly than had been anticipated. This discovery made a westward journey to the East appear more attractive. Furthermore, in January 1492, the Spanish Christians defeated the Moorish Muslims in Granada, thereby ending years of warfare in southern Spain. The Spaniards also banished all Jews from the land. Once freed from the expense of this costly civil war, the Spanish monarchs, Ferdinand and Isabella, now had the luxury of gambling their fortunes on Columbus's scheme. They supplied Columbus with three ships and a crew, an elaborate title, and a diplomatic passport intended to introduce him to the kings he expected to meet in the Orient.

A woodcut published with the 1493 edition of Columbus's letter. King Ferdinand is the figure on the left side. Columbus is the little figure in the boat meeting the much larger inhabitants of Hispaniola. In much medieval and early modern art, the size of the figures in artistic renderings implied something about the relationship of the figure to God and the viewer. Often, saints and other important people were larger than commoners. What do you think this artist was implying by making the Taino Indians larger than Columbus and approximately the same size as King Ferdinand? (Rare Books Division, The New York Public Library, Astor, Lenox and Tilden Foundations)

In return for this sponsorship, the Spanish Crown was to receive 90 percent of all income gained from the enterprise.

Although it was not required or even customary for Spanish sea captains at this time to keep a travel log, Columbus decided to document his historic search for the Orient. Writing for his monarchs but with an eye to history, Columbus produced a narrative of the voyage, a document that included a prologue detailing the objectives of the mission, as well as daily journal entries describing the preparation of the fleet, the outward voyage, landfall, exploration, and the homeward journey. On returning to Spain, Columbus presented his narrative to Queen Isabella, who copied it, kept the original, and returned the copy to Columbus. The original was subsequently lost, and Columbus's copy passed on his death to his eldest son, and later to Luis, one of his grandsons. Although Luis had permission to publish the journal, he never did, and some scholars have been led to conclude that he sold it to subsidize his legendary debauchery. At any rate, both the original and the only known copy of Columbus's journal disappeared before the historic text could be published.

Fortunately, however, in the 1530s Bartolomé de Las Casas came into contact with one of the copies of the journal while he was conducting research for his own *History of the Indies*. Las Casas took extensive notes from the journal, summarizing portions of it and copying other sections word for word. Las Casas's transcription, which itself was not published until 1825, is the closest we are likely to get to Columbus's original 1492–1493 narrative.

In addition to providing us with the only extant version of Columbus's journal, Las Casas also left a passionate description of the consequences of the first half-century of Spanish colonization. Las Casas became interested in the peoples of the New World at an early age. In 1493, while only eight years old, he saw Columbus parade through the streets of Seville during a triumphant tour showcasing Columbus's first voyage. Six months later, Las Casas's father and three of his uncles sailed with Columbus on the second of Columbus's four transatlantic voyages. As a young teenager, Las Casas received from his father an unusual souvenir gift: a Taino boy, a servant who was subsequently freed and returned to the Indies on the order of Queen Isabella. In 1502, Las Casas made the first of what would be ten trips across the Atlantic. Initially as a *doctrinero* (or teacher of Christian doctrine to the Indians) and later as the first Roman Catholic priest ordained in the New World, Las Casas began to see the moral inequities within a colonial system that granted Spanish settlers—in return for promising to instruct the natives in Christian doctrine—the right to the fields, mines, and labor of Native American subjects. Between 1514, when Las Casas first spoke against the horrors of Spanish exploitation, and his death in 1564, he carried on a gallant if sometimes frustrating crusade for Native American rights.

THE DOCUMENTS

While reading the following documents, rethink the meaning of the "Age of Contact and Conquest." Re-create the moment of encounter. In what ways were the Old and New Worlds and their peoples alike and not alike? What did the word *discovery* mean to Columbus and the subsequent colonists, and what did it mean to the Native Americans who encountered alien creatures invading their lands? Also, reflect on the consequences of the Spanish colonization efforts. How did the Spanish justify colonization, and how valid were these justifications?

Introduction to Documents 1 and 2

The following are excerpts from the writings of the Spanish monarchs, Ferdinand and Isabella, and Christopher Columbus. The first document, "Privileges and Prerogatives Granted by Their Catholic Majesties," offers insights into what the Spanish monarchs expected Columbus to accomplish on his maiden voyage. The second document is taken from the prologue and journal of Columbus's first voyage. Recall that Columbus found land as he had anticipated, when about twenty-four hundred miles out into the Atlantic. The people and environs he encountered, however, were not expected. Whereas he anticipated the busy ports and elegantly robed subjects that had been described in the writings of Marco Polo, he instead found naked strangers and few signs of commerce. His words suggest a bewildered man struggling to reconcile the known with the unknown. Note: *Grand Khan* and *Cathay* refer to Asia.

🪶 DOCUMENT 1 *Privileges and Prerogatives Granted by Their Catholic Majesties to Christopher Columbus: 1492*

FERDINAND and ELIZABETH, by the Grace of God, King and Queen of Castile, of Leon, of Arragon, of Sicily, of Granada, of Toledo, of Valencia, of Galicia, of Majorca, of Minorca, of Sevil, of Sardinia, of Jaen, of Algarve, of Algezira, of Gibraltar, of the Canary Islands, Count and Countess of Barcelona, Lord and Lady of Biscay and Molina, Duke and Duchess of Athens and Neopatria, Count and Countess of Rousillion and Cerdaigne, Marquess and Marchioness of Oristan and Gociano, &c.

For as much of you, Christopher Columbus, are going by our command, with some of our vessels and men, to discover and subdue some Islands and Continent in the ocean, and it is hoped that by God's assistance, some of the said Islands and Continent in the ocean will be discovered and conquered by your means and conduct, therefore it is but just and reasonable, that since you expose yourself to such danger to serve us, you should be rewarded for it. And we being willing to honor and favor You for the reasons aforesaid: Our will is, That you, Christopher Columbus, after discovering and conquering the said Islands and Continent in the said ocean, or any of them, shall be our Admiral of the said Islands and Continent you shall so discover and conquer; and that you be our Admiral, Vice-Roy, and Governor in them, and that for the future, you may call and style yourself, D. Christopher Columbus, and that your sons and successors in the said employment, may call themselves Dons, Admirals, Vice-Roys, and Governors of them; and that you may exercise the office of Admiral, with the charge of Vice-Roy and Governor of the said Islands and Continent, which you and your Lieutenants shall conquer, and freely decide all causes, civil and criminal, appertaining to the said employment of Admiral, Vice-Roy, and Governor, as you shall think fit in justice, and as the Admirals of our kingdoms use to do; and that you have power to punish offenders; and you and your Lieutenants exercise the employments of Admiral, Vice-Roy, and Governor, in all things belonging to the said offices, or any of them; and that you enjoy the perquisites and salaries belonging to the said employments, and to each of them, in the same manner as the High Admiral of our kingdoms does. . . .

GIVEN at Granada, on the 30th of April, in the year of our Lord, 1492.-
I, THE KING, I, THE QUEEN.

🪶 DOCUMENT 2 *Journal of Christopher Columbus's First Voyage*

. . . This present year of 1492, after Your Highnesses had brought to an end the war with the Moors who ruled in Europe and had concluded the war in the very great city of Granada, where this present year on the second day of the month of January I saw the Royal Standards of Your Highnesses placed by force of arms on the towers of the Alhambra, which is the fortress of the said city; and I saw the Moorish King come out to the gates of the city and kiss the Royal Hands of Your Highnesses and of the Prince my Lord; and later in that same month, because of the report that I had given to Your Highnesses about the lands of India and about a prince who is called "Grand Khan," which means in our Spanish language "King of Kings"; how, many times, he and his predecessors had sent to Rome to ask for men learned in our Holy Faith in order that they might instruct him in it and how the Holy Father had never provided them; and thus so many peoples were lost, falling into idolatry and accepting false and harmful religions; and Your Highnesses, as Catholic Christians and Princes, lovers and promoters of the Holy Christian Faith, and enemies of the false doctrine of Mahomet and of all idolatries and heresies, you thought of sending me, Christóbal Colón, to the said regions of India to see the said princes and the peoples and the lands, and the characteristics of the lands and of everything, and to see how their conversion to our Holy Faith might be undertaken. And you commanded that I should not go to the East by land, by which way it is customary to go, but by the route to the West, by which route we do not know for certain that anyone previously has passed. So, after having expelled all the Jews from all of your Kingdoms and Dominions, in the same month of January Your Highnesses commanded me to go, with a suitable fleet, to the said regions of India. And for that you granted me great favors and ennobled me so that from then on I might call myself "Don" and would be Grand Admiral of the Ocean Sea and Viceroy and perpetual Governor of all the islands and lands that I might discover and gain and [that] from now on might be discovered and gained in the Ocean Sea; and likewise my eldest son would succeed me and his son him, from generation to generation forever. And I left the city of Granada on the twelfth day of May in the same year of 1492 on Saturday, and I came to the town of Palos, which is a seaport, where I fitted out three vessels very well suited for such exploits; and I left the said port, very well provided with supplies and with many seamen, on the third day of August of the said year, on a Friday, half an hour before sunrise; and I took the route to Your Highnesses' Canary Islands, which are in the said Ocean Sea, in order from there to take my course and sail so far that I would reach the Indies and give Your Highnesses' message to those princes and thus carry out that which you had commanded me to do. And for this purpose I thought of writing on this whole voyage, very diligently, all that I would do and see and experience, as will be seen further along. . . .

Wednesday 10 October

He* steered west-southwest; they traveled ten miles per hour and at times 12 and for a time seven and between day and night made 59 leagues; he told the men only 44 leagues. Here the men could no longer stand it; they complained of the long voyage. But the Admiral encouraged them as best he could, giving them good hope of the benefits that they would be able to secure. And he added that it was useless to complain since he had come to find the Indies and thus had to continue the voyage until he found them, with the help of Our Lord.

Thursday 11 October

He steered west-southwest. They took much water aboard, more than they had taken in the whole voyage. They saw petrels and a green bulrush near the ship. The men of the caravel *Pinta* saw a cane and a stick, and took on board another small stick that appeared to have been worked with iron, and a piece of cane, and other vegetation originating on land, and a small plank. The men of the caravel *Niña* also saw other signs of land and a

---

*Note that Columbus sometimes referred to himself in the third person.

small stick loaded with barnacles. With these signs everyone breathed more easily and cheered up. On this day, up to sunset, they made 27 leagues.

After sunset he steered on his former course to the west. They made about 12 miles each hour and, until two hours after midnight, made about 90 miles, which is twenty-two leagues and a half. And because the caravel *Pinta* was a better sailer and went ahead of the Admiral it found land and made the signals that the Admiral had ordered. A sailor named Rodrigo de Triana saw this land first, although the Admiral, at the tenth hour of the night, while he was on the sterncastle, saw a light, although it was something so faint that he did not wish to affirm that it was land. But he called Pero Gutierrez, the steward of the king's dais, and told him that there seemed to be a light, and for him to look: and thus he did and saw it. He also told Rodrigo Sánchez de Segovia, whom the king and queen were sending as *veedor*† of the fleet, who saw nothing because he was not in a place where he could see it. After the Admiral said it, it was seen once or twice; and it was like a small wax candle that rose and lifted up, which to few seemed to be an indication of land. But the Admiral was certain that they were near land, because of which when they recited the *Salve*, which sailors in their own way are accustomed to recite and sing, all being present, the Admiral entreated and admonished them to keep a good lookout on the forecastle and to watch carefully for land; and that to the man who first told him that he saw land he would later give a silk jacket in addition to the other rewards that the sovereigns had promised, which were ten thousand *maravedis* as an annuity to whoever should see it first. At two hours after midnight the land appeared, from which they were about two leagues distant. They hauled down all the sails and kept only the *treo*, which is the mainsail without bonnets, and jogged on and off, passing time until daylight Friday, when they reached an islet of the Lucayas, which was called Guanaham in the language of the Indians. Soon they saw naked people; and the Admiral went ashore in the armed launch, and Martin Alonso Pinzón and his brother Vicente Anes, who was captain of the *Niña*. The Admiral brought out the royal banner and the captains two flags with the green cross, which the Admiral carried on all the ships as a standard, with an F and a Y, and over each letter a crown, one on one side of the † and the other on the other. Thus put ashore they saw very green trees and many ponds and fruits of various kinds. The Admiral called to the two captains and to the others who had jumped ashore and to Rodrigo Descobedo, the *escrivano* [secretary] of the whole fleet, and to Rodrigo Sánchez de Segovia; and he said that they should be witnesses that, in the presence of all, he would take, as in fact he did take, possession of the said island for the king and for the queen his lords, making the declarations that were required, and which at more length are contained in the testimonials made there in writing. Soon many people of the island gathered there. What follows are the very words of the Admiral in his book about his first voyage to, and discovery of, these Indies. I, he says, in order that they would be friendly to us—because I recognized that they were people who would be better freed [from error] and converted to our Holy Faith by love than by force—to some of them I gave red caps, and glass beads which they put on their chests, and many other things of small value, in which they took so much pleasure and became so much our friends that it was a marvel. Later they came swimming to the ships' launches where we were and brought us parrots and cotton thread in balls and javelins and many other things, and they traded them to us for other things which we gave them, such as small glass beads and bells. In sum, they took everything and gave of what they had very willingly. But it seemed to me that they were a people very poor in everything. All of them go around as naked as their mothers bore them; and the women also, although I did not see more than one quite young girl. And all those that I saw were young people, for none did I see of more than 30 years of age. They are very well formed, with handsome bodies and good faces. Their hair [is] coarse—almost

†A *veedor*, or comptroller, was appointed by the sovereigns.

like the tail of a horse—and short. They wear their hair down over their eyebrows except for a little in the back which they wear long and never cut. Some of them paint themselves with black, and they are of the color of the Canarians, neither black nor white; and some of them paint themselves with white, and some of them with red, and some of them with whatever they find. And some of them paint their faces, and some of them the whole body, and some of them only the eyes, and some of them only the nose. They do not carry arms nor are they acquainted with them, because I showed them swords and they took them by the edge and through ignorance cut themselves. They have no iron. Their javelins are shafts without iron and some of them have at the end a fish tooth. . . . All of them alike are of good-sized stature and carry themselves well. I saw some who had marks of wounds on their bodies and I made signs to them asking what they were; and they showed me how people from other islands nearby came there and tried to take them, and how they defended themselves; and I believed and believe that they come here from *tierra firme** to take them captive. They should be good and intelligent servants, for I see that they say very quickly everything that is said to them; and I believe that they would become Christians very easily, for it seemed to me that they had no religion. Our Lord pleasing, at the time of my departure I will take six of them from here to Your Highnesses in order that they may learn to speak. . . .

. . . They came to the ship with dugouts that are made from the trunk of one tree, like a long boat, and all of one piece, and worked marvelously in the fashion of the land, and so big that in some of them 40 and 45 men came. And others smaller, down to some in which came one man alone. They row with a paddle like that of a baker and go marvelously. And if it capsizes on them they then throw themselves in the water, and they right and empty it with calabashes [bowls] that they carry. They brought balls of spun cotton and parrots and javelins and other little things that it would be tiresome to write down, and they gave everything for anything that was given to them. I was attentive and labored to find out if there was any gold; and I saw that some of them wore a little piece hung in a hole that they have in their noses. And by signs I was able to understand that, going to the south or rounding the island to the south, there was there a king who had large vessels of it and had very much gold. . . . This island is quite big and very flat and with very green trees and much water and a very large lake in the middle and without any mountains; and all of it so green that it is a pleasure to look at it. And these people are very gentle, and because of their desire to have some of our things, and believing that nothing will be given to them without their giving something, and not having anything, they take what they can and then throw themselves into the water to swim. . . .

Sunday 14 October

As soon as it dawned I ordered the ship's boat and the launches of the caravels made ready and went north-northeast along the island in order to see what there was in the other part, which was the eastern part. And also to see the villages, and I soon saw two or three, as well as people, who all came to the beach calling to us and giving thanks to God. Some of them brought us water; others, other things to eat; others, when they saw that I did not care to go ashore, threw themselves into the sea swimming and came to us, and we understood that they were asking us if we had come from the heavens. And one old man got into the ship's boat, and others in loud voices called to all the men and women: Come see the men who came from the heavens. Bring them something to eat and drink. Many men came, and many women, each one with something, giving thanks to God, throwing themselves on the ground; and they raised their hands to heaven, and afterward they called to us in loud voices to come ashore. But I was afraid, seeing a big stone reef that encircled that island all around. And in between the reef and shore there was depth

Tierra firme literally means "firm earth." In this context, however, it means the mainland.

and harbor for as many ships as there are in the whole of Christendom, and the entrance to it is very narrow. . . . And I saw a piece of land formed like an island, although it was not one, on which there were six houses. This piece of land might in two days be cut off to make an island, although I do not see this to be necessary since these people are very naive about weapons, as Your Highnesses will see from seven that I caused to be taken in order to carry them away to you and to learn our language and to return them. Except that, whenever Your Highnesses may command, all of them can be taken to Castile or held captive in this same island; because with 50 men all of them could be held in subjection and can be made to do whatever one might wish. And later [I noticed], near the said islet, groves of trees, the most beautiful that I saw and with their leaves as green as those of Castile in the months of April and May, and lots of water. I looked over the whole of that harbor and afterward returned to the ship and set sail, and I saw so many islands that I did not know how to decide which one I would go to first. And those men whom I had taken told me by signs that they were so very many that they were numberless. And they named by their names more than a hundred. Finally I looked for the largest and to that one I decided to go and so I am doing. It is about five leagues distant from this island of San Salvador, and the others of them some more, some less. All are very flat without mountains and very fertile and all populated and they make war on one another, even though these men are very simple and very handsome in body. . . .

Tuesday 30 October

He went out of the Rio de Mares to the northwest and, after he had gone 15 leagues, saw a cape full of palms and named it Cabo de Palmas. The Indians in the caravel *Pinta* said that behind that cape there was a river and that from the river to Cuba was a four-day journey. And the captain of the *Pinta* said that he understood that this Cuba was a city and that that land was a very big landmass that went far to the north, and that the king of that land was at war with the Grand Khan, whom they call *cami*, and his land or city, Faba, and many other names. The Admiral decided to go to that river and to send a present to the king of the land and to send him the letter of the sovereigns. And for this purpose he had a sailor who had gone on the same kind of mission in Guinea, and certain Indians from Guanahani wished to go with him so that afterward they would be returned to their own land. In the opinion of the Admiral he was distant from the equinoctial line 42 degrees toward the northern side (if the text from which I took this is not corrupt). And he says that he must strive to go to the Grand Khan, whom he thought was somewhere around there, or to the city of Cathay, which belongs to the Grand Khan. For he says that it is very large, according to what he was told before he left Spain. All this land, he says, is low and beautiful, and the sea deep. . . .

Sunday 4 November

. . . The Admiral showed cinnamon and pepper to a few of the Indians of that place (it seems from the samples that he was bringing from Castile) and he says that they recognized it; and they said by signs that nearby to the southeast there was a lot of it. He showed them gold and pearls, and certain old men answered that in a place that they called Bohío there was a vast amount and that they wore it on neck and in ears and on arms and legs; and also pearls. Moreover, he understood that they said that there were big ships and much trade and that all of this was to the southeast. He understood also that, far from there, there were one-eyed men, and others, with snouts of dogs, who ate men, and that as soon as one was taken they cut his throat and drank his blood and cut off his genitals. The Admiral decided to return to the ship to wait for the two men whom he had sent and to decide whether to leave and seek those lands, unless the two men brought good news of that which they desired. . . .

Tuesday 6 November

. . . They saw many kinds of trees and plants and fragrant flowers; they saw birds of many kinds, different from those of Spain, except partridges and nightingales, which sang, and geese, for of these there are a great many there. Four-footed beasts they did not see, except dogs that did not bark. The earth was very fertile and planted with those *mañes* and bean varieties very different from ours, and with that same millet. And they saw a large quantity of cotton collected and spun and worked; and in a single house they had seen more than five hundred *arrobas;* and that one might get there each year four thousand *quintales* [of it]. The Admiral says that it seemed to him that they did not sow it and that it produces fruit [i.e., cotton] all year. It is very fine and has a large boll. Everything that those people have, he says, they would give for a very paltry price, and that they would give a large basket of cotton for the tip of a lacing or anything else given to them. They are people, says the Admiral, quite lacking in evil and not warlike; [and] all of them, men and women [are] naked as their mothers bore them. It is true that the women wear a thing of cotton only so big as to cover their genitals and no more. And they are very respectful and not very black, less so than Canarians. I truly believe, most Serene Princes (the Admiral says here), that, given devout religious persons knowing thoroughly the language that they use, soon all of them would become Christian. And so I hope in Our Lord that Your Highnesses, with much diligence, will decide to send such persons in order to bring to the Church such great nations and to convert them, just as you have destroyed those that did not want to confess the Father and the Son and the Holy Spirit, and that after your days (for all of us are mortal) you will leave your kingdoms in a tranquil state, free of heresy and evil, and will be well received before the Eternal Creator, may it please Whom to give you long life and great increase of your kingdoms and dominions and the will and disposition to increase the Holy Christian Religion, as up to now you have done, amen. Today I pulled the ship off the beach and made ready to leave on Thursday, in the name of God, and to go to the southeast to seek gold and spices and to explore land. All these are the Admiral's words. He intended to leave on Thursday, but because a contrary wind came up he could not leave until the twelfth of November. . . .

Introduction to Document 3

The second document comes from a Catholic priest who dared to challenge the justice of Spanish conduct in the New World. Bartolomé de Las Casas wrote his *Very Brief Account of the Destruction of the Indies* in 1542 to be read aloud in a court called by Holy Roman Emperor Charles V to consider Spanish colonial reforms. Las Casas's objective was to shock his audience with gruesome details of Spanish cruelty. His account was later translated into six European languages and was circulated widely by the enemies of Spain. The passages reprinted here describe the island of Hispaniola (modern-day Haiti and the Dominican Republic), which Columbus described in his journal.

DOCUMENT 3 *From* **The Destruction of the Indies**

A BRIEF ACCOUNT

Bartolomé de Las Casas

The Indies were discovered in the year one thousand four hundred and ninety-two. In the following year a great many Spaniards went there with the intention of settling the land.

Thus, forty-nine years have passed since the first settlers penetrated the land, the first so-claimed being the large and most happy isle called Hispaniola, which is six hundred leagues in circumference. Around it in all directions are many other islands, some very big, others very small, and all of them were, as we saw with our own eyes, densely populated with native peoples called Indians. This large island was perhaps the most densely populated place in the world. There must be close to two hundred leagues of land on this island, and the seacoast has been explored for more than ten thousand leagues, and each day more of it is being explored. And all the land so far discovered is a beehive of people; it is as though God had crowded into these lands the great majority of mankind.

And of all the infinite universe of humanity, these people are the most guileless, the most devoid of wickedness and duplicity, the most obedient and faithful to their native masters and to the Spanish Christians whom they serve. They are by nature the most humble, patient, and peaceable, holding no grudges, free from embroilments, neither excitable nor quarrelsome. These people are the most devoid of rancors, hatreds, or desire for vengeance of any people in the world. And because they are so weak and complaisant, they are less able to endure heavy labor and soon die of no matter what malady. The sons of nobles among us, brought up in the enjoyments of life's refinements, are no more delicate than are these Indians, even those among them who are of the lowest rank of laborers. They are also poor people, for they not only possess little but have no desire to possess worldly goods. For this reason they are not arrogant, embittered, or greedy. Their repasts are such that the food of the holy fathers in the desert can scarcely be more parsimonious, scanty, and poor. As to their dress, they are generally naked, with only their pudenda covered somewhat. And when they cover their shoulders it is with a square cloth no more than two varas in size. They have no beds, but sleep on a kind of matting or else in a kind of suspended net called *bamacas*. They are very clean in their persons, with alert, intelligent minds, docile and open to doctrine, very apt to receive our holy Catholic faith, to be endowed with virtuous customs, and to behave in a godly fashion. And once they begin to hear the tidings of the Faith, they are so insistent on knowing more and on taking the sacraments of the Church and on observing the divine cult that, truly, the missionaries who are here need to be endowed by God with great patience in order to cope with such eagerness. Some of the secular Spaniards who have been here for many years say that the goodness of the Indians is undeniable and that if this gifted people could be brought to know the one true God they would be the most fortunate people in the world.

Yet into this sheepfold, into this land of meek outcasts there came some Spaniards who immediately behaved like ravening wild beasts, wolves, tigers, or lions that had been starved for many days. And Spaniards have behaved in no other way during the past forty years, down to the present time, for they are still acting like ravening beasts, killing, terrorizing, afflicting, torturing, and destroying the native peoples, doing all this with the strangest and most varied new methods of cruelty, never seen or heard of before, and to such a degree that this Island of Hispaniola, once so populous (having a population that I estimated to be more than three million), has now a population of barely two hundred persons.

The island of Cuba is nearly as long as the distance between Valladolid and Rome; it is now almost completely depopulated. San Juan [Puerto Rico] and Jamaica are two of the largest, most productive and attractive islands; both are now deserted and devastated. On the northern side of Cuba and Hispaniola lie the neighboring Lucayos comprising more than sixty islands including those called *Gigantes*, beside numerous other islands, some small some large. The least felicitous of them were more fertile and beautiful than the gardens of the King of Seville. They have the healthiest lands in the world, where lived more than five hundred thousand souls; they are now deserted, inhabited by not a single living creature. All the people were slain or died after being taken into captivity and brought to the Island of Hispaniola to be sold as slaves. When the Spaniards saw that some of these had escaped, they sent a ship to find them, and it voyaged for three years among the islands searching for those who had escaped being slaughtered, for a good Christian had helped them escape, taking pity on them and had won them over to Christ; of these there were eleven persons and these I saw.

More than thirty other islands in the vicinity of San Juan are for the most part and for the same reason depopulated, and the land laid waste. On these islands I estimate there are 2,100 leagues of land that have been ruined and depopulated, empty of people.

As for the vast mainland, which is ten times larger than all Spain, even including Aragon and Portugal, containing more land than the distance between Seville and Jerusalem, or more than two thousand leagues, we are sure that our Spaniards, with their cruel and abominable acts, have devastated the land and exterminated the rational people who fully inhabited it. We can estimate very surely and truthfully that in the forty years that have passed, with the infernal actions of the Christians, there have been unjustly slain more than twelve million men, women, and children. In truth, I believe without trying to deceive myself that the number of the slain is more like fifteen million.

The common ways mainly employed by the Spaniards who call themselves Christian and who have gone there to extirpate those pitiful nations and wipe them off the earth is by unjustly waging cruel and bloody wars. Then, when they have slain all those who fought for their lives or to escape the tortures they would have to endure, that is to say, when they have slain all the native rulers and young men (since the Spaniards usually spare only the women and children, who are subjected to the hardest and bitterest servitude ever suffered by man or beast), they enslave any survivors. With these infernal methods of tyranny they debase and weaken countless numbers of those pitiful Indian nations.

Their reason for killing and destroying such an infinite number of souls is that the Christians have an ultimate aim, which is to acquire gold, and to swell themselves with riches in a very brief time and thus rise to a high estate disproportionate to their merits. It should be kept in mind that their insatiable greed and ambition, the greatest ever seen in the world, is the cause of their villainies. And also, those lands are so rich and felicitous, the native peoples so meek and patient, so easy to subject, that our Spaniards have no more consideration for them than beasts. And I say this from my own knowledge of the acts I witnessed. But I should not say "than beasts" for, thanks be to God, they have treated beasts with some respect; I should say instead like excrement on the public squares. And thus they have deprived the Indians of their lives and souls, for the millions I mentioned have died without the Faith and without the benefit of the sacraments. This is a well-known and proven fact which even the tyrant Governors, themselves killers, know and admit. And never have the Indians in all the Indies committed any act against the Spanish Christians, until those Christians have first and many times committed countless cruel aggressions against them or against neighboring nations. For in the beginning the Indians regarded the Spaniards as angels from Heaven. Only after the Spaniards had used violence against them, killing, robbing, torturing, did the Indians ever rise up against them. . . .

On the Island Hispaniola was where the Spaniards first landed, as I have said. Here those Christians perpetrated their first ravages and oppressions against the native peoples. This was the first land in the New World to be destroyed and depopulated by the Christians, and here they began their subjection of the women and children, taking them away from the Indians to use them and ill use them, eating the food they provided with their sweat and toil. The Spaniards did not content themselves with what the Indians gave them of their own free will, according to their ability, which was always too little to satisfy enormous appetites, for a Christian eats and consumes in one day an amount of food that would suffice to feed three houses inhabited by ten Indians for one month. And they committed other acts of force and violence and oppression which made the Indians realize that these men had not come from Heaven. And some of the Indians concealed their foods while others concealed their wives and children and still others fled to the mountains to avoid the terrible transactions of the Christians.

And the Christians attacked them with buffets and beatings, until finally they laid hands on the nobles of the villages. Then they behaved with such temerity and shamelessness that the most powerful ruler of the islands had to see his own wife raped by a Christian officer.

From that time onward the Indians began to seek ways to throw the Christians out of their lands. They took up arms, but their weapons were very weak and of little service in offense and still less in defense. (Because of this, the wars of the Indians against each other are little more than games played by children.) And the Christians, with their horses and swords and pikes began to carry out massacres and strange cruelties against them. They attacked the towns and spared neither the children nor the aged nor pregnant women nor women in childbed, not only stabbing them and dismembering them but cutting them to pieces as if dealing with sheep in the slaughter house. They laid bets as to who, with one stroke of the sword, could split a man in two or could cut off his head or spill out his entrails with a single stroke of the pike. They took infants from their mothers' breasts, snatching them by the legs and pitching them headfirst against the crags or snatched them by the arms and threw them into the rivers, roaring with laughter and saying as the babies fell into the water, "Boil there, you offspring of the devil!" Other infants they put to the sword along with their mothers and anyone else who happened to be nearby. They made some low wide gallows on which the hanged victim's feet almost touched the ground, stringing up their victims in lots of thirteen, in memory of Our Redeemer and His twelve Apostles, then set burning wood at their feet and thus burned them alive. To others they attached straw or wrapped their whole bodies in straw and set them afire. With still others, all those they wanted to capture alive, they cut off their hands and hung them round the victim's neck, saying, "Go now, carry the message," meaning, Take the news to the Indians who have fled to the mountains. They usually dealt with the chieftains and nobles in the following way: they made a grid of rods which they placed on forked sticks, then lashed the victims to the grid and lighted a smoldering fire underneath, so that little by little, as those captives screamed in despair and torment, their souls would leave them. . . .

After the wars and the killings had ended, when usually there survived only some boys, some women, and children, these survivors were distributed among the Christians to be slaves. The *repartimiento* or distribution was made according to the rank and importance of the Christian to whom the Indians were allocated, one of them being given thirty, another forty, still another, one or two hundred, and besides the rank of the Christian there was also to be considered in what favor he stood with the tyrant they called Governor. The pretext was that these allocated Indians were to be instructed in the articles of the Christian Faith. As if those Christians who were as a rule foolish and cruel and greedy and vicious could be caretakers of souls! And the care they took was to send the men to the mines to dig for gold, which is intolerable labor, and to send the women into the fields of the big ranches to hoe and till the land, work suitable for strong men. Nor to either the men or the women did they give any food except herbs and legumes, things of little substance. The milk in the breasts of the women with infants dried up and thus in a short while the infants perished. And since men and women were separated, there could be no marital relations. And the men died in the mines and the women died on the ranches from the same causes, exhaustion and hunger. And thus was depopulated that island which had been densely populated.

Introduction to Document 4

There is no way to tell the story of the coming of Europeans in the words of Caribbean peoples; their impressions are lost to history. But written records have survived from the most powerful native group, the Aztecs. On November 8, 1519,

Hernán Cortés, accompanied by six hundred Spanish soldiers, as well as many indigenous allies, entered the Aztec capitol of Tenochtitlán (today, Mexico City). On first seeing the city, Bernal Díaz del Castillo, one of the conquistadors, thought he must be dreaming; the temples and towers and fortresses all gleaming white were "a wonderful thing to behold." The Spaniards were greeted by Motecuhzoma (better known to us as Montezuma), the Aztec King. Motecuhzoma believed that Cortés must be Quetzalcoatl, the god who it had been prophesied would return some day from across the waters. The following account was recorded in Nahuatl, the Aztec language, by students of the Franciscan friar Bernadino de Sahagún. Called the *Florentine Codex*, these narratives were taken down a few decades after the conquest and were based on the reminiscences of Aztecs who had lived through those events.

DOCUMENT 4   *The Aztec Account of the Spanish Conquest, Florentine Codex, as Collected by Bernadino de Sahagún*

The Spaniards arrived in Xoloco, near the entrance to Tenochtitlán. That was the end of the march, for they had reached their goal.

Motecuhzoma now arrayed himself in his finery, preparing to go out to meet them. The other great princes also adorned their persons, as did the nobles and their chieftains and knights. They all went out together to meet the strangers.

They brought trays heaped with the finest flowers—the flower that resembles a shield; the flower shaped like a heart; in the center, the flower with the sweetest aroma; and the fragrant yellow flower, the most precious of all. They also brought garlands of flowers, and ornaments for the breast, and necklaces of gold, necklaces hung with rich stones, necklaces fashioned in the petatillo style.

Thus Motecuhzoma went out to meet them, there in Huitzillan. He presented many gifts to the Captain and his commanders, those who had come to make war. He showered gifts upon them and hung flowers around their necks; he gave them necklaces of flowers and bands of flowers to adorn their breasts; he set garlands of flowers upon their heads. Then he hung the gold necklaces around their necks and gave them presents of every sort as gifts of welcome.

When Motecuhzoma had given necklaces to each one, Cortés asked him: "Are you Motecuhzoma? Are you the king? Is it true that you are the king Motecuhzoma?"

And the king said: "Yes, I am Motecuhzoma." Then he stood up to welcome Cortés; he came forward, bowed his head low and addressed him in these words: "Our lord, you are weary. The journey has tired you, but now you have arrived on the earth. You have come to your city, Mexico. You have come here to sit on your throne, to sit under its canopy.

"The kings who have gone before, your representatives, guarded it and preserved it for your coming. The kings Itzcoatl, Motecuhzoma the Elder, Axayacatl, Tizoc and Ahuitzol ruled for you in the City of Mexico. The people were protected by their swords and sheltered by their shields. . . .

"No, it is not a dream. I am not walking in my sleep. I am not seeing you in my dreams. . . . I have seen you at last! I have met you face to face! I was in agony for five days, for ten days, with my eyes fixed on the Region of the Mystery. And now you have come out of the clouds and mists to sit on your throne again.

"This was foretold by the kings who governed your city, and now it has taken place. You have back to us; you have come down from the sky. Rest now, and take possession of your royal houses. Welcome to your land, my lords!"

When Motecuhzoma had finished, La Malinche translated his address into Spanish so that the Captain could understand it. Cortés replied in his strange and savage tongue, speaking first to La Malinche: "Tell Motecuhzoma that we are his friends. There is nothing to fear. We have wanted to see him for a long time, and now we have seen his face and heard his words. Tell him that we love him well and that our hearts are contented." . . .

When the Spaniards entered the Royal House, they placed Motecuhzoma under guard and kept him under their vigilance. They also placed a guard over Itzcuauhtzin, but the other lords were permitted to depart.

Then the Spaniards fired one of their cannons, and this caused great confusion in the city. The people scattered in every direction; they fled without rhyme or reason; they ran off as if they were being pursued. It was as if they had eaten the mushrooms that confuse the mind, or had seen some dreadful apparition. They were all overcome by terror, as if their hearts had fainted. And when night fell, the panic spread through the city and their fears would not let them sleep.

In the morning the Spaniards told Motecuhzoma what they needed in the way of supplies: tortillas, fried chickens, hens' eggs, pure water, firewood and charcoal. Also: large, clean cooking pots, water jars, pitchers, dishes and other pottery. Motecuhzoma ordered that it be sent to them. The chiefs who received this order were angry with the king and no longer revered or respected him. But they furnished the Spaniards with all the provisions they needed—food, beverages and water, and fodder for the horses. . . .

When the Spaniards were installed in the palace, they asked Motecuhzoma about the city's resources and reserves and about the warriors' ensigns and shields. They questioned him closely and then demanded gold.

Motecuhzoma guided them to it. They surrounded him and crowded close with their weapons. He walked in the center, while they formed a circle around him.

When they arrived at the treasure house called Teucalco, the riches of gold and feathers were brought out to them: ornaments made of quetzal feathers, richly worked shields, disks of gold, the necklaces of the idols, gold nose plugs, gold greaves and bracelets and crowns.

The Spaniards immediately stripped the feathers from the gold shields and ensigns. They gathered all the gold into a great mound and set fire to everything else, regardless of its value. Then they melted down the gold into ingots. As for the precious green stones, they took only the best of them; the rest were snatched up by the Tlaxcaltecas [a neighboring people]. The Spaniards searched through the whole treasure house, questioning and quarreling, and seized every object they thought was beautiful. . . .

Next they went to Motecuhzoma's storehouse, in the place called Totocalco [Place of the Palace of the Birds], where his personal treasures were kept. The Spaniards grinned like little beasts and patted each other with delight.

When they entered the hall of treasures, it was as if they had arrived in Paradise. They searched everywhere and coveted everything; they were slaves to their own greed. All of Motecuhzoma's possessions were brought out: fine bracelets, necklaces with large stones, ankle rings with little gold bells, the royal crowns and all the royal finery—everything that belonged to the king and was reserved to him only. They seized these treasures as if they were their own, as if this plunder were merely a stroke of good luck. And when they had taken all the gold, they heaped up everything else in the middle of the patio. . . .

The Aztecs begged permission of their king to hold the fiesta of Huitzilopochtli. The Spaniards wanted to see this fiesta to learn how it was celebrated. A delegation of the celebrants came to the palace where Motecuhzoma was a prisoner, and when their spokesman asked his permission, he granted it to them.

As soon as the delegation returned, the women began to grind seeds of the chicalote. These women had fasted for a whole year. They ground the seeds in the patio of the temple.

The Spaniards came out of the palace together, dressed in armor and carrying their weapons with them. They stalked among the women and looked at them one by one; they stared into the faces of the women who were grinding seeds. After this cold inspection, they went back into the palace. It is said that they planned to kill the celebrants if the men entered the patio. . . .

[The Aztecs celebrated the fiesta of Toxcatl in honor of the god Huitzilopochtli. Bernadino de Sahagún observed that this spring festival was one of the most important in the calendar, much like the Spaniard's Easter. The incidents described in this passage took place when Cortés was away from Tenochtitlán, and the Spanish soldiers were commanded in his absence by Pedro de Alvarado.]

On the evening before the fiesta of Toxcatl, the celebrants began to model a statue of Huitzilopochtli. They gave it such a human appearance that it seemed the body of a living man. Yet they made the statue with nothing but a paste made of the ground seeds of the chicalote, which they shaped over an armature of sticks.

When the statue was finished, they dressed it in rich feathers, and they painted crossbars over and under its eyes. They also clipped on its earrings of turquoise mosaic; these were in the shape of serpents, with gold rings hanging from them. Its nose plug, in the shape of an arrow, was made of gold and was inlaid with fine stones.

They placed the magic headdress of hummingbird feathers on its head. They also adorned it with an *anecuyotl*, which was a belt made of feathers, with a cone at the back. Then they hung around its neck an ornament of yellow parrot feathers, fringed like the locks of a young boy. Over this they put its nettleleaf cape, which was painted black and decorated with five clusters of eagle feathers.

Next they wrapped it in its cloak, which was painted with skulls and bones, and over this they fastened its vest. The vest was painted with dismembered human parts: skulls, ears, hearts, intestines, torsos, breasts, hands and feet. They also put on its *maxtlatl*, or loincloth, which was decorated with images of dissevered limbs and fringed with amate paper. This *maxtlatl* was painted with vertical stripes of bright blue. . . .

Early the next morning, the statue's face was uncovered by those who had been chosen for that ceremony. They gathered in front of the idol in single file and offered it gifts of food, such as round seedcakes or perhaps human flesh. But they did not carry it up to its temple on top of the pyramid.

All the young warriors were eager for the fiesta to begin. They had sworn to dance and sing with all their hearts, so that the Spaniards would marvel at the beauty of the rituals.

The procession began, and the celebrants filed into the temple patio to dance the Dance of the Serpent. When they were all together in the patio, the songs and the dance began. Those who had fasted for twenty days and those who had fasted for a year were in command of the others. . . .

At this moment in the fiesta, when the dance was loveliest and when song was linked to song, the Spaniards were seized with an urge to kill the celebrants. They all ran forward, armed as if for battle. They closed the entrances and passageways, all the gates of the patio: the Eagle Gate in the lesser palace, the Gate of the Canestalk and the Gate of the Serpent of Mirrors. They posted guards so that no one could escape, and then rushed into the Sacred Patio to slaughter the celebrants. They came on foot, carrying their swords and their wooden or metal shields.

They ran in among the dancers, forcing their way to the place where the drums were played. They attacked the man who was drumming and cut off his arms. Then they cut off his head, and it rolled across the floor.

They attacked all the celebrants, stabbing them, spearing them, striking them with their swords. They attacked some of them from behind, and these fell instantly to the

The Spanish massacre of the Aztecs in the main temple, Tenochtitlán.
(Adapted from paintings in the Aztec Codex Duran by Alberto Bertran.)

ground with their entrails hanging out. Others they beheaded: they cut off their heads, or split their heads to pieces.

They struck others in the shoulders, and their arms were torn from their bodies. They wounded some in the thigh and some in the calf. They slashed others in the abdomen, and their entrails all spilled to the ground. Some attempted to run away, but their intestines dragged as they ran; they seemed to tangle their feet in their own entrails. No matter how they tried to save themselves, they could find no escape.

Some attempted to force their way out, but the Spaniards murdered them at the gates. Others climbed the walls, but they could not save themselves. Those who ran into the communal houses were safe there for a while; so were those who lay down among the victims and pretended to be dead. But if they stood up again, the Spaniards saw them and killed them.

The blood of the warriors flowed like water and gathered into pools. The pools widened, and the stench of blood and entrails filled the air. The Spaniards ran into the communal houses to kill those who were hiding. They ran everywhere and searched everywhere; they invaded every room, hunting and killing.

. . . And they shackled Motecuhzoma in chains. . . .

POSTSCRIPT

The Aztecs were formidable opponents; it took the Spanish nearly two years to conquer them, as the native warriors inflicted heavy casualties and sometimes drove their enemies before them. But superior technology and the European diseases that ravaged the population finally did their work. The Aztecs mourned for their lost city:

> Broken spears lie in the roads;
> we have torn our hair in our grief.
> The houses are roofless now, and their walls
> are red with blood.
>
> Worms are swarming in the streets and plazas,
> and the walls are splattered with gore.
> The water has turned red, as if it were dyed
> and when we drink it,
> it has the taste of brine.
>
> We have pounded our hands in despair
> against the adobe walls,
> for our inheritance, our city, is lost and dead.
> The shields of our warriors were its defense,
> but they could not save it. . . .

QUESTIONS

Defining Terms

Identify in the context of the chapter each of the following:

James Gibbons	Grand Admiral of the Ocean Sea
genocide	Huitzilopochtli
Guanaham	Motecuhzoma
Hispaniola	fiesta of Toxcatl
Bartolomé de Las Casas	*Florentine Codex*

Probing the Sources

1. Contrast the celebrations of "Discovery Day" in 1892 and 1992. How do you explain the differences?

2. What were the scientific, economic, diplomatic, and religious objectives of the Columbus mission?

3. Compare the ways Columbus and Las Casas described the environment and peoples of the New World. How do you explain the similarities and differences in their observations?

4. To what degree did religion influence Spanish exploration and colonization?

5. In what ways did the Spanish conquest of the New World affect the political, economic, social, agricultural, and dietary patterns of the two continents?

Interpreting the Sources

1. Using all three sources, retell the story of Columbus as if you were living in the Caribbean when the Spanish arrived.

2. What label—hero, villain, victim, product of his time, or some other term—best captures your feelings about each of the following: (a) Columbus, (b) Las Casas, (c) Motecuhzoma? Justify your responses.

3. How do you think Americans should celebrate Columbus Day?

ADDITIONAL READING

An older yet still insightful and entertaining biography of Columbus is Samuel Eliot Morrison's *Admiral of the Ocean Sea* (1942). The definitive edition of the journal of the first voyage is Oliver Dunn and James E. Kelley, eds., *The Diario of Christopher Columbus's First Voyage to America, 1492–93* (1989). An interesting introduction to Las Casas, as well as a translation of his writings, is in George Sanderlin, ed., *Bartolomé de Las Casas* (1971).

An excellent study that details the important biological consequences produced by the interaction of the European and Native American cultures is Alfred W. Crosby, Jr.'s *The Columbian Exchange* (1972). Also of interest are the three short volumes produced for the Quincentennial by the American Historical Association: James Axtell, *Imagining the Other: First Encounters in North America* (1991); William D. Phillips, Jr., *Before 1492: Christopher Columbus's Formative Years* (1992); and Karen Ordahl Kupperman, *North America and the Beginnings of European Colonization* (1992). On North America before Columbus, see Alvin M. Josephy, *America in 1492: The World of the Indian Peoples Before the Arrival of Columbus* (1992); and Francis Jennings, *The Founders of America* (1993).

2

Dying and Surviving in Virginia

Historical Context

Historians are detectives, storytellers, and occasionally, mythmakers. As detectives we search for clues about past events, ideas, or people that interest us. Most generally, we gather these clues from documents that, by either planning or happenstance, have survived the ravages of time. From a study of these documents—a task that involves discounting some evidence in order to make sense of the whole—we attempt to piece together a meaningful story.

Often the stories we tell provoke interest only among other lovers of history. Some accounts temporarily gain wide popularity but are soon forgotten. On rare occasions, however, narratives of the past (or more likely, retold, simplified versions of an original tale) evoke broad, enduring emotional responses. These accounts are passed forward from generation to generation and become ingrained in the collective memory of a people. Citizens who fail to understand them are considered alien or culturally illiterate. At some point these enduring stories may transcend history and enter the realm of "myth." In labeling a story a myth, we are not implying that it is necessarily untrue. Rather, we simply mean that the story has become a traditional tale, shared by all members of a community, that purports to explain the origins, customs, and institutions of a people.

The early history of Virginia has become an American myth. Most of us can recall stories about Jamestown, the first permanent English colony in America. We can recite tales learned in childhood about Captain John Smith, the savior of the colony, who transformed the lazy colonists into hardened work crews. We remember the man, if not the name, of Powhatan, the powerful Algonquian chief who shared the secret of growing corn with the early colonists. And we remember Pocahontas, the Algonquian princess who pleaded with her father to spare the life of John Smith, and who later married the Englishman John Rolfe and converted to his Christian religion.

Augmenting these real-life adventures of daring individuals is the inspirational collective history of the colony. Established as a business enterprise, early Jamestown was the property of Virginia Company stockholders who risked their personal assets in pursuit of profit. While their original plan to find gold failed, the stockholders learned from their mistakes, altered their policies, and prepared the way for future investors to extract great wealth from Virginia's plentiful tobacco harvests. Moreover, in 1619, the company instituted the House of Burgesses in Virginia and thereby planted in American soil the seed of democratic government. Altogether, the colony of Jamestown overcame early set-backs, survived, and left a grand legacy for the American people. More than simply England's first permanent colony in the New World, Jamestown has become for many a symbol of American achievement. It was a place where courageous and enterprising individuals overcame hardships, tamed the forces of nature, brought glory to their country, and fulfilled their personal dreams.

Our memory of colonial Virginia, as previously described, is not necessarily incorrect, but it is highly selective. After all, the story of English settlement in the land named for the "virgin" queen Elizabeth does not begin in Jamestown in 1607 but in the failed colonies of Roanoke (today, part of North Carolina) in the 1580s. Notwithstanding the inspiration we draw from Jamestown, for both its sponsors and its settlers, early Virginia was a disaster that cost investors their fortunes and colonists their lives.

For nearly a century following Columbus's first voyage, Spain was the dominant nation on earth. No peoples, either in Europe or in the Americas, were able to challenge Spain's power in the New World. Midway into Queen Elizabeth's reign, however, the English monarch quietly gave two half-brothers, Humphrey Gilbert and Walter Raleigh, permission to establish an English settlement in any land not actually possessed by a "Christian prince." In the careful wording of this license, Elizabeth avoided directly challenging Philip II, who had claimed all of North America for Spain, but who actually possessed as his northern-most outpost only a lonely fort in Saint Augustine, Florida. The English queen did not worry herself about affronting the chieftains of the indigenous peoples of North America who occupied the vast majority of the continent.

In 1583, Gilbert attempted to establish an English outpost in Newfoundland. After one winter in the northern climate, Gilbert decided to relocate further to the south. While returning to England for supplies, however, Gilbert's ship was lost at sea. Undaunted, Raleigh sent a 1584 exploration party to find a more suitable location for an English settlement. This party, under the command of Philip Amadas and Arthur Barlowe, explored the Chesapeake Bay area of North America. After receiving the reports of this reconnaissance mission, Raleigh sent in 1585 about one hundred would-be English colonists, most of whom were soldiers, to the region, now renamed Virginia. The colonists built a fort at Roanoke Island on the Carolina outer banks.

Although the English settlers were intruders on land inhabited by the Carolina Algonquian Indians, at least initially a spirit of goodwill existed among the English and the Native Americans. With vastly different languages, customs, and technologies, the two peoples were fascinated by the strange sounds, behavior, and objects of each other. At first, mutual curiosity and the natural desire to learn by exchanging gifts—Native American food for English metals—fostered a semblance of friendship among two peoples. Within a year, however, cooperation gave way to conflict. When the disgruntled English settlers decided to abort the colony and return to England, the Algonquians were happy to see them leave.

In 1587, a second group made up of 155 English recruits, including 17 women and 11 children, reestablished the settlement at Roanoke. These colonists, mainly persons of small resources, hoped to plant an English community of men, women, and children in the New World and to concentrate on subsistence farming rather

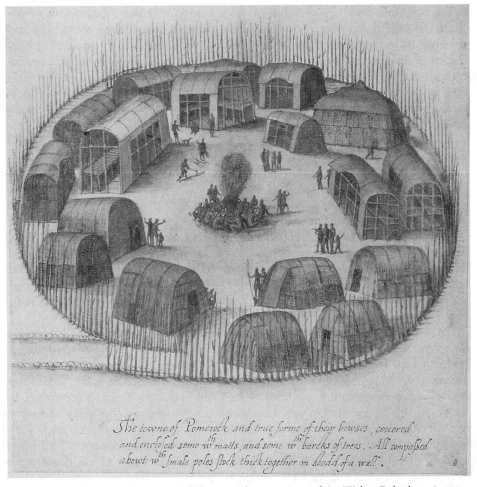

The towne of Pomeiock and true forme of their howses, couered and enclosed some w:th matts and some w:th barcks of trees. All compassed abowt w:th smale poles stock thick together in steedd of a wall.

This drawing by John White, an English artist who accompanied Sir Walter Raleigh to America in 1585, depicts the typical Algonquian village of Pemiock. Many eastern groups of Native Americans settled in semipermanent villages like this one, composed of domed houses made from woven mats and tree bark and surrounded by a defensive wooden palisade. (Reproduced by courtesy of the Trustees of the British Museum. © The British Museum)

than on the exploitation of resources for export. Despite their limited ambitions and peaceful intentions, they, too, found surviving in the American wilderness difficult. Just one month after their arrival, they persuaded their governor, John White, to return to England for additional supplies. Keeping a small band of settlers on the island, a group that included White's daughter and newborn granddaughter, Virginia Dare, Governor White left for England, hoping to secure from Raleigh the needed supplies and to return promptly to Roanoke. England's war against the great Spanish Armada (1588), however, delayed his return voyage. When White finally arrived at Roanoke in 1590, he found the colony utterly deserted. What became of the "lost colony" is still a mystery.

The twice-failed venture at Roanoke did not destroy England's ambitions for Virginia, but it did demonstrate how risky and expensive colonization could be. Future colonization efforts would be undertaken not by individual promoters such as Gilbert or Raleigh, but by joint-stock companies, the forerunners of the modern-day corporation. These companies, which generally secured from the Crown special trading privileges, raised funds to support the enterprise by selling shares to investors who preferred to divide among themselves the financial risks as well as the anticipated profits.

In 1606, three years after James I had succeeded Elizabeth as the English monarch, two groups of merchants—one from London and one from Plymouth—persuaded the new king to grant them exclusive rights to colonize in Virginia. The Plymouth Company, which received a charter to settle the northern half of the region, sent a party to a site in the present-day state of Maine. Like the aborted efforts in Newfoundland and Roanoke, however, this colony was soon abandoned.

Meanwhile, the investors from London recruited about 140 colonists to build a colony in the Chesapeake Bay region. Shortly before Christmas 1606, three ships, the *Susan Constant,* the *Godspeed,* and the *Discovery,* left England in hopes of an early spring arrival. Barely off the English coast, the winds stilled and the ships sat stranded in the water. For six weeks the men waited. Tempers flared, fevers spread, and precious rations were consumed.

On April 26, 1607, those who had survived the passage entered Chesapeake Bay. After spending about two weeks scouting the region, they selected an encampment 60 miles up a river that they named James in honor of their king. The chosen site was a peninsula about two miles long and one mile wide, with a narrow isthmus connecting it to the bank of the river. Surrounded almost completely by water, the site of Jamestown was chosen because it had a deep water shoreline, had an abundance of trees and game, and, most important, could be readily defended from Spanish attack. Unfortunately, Jamestown lacked adequate freshwater springs, and the high ground rimming its shores made much of the peninsula a marshland—an ideal habitat for malaria-bearing mosquitoes.

The Spanish never attacked, but the mosquitoes and Native Americans did. By the time a second shipment of supplies arrived in January 1608, only 38 of the original group remained alive. Later English recruits swelled the population to about five hundred, but all save 60 of these died during the "starving time" of the winter of 1609–1610.

Many of the earliest settlers were gentlemen, who expected to lead rather than work, or the servants and craftsmen of gentlemen, who were accustomed to labor but did not consider field cultivation their line of work. Having come to Virginia with unrealistic expectations, they found the environment unfamiliar and hostile. Ill prepared and ill supplied, they quickly lost both health and spirit. The dictatorial controls of such leaders as John Smith and Sir Thomas Dale kept the colony afloat for a while, but even during the best of times, survival—not the pursuit of happiness—was the only realistic goal. In the worst of times, some resorted to cannibalism in order to survive.

The colony ultimately endured largely because the stockholders back home refused to concede defeat. Although always short of the capital needed to fund the project adequately, the company kept sending new recruits to the wasteland in the hope of making a return on their investment. These latter settlers came largely from the ranks of ordinary English working people. Most were male, typically young, between the ages of 15 and 24, and without skills or wealth. By the second decade of the venture, the great majority of the immigrants came as "indentured servants," that is, as bound laborers who, in exchange for the price of passage, legally committed themselves to work a set number of years (generally four to seven) for their masters.

In a desperate search for profits, the stockholders in England censored colonial publications and lied about life in Virginia. They secured permission from the king to hold public lotteries to fill company coffers; they brought Pocahontas to England (and to her death!) for promotional purposes; they recruited shiploads of unmarried English women and auctioned them off for tobacco as wives for the Virginia bachelors; they invoked martial law in the colony, and when they deemed it to be to their financial advantage, they instituted a House of Burgesses that gave the Virginians some say in local affairs—subject, of course, to the veto of the company. They searched for, but never discovered, the secret of extracting treasures from American soil. And after the Indian uprising of 1622 eliminated one-third of the white population in Virginia, even the most optimistic of the investors fell into despair. By 1624, when King James finally revoked the company's charter, the stockholders had lost about 100,000 pounds in the company, an equivalent of $12 million in today's currency! Jamestown was the first permanent English colony in the New World. It also, however, was a death trap and a financial bust. The colony survived, but most of the colonists and investors did not.

THE DOCUMENTS

This chapter includes descriptions of life in colonial Virginia during the first half-century of attempted settlement by English colonists. The earliest reports, which portrayed Virginia as an earthly paradise, shifted over time to more sordid accounts of disease, starvation, violence, brutality, and managerial incompetence. Read the following documents written by those who participated in these historic ventures, and ask yourself what were the principal concerns of the sponsors and settlers of the first English colonies. To what degree do these descriptions of early Virginia correspond to your preconceived notions? How do you explain the discrepancies?

Introduction to Documents 1, 2, and 3

The first document is an excerpt from Queen Elizabeth's 1584 charter to Sir Walter Raleigh. Note the references in the document to land "not actually possessed of any Christian Prince, nor inhabited by Christian People." The next two documents are taken from a collection of narratives published in 1589 by Richard Hakluyt, a friend of Raleigh's colonization ventures. Do note, however, that the language has been modernized. Although the documents were written by Englishmen with European biases and were edited to fit the propaganda needs of Raleigh, the texts are important, for they provide us with the first view of North America before English occupation. The excerpts from Arthur Barlowe's "Narrative of the 1584 Voyage" describe the landscape and peoples of the North American seacoast at the time of contact. (Spelling and grammar have been modernized.) The selections from Thomas Harriot's *A Brief and True Report of the New Found Land of Virginia* detail sympathetic observations of the inner life and beliefs of the native peoples. Harriot's descriptions of the mysterious epidemics that marked his travels also inform us of one of the appalling results of contact: the spread of European diseases among the aboriginal populations. Compare these descriptions of contact in Virginia with Columbus's initial impressions of the Caribbean. In what ways are the accounts similar and different?

DOCUMENT 1 *Charter to Sir Walter Raleigh: 1584*

ELIZABETH by the Grace of God of England, France and Ireland Queen, defender of the faith, &c. To all people to whom these presents shall come, greeting.

Know ye that . . . we give and grant to our trustee and well-beloved servant Walter Raleigh, Esquire, and to his heirs assignee forever, free liberty and license from time to time, and at all times forever hereafter, to discover, search, find out, and view such remote, heathen and barbarous lands, countries, and territories, not actually possessed of any Christian Prince, nor inhabited by Christian People. . . .

And further that the said Walter Raleigh . . . shall have hold, occupy, and enjoin to him, his heirs and assignee, and every of them forever, all the soil of all such lands, territories, and Countries, so to be discovered and possessed as aforesaid, and of all such Cities, castles, towns, villages, and places in the same, with the right, royalties, franchises, and jurisdictions . . . reserving always to us, our heirs and successors, for all services, duties, and demands, the fifth part of all the ore of gold and silver, that from time to time, and at all times after such discovery, subduing and possessing, shall be there gotten and obtained: All which lands, Countries, and territories, shall forever beholden of the said Walter Raleigh, his heirs and assignee, of us, our heirs and successors, by homage, and by the said payment of the said fifth part, reserved only for all services.

And moreover, we give and grant license to the said Walter Raleigh . . . for his and their defense, [the authority to] encounter and expulse, repel and resist . . . all, and every such person and persons whatsoever . . . [who] shall attempt to inhabit within the said Countries, or any of them, or within the space of two hundred leagues near to the place or places within such Countries as aforesaid (if they shall not be before planted or inhabited within the limits as aforesaid with the subjects of any Christian Prince being in amity with us) where the said Walter Raleigh, his heirs, or assignee, or any of them, or his, or their or any of their associates or company, shall within sine [six?] years (next ensuing) make their dwellings. . . .

In witness whereof, we have caused these our letters to be made patents. Witness our selves, at Westminster, the 25. day of March, in the six and twentieth year of our Reign.

DOCUMENT 2 *"Narrative of the 1584 Voyage"*

Arthur Barlowe

The first voyage made to the coasts of America, with two boats, were Captains Master Philip Amadas and Master Arthur Barlowe, who discovered part of the country now called Virginia, in 1584: Written by one of the said Captains and sent to Sir Walter Raleigh, knight, at whose charge and direction the voyage was set forth.

On the 27th day of April, in the year of our redemption 1584, we departed the west of England with two boats well furnished with men and victuals. . . .

On the tenth of May we arrived at the Canaries, and on the tenth of June in this present year, we were fallen with the Islands of the West Indies. . . .

The next day there came upon us diverse boats, and in one of them, the King's brother, accompanied with forty or fifty men, very handsome and goodly people, and in their behavior as mannerly and civil as any of Europe. His name was Granganimeo, and the King is called Wingina, the country Wingandacoa, (and now by her Majesty, Virginia). . . .

The King is greatly obeyed, and his brothers and children reverenced. The King himself was sorely wounded in a fight which he had with the King of the next country. . . . A day or two after this, we fell to trading with them, exchanging some things that we had for chamous leather, elk and deer skins. When we showed him all our packet of merchandise, of all the things that he saw, a bright tin dish most pleased him. He presently took it up, clapt it before his breast, and afterward made a hole in the brim thereof, and hung it about his neck, making signs that it would defend him against his enemies arrows. Those people maintain a deadly and terrible war with the people and King adjoining.

[The people] are of color yellowish, and their hair black for the most, and yet we saw children that had very fine auburn and chestnut color hair. . . . No people in the world carry more respect to their King, Nobility and Governors than these do. The King's brother's wife, when she came to us, as she did many times, was always followed with forty or fifty women. . . .

The King's brother had great liking of our armor, a sword, and divers other things which we had, and offered to lay a great box of pearl in exchange for them. But we refused it for this time because we would not make them know that we esteemed it until we had understood in what places of the country the pearl grew (which now your worship does very well understand). He was very just in his promise, for many times we delivered him merchandise upon his word and always he came within the day and performed his promise. He sent us every day a brace or two of fat bucks, conies, hares, fish, the best of the world. He sent us divers kinds of fruits, melons, walnuts, cucumbers, gourds, peas, and divers roots, and fruits very excellent good, and of their country corn, which is very white, fair and well tasted and grows three times in five months. In May they sow, in July they reap; in June they sow, in August they reap; in July they sow, in September they reap. They only cast the corn into the ground, breaking a little of the soft turf with a wooden mattock or pick ax. We proved the soil and put some of our peas into the ground. In ten days they were of fourteen inches high. They have also beans very fair, of divers colors and wonderful plenty, some growing naturally and some in their gardens. And so have they both wheat and oats.

The soil is the most plentiful, sweet, fruitful and wholesome of all the world. There are above fourteen several sweet smelling timber trees. . . . They have those oaks that we have, but far greater and better. . . .

The following evening we came to an island which they call Roanoke. [It was] distant from the harbor by which we entered, seven leagues. At the north end thereof, there was a village of nine houses, built of cedar and fortified round about with sharp trees to keep out their enemies. The entrance into it made it like a turnpike very artificially. When we came towards it, standing near unto the waters side, the wife of Grangyno, the King's brother, came running out to meet us very cheerfully and friendly. Her husband was not then in the village. Some of her people she commanded to draw our boat on the shore for the beating of the billow. Others she appointed to carry us on their backs to the dry ground and others to bring our oars into the house for fear of stealing. When we were come into the outer room, having five rooms in her house, she caused us to sit down by a great fire, and after took off our clothes and washed them and dried them again. Some of the women pulled off our stockings and washed them. Some washed our feet in warm water, and she herself took great pains to see all things ordered in the best manner she could, making great haste to dress some meat for us to eat. . . . We were entertained with all love and kindness, and with as much bounty, after their manner, as they could possible devise. We found the people most gentle, loving and faithful, void of all guile and treason, and such as lived after the manner of the golden age. The earth brings forth all things in abundance as in the first creation, without toil or labor. The people only care to defend themselves from the cold in their short winter, and to feed themselves with such meat as the soil affords. Their meat is very well sodden, and they make broth very sweet and savory. Their vessels are earthen pots, very large, white and sweet. Their dishes are wooden platters of sweet timber. Within the place where they feed was their lodging, and within that their Idol, which they worship, of which they speak incredible things. . . .

DOCUMENT 3 *From* A Brief and True Report of the New Found Land of Virginia

Thomas Harriot

Within a few days after our departure from every . . . town, the people began to die very fast, and many in short space, in some towns about twenty, in some fourty and in one six score, which in truth was very many in respect of their numbers. . . . The disease also so strange, that they neither knew what it was, nor how to cure it, the like by report of the oldest men in the country never happened before, time out of mind. A thing especially observed by us, as also by the natural inhabitants themselves.

Insomuch that when some of the inhabitants which were our friends, and especially the Wiroans Wingina, had observed such effects in four or five towns to follow their wicked practices, they were persuaded that it was the work of our God through our means, and that we by him might kill and slay whom we would without weapons, and not come near them. . . .

This marvelous accident in all the country wrought so strange opinions of us, that some people could not tell whether to think us gods or men, and the rather because that all the space of their sickness, there was no man of ours known to die, or that was especially sick. They noted also that we had no women amongst us, neither that we did care for any of theirs.

Some therefore were of opinion that we were not borne of women, and therefore not mortal, but that we were men of an old generation many years past, then risen again to immortality.

Some would likewise seem to prophecy, that there were more of our generation yet to come, to kill theirs and take their places, as some thought the purpose was, by that which was already done.

Introduction to Document 4

The next document is taken from John White's "Narrative of the 1590 Virginia Voyage." This return voyage to Roanoke reached Virginia on August 17, 1590. High winds destroyed one of the boats as it approached the island. Seven sailors perished in the accident, and crew morale among the survivors plummeted. It was dark before the party came ashore. The following excerpts detail what White found when he reached the deserted colony. (Once again, spelling and grammar have been modernized.) What clues does this account provide to the fate of the famous "lost colony"?

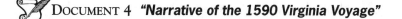

Document 4 *"Narrative of the 1590 Virginia Voyage"*

John White

It was so exceedingly dark that we overshot the place a quarter of a mile. There we spied towards the north end of the island the light of a great fire through the woods, to which we presently rowed. When we came right over against it, we let fall our Grapnel near the shore and sounded with a trumpet a call, and afterward many familiar English tunes of songs, and called to them friendly. But we had no answer. We therefore landed at daybreak, and coming to the fire we found the grass and sundry rotten trees burning about the place. From hence we went through the woods to that part of the island directly over against Dasamongwepeuk, and from thence we returned by the water side, round about the North-point of the island, until we came to the place where I left our colony in the year 1586.* In all this way we saw in the sand the print of the savage feet of 2 or 3 sorts trod that night, and as we entered up the sandy bank, upon a tree in the very brow thereof were curiously carved these fair Roman letters CRO: which letters presently we knew to signify the place where I should find the planters seated, according to a secret token agreed upon between them and me at my last departure from them, which was, that in anyway they should not fail to write or carve on the trees or posts of the doors the name of the place where they should be seated; for at my coming away they were prepared to remove from Roanoak 50 miles into the mainland. Therefore at my departure from them in 1587 I willed them, that if they should happen to be distressed in any of those place, that then they should carve over the letters or name, a cross † in this form, but we found no such sign of distress. And having well considered of this, we passed toward the place where they were left in sundry houses, but we found the houses taken down, and the places very strongly enclosed with a high palisade of great trees with curtains and flankers very fort-like. One of the chief trees or posts at the right side of the entrance had the bark taken off, and 5 foot from the ground in fair capital letters was engraved CROATOAN without any cross or sign of distress; this done, we entered into the palisade where we found many bars of iron, two pigs of lead, four iron fowlers, iron sacker-shot, and such like heavy things, thrown here and there, almost overgrown with grass and weeks. From thence we went along by the water side, towards the point of the creek to see if we could find any of their boats or Pinnissee, but we could perceive no sign of them, nor any of the last falkons and small ordinance which were left with them at my departure from them. At our return from the creek, some of our sailors meeting us told us that they had found where divers chests had been hidden, and long since dug up again and broken-up, and much of the goods in them spoiled and scattered about, but nothing left. . . .

Introduction to Documents 5, 6, and 7

The following documents are written by two of the fortunate survivors of early Jamestown: George Percy and John Smith. The spelling and grammar of these documents have been modernized. Percy's observations on Jamestown in 1607 describe the tenuous relationships between the English and their Algonquian neighbors. Smith's account details the "starving time" of 1609. These documents reveal the

---

*White's date is inaccurate. The correct date is 1587.

horrors of the early settler's struggle for survival. The third document in this section is Smith's recollection of a 1609 speech by Chief Powhatan. In this speech to Smith, Powhatan expresses concerns about his relationship with the Anglos and with the neighboring Namesmond Indians. As this document reveals, the struggle for survival in early Virginia was not limited to the Anglo settlers of Jamestown.

DOCUMENT 5 *"Discourse"*

George Percy

[April 26, 1607] about four o'clock in the morning, we described [detected] the land of Virginia. The same day we entered into the Bay of Chesapeake directly, without any let or hindrance. There we landed and discovered a little way, but we could find nothing worth speaking of but fair meadows and goodly tall trees. With such fresh waters running through the woods, I was almost ravished at the first sight thereof.

At night, when we were going aboard, there came the savages creeping upon all fours from the hills like bears, with their bows in their mouths. [They] charged us [looking] very desperately in their faces, hurt Captain Gabrill Archer in both his hands and a sailor in two very dangerous places of the body. After they had spent their arrows, and felt the sharpness of our shot, they retired into the woods with a great noise. . . .

On the twenty-ninth day we set up a cross at Chesapeake Bay, and named that place Cape Henry. On the thirtieth, we came with our ships to Cape Comfort where we saw five savages running on the shore. Presently the Captain caused the shallop to be manned. Rowing to the shore, the Captain called to them in a sign of friendship, but they were at first very timorsome [fearful] until they saw the Captain lay his hand on his heart. Upon that, they laid down their bows and arrows and came very boldly to us, making signs to come ashore to their town, which is called by the savages Kecoughtan. We coasted to their town, rowing over a river running into the main. The savages swam over with their bows and arrows in their mouths.

When we came over to the other side, there were many other savages which directed us to their town where we were entertained by them very kindly. When we came first ashore, they made a doleful noise, laying their faces go the ground, scratching the earth with their nails. We thought they had been at their idolatry. When they ended their ceremonies, they went into their houses and brought out mats and laid [them] upon the ground. The chiefest of them sat all in a rank. The meanest sort brought us such dainties as they had: bread which they make of maize or guinea wheat. They would not suffer us to eat unless we sat down, which we did on a mat right against them. After we were well satisfied, they gave us of their tobacco, which they took in an artificial pipe made of earth like ours are, but far bigger, with the bowl fashioned together with a piece of fine copper. After they had feasted us, they show us, in welcome, their manner of dancing, which was in this fashion. One of the savages was standing in the midst singing, beating one hand against another. All the rest were dancing about him, shouting, howling, and stamping against the ground with many antic tricks and faces, making noise like so many wolves or devils. One thing of them I observed: when they were in their dance, they kept stroke with their feet just one with another. But with their hands, heads, faces and bodies, every one of them had a separate gesture. They continued for the space of half an hour. When they had ended their dance, the Captain gave them beads and other trifling jewels. They hang through their ears fowls' legs. They shave the right side of their heads with a shell. On the left side they wear an ell long tied up with an artificial knot, with many fowls's feathers sticking in it. They go altogether naked, but their privates are covered with beasts skins beset commonly with little bones or beasts teeth. Some paint their bodies black, some red, with artificial knots of sundry lively colors, very beautiful and pleasing to the eye, in a braver fashion than they in the West Indies. . . .

At Port Cottage in our voyage up the river, we saw a savage boy about the age of ten years with a head of hair of perfect yellow and a reasonable white skin, which is a miracle amongst all savages.

This river which we have discovered is one of the most famous rivers ever found by any Christian. It ebbs and flows a hundred and threescore miles where ships of great burden may harbor in safety. Where ever we landed upon this river, we saw the goodliest woods: beech, oak, cedar, cypress, walnuts, sassafras and vines in great abundance in great clusters on many trees, and other trees unknown. All the grounds are bespread with many sweet and delicate flowers of diverse colors and kinds. There are also many fruits: strawberries, mulberries, raspberries and fruits unknown. There are many branches of this river which run flowing through the woods with great plenty of all kinds of fish. As for sturgeon, all the world cannot compare to it. In this country I have seen many great and large meadows having excellent good pasture for any cattle. There is also great store of deer, both red and fallow. There are bears, foxes, otters, beavers, muskrats, and wild beasts unknown.

The twenty-fourth day we set up a cross at the head of this river, naming it Kings River, where we proclaimed James King of England to have the most right unto it. When we had finished and set up our cross, we shipped our men and made for James Fort. By the way we came to Pohatan's Tower where the Captain went ashore, suffering none to go with him. He presented the commander of this place with a hatchet. He took it joyfully and was well pleased.

But yet the savages murmured at our planting in the country, whereupon this Werowance made answer again very wisely of a savage. Why should you be offended with them as long as they hurt you not, nor take anything away by force? They take but a little waste ground which doth you nor any of us any good.

I saw bread made by their women which do all their drudgery. The men take their pleasure in hunting and their wars, which they are in continually one kingdom against another. Their manner of baking of bread is thus: after they pound their wheat into flour with hot water, they make it into paste, and work it into round balls and cakes. Then they put it into a pot of seething water. When it is sod thoroughly, they lay it on a smooth stone. There they harden it as well as in an oven. . . .

Captain Newport being gone for England, leaving us (one hundred and four persons) very bare, scanty of victuals and wares and in danger of the savages. We hoped after a supply which Captain Newport promised within twenty weeks. But if the beginners of this action do carefully further us, the country being so fruitful, it would be as great a profit to the realm of England as the Indies to the King of Spain. If this river which we have found had been discovered in the time of war with Spain, it would have been a commodity to our realm and a great annoyance to our enemies.

On the twenty-seventh of July the King of Rapahanna demanded a canoe which was restored. He lifted up his hand to the sun, which they worship as their god. Then he laid his hand on his heart [to affirm] that he would be our special friend. It is a general rule of these people when they swear by their god which is the sun. No Christian will keep their oath better upon this promise. These people have a great reverence to the sun above all other things. At its rising and setting, they sit down lifting up their hands and eyes to the sun. Making a round circle on the ground with dried tobacco, they began to pray making many devilish gestures with a hellish noise, foaming at the mouth, staring with their eyes, wagging their heads and hands in such a fashion and deformity as it was monstrous to behold.

On August 6th died John Asbie of the bloody flux. On the ninth died George Flower of the swelling. On the tenth died William Bruster, Gentleman, of a wound given by the savages, and was buried the eleventh. On the fourteenth, Jerome Alikock,

Ancient, died of a wound. The same day Francis Midwinter, Edward Moris, Corporal, died suddenly. . . . The fourth day of September died Thomas Jacob, Sergeant. The fifth day died Benjamin Beast. Our men were destroyed with cruel diseases as swellings, fluxes, burning fevers, and by wars. Some departed suddenly, but for the most part they died of mere famine.

There were never Englishmen left in a foreign country in such misery as we were in this new discovered Virginia. We watched every three nights lying on the bare cold ground what weather soever came warded all the next day, which brought our men to be most feeble wretches. Our food was but a small can of barley sod in water to five men a day. Our drink was cold water taken out of the river, which was at a flood very salt, at a low tide, full of slime and filth, which was the destruction of many of our men. Thus we lived for the space of five months in this miserable distress, not having five able men to man our bulwarks upon any occasion. If it had not pleased god to have put a terror in the savages' hearts, we had all perished by those wild and cruel pagans. Being in that weak estate as we were, our men night and day groaning in every corner of the fort [were] most pitiful to hear. If there were any conscience in men, it would make their hearts to bleed to hear the pitiful murmuring and outcries of our sick men without relief every night and day for the space of six weeks. Some departing from our world, many times three or four in a night; in the morning their bodies were trailed out of their cabins like dogs to be buried. In this sort did I see the mortality of diverse of our people.

It pleased God, after a while, to send those people which were our mortal enemies to relieve us with victuals, as bread, corn, fish, and flesh were in great plenty, which was the setting up of our feeble men. Otherwise we had all perished. Also we were frequented by diverse kings in the country, bringing us store of provision to our great comfort.

 DOCUMENT 6 *From* Journal

John Smith

. . . As for corn, provision and contribution from the savages, we had nothing but mortal wounds, with clubs and arrows; as for our hogs, hens, goats, sheep, horse, or what lived, our commanders, officers and savages daily consumed them, some small proportions sometimes we tasted, till all was devoured; then swords, arms, pieces, or anything, we traded with the savages, whose cruel fingers were so oft imbrued in our blood, that what by their cruelty, our Governor's indiscretion, and the loss of our ships, of five hundred within six months after Captain Smith's* departure, there remained not past sixty men, women and children, most miserable and poor creatures; and those were preserved for the most part, by roots, herbs, acorns, walnuts, berries, now and then a little fish: they that had starch in these extremities, made no small use of it; yea, even the very skins of our horses. Nay, so great was our famine, that a savage we slew, and buried, the poorer sort took him up again and ate him, and so did diverse one another boiled and stewed with roots and herbs: and one amongst the rest did kill his wife, powdered [i.e., salted] her, and had eaten part of her before it was known, for which he was executed, as he well deserved; now whether she was better roasted, boiled or carbonadoed [i.e., grilled], I know not, but of such a dish as powdered wife I never heard of. This was that time, which still to this day we called the starving time; it were too vile to say, and scarce to be believed, what we endured: but the occasion was our own, for want of providence, industry, and government, and not the barrenness and defect of the country, as is generally supposed; for till then in

*Note that Smith writes in the third person.

three years, for the numbers were landed us, we had never from England provision sufficient for six months, though it seemed by the bills of loading sufficient was sent us, such a
glutton is the sea, and such good fellows the mariners; we as little tasted of the great proportion sent us, as they of our want and miseries, yet notwithstanding they ever over-
swayed and ruled the business, though we endured all that is said, and chiefly lived on
what this good country naturally afforded; yet had we been even in paradise itself with
these governors, it would not have been much better with us; yet there was amongst us,
who had they had the government as Captain Smith appointed, but that they could not
maintain it, would surely have kept us from those extremities of miseries. This in ten days
more, would have supplanted us all with death.

But God that would not this country should be unplanted, sent Sir Thomas Gates,
and Sir George Sommers with one hundred and fifty people most happily preserved by
the Bermudas to preserve us. . . .

DOCUMENT 7 *Powhatan's Speech to Captain John Smith: 1609*

Captain Smith, you may understand that I having seen the death of all my people
thrice, and not any one living of these three generations by myself; I know the difference of Peace and War better than any in my Country. But now I am old and ere long
must die, my brethren, namely Opitchapam, Opechancanough, and Kekataugh, my two
sisters, and their two daughters, are distinctly each other's successors. I wish their experience no less than mine, and your love to them no less than mine to you. But this brut
from Nansemond, that you are come to destroy my Country, so much frightens all my
people as they dare not visit you. What will it avail you to take by force [that which]
you may quickly have by love, or to destroy them that provide you food? What can you
get by war, when we can hide our provisions and fly to the woods? whereby you must
famish by wronging us your friends. And why are you thus jealous of our lives seeing us
unarmed, and both do, and are willing still to feed you, with that you cannot get but by
our labors? Think you I am so simple, not to know it is better to eat good meat, lie well,
and sleep quietly with my women and children, laugh and be marry with you, have copper, hatchets, or what I want being your friend: then be forced to flee from all, to lie
cold in the woods, feed upon acorns, roots, and such trash, and be so hunted by you,
that I can neither rest, eat, nor sleep; but my tired men must watch, and if a twig but
break, everyone cries, there comes Captain Smith: then must I fly I know not whether:
and thus with miserable fear, end my miserable life, leaving my pleasures to such youths
as you, which through your rash unadvisedness may quickly as miserably end, for want
of that, you never know where to find. Let this therefore assure you of our loves, and
every year our friendly trade shall furnish you with corn; and now also, if you would
come in friendly manner to see us, and not thus with your guns and swords as to invade
your foes.

Introduction to Documents 8 and 9

Between 1610 and 1616, Virginia's survival was the result of the stern governments of Sir Thomas Gates and Sir Thomas Dale. The regulations imposed by Dale
were codified and published in 1611 by William Strachey as *Lawes Divine, Morall
and Martiall.* Meanwhile, in England, the Virginia Company published and circulated the tract *Nova Britannia* in an attempt to persuade the general public to purchase shares in the venture. Selections from each document follow. Compare the
two documents. How do their descriptions of Virginia differ? Why?

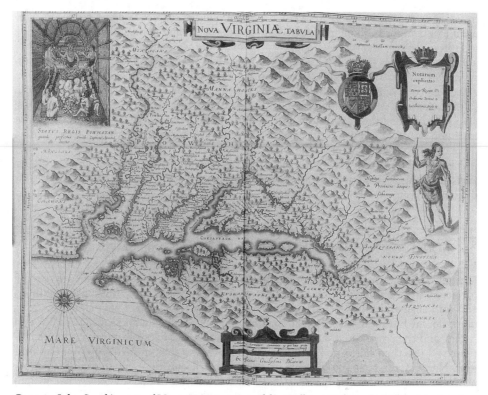

Captain John Smith's map of Virginia was engraved by William Hole and published in London in 1612. The map, with crosses to mark the farthest extent of Smith's own exploration, details the intricacies of the Virginia landscape and the distribution of Native Americans. (Courtesy of the Edward E. Ayer Collection, The Newberry Library, Chicago)

DOCUMENT 8 *From* **Nova Britannia:** *1609*

The country itself is large and great assuredly, though as yet, no exact discovery can be made of all. It is also commendable and hopeful every way, the air and climate most sweet and wholesome, and very agreeable to our nature. It is inhabited with wild and savage people, that live and lie up and down in troupes like herds of deer in a forest; they have no law but nature, their apparel, skins of beasts, but most go naked; the better sort have houses, but poor ones; they have no arts nor sciences, yet they live under superior command such as it is; they are generally very loving and gentle, and do entertain and relieve our people with great kindness; the land yieldeth naturally for the sustenance of man, abundance of fish, infinite store of deer, and hares, with many fruits and roots.

There are valleys and plains streaming with sweet springs, there are hills and mountains making a sensible proffer of hidden treasure, never yet searched; the land is full of minerals, plenty of woods; the soil is strong and sends out naturally fruitful vines running upon trees, and shrubs: it yields also resin, turpentine, pitch and tar, sassafras, mulberry trees and silkworms, many skins and rich furs, many sweet woods, and costly dyes; plenty of sturgeon, timber for shipping. But of this that I have said, if bare nature be so amiable in its naked kind, what may be hope, when art and nature both shall join and strive together, to give best content to man and beast? . . .

. . . As for supplanting the savages, we have such intent: Our intrusion into their possessions shall tend to their great good; and no way to their hurt, unless as unbridled beasts, they procure it to themselves. We purpose to proclaim and make it known to them all, by some public interpretation, that our coming hither is to plant ourselves in their country; yet not to supplant and root them out, but to bring them from their base condition to a far better: First, in regard of God the Creator, and of Jesus Christ their Redeemer, if they will believe in Him. And secondly, in respect of earthly blessing, whereof they have now no comfortable use, but in beastly brutish manner, with promise to defend them against all public and private enemies.

We require nothing at their hands, but a quiet residence to us and ours, that by our own labor and toil, we may work this good unto them and recompense our own adventures, costs, and travels in the end; wherein, they shall be most friendly welcome to join their labors with ours, and shall enjoy equal privileges with us, in whatsoever good success, time or means may bring to pass. To which purpose, we may verily believe that God has reserved in this last age of the world, an infinite number of those lost and scattered sheep, to be won and recovered by our means. . . .

And as for the general sort that shall go to be planters, be they never so poor, so they be honest, and take pains, the place will make them rich. . . . They shall have there employment enough for there is a world of means to set many thousands awork, partly in such things as I mentioned before, and many other profitable works, for no man must live idle there.

And by this employment, we may happily stop the course of those irregular youths of no religion, that daily run from us to Rome and Rhemes for exhibition, which after a little hammering and training there by Parson and his imps, they become pliable for the impression of any villainy whatsoever, as appears by their positions and practices at home and abroad.

And hereby our mariners shall not lie idle, nor our owners sell their ships for want of freight: you know how many good ships are daily sold, and made away to foreign nations; how many men for want of employment, betake themselves to Tunis, Spain, and Florence, and to serve in courses not warrantable, which would better beseem, our own walls and borders to be spread with such branches, than their native country.

The thing to make this plantation is money, to be raised among the adventurers [stockholders], wherein the sooner and more deeply men engage them selves, their charge will be the shorter, and their gain the greater.

First you shall understand that his Majesty has granted us an enlargement of our charter, with many ample privileges, wherein we have knights and gentlemen of good place, named for the King's Council of Virginia to govern us. As also every planter and adventurer shall be inserted in the patent by name. This ground being laid, we purpose presently to make supply of men, women, and children (so many as we can) to make the plantation. We call those planters that go in their persons to dwell there and those adventurers that adventure their money and go not in person, and both do make the members of one colony. We do account twelve pound ten shillings to be a single share adventured. Every ordinary man or woman, if they will go and dwell there, and every child above ten years that shall be carried thither to remain, shall be allowed for each of their persons a single share, as if they had adventured twelve pound ten shillings in money. Every extraordinary man, as divines, governors, ministers of state and justice, gentlemen, physicians, and such as be men of worth for special services, are all to go as planters, and to execute their several functions in the colony, and are to be maintained at the common charge, and are to receive their dividend (as others do) at seven years end, and they are to be agreed with all before they go, and to be rated by the council, according to the value of their persons, which shall be set down and registered in a book, that it may always appear what people have gone to the plantation, at what time they went, and how their persons were valued. And likewise, if any that go to be planters will lay down money to the treasurer, it shall be also registered and their shares enlarged accordingly, be it for more or less. All charges of settling and maintaining the plantation and of making supplies shall be born in a joint stock of the adventurers for seven years; we supply from here at our own charge all necessary food and apparel, for fortifying and building of houses in a joint stock, so they are also to return from thence the increase and fruits of their labors, for the use and advancement of the same joint stock, till the end of seven years; at which time we purpose (God willing) to make a division by commissioners appointed, of all the lands granted unto us by his Majesty, to every of the colony, according to each man's several adventure, agreeing with our register book, which we doubt not will be for every share of twelve pound ten shillings, five hundred acres at least. And as for the value and little worth now of those grounds in Virginia, we know that in England within these thirty or forty years, the yearly rent of those grounds (in many places) were not worth five shillings, that now go for forty or more.

DOCUMENT 9 *From* Laws Divine, Moral and Martial, *1611*

1. First since we owe our highest and supreme duty, our greatest, and all our allegiance to him, from whom all power and authority is derived, and flows as from the first, and only fountain, and being especial soldiers impressed in this sacred cause, we must alone expect our success from him, who is only the blesser of all good attempts, the king of kings, the commander of commanders, and Lord of Hosts, I do strictly command and charge all captains and officers, of what quality or nature soever, whether commanders in the field, or in town, or towns, forts or fortresses, to have a care that the Almighty God be duly and daily served. . . .

6. Every man and woman duly twice a day upon the first tolling of the bell shall upon the working days repair unto the church, to hear divine service upon pain of losing his or her day's allowance for the first omission, for the second to be whipped, and for the third to be condemned to the galleys for six months. Likewise no man or woman shall dare to violate or break the Sabbath by any gaming, public, or private abroad, or at home, but duly sanctify and observe the same, both himself and his family, by preparing themselves at home with private prayer, that they may be the better fitted for the public, according to the commandments of God. . . .

9. No man shall commit the horrible, and detestable sins of sodomy upon pain of death; and he or she that can be lawfully convicted of adultery shall be punished with death. No man shall ravish or force any woman, maid or Indian, or other, upon pain of death, and know the[e] that he or she, that shall commit fornication, and evident proof made thereof, for their first fault shall be whipped, for their second they shall be whipped, and for their third they shall be whipped three times a week for one month, and ask public forgiveness in the assembly of the congregation. . . .

13. No manner of person whatsoever . . . shall detract, slander, calumniate, murmur, mutiny, resist, disobey, or neglect the commandments, either of the Lord Governor, and Captain General, the Lieutenant General, the Marshal, the Council, or any authorized captain, commander or public officer, upon pain for the first time so offending to be whipped three several times, and upon his knees to acknowledge his offense, with asking forgiveness upon the Sabbath day in the assembly of the congregation, and for the second time so offending to be condemned to the galley for three years: and for the third time so offending to be punished with death. . . .

15. No man of what condition soever shall barter, truck, or trade with the Indians, except he be thereunto appointed by lawful authority, upon pain of death.

16. No man shall rifle or despoil, by force or violence, take away anything from any Indian coming to trade, or otherwise, upon pain of death.

17. No cape merchant, or provant [i.e., provision] master, or munition master, or truck master, or keeper of any store, shall at any time embezzle, sell, or give away anything under his charge to any favorite of his, more than unto any other, whom necessity shall require in that case to have extraordinary allowance of provisions, nor shall they give a false account unto the Lord Governor, and Captain General, unto the Lieutenant General, unto the Marshal, or any deputed governor, at any time having the command of the colony, with intent to defraud the said colony, upon pain of death. . . .

20. No captain, master, mariner, or sailor, or what officer else belonging to any ship, or ships, now within our river, or hereafter which shall arrive, shall dare to bargain, exchange, barter, truck, trade, or sell, upon pain of death, unto any one landman member of this present colony, any provisions of what kind soever, above the determined valuations, and prices, set down and proclaimed, and sent therefore unto each of your several ships, to be fixed upon your main mast, to the intent that want of due notice, and ignorance in this case, be no excuse, or plea, for any one offender herein. . . .

23. No man shall embezzle, lose, or willingly break, or fraudulently make away, either spade, shovel, hatchet, axe, mattock, or other tool or instrument upon pain of whipping.

25. Every man shall have an especial and due care, to keep his house sweet and clean, as also so much of the street, as lieth before his door, and especially he shall so provide, and set his bedstead whereon he lieth, that it may stand three feet at least from the ground, as he will answer the contrary at a martial court. . . .

31. What man or woman soever, shall rob any garden, public or private, being set to weed the same, or willfully pluck up therein any root, herb, or flower, to spoil and waste or steal the same, or rob any vineyard, or gather up the grapes, or steal any ears of the corn growing, whether in the ground belonging to the same fort or town where he dwelleth, or in any other, shall be punished with death. . . .

Introduction to Document 10

In the early 1620s, disgruntled investors sent investigating committees to Virginia to assess the poor financial condition of the colony. While the various factions of stockholders were arguing among themselves about who was at fault, the infamous massacre of 1622 claimed the lives of 347 Virginians. Why had the company been unable to prevent the massacre? The following document, "The State of the Colony in Virginia," was written in 1622 by company officials to defend themselves against charges of neglect. How credible is their defense?

DOCUMENT 10 *"The State of the Colony in Virginia," 1622*

That all men may see the impartial ingenuity of this discourse, we freely confess, that the country is not so good, as the natives are bad, whose barbarous selves need more cultivation than the ground itself, being more overspread with incivility and treachery, than that with briars. . . . The plantations of particular adventurers and planters were placed scatteringly and stragglingly as a choice vein of rich ground invited them, and the further from neighbors held the better. The houses generally set open to the savages, who were always friendly entertained at the tables of the English, and commonly lodged in their bedchambers. The old planters (as they thought now come to reap the benefit of their long travels) placed with wonderful content upon their private lands, and their familiarity with the natives, seeming to open a fair gate for their conversion to Christianity.

The country being in this estate, an occasion was ministered of sending to Opach ankano, the King of these savages, about the middle of March last, what time the messenger returned back with these words from him, that he held the peace concluded so firm as the sky should sooner fall than it dissolve. Yea, such was the treacherous dissimulation of that people who then had contrived our destruction, that even two days before the massacre, some of our men were guided through the woods by them in safety. Yea, they borrowed our own boats to convey themselves across the river (on the banks of both sides whereof all our plantations were) to consult of the devilish murder that ensued, and of our utter extirpation, which God of His mercy (by the means of themselves converted to Christianity) prevented. And as well on the Friday morning (the fatal day) the twenty-second of March, as also in the evening, as on other days before, they came unarmed into our houses, without bows or arrows, or other weapons, with deer, turkey, fish, fur, and other provisions to sell and trade with us for glass, beads, and other trifles. Yet in some places, they sat down at breakfast with our people at their tables, whom immediately with their own tools and weapons either laid down, or standing in their houses, they basely and barbarously murdered, not sparing either age or sex, man, woman, or child, so sudden in their cruel execution that few or none discerned the weapon or blow that brought them to destruction. In which manner they also slew many of our people then at their several work and husbandries in the fields, and without their houses, some in planting corn and tobacco, some in gardening, some in making brick, building, sawing, and other kinds of husbandry, they well knowing in what places and quarters each of our men were, in regard of their daily familiarity and resort to us for trading and other negotiations, which the more willingly was by us continued and cherished for the desire we had of effecting that great masterpiece of works, their conversion. And by this means that fatal Friday morning, there fell under the bloody and barbarous hands of that perfidious and inhuman people, contrary to all laws of God and men, of nature and nations, three hundred forty seven men, women, and children, most by their own weapons. And not being content with taking away life alone, they fell after again upon the dead, making as well as they could, a fresh murder, defacing, dragging, and mangling the dead carcasses into many pieces, and carrying some parts away in derision, with base and brutish triumph. That the slaughter had been universal, if God had not put it into the heart of an Indian belonging to one Perry to disclose it, who living in the house of one Pace, was urged by another Indian his brother (who came the night before and lay with him) to kill Pace. Telling further that by such an hour in the morning a number would come from different places to finish the execution, who failed not at the time, Perry's Indian rose out of his bed and revealed it to Pace, that used him as a son. And thus the rest of the colony that had warning given them by this means was saved. Such was (God be thanked for it) the good fruit of an infidel converted to Christianity. For though three hundred and more of ours died by many of these pagan infidels, yet thousands of ours were saved by the means of one of them alone which was made a Christian. Blessed be God forever, whose mercy endureth forever.

Thus have you seen the particulars of this massacre, wherein treachery and cruelty have done their worst to us, or rather to themselves; for whose understanding is so shallow, as not to perceive that this must needs be for the good of the plantation after, and the loss of this blood to make the body more healthful, as by these reasons may be manifest.

First, because betraying innocence never rests unpunished.

Secondly, because our hands, which before were tied with gentleness and fair usage, are now set at liberty by the treacherous violence of the savages, not untying the knot, but cutting it. So that we, who hitherto have had possession of no more ground than their waste, and our purchase at a valuable consideration to their own contentment gained, may now, by right of war and law of nations, invade the country, and destroy them who sought to destroy us. Whereby we shall enjoy their cultivated places, possessing the fruits of others' labors. Now their cleared grounds in all their villages (which are situated in the fruitfulest places of the land) shall be inhabited by us, whereas heretofore the grubbing of woods was the greatest labor.

Thirdly, because those commodities which the Indians enjoyed as much or rather more than we, shall now also be entirely possessed by us. The deer and other beasts will be in safety, and infinitely increase, which heretofore not only in the general huntings of the King, but by each particular Indian were destroyed at all times of the year, without any difference of male, dame, or young.

There will be also a great increase of wild turkeys, and other weighty fowl, for the Indians never put difference of destroying the hen, but kill them whether in season or not, whether in breeding time, or sitting on their eggs, or having new hatched, it is all one to them.

Fourthly, because the way of conquering them is much more easy than of civilizing them by fair means, for they are a rude, barbarous, and naked people, scattered in small companies, which are helps to victory, but hindrance to civility. Besides that, a conquest may be of many, and at once; but civility is in particular and slow, the effect of long time, and great industry. Moreover, victory of them may be gained many ways: by force, by surprise, by famine in burning their corn, by destroying and burning their boats, canoes, and houses, by breaking their fishing wares, by assailing them in their huntings, whereby they get the greatest part of their sustenance in winter, by pursuing and chasing them with our horses and bloodhounds to draw after them, and mastiffs to tear them.

Introduction to Document 11

The final document in this chapter is a letter written in 1623 by a young indentured servant to his family back in England. This pathetic appeal contrasts with the more favorable accounts of Virginia presented by its investors. To what degree did one's perception of life in early Virginia depend on one's socioeconomic position?

DOCUMENT 11 *An Indentured Servant Describes Life in Virginia in a Letter to His Parents*

Richard Frethorne

Loving and kind father and mother:

My most humble duty remembered to you, hoping in God of your good health, as I myself am at the making hereof. This is to let you understand that I your child am in a most heavy case by reason of the nature of the country, [which] is such that it causeth much sickness, [such] as the scurvy and the bloody flux and diverse other diseases, which maketh the body very poor and weak. And when we are sick there is nothing to comfort us; for since I came out of the ship I never ate anything but peas, and loblollie (that is, water gruel). As for deer or venison I never saw any since I came into this land. There is indeed some fowl, but we are not allowed to go and get it, but must work hard both early and late for a mess of water gruel and a mouthful of bread and beef. A mouthful of bread for a penny loaf must serve for four men which is most pitiful. [You would be grieved] if you did know as much as I [do], when people cry out day and night—Oh! that they were in England without their limbs—and would not care to lose any limb to be in England again, yea, though they beg from door to door. For we live in fear of the enemy every hour, yet we have had a combat with them on the Sunday before Shrovetide, and we took two alive and made slaves of them. But it was by policy, for we are in great danger; for our plantation is very weak by reason of the death and sickness of our company. For we came but twenty for the merchants, and they are half dead just; and we look every hour when two more should go. Yet there came some four other men yet to live with us, of which there is but one alive; and our Lieutenant is dead, and [also] his father and his brother. And there was some five or six of the last year's twenty, of which there is but three left, so that we are fain to get other men to plant with us; and yet we are but 32 to fight against 3000 if they should come. And the nighest help that we have is ten miles of us, and when the rogues overcame this place [the] last [time] they slew 80 persons. How then shall we do, for we lie even in their teeth? They may easily take us, but [for the fact] that God is merciful and can save with few as well as with many, as he showed to Gideon. And like Gideon's soldiers, if they lapped water, we drink water which is but weak.

And I have nothing to comfort me, nor is there nothing to be gotten here but sickness and death, except [in the event] that one had money to lay out in some things for profit. But I have nothing at all—no, not a shirt to my back but two rags (2), nor no clothes but one poor suit, nor but one pair of shoes, but one pair of stockings, but one cap, [and] but two bands. My cloak is stolen by one of my own fellows, and to his dying hour [he] would not tell me what he did with it; but some of my fellows saw him have butter and beef out of a ship, which my cloak, I doubt [not], paid for. So that I have not a penny, not a penny worth, to help me to either spice or sugar or strong waters, without the which one cannot live here. For as strong beer in England doth fatten and strengthen them, so water here doth wash and weaken these here [and] only keeps [their] life and soul together. But I am not half [of] a quarter so strong as I was in England, and all is for want of victuals; for I do protest unto you that I have eaten more in [one] day at home than I have allowed me here for a week. You have given more than my day's allowance to a beggar at the door; and if Mr. Jackson had not relieved me, I should be in a poor case. But he like a father and she like a loving mother doth still help me.

. . . Oh, they be very godly folks, and love me very well, and will do anything for me. And he much marvelled that you would send me a servant to the Company; he saith I had been better knocked on the head. And indeed so I find it now, to my great grief and misery; and [I] saith that if you love me you will redeem me suddenly, for which I do entreat and beg. And if you cannot get the merchants to redeem me for some little money, then for God's sake get a gathering or entreat some good folks to lay out some little sum of money in meal and cheese and butter and beef. Any eating meat will yield great profit. Oil and vinegar is very good; but, father, there is great loss in leaking. But for God's sake send beef and cheese and butter, or the more of one sort and none of another. But if you send cheese, it must be very old cheese; and at the cheesemonger's you may buy very good cheese for twopence farthing or halfpenny, that will be liked very well. But if you send cheese, you must have a care how you pack it in barrels; and you must put cooper's chips between every cheese, or else the heat of the hold will rot them. And look whatsoever you send me—be it never so much—look, what[ever] I make of it, I will deal truly with you. I will send it over and beg the profit to redeem me; and if I die before it come, I have entreated Goodman Jackson to send you the worth of it, who hath promised he will. If you send, you must direct your letters to Goodman Jackson, at Jamestown, a gunsmith. (You must set down his freight, because there be more of his name there.) Good father, do not forget me, but have mercy and pity my miserable case. I know if you did but see me, you would weep to see me; for I have but one suit. (But [though] it is a strange one, it is very well guarded.) Wherefore, for God's sake, pity me. I pray you to remember my love to all my friends and kindred. I hope all my brothers and sisters are in good health, and as for my part I have set down my resolution that certainly will be; that is, that the answer of this letter will be life or death to me. Therefore, good father, send as soon as you can; and if you send me any thing let this be the mark.

Richard Frethorne
Martin's Hundred

POSTSCRIPT

While the early years of Virginia were notably unsuccessful, things began to change. In 1619, settler John Rolfe (who had married Pocahontas) wrote, "About the last of August came in a dutch man of warre that sold us twenty Negars." The enslavement of Africans by Europeans had been going on for decades, but Rolfe's offhanded comment is the first indication of a black presence in Virginia. It is unclear whether, in the early years, those Africans were treated more like slaves or like indentured servants. We do know that, by 1660, servitude that lasted a lifetime and extended to one's children was the fate of Virginia blacks.

But why were these people brought to the troubled colony? Tobacco was the answer. In the very year that the Dutch ship dropped off its African cargo (1619), 45,000 pounds of tobacco were exported to England from Virginia and the British colony of Bermuda. Five years earlier, not a pound had been shipped, but just one year later, in 1620, over 100,000 pounds passed through London. It was the very same John Rolfe who noted the coming of the first twenty blacks who had also procured tobacco seeds from the Spanish West Indies, a variety of the plant favored by the English. King James publicly condemned the "sot-weed," but he was not about to ban a product that generated rich customs duties.

By the 1620s, tobacco brought boom times to Virginia, as men engaged in a ruthless scramble for wealth. In the 1630s and 1640s, prices stabilized, and planters began to raise more corn and cattle. As food supplies increased, mortality rates declined. The planter elites who had gained their wealth during the tobacco boom came to dominate colony politics. Some of their economic inferiors also prospered, although to a lesser degree. Many former indentured servants, after working several years as tenant farmers, were able to save sufficient funds to purchase their own land and became independent planters themselves (Richard Frethorne, alas, was not so lucky; he died in poverty shortly after sending his letter). By the middle of the seventeenth century, the Virginia population reached fifteen thousand, with more immigrants coming every year. This growth, coupled with the need for fresh acreage by those who planted soil-depleting tobacco, encouraged more English encroachments on Indian lands. The resulting wars dramatically reduced the native population. By 1680, there were fewer than one thousand Native Americans in all of Virginia.

Tobacco had become so profitable that it justified a heavy investment in labor. Although white indentured servants continued to be sorely exploited, they also proved hard to control, and even rebellious. But black slaves could be made to tend crops through the long growing season, and they could be exploited more thoroughly than white laborers. By the third generation after the settlement of Jamestown, a relative handful of powerful white men controlled the best land and owned the majority of slaves. It was these men and their descendants in the eighteenth century who began to create a gracious life on their plantations. After decades of failure, then, it could be said that Virginia grew to be England's largest and most populous colony out of the labor of enslaved Africans and the cravings of Europeans for nicotine.

QUESTIONS

Defining Terms

Identify in the context of the chapter each of the following:

Sir Walter Raleigh	CRO
Algonquians	John Rolfe
joint-stock companies	indentured servants
Arthur Barlowe	Opachankano
Roanoke Island	House of Burgesses

Probing the Sources

1. Compare Columbus's initial impressions of the New World with those of the English settlers. Account for the similarities and differences in their observations.
2. Compare the technologies and military strength of the English with those of the Native Americans. Why did Powhatan not eliminate the English during the early years of settlement?
3. Describe the hardships faced by the original settlers of Jamestown. Why was the first decade of settlement so difficult?
4. How did the relationships between the Native Americans and the English change over time? Account for these changes.

Interpreting the Sources

1. What do you think happened to the "lost" colonists at Roanoke?
2. Define *racism*. To what degree was racism prevalent in early Virginia?
3. When you weigh all the sources, how would you describe life in early Virginia?
4. What were the causes and consequences of the uprising of 1622?

ADDITIONAL READING

David B. and Alison M. Quinn's *The First Colonists* (1982) and Karen Ordahl Kupperman's *Captain John Smith* (1988) provide excellent introductions to the writings of some of the most colorful figures in early America. An often asked question is addressed in J. A. Leo Lemay's *Did Pocahontas Save Captain John Smith?* (1992). Other interesting studies discussing race relations in Virginia include Ben C. McCary's *Indians in Seventeenth Century Virginia* (1992) and Frank Craven's *White, Red, and Black: The Seventeenth-Century Virginia* (1971). For straightforward narratives of early Virginia from an English point of view, see Alden Vaughan, *American Genesis: Captain John Smith and the founding of Virginia* (1975) and Carl Bridenbaugh, *Jamestown, 1544–1699* (1980).

3

The Puritan Experience
in New England

HISTORICAL CONTEXT

Few peoples have been more praised or more denounced than the New England Puritans. As far back as 1920, Charles Beard poked fun at his fellow historians for their stereotypical portrayals of the early settlers of New England. Contrary to popular legend and much contemporary scholarship, Beard asserted, the masses of New England Puritans were neither saintly heroes who brought civilization to American shores nor liberty-hating bigots who opposed all forms of pleasure and creative thought. Over the years, scholars have described these seventeenth-century settlers in a great variety of ways: as moral athletes and moral busybodies, as utopian communitarians and enterprising capitalists, as concerned Christians committed to making converts and as genocidal zealots committed to exterminating their Native American neighbors.

Perhaps our fascination with the Puritan past stems from a curiosity about the exotic and the contradictory in life. While all societies are beset with inner tensions that demand resolution, the soul-wrenching struggle of the Puritans to find purpose in a world that was changing before their eyes was particularly intense, and consequently, their history remains extraordinarily intriguing. In many ways, the world of the Puritan settlers was vastly different from our own. Seventeenth-century Puritans viewed the earth as God's temporal kingdom, where humans were placed to carry out divine purposes. For Puritan thinkers, there simply was no such thing as accident or happenstance. Every event and every creature somehow related to God's cosmic plan. Part of this scheme included a gigantic struggle between the forces of Good and Evil. In this world, evidences of God's remarkable providence were everywhere to be found, but so, too, were the manifestations of Satan, a real and frightful being who infested the world with demons to lure humans into cooperation with his evil designs. The earthly kingdom, therefore, was not a paradise but a spiritual battleground, where those of God warred against those in league with the Devil. Ultimate victory and heavenly bliss were promised to God's chosen saints. Conversely, those who succumbed to the Devil could also expect their just rewards: suffering and death on Earth and eternal damnation in Hell.

Many of the earliest settlers of New England were devout folk who emigrated to the New World for largely religious purposes. Like the famous Pilgrims who settled Plymouth Colony in 1620, the Massachusetts Bay Puritans disliked the theology, government, and lack of discipline within the Church of England. Unlike the Separatist Pilgrims, however, these Puritans believed that the Anglican church was still God's church and could be purified. When political circumstances in England frustrated their attempts at reform, Puritan leaders devised an ambitious plan to establish a model "Christian commonwealth" in Massachusetts Bay. Confident that it was the nature of God to punish sin and reward obedience, these Non-Separatist Puritans hoped to save their church and nation from impending calamity by setting an example for Old England to imitate.

For these visionaries, the New World was a New Canaan, and they were God's chosen people sent on an errand into the wilderness. Their goal was not worldly success but the establishment of a colony dedicated to the glory of God. This mission, they believed, would succeed if each individual found his or her "particular & personal calling" and lived "a certain kind of life, ordained and imposed on man by God, for the common good." According to the pleadings of their leaders, in this Bible commonwealth the "care of the public must oversway all private respects," and everyone must strive "to do justly, to love mercy, to walk humbly with our God."

Creating a colony with such a lofty objective was not easy. Maintaining it was even harder. The seriousness of the Puritan's mission encouraged them to suppress dissent, to limit voting rights to church members, to punish moral laxity among both believers and nonbelievers, to demand hard labor from everyone, and to prevent extravagance. Nonetheless, the Puritans were not colorless and sexually repressed prigs. Like other seventeenth-century English subjects, they dressed according to their social class and pocketbook. The poor—whether Puritan or non-Puritan—wore dark, drab clothing, while the well-to-do purchased brightly colored apparel along with other luxury items commensurate with their class. Puritans refused to observe Christmas, Easter, and Maypole celebrations because they believed these practices were pagan in origin. They did not prohibit seasonal times of feasting and merriment, however, nor did they condemn the drinking of beer or wine in moderation. Furthermore, the Puritans adamantly rejected the doctrine that sex was intended solely for procreation. Rather, they viewed sex within marriage as a gift from God to be enjoyed. They discouraged all extramarital affairs—punishing severely adulterous and homosexual relationships—but they treated premarital sex, which was common, with considerable leniency. To protect the sanctity of the "marriage bed," they required married men unaccompanied by their wives to provide for their wives' passage to America or else to leave the colony. They also permitted divorces for those whose spouses were impotent, too long absent, or cruel.

If not repressed zealots, they also were not always flawless citizens and compassionate neighbors. Holding fast to the Calvinistic doctrine that all humans deserved damnation but that God in His mercy had "predestined" some for salvation, the Puritans relegated the nonelect—who soon made up a majority of the population even in New England—to a subordinate status on earth and to eternal affliction in Hell. As their numbers grew, the Puritans were also quick to seize additional lands from the Indians and then to justify their expansion as the sign of God's favor. In 1633, for instance, when a smallpox epidemic devastated the nearby Indian population, the pious governor John Winthrop smugly dismissed the disaster, asking, "If God were not pleased with our inheriting these parts, why did he drive the natives before us? And why doth he still make room for us by diminishing them as we increase?"

In regard to their relations with the Native Americans, the Puritans viewed their neighbors as cultural inferiors. They believed the Native Americans to be the descendants of one of the Ten Lost Tribes of Israel, whose original white skin coloring had been darkened naturally by the sun and unnaturally by degenerate customs. This interpretation encouraged Puritan missionaries such as John Eliot to translate the Bible into the Algonquian language and to seek Christian converts among the natives. New England missionaries won fewer Indians to Christianity than the Jesuits did in New France, largely because the Puritans held high and rigid standards that included a knowledge of complex theological issues and a prescribed conversion experience.

Despite their alleged concern about the salvation of the Algonquian peoples, at times the Puritans turned violently against their neighbors. In 1636–1637, the Puritans launched a clandestine assault against the Pequots that can best be described as a wholesale massacre. An even more deadly confrontation erupted in 1675 between the Wampanoag chieftain Metacomet and the descendants of the Plymouth Pilgrims. Angered by English encroachments on his ancestral homeland, and humiliated by English attempts to intimidate him into submission, Metacomet (known among the Puritans as King Philip) forged a military alliance with the Narragansett and Nipmuck peoples and began raiding towns along the Massachusetts-Connecticut frontier. The ensuing struggle, dubbed by the English King Philip's War, had a devastating impact on the region's population and morale. Within two years, nearly 10 percent of the adult white male and 30 percent of the Native American population had died in the fighting or from the disease and starvation that followed. The war also destroyed what goodwill remained between the two peoples. John Eliot's vision of Christianized Native Americans living harmoniously within a "civilized" English society was replaced by the attitude summarized centuries later in the jingoistic expression, "The only good Indian is a dead Indian."

King Philip's War forced the Puritans to reexamine themselves and their mission. In the first half-century of settlement, New England had prospered in many ways. Virtually everyone in the region could read and write, an achievement unequaled by other seventeenth-century cultures. The average adult life expectancy in New England was about sixty-five years, more than ten years longer than in Old England, and twenty years longer than in Virginia. Longer life meant more working years and the potential for more money; it meant longer marriages and more children. But for Puritans on a holy mission, prosperity had its drawbacks. From the outset, the religious values of the founders had been threatened by the non-Puritans who had come to New England solely for commercial reasons. With the passing years, these enterprising emigrants were joined by increasing numbers of second- and third-generation New Englanders who also preferred pursuing earthly rather than heavenly treasures. For the pious remnant, the alarming drop in church membership (especially among the males), the growing lack of interest of the youth in spiritual matters, and the disconcerting tendency of the adults to place economic gain above community concerns were signs of spiritual "declension." In 1662, Puritan clergymen responded to the crisis by proposing the Half Way Covenant, a compromise solution that permitted the unconverted children and grandchildren of full church members to enjoy some church privileges. This easier halfway church membership, while preserving the semblance of a God-centered society, merely dramatized to many how far New England had fallen from the ideals of its founders. Strict Puritans ridiculed the compromise, which in practice failed to improve church vitality.

In the latter decades of the seventeenth century, Puritan preachers, in sermons known as *jeremiads,* wailed against the waning piety of their generation and called the people to public and private repentance. Meanwhile, political troubles in England compounded the anxieties of the builders of Zion. In 1684, Charles II revoked the charter of Massachusetts Bay. The next year, a new king, James II, abolished the colonial assemblies and combined all the New England colonies into a single "Dominion of New England." This hated reorganization plan lasted only briefly, for in 1688, the "Glorious Revolution" in England ousted James II from the throne. The new Protestant monarchs, William and Mary, however, disappointed the Puritan rulers when they proclaimed Massachusetts a royal colony. The new charter of 1691 forced Massachusetts to drop the religious qualification for the right to vote and gave the English Crown authority to appoint its governor.

With power now in the hands of the Crown and colonial merchants, concerned Puritans could not help but wonder if their misfortunes were punishments from God. Had He forsaken the people of New England? Was there still hope for their redemption? As they pondered these haunting questions, the seaport town of Salem appeared to be invaded by a swarm of witches. For many, this crisis of 1692 was yet another ominous sign of God's displeasure with His people.

THE DOCUMENTS

This chapter includes a rich collection of documents written by Puritan men and women during the first three generations of their settlement. The assortment of texts touches on a variety of topics, including the original purpose of the colony, community and family life in New England, Puritan-Indian conflicts, and the battle against Satan at Salem. As you read each selection, try to identify both the changing and the unchanging elements within the Puritan experience. What was it that united and divided the people of Massachusetts Bay? To what—family, religion, business, education, township, colony, or race—did they give their allegiance? And how did they react when what they valued was threatened? In probing these facets of the New England mind and soul, you may discover that the mysterious world of the seventeenth century is not so foreign to us after all.

Introduction to Document 1

In 1630, while aboard the flagship *Arbella,* Governor John Winthrop finished writing and delivered "A Model of Christian Charity." Although the document reads like a Puritan sermon, Winthrop was not a Puritan minister, and his intent was not simply to present a Sabbath day religious homily. Rather, as governor of Massachusetts Bay, Winthrop took the occasion to articulate the hopes, fears, and dreams of the colony's organizers. His speech was an elaborate statement about how people must act, socially and economically, for the colony to succeed. What is the essence of Winthrop's message, and the paradox within his argument? In particular, what was his attitude toward the prospects of upward mobility in Massachusetts Bay?

DOCUMENT 1   *"A Model of Christian Charity"*

John Winthrop

God Almighty, in his most holy and wise providence, hath so disposed of the condition of mankind, as in all times some must be rich, some poor, some high and eminent in power and dignity, others mean and in subjection.

The Reason Hereof

First, to hold conformity with the rest of his works. Being delighted to show forth the glory of his wisdom in the variety and difference of the creatures; and the glory of his power, in ordering all these differences for the preservation and good of the whole; and the glory of his greatness. . . .

Secondly, that he might have the more occasion to manifest the work of his Spirit. First, upon the wicked, in moderating and restraining them: so that the rich and mighty should not eat up the poor, nor the poor and despised rise up against their superiors and shake off their yoke. Secondly, in the regenerate, in exercising his graces in them: as in the great ones, their love, mercy, gentleness, temperance etc.; in the poor and inferior sort, their faith, patience, obedience etc.

Thirdly, that every man might have need of other, and from hence they might be all knit more nearly together in the bond of brotherly affection. From hence it appears plainly that no man is made more honorable than another, or more wealthy etc., out of any particular and singular respect to himself, but for the glory of his creator and the common good of the creature, man. Therefore God still reserves the property of these gifts to himself, as [in] Ezekiel, 16. 17: he there calls wealth *his* gold and *his* silver; [in] Proverbs, 3. 9: he claims their service as his due: honor the Lord with thy riches etc. All men being thus (by divine providence) ranked into two sorts, rich and poor, under the first are comprehended all such as are able to live comfortably by their own means duly improved; and all others are poor, according to the former distribution. . . .

Question: What rule shall a man observe in giving, in respect of the measure?
Answer: If the time and occasion be ordinary he is to give out of his abundance— let him lay aside, as God hath blessed him. If the time and occasion be extraordinary he must be ruled by them, taking this withal: that then a man cannot likely do too much, especially if he may leave himself and his family under probable means of comfortable subsistence. . . .
Question: What rule must we observe in lending?
Answer: Thou must observe whether thy brother hath present or probable or possible means of repaying thee; if there be none of these, thou must give him according to his necessity, rather than lend him as he requires. If he hath present means of repaying thee, thou art to look at him, not as an act of mercy, but by way of commerce, wherein thou art to walk by the rule of Justice. But if his means of repaying thee be only probable or possible, then is he an object of thy mercy—thou must lend him, though there be danger of losing it, Deuteronomy, 15. 7: If any of thy brethren be poor etc., thou shalt lend him sufficient. . . . And because some might object, why so I should soon impoverish myself and my family? He adds, with all thy work etc., for our saviour. Matthew, 5. 42: "From him that would borrow of thee, turn not away."
Question: What rule must we observe in forgiving?

Answer: Whether thou didst lend by way of commerce or in mercy, if he have nothing to pay thee [thou] must forgive him (except in case where thou hast a surety or a lawful pledge), Deuteronomy, 15. 2. . . . In all these and like cases, Christ was a general rule, Matthew, [7. 12]: Whatsoever ye would that men should do to you, do ye the same to them also. . . .

Thus stands the cause between God and us. We are entered into covenant with him for this work, we have taken out a commission, the Lord hath given us leave to draw our own articles, we have professed to enterprise these actions, upon these and those ends, we have hereupon besought him of favor and blessing. Now if the Lord shall please to hear us, and bring us in peace to the place we desire, then hath he ratified this covenant and sealed our commission, [and] will expect a strict performance of the articles contained in it. But if we shall neglect the observation of these articles, which are the ends we have propounded, and, dissembling with our God, shall fall to embrace this present world and prosecute our carnal intentions, seeking great things for ourselves and our posterity, the Lord will surely break out in wrath against us, be revenged of such a perjured people and make us know the price of the breach of such a covenant.

Now the only way to avoid this shipwreck, and to provide for our posterity, is to follow the counsel of Micah: to do justly, to love mercy, to walk humbly with our God. For this end, we must be knit together in this work as one man, we must entertain each other in brotherly affection, we must be willing to abridge ourselves of our superfluities, for the supply of others' necessities, we must uphold a familiar commerce together in all meekness, gentleness, patience and liberality; we must delight in each other, make others' conditions our own, rejoice together, mourn together, labor and suffer together, always having before our eyes our commission and community in the work, our community as members of the same body. So shall we keep the unity of the spirit in the bond of peace. The Lord will be our God, and delight to dwell among us as his own people, and will command a blessing upon us in all our ways, so that we shall see much more of his wisdom, power, goodness and truth, than formerly we have been acquainted with. We shall find that the God of Israel is among us, when ten of us shall be able to resist a thousand of our enemies; when he shall make us a praise and glory that men shall say of succeeding plantations: "the Lord make it like that of NEW ENGLAND." For we must consider that we shall be as a city upon a hill: The eyes of all people are upon us, so that if we shall deal falsely with our God in this work we have undertaken, and so cause him to withdraw his present help from us, we shall be made a story and a by-word through the world: we shall open the mouths of enemies to speak evil of the ways of God and all professors for God's sake. We shall shame the faces of many of God's worthy servants, and cause their prayers to be turned into curses upon us, till we be consumed out of the good land whither we are going.

And to shut up this discourse with that exhortation of Moses, that faithful servant of the Lord, in his last farewell to Israel, Deuteronomy, 30: beloved, there is now set before us life and good, death and evil, in that we are commanded this day to love the Lord our God, and to love one another, to walk in his ways and to keep his commandments and his ordinance and his laws, and the articles of our covenant with him, that we may live and be multiplied, and that the Lord our God may bless us in the land whither we go to possess it. But if our hearts shall turn away, so that we will not obey, but shall be seduced, and worship other Gods—our pleasures and profits—and serve *them*, it is propounded unto us this day, we shall surely perish out of the good land whither we pass over this vast sea to possess it:

Therefore let us choose life,
that we and our seed

may live by obeying His
voice and cleaving to Him,
for He is our life, and
our prosperity.

Introduction to Documents 2 and 3

Notwithstanding Winthrop's call for Christian unity, not all settlers to Massachusetts embraced either Winthrop's mission or methods. The following documents express the opinions of two of Winthrop's adversaries, Anne Hutchinson and Robert Keayne. Hutchinson was a pious Puritan woman who accused the colonial ministers of teaching that one can get to heaven by doing good works. Puritans rejected this teaching, insisting that salvation comes from grace through faith, not through good works. For accusing the ministers of this false teaching, Hutchinson was brought to court and tried for sedition. Document 2 contains some excerpts from her trial. According to these passages, how did Hutchinson defend her understanding of divine truth, and for what was she banished from Massachusetts?

Document 3 contains some excerpts from the Last Will and Testament of the eminently successful New England merchant, Robert Keayne. Throughout his career, Keayne was hounded by Puritan authorities who claimed that he had secured his wealth by corrupt practices, which included lending money on interest, selling goods at rates determined by market factors, and pursuing his self-interest rather than the common good of the community. For these practices, Keayne was brought before the court and fined £200. In the following passages, Keayne defends himself against the charges of price gouging and of failing to support the common good. Compare Keayne's defense with Winthrop's address to the Puritans aboard the *Arabella*. To what degree were Keayne's capitalistic business practices and Winthrop's Puritan mission compatible?

DOCUMENT 2 *Excerpts from the Trial of Anne Hutchinson*

Mrs. Hutchinson: If you please to give me leave I shall give you the ground of what I know to be true. Being much troubled to see the falseness of the constitution of the church of England, I had like to have turned separatist; whereupon I kept a day of solemn humiliation and pondering of the things; this scripture was brought upon me—he that denies Jesus Christ to be come in the flesh is the antichrist—This I considered of and in considering found that the papists did not deny him to be come in the flesh, nor we did not deny him—who then was antichrist? Was the Turk antichrist only? The Lord knows that I could not open scripture; he must by his prophetical office open it unto me. So after that being unsatisfied in the things, the Lord was please to bring this scripture out of the Hebrews. He that denies the testament denies the testator, and in this did open unto me and give me to see that those which did not teach the new covenant had the spirit of antichrist, and upon this he did discover the ministry unto me and ever since, I bless the Lord, he hath let me see which was the clear ministry and which the wrong. Since that time I confess I have been more choice and he hath left me to distinguish between the voice of my beloved and the voice of Moses, the voice of John Baptist and the voice of the antichrist, for all those voice are spoken of in scripture. Now if you do condemn me for speaking what in my conscience I know to be truth I must commit myself unto the Lord.

Mr. Nowel: How do you known that that was the spirit?

Mrs. Hutchinson: How did Abraham know that it was God that bid him offer his son, being a breach of the sixth commandment?

Dep. Gov: By an immediate voice.

Mrs. Hutchinson: So to me by an immediate revelation.

Dep. Gov: How! an immediate revelation.

Mrs. Hutchinson: By the voice of his own spirit to my soul. . . .

. . . After more testimony, the court rendered its verdict.

Gov: Mrs. Hutchinson, the sentence of the court you hear is that you are banished from out of our jurisdiction as being a woman not fit for our society, and are to be imprisoned till the court shall send you away.

DOCUMENT 3 *From* The Apologia of Robert Keayne

[My effort] to promote the good of this place has been answered by divers here with unchristian, uncharitable, and unjust reproaches and slanders since I came hither, as if men had the liberty of their tongues to reproach any that were not beneficial to them. [These attacks came] together with that deep and sharp censure that was laid upon me in the country and carried on with so much bitterness and indignation of some, contrary both to law or any foregoing precedent if I mistake not, and, I am sure, contrary or beyond the quality and desert of the complaints that came against me, which indeed were rather shadows of offense, out of a desire of revenge made great by the aggravations of some to make them heinous and odious than that they were so indeed, and this not in my own judgments only (which may be looked at as partial) but in the judgments of hundreds that have expressed themselves, both then and especially since. Yet by some it was carried on with such violence and pretended zeal as if they had had some of the greatest sins in the world to censure. . . . Had it been in their power or could they have carried it they would not have corrected or reformed but utterly have ruined myself and all that I had, as if no punishment had been sufficient to expiate my offense [of] selling a good bridle for 2 s. that now worse are sold without offense for 3 s., 6 d. nails for 7 d., and 8 d. nails for 10 d. per hundred, which since and to this day are frequently sold by many for a great deal more. And so [it was] in all other things proportionably, as selling gold buttons for two shilling nine pence a dozen that cost above 2 in London and yet were never paid for by them that complained.

These were the great matters in which I had offended, when myself have often seen and heard offenses, complaints, and crimes of a high nature against God and men, such as filthy uncleanness, fornications, drunkenness, fearful oaths, quarreling, mutinies, sabbath breakings, thefts, forgeries, and such like, which hath passed with fines or censures so small or easy as hath not been worth the naming or regarding.

I did submit to the censure, I paid the fine to the uttermost, which is not nor hath been done by many (nor so earnestly required as mine was) though for certain and not supposed offenses of far higher nature, which I can make good not by hearsay only but in my own knowledge, yea offenses of the same kind. [My own offense] was so greatly aggravated and with such indignation pursued by some, as if no censure could be too great or too severe, as if I had not been worthy to have lived upon the earth. [Such offenses] are not only now common almost in every shop and warehouse but even then and ever since with a higher measure of excess, yea even by some of them that were most zealous and had their hands and tongues deepest in my censure. [At that time] they were buyers, [but since then] they are turned sellers and peddling merchants themselves, so that they are become no offenses now nor worthy questioning nor taking notice of in others. Yet [they cried] oppression and excessive gains, [when] considering the time that they kept the goods bought in their hands before they could or would pay and the quality or rather the business of their pay for kind, contrary to their own promises, instead of gains there was apparent loss without any gains to the seller.

The oppression lay justly and truly on the buyer's hand rather than on the seller; but then the country was all buyers and few sellers, though it would not be seen on that side then. For if the lion will say the lamb is a fox, it must be so, the lamb must be content to leave it. But now the country hath got better experience in merchandise, and they have soundly paid for their experience since, so that it is now and was many years ago become a common proverb amongst most buyers that knew those times that my goods and prices were cheap pennyworths in comparison of what hath been taken since and especially [in comparison with] the prices of these times. Yet I have borne this patiently and without disturbance or troubling the Court with any petitions for remission or abatement of the fine, though I have been advised by many friends, yea and some of the same Court, so to do, as if they would be willing to embrace such an occasion to undo what was then done in a hurry and in displeasure, or at least would lessen or mitigate it in a great measure. But I have not been persuaded to it because the more innocently that I suffer, the more patiently have I borne it, leaving my cause therein to the Lord. . . .

Therefore, I would make this request to the overseers of this my will, that all or some of them would (if they in their wisdom judge it not very inconvenient) to take a seasonable time to move the General Court about it, to recall or repeal that sentence and to return my fine again after all this time of enjoying it, . . . And if upon this motion of my overseers the Court shall be pleased to consent, . . . my will is that what is so returned by them may be given to Harvard College at Cambridge, according as I have proposed in my former gifts to that place, or [to] any other work more needful upon which it may be disposed of to more good or public use or service. This I leave to the discretion of my overseers with the consent of my executors.

Introduction to Documents 4 and 5
Education and Literacy

The next two documents offer clues about education in Puritan New England. The Massachusetts School Law of 1647, sometimes called the old deluder Satan law, established the first system of public education in the colonies. The second document, a page from *The New England Primer* (1687), illumines the method and content of early childhood instruction. From the evidence provided in these readings, speculate about the purpose of schooling in colonial Massachusetts.

DOCUMENT 4   *Massachusetts School Law of 1647*

It being one chief project of the old deluder, Satan, to keep men from the knowledge of the Scriptures, as in former times by keeping them in an unknown tongue, and in these later times by persuading [them] from the use of tongues, so that at least the true sense and meaning of the original might be clouded by false glosses of saint seeming deceivers, that learning may not be buried in the grave of our fathers in the church and commonwealth, the Lord assisting our endeavors:

It is therefore ordered that every township in this jurisdiction after the Lord has increased their number to fifty householders shall then forthwith appoint one in their town to teach all such children as shall resort to him to write and read, whose wages shall be paid either by the parents or masters of such children or by the inhabitants in general, by way of supply, as most part of those that ordered these judgments shall appoint; provided those that send their children be not oppressed by paying much more than they can have them taught for in other towns; and it is further ordered that where any town shall increase to the number of 100 families or householders, they shall set up a grammar school, the master thereof being able to instruct youth so far as they shall be fitted for the university, provided that if any town neglect the performance hereof above one year, that each and every such town shall pay five pounds to the next school until they have performed this order.

DOCUMENT 5   The New England Primer, *c. 1687*

In *Adam's* fall
We sinned all.

Thy life to mend
This *Book* attend.

The *Cat* doth play
And after slay.

A *Dog* will bite
The thief at night.

An *Eagle's* flight
Is out of sight.

The idle *Fool*
Is whipped at school.

As runs the *Glass*,
Man's life doth pass.

My *Book* and *Heart*
Shall never part.

Job feels the rod,
Yet blesses GOD.

Our *KING* the good,
no man of blood.

The *Lion* bold
The *Lamb* doth hold.

The *Moon* gives light
In time of night.

Nightingales sing
In time of spring.

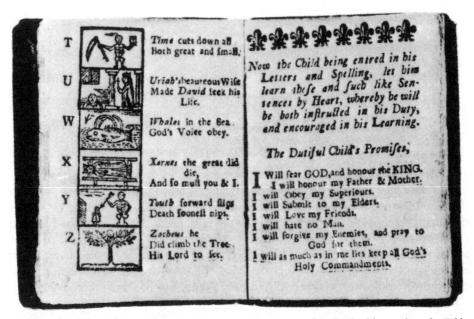

The Puritans believed that the word of God must come to each individual by reading the Bible, so they considered literacy essential. The New England Primer, with its didactic style and moral lessons, was the main textbook for children. (Rare Books Division, The New York Public Library, Astor, Lenox and Tilden Foundations)

The *Royal Oak* it was the tree
That saved His Royal Majesty.

Peter denies
His Lord and cries.

Queen Esther comes in royal state
To save the JEWS from dismal fate.

Rachel doth mourn
For her first born.

Samuel anoints
Whom God appoints.

Time cuts down all
Both great and small.

Uriah's beautous wife
Made David seek his life.

Whales in the sea
God's voice obey.

Xerxes the great did die,
And so must you and I.

Youth forward slips,
Death soonest nips.

Zacheus he
Did climb the tree
His Lord to see.

Introduction to Documents 6 and 7

Home and Family

Although the Puritans generally disliked literary works that celebrated the human writer rather than the "Divine Author of all things," they looked favorably on poetic efforts used to promote their understanding of divine Truth. Anne Bradstreet, America's first and best-known Puritan poet, wrote a book of poetry that was first published in London in 1650. The following two selections from this work are love poems that illustrate the anxieties as well as the affections of a devoted Puritan wife and mother. From a very different perspective, the Reverend Increase Mather's letter to Michael Wigglesworth (dated May 8, 1679) also touches on Puritan attitudes toward love, sex, and marriage.

DOCUMENT 6 *The Poetry of Anne Bradstreet*

To my Dear and Loving Husband

If ever two were one, then surely we.
If ever man were loved by wife, then thee;
If ever wife was happy in a man,
Compare with me, ye women, if you can.
I prize thy love more than whole mines of gold
Or all the riches that the East doth hold.
My love is such that rivers cannot quench,
Nor ought but love from thee, give recompense.
Thy love is such I can no way repay,
The heavens reward thee manifold, I pray.
Then while we live, in love let's so persevere
That when we live no more, we may live ever.

Before the Birth of One of Her Children

All things within this fading world hath end,
Adversity doth still our joys attend;
No ties so strong, no friends so dear and sweet,
But with death's parting blow is sure to meet.
The sentence past is most irrevocable,
A common thing, yet oh, inevitable.
How soon my Dear, death may my steps attend,
How soon't may be thy lot to lose thy friend,
We both are ignorant, yet love bids me
These farewell lines to recommend to thee,
That when that knot's untied that made us one,

I may seem thine, who in effect am none.
And if I see not half my days that's due,
What nature would, God grant to yours and you;
The many faults that well you know I have
Let be interred in my oblivious grave;
If any worth or virtue were in me,
Let that live freshly in thy memory
And when thou feel'st no grief, as I no harms,
Yet love thy dead, who long lay in thine arms.
And when thy loss shall be repaid with gains,
Look to my little babes, my dear remains.
And if thou love thyself, or loved'st me,
These O protect from step-dame's injury.
And if chance to thine eyes shall bring this verse,
With some sad sighs honour my absent hearse;
And kiss this paper for thy love's dear sake,
Who with salt tears this last farewell did take.

DOCUMENT 7 *Increase Mather to Michael Wigglesworth*

Reverend Sir,—Since I saw you the last in B. one that doth unfeignedly desire your welfare hath bin with mee, expressing grief of heart with reference unto a matter wherein yourselfe is concerned. I owe you that respect (& much more) as to informe you what I have bin told. The Report is, that you are designing to marry with your servant mayd, & that she is one of obscure parentage, & not 20 years old, & of no Church, nor so much as Baptised. If it be as is related, I would humbly entreat you (before it be too late) to consider of these arguments in opposition: 1. For you to doe this, which will be a grief of heart to your dear Relations. . . . 2. I doubt that considering her youth, & your age, & great bodily infirmities, such a change of your condition, if that which is intimated by the Holy Apostle, 1 Cor. 7, 3, should be attended, your days would be shortned, & consequently the 5th Commandment broken. 3. Such general Rules as those, Phil. 4, 8, doe concern as all christians, so eminently Ministers of Christ. . . . 4. The ministry will be blamed, which wee should be very carefull to prevent. 2 Cor. 6, 3. The mouths of carnal ones will be opened, not onely to censure you, but your brethren in the ministry will be condemned also. . . . 5. I am afraid that if you should proceed, that Rule, 2 Cor. 6, 14, will be transgressed. It useth to be said *nube pari*, but to marry with one so much your Inferior on all accounts, is not *nubere pari*. And to take one that was never baptised into such neerness of Relation, seemeth contrary to the Gospell; especially for a Minister of Christ to doe it. The like never was in N. E. Nay, I question whether the like hath bin known in the christian world. 6. Doth not that Script. 1 Tim. 3, 11, with others of the like importance, prohibit such proceedings?

Thus have I made bold to suggest my thoughts unto you. And if I had not respected the interest of Religion, & your credit & comfort, I should have bin wholly silent in a matter that concerns another & not me, further than as I am bound to seeke your welfare, & doe what I may to prevent trouble from coming upon my neighbor, & brother, especially such an one, whose Name hath bin, & I hope may still be, of precious esteem with the Lord's people.

Though your affections should be too far gone in this matter, I doubt not but if you put the object out of your sight, & looke up to the Lord Jesus for supplies of grace, you will be enabled to overcome these Temptations. The Lord be with you, I am

Yours unfeignedly,
Increase Mather.

Introduction to Document 8
Puritans and Indians

When Rip Van Winkle, in Washington Irving's classic American tale (1819–1820), did not return from a hunting trip into the Catskills, it was assumed that he had been "carried away by the Indians." That Irving needed no further explanation for Rip's disappearance demonstrates the degree to which readers of his day accepted the possibility of being kidnapped by hostile Indians. This kind of captivity, of course, was a historic reality that a small number of Americans knew firsthand. Most Americans, however, experienced vicariously the emotions and fear of capture by Native Americans through the reading of captivity narratives—the most popular literary genre of late colonial times.

Stories of captivity by an alien culture have long excited the public imagination. The first and perhaps the best of the Puritan captivity narratives was written by Mary Rowlandson, the wife of a clergyman who was captured during King Philip's War. Published in 1682, this piece sold quickly and went through some thirty future editions, preparing the way for many other captivity stories, which also became the best-sellers of their day. This narrative was popular in part because it was a thrilling personal-adventure story placed in an exotic context. But for the Puritans, it was also a religious epic that described how God had punished but not forgotten His people: The personal story of Rowlandson was in microcosm the story of all Puritans whom God had tested but was ultimately willing to redeem. While offering some insights into the culture of the Algonquians, these selections from Rowlandson's *The Sovereignty and Goodness of God* reveal even more about the New England mind and the tensions within a conflicted Puritan society.

DOCUMENT 8   *From* **The Sovereignty and Goodness of God**

Mary Rowlandson

On the tenth of February 1675 came the Indians with great numbers upon Lancaster. Their first coming was about sunrising. Hearing the noise of some guns, we looked out; several houses were burning and the smoke ascending to heaven. There were five persons taken in one house; the father and the mother and a sucking child they knocked on the head; the other two they took and carried away alive. There were two others, who being out of their garrison upon some occasion were set upon; one was knocked on the head, the other escaped. Another there was who running along was shot and wounded and fell down; he begged of them his life, promising them money (as they told me), but they would not hearken to him but knocked him in [the] head, stripped him naked, and split open his bowels. Another, seeing many of the Indians about his barn, ventured and went out but was quickly shot down. There were three others belonging to the same garrison who were killed; the Indians, getting up upon the roof of the barn, had advantage to shoot down upon them over their fortification. Thus these murderous wretches went on, burning and destroying before them.

At length they came and beset our own house, and quickly it was the dolefullest day that ever mine eyes saw. The house stood upon the edge of a hill. Some of the Indians got behind the hill, others into the barn, and others behind anything that could shelter them; from all which places they shot against the house so that the bullets seemed to fly like hail; and quickly they wounded one man among us, then another, and then a third. About two hours (according to my observation in that amazing time) they had been about the house before they prevailed to fire it (which they did with flax and hemp which they brought out of the barn, and there being no defense about the house, only two flankers at two opposite corners and one of them not finished). They fired it once, and one ventured out and quenched it, but they quickly fired it again and that took.

Now is that dreadful hour come that I have often heard of (in time of war as it was the case of others), but now mine eyes see it. Some in our house were fighting for their lives, others wallowing in their blood, the house on fire over our heads, and the bloody heathen ready to knock us on the head if we stirred out. Now might we hear mothers and children crying out for themselves and one another, "Lord, what shall we do?" Then I took my children (and one of my sisters, hers) to go forth and leave the house, but as soon as we came to the door and appeared, the Indians shot so thick that the bullets rattled against the house as if one had taken an handful of stones and threw them so that we were fain to give back. We had six stout dogs belonging to our garrison, but none of them would stir although another time, if any Indian had come to the door, they were ready to fly upon him and tear him down. The Lord hereby would make us the more to acknowledge His hand and to see that our help is always in Him. But out we must go, the fire increasing and coming along behind us roaring, and the Indians gaping before us with their guns, spears, and hatchets to devour us. No sooner were we out of the house, but my brother-in-law [John Divoll] (being before wounded, in defending the house, in or near the throat) fell down dead; whereat the Indians scornfully shouted, hallooed, and were presently upon him, stripping off his clothes. The bullets flying thick, one went through my side, and the same (as would seem) through the bowels and hand of my dear child in my arms. One of my elder sister's children, named William [Kerley], had then his leg broken, which the Indians perceiving, they knocked him on the head. Thus were we butchered by those merciless heathen, standing amazed, with the blood running down to our heels.

My eldest sister [Elizabeth] being yet in the house and seeing those woeful sights, the infidels hailing mothers one way and children another and some wallowing in their blood, and her elder son telling her that her son William was dead and myself was wounded, she said, "And, Lord, let me die with them." Which was no sooner said, but she was struck with a bullet and fell down dead over the threshold. I hope she is reaping the fruit of her good labors, being faithful to the service of God in her place. In her younger years she lay under much trouble upon spiritual accounts till it pleased God to make that precious scripture take hold of her heart, 2 Cor. 12:9, "And he said unto me, my grace is sufficient for thee." More than twenty years after I have heard her tell how sweet and comfortable that place was to her. But to return: the Indians laid hold of us, pulling me one way and the children another, and said, "Come go along with us." I told them they would kill me. They answered, if I were willing to go along with them they would not hurt me.

Oh, the doleful sight that now was to behold at this house! "Come, behold the works of the Lord, what desolation He has made in the earth." Of thirty-seven persons who were in this one house none escaped either present death or a bitter captivity save only one, who might say as he, Job 1:15, "And I only am escaped alone to tell the news." There were twelve killed, some shot, some stabbed with their spears, some knocked down with their hatchets. When we are in prosperity, oh, the little that we think of such dreadful sights, and to see our dear friends and relations lie bleeding out their heart-blood upon the ground! There was one who was chopped into the head with a hatchet and stripped naked, and yet was crawling up and down. It is a solemn sight to see so many Christians lying in their blood, some here and some there, like a company of sheep torn by wolves, all of them stripped naked by a company of hellhounds, roaring, singing, ranting and insulting, as if they would have torn our very hearts out. Yet the Lord by his almighty power preserved a number of us from death, for there were twenty-four of us taken alive and carried captive.

I had often before this said that if the Indians should come I should choose rather to be killed by them than taken alive, but when it came to the trial, my mind changed; their glittering weapons so daunted my spirit that I chose rather to go along with those (as I may say) ravenous beasts than that moment to end my days. And that I may the better declare what happened to me during that grievous captivity, I shall particularly speak of the several removes we had up and down the wilderness.

The First Remove

Now away we must go with those barbarous creatures with our bodies wounded and bleeding and our hearts no less than our bodies. About a mile we went that night up upon a hill within sight of the town where they intended to lodge. There was hard by a vacant house (deserted by the English before for fear of the Indians). I asked them whether I might not lodge in the house that night, to which they answered, "What, will you love English men still?" This was the dolefullest night that ever my eyes saw. Oh, the roaring and singing and dancing and yelling of those black creatures in the night, which made the place a lively resemblance of hell. And as miserable was the waste that was there made of horses, cattle, sheep, swine, calves, lambs, roasting pigs, and fowl (which they had plundered in the town), some roasting, some lying and burning, and some boiling to feed our merciless enemies who were joyful enough though we were disconsolate. To add to the dolefulness of the former day and the dismalness of the present night, my thoughts ran upon my losses and sad bereaved condition. All was gone: my husband gone (at least separated from me, he being in the Bay, and to add to my grief, the Indians told me they would kill him as he came homeward), my children gone, my relations and friends gone, our house and home and all our comforts within door and without, all was gone except my life, and I knew not but the next moment that might go too. There remained nothing to me but one poor wounded babe, and it seemed at present worse than death that it was in such a pitiful condition bespeaking compassion, and I had no refreshing for it nor suitable things to revive it. . . .

The Third Remove

. . . This day in the afternoon about an hour by sun we came to the place where they intended, viz. an Indian town called Wenimesset, nor[th]ward of Quabaug. When we were come, oh, the number of pagans (now merciless enemies) that there came about me that I may say as David, Psal. 27:13, "I had fainted, unless I had believed," etc. The next day was the Sabbath. I then remembered how careless I had been of God's holy time, how many Sabbaths I had lost and misspent and how evilly I had walked in God's sight, which lay so close unto my spirit that it was easy for me to see how righteous it was with God to cut the thread of my life and cast me out of His presence forever. Yet the Lord still showed mercy to me and upheld me, and as He wounded me with one hand, so He healed me with the other. . . .

. . . I sat much alone with a poor wounded child in my lap, which moaned night and day, having nothing to revive the body or cheer the spirits of her, but instead of that sometimes one Indian would come and tell me one hour that, "Your master will knock your child in the head." And then a second, and then a third, "Your master will quickly knock your child in the head."

This was the comfort I had from them. "Miserable comforters are ye all," as He said. Thus nine days I sat upon my knees with my babe in my lap till my flesh was raw again; my child being even ready to depart this sorrowful world, they bade me carry it out to another wigwam (I suppose because they would not be troubled with such spectacles), whither I went with a heavy heart, and down I sat with the picture of death in my lap. About two hours in the night my sweet babe like a lamb departed this life on Feb. 18, 1675, it being about six years and five months old. It was nine days from the first wounding in this miserable condition without any refreshing of one nature or other except a little cold water. I cannot but take notice how at another time I could not bear to be in the room where any dead person was, but now the case is changed; I must and could lie down by my dead babe side by side all the night after. I have thought since of the wonderful goodness of God to me in preserving me in the use of my reason and senses in that distressed time that I did not use wicked and violent means to end my own miserable life. . . .

I cannot but take notice of the wonderful mercy of God to me in those afflictions in sending me a Bible. One of the Indians that came from Medfield fight [who] had brought some plunder came to me and asked me if I would have a Bible; he had got one in his basket. I was glad of it and asked him whether he thought the Indians would let me read. He answered, "Yes." So I took the Bible, and in that melancholy time it came into my mind to read first the 28 chapter of Deut., which I did, and when I had read it, my dark heart wrought on this manner, that there was no mercy for me, that the blessings were gone and the curses come in their room, and that I had lost my opportunity. But the Lord helped me still to go on reading till I came to chapter 30, the seven first verses, where I found there was mercy promised again if we would return to him by repentance, and, though we were scattered from one end of the earth to the other, yet the Lord would gather us together and turn all those curses upon our enemies. I do not desire to live to forget this scripture and what comfort it was to me. . . .

The Twentieth Remove

It was their usual manner to remove when they had done any mischief, lest they should be found out, and so they did at this time. We went about three or four miles, and there they built a great wigwam big enough to hold a hundred Indians, which they did in preparation to a great day of dancing. . . .

In my travels an Indian came to me and told me if I were willing, he and his squaw would run away and go home along with me. I told him no. I was not willing to run away but desired to wait God's time that I might go home quietly and without fear. And now God hath granted me my desire. O, the wonderful power of God that I have seen and the experience that I have had! I have been in the midst of those roaring lions and savage bears that feared neither God nor man nor the devil, by night and day, alone and in company, sleeping all sorts together, and yet not one of them ever offered me the least abuse of unchastity to me in word or action. Though some are ready to say I speak it for my own credit, I speak it in the presence of God and to His glory. God's power is as great now and as sufficient to save as when He preserved Daniel in the lion's den or the three children in the fiery furnace. I may well say as his Psal. 107:12, "Oh, give thanks unto the Lord for He is good, for His mercy endureth forever." Let the redeemed of the Lord say so whom He hath redeemed from the hand of the enemy, especially that I should come away in the midst of so many hundreds of enemies quietly and peaceably and not a dog moving his tongue. . . .

I have seen the extreme vanity of this world. One hour I have been in health and wealth, wanting nothing, but the next hour in sickness and wounds and death, having nothing but sorrow and affliction. Before I knew what affliction meant, I was ready sometimes to wish for it. When I lived in prosperity, having the comforts of the world about me, my relations by me, my heart cheerful, and taking little care for anything, and yet seeing many whom I preferred before myself under many trials and afflictions, in sickness, weakness, poverty, losses, crosses, and cares of the world, I should be sometimes jealous lest I should have my portion in this life, and that scripture would come to mind, Heb. 12:6, "For whom the Lord loveth he chasteneth and scourgeth every son whom he receiveth." But now I see the Lord had His time to scourge and chasten me. The portion of some is to have their afflictions by drops, now one drop and then another, but the dregs of the cup, the wine of astonishment, like a sweeping rain that leaveth no food, did the Lord prepare to be my portion. Affliction I wanted and affliction I had, full measure (I thought) pressed down and running over. Yet I see when God calls a person to anything and through never so many difficulties, yet He is fully able to carry them through and make them see and say they have been gainers thereby. And I hope I can say in some measure, as David did, "It is good for me that I have been afflicted."

The Lord hath showed me the vanity of these outward things. That they are the vanity of vanities and vexation of spirit, that they are but a shadow, a blast, a bubble, and things of no continuance. That we must rely on God himself and our whole dependence must be upon Him. If trouble from smaller matters begin to arise in me, I have something at hand to check myself with and say, why am I troubled? It was but the other day that if I had had the world I would have given it for my freedom or to have been a servant to a Christian. I have learned to look beyond present and smaller troubles and to be quieted under them, as Moses said, Exod. 14:13, "Stand still and see the salvation of the Lord."

Introduction to Documents 9–12
Salem's Struggle with Satan

In early 1692, several Salem girls showed hysterical behavior and accused certain individuals of bewitching them. When the local magistrates and minister demanded that something be done, the Massachusetts governor appointed a special court to try the cases against the accused witches. Before the court was adjourned, more than 150 residents had been accused of witchcraft, one man had been crushed to death in an attempt to force him into a confession, and 19 persons had been hanged.

Presented next are selections from documents related to the Salem witchcraft trials. The first selection is from a sermon of Samuel Parris, the minister of Salem. Parris was the father of one of the afflicted girls and the owner of an African slave named Tituba, who was accused on using her power to bring Satan into the community. The second document comes from the narratives of the trials. Note how these first two documents dwell off the pervasiveness and insidiousness of evil. The final selections consist of the 1692 deposition and the 1706 confession of Ann Putnam, one of the girls allegedly victimized by the witches of Salem. Search the documents for evidence of tensions within this Puritan community. How do you explain the tragic witchcraft episode?

DOCUMENT 9   *"Christ Knows How Many Devils There Are,"* 1692

Samuel Parris

27 March 1691/92, Sacrament day.

. . . John 6:70. "Have not I chosen you twelve, and one of you is a Devil.". . . .

Doctrine: *Our Lord Jesus Christ knows how many Devils there are in his Church, and who they are.*

1. There are devils as well as saints in Christ's Church.
2. Christ knows how many of these devils there are.
3. Christ knows who these devils are.

Proposition 1: There are devils as well as saints in Christ's church. Here three things may be spoken to: (1) Show you what is meant here by *devils*; (2) That there are such devils in the church; (3) That there are also true saints in such churches. . . .

. . . Let none then be stumbled at religion, because too often there are devils found among the saints. You see, here was a true church, sincere converts and sound believers; and yet here was a devil among them.

. . . Terror to hypocrites who profess much love to Christ but indeed are in league with their lusts, which they prefer above Christ. Oh! remember that you are devils in Christ's account. Christ is lightly esteemed of you, and you are vilely accounted for by Christ. Oh! if there be any such among us, forbear to come this day to the Lord's table, lest Satan enter more powerfully into you—lest while the bread be between your teeth, the wrath of the Lord come pouring down upon you (Psalm 78:30–31). . . .

. . . Examine we ourselves well, what we are—what we church members are. We are either saints or devils: the Scripture gives us no medium. The Apostle tells us we are to examine ourselves (2 Cor. 13:5). Oh! it is a dreadful thing to be a devil, and yet to sit down at the Lord's table (1 Cor. 10:21). Such incur the hottest of God's wrath (as follows—v. 22). Now, if we would not be devils, we must give ourselves wholly up to Christ, and not suffer the predominancy of one lust—and particularly that of covetousness, which is made so light of, and which so sorely prevails in these perilous times. Why, this one lust made Judas a devil (John 12:6, Matth. 26:15). And no doubt it has made more devils than one. For a little pelf [money], men sell Christ to his enemies, and their souls to the devil. But there are certain sins that make us devils; see that we be not such:

1. A liar or murderer (John 8:44)
2. A slanderer or an accuser of the godly
3. A tempter to sin
4. An opposer of godliness, as Elymos (Acts 13:8 etc.)
5. Envious persons as witches
6. A drunkard (I Sam. 1: 15–16)
7. A proud person

DOCUMENT 10 *Narratives of the Witchcraft Cases*

Martha Carrier was indicted for the bewitching of certain persons, according to the form usual in such cases pleading not guilty to her indictment. There were first brought in a considerable number of the bewitched persons, who not only made the court sensible to an horrid witchcraft committed upon them, but also deposed that it was Martha Carrier, or her shape, that grievously tormented them by biting, pricking, pinching, and choking of them. It was further deposed that while this Carrier was on her examination before the magistrates, the poor people were so tortured that every one expected their death upon the very spot, but that upon the binding [arrest] of Carrier they were eased. . . .

Before the trial of this prisoner, several of her own children had frankly and fully confessed, not only that they were witches themselves, but that this, their mother, had made them so. This confession they made with great shows of repentance, and with much demonstration of truth. They related place, time, occasion; they gave an account of journeys, meetings, and mischiefs by them performed, and were very credible in what they said. . . .

Benjamin Abbot gave in his testimony that . . . this Carrier was very angry with him upon laying out some land near her husband's. Her expressions in this anger were that she "would stick as close to Abbot as the bark stuck to the tree; and that he should repent of it afore seven years came to an end, so as Doctor Prescot should never cure him." . . . Presently after this he was taken with a swelling in his foot, and then with a pain in his side, and exceedingly tormented. It bred into a sore, which was lanced by Doctor Prescot, and several gallons of corruption [pus] ran out of it. For six weeks it continued very bad, and then another sore bred in his groin, which was also lanced by Doctor Prescot. Another sore then bred in his groin, which was likewise cut, and put him to very great misery. He was brought unto death's door, and so remained until Carrier was taken and carried away by the constable, from which very day he began to mend and so grew better every day, and is well ever since.

Sarah Abbot also, his wife, testified that her husband was not only all this while afflicted in his body, but also that strange, extraordinary, and unaccountable calamities befell his cattle, their death being such as they could guess at no natural reason for. . . .

One Foster, who confessed her own share in the witchcraft for which the prisoner stood indicted, affirmed that she had seen the prisoner at some of their witch meetings, and that it was this Carrier who persuaded her to be a witch. She confessed that the devil carried them on a pole to a witch meeting; but the pole broke, and she hanging about Carrier's neck, they both fell down, and she then received an hurt by the fall whereof she was not at this very time recovered.

DOCUMENT 11 *Ann Putnam's Deposition, 1692*

Who testifyith and saith that on 20th of April, 1692, at evening she saw the Apparition of a minister at which she was grievously affrighted and cried out, Oh dreadful: Dreadful here is a minister come, what are Minister's witches to: Whence come you and What is your name? For I will complain of you though you be a Minister. If you be a wizard . . . and immediately I was tortured by him, being Racked and almost choked by him. And he tempted me to write in his book which I Refused with loud cries and said I would not write in his book though he tore me all to pieces but told him that it was a dreadful thing, that he which was a Minister that should teach children to fear God should come to persuade poor creatures to give their souls to the devil. Oh, dreadful, dreadful, tell me your name so that I may know who you are. Then again he tortured me and urged me to write in his book, which I refused and then presently he told me that his name was George Burroughs, and that he had had three wives and that he had bewitched the two first of them to death and that he had killed Miss T. Lawson because she was so unwilling to go from the village and also killed Mr. Lawson's child because he went to the eastward with Sir Edmon and preached to the soldiers and that he had made Abigail Hobs a witch and several witches more, and he has continued every since, by times tempting me to write in his book and grievously torturing me by beating, pinching, and almost choking me several times a day and he also told me that he was above a witch, he was a conjurer.

DOCUMENT 12 *Ann Putnam's Confession, 1706*

"I desire to be humbled before God for that sad and humbling providence that befell my father's family in the year about '92; that I, then being in my childhood, should, by such a providence of God, be made an instrument for the accusing of several persons of a griev-ous crime, whereby their lives were taken away from them, whom now I have just grounds and good reason to believe they were innocent persons; and that it was a great delusion of Satan that deceived me in that sad time, whereby I justly fear I have been instrumental, with others, though ignorantly and unwittingly, to bring upon myself and this land the guilt of innocent blood; though what was said or done by me against any person I can truly and uprightly say, before God and man, I did it not out of any anger, malice, or ill-will to any person, for I had no such thing against one of them; but what I did was igno-rantly, being deluded by Satan. And particularly, as I was a chief instrument of accusing of Goodwife Nurse and her two sisters, I desire to lie in the dust, and to be humbled for it, in that I was a cause, with others, of so sad a calamity to them and their families; for which cause I desire to lie in the dust, and earnestly beg forgiveness of God, and from all those unto whom I have given just cause of sorrow and offence, whose relations were taken away or accused.

[Signed]

"This confession was read before the congregation, together with her relation, Aug. 25, 1706; and she acknowledged it.

"J. Green, Pastor."

QUESTIONS

Defining Terms

Identify in the context of the chapter each of the following:

Calvinism	Robert Keayne
Half Way Covenant	"the old deluder Satan law"
John Winthrop	Anne Bradstreet
Metacomet (King Philip)	Mary Rowlandson
jeremiads	"a city upon a hill"

Probing the Sources

1. How did the ideas expressed in Winthrop's "A Model of Christian Charity" inhibit and promote business activities in Massachusetts?

2. Discuss the characteristics of family life in colonial New England.

3. What was Rowlandson's purpose for writing *The Sovereignty and Goodness of God?* To what degree is her account an accurate description of Algonquian culture?

4. Discuss the ways in which Puritan ideas about education, love, family, work, and com-munity related to their religious worldview?

Interpreting the Sources

1. Define Puritanism. To what degree has the Puritan past shaped the development of American culture?

2. Compare the reasons for establishing Virginia and Massachusetts Bay. Account for the similarities and the differences.

3. Compare the descriptions of Native Americans in the writings of Rowlandson, Columbus, Las Casas, Barlowe, and Percy. How do you explain the similarities and the differences?

4. Was Massachusetts Bay a successful colony? Justify your answer.

ADDITIONAL READING

An excellent introduction to the study of Winthrop and New England Puritanism is Edmund S. Morgan, *The Puritan Dilemma: The Story of John Winthrop* (1985). For Puritan understandings of providence and government of God in later decades, see Michael P. Winship's *Seers of God: Puritan Providentialism in the Restoration and Early Enlightenment* (1996). Other insightful examinations into Puritan culture include Harry S. Stout, *The New England Soul: Preaching and Religious Culture* (1986), Stephen Innes, *Creating the Commonwealth: The Economic Culture of Puritan New England* (1995), and Pascal Covici, Jr., *Humor and Revelation in American Literature: The Puritan Connection* (1997). The female Puritan experience is vividly discussed in Lyle Koehler's *A Search for Power: The "Weaker Sex" in Seventeenth-Century New England* (1980) and Amanda Porterfield's *Female Piety in Puritan New England: The Emergence of Religious Humanism* (1992). For discussions of Puritan-Indian relations, see James Axtell, *The European and the Indian: Essays in the Ethnohistory of Colonial North America* (1981), and Alden Vaughan, *New England Frontier: Puritans and Indians, 1620–1675* (1965).

Eighteenth-Century
American Voices

HISTORICAL CONTEXT

Before 1776, most colonists thought of themselves as English. They were proud of
England, proud to be part of the empire. True, Germans, Africans, Scots, Native
Americans, and others retained many of their old ways. But more than those of any
other single group, English language, religion, customs, and folkways predomi-
nated from Florida to Maine. Alongside colonists' pride in their Englishness, however, a growing sense of American identity was emerging. Perhaps it was
inevitable that 100 years of settlement and three thousand miles of distance would
engender feelings of American distinctiveness. The mixing of so many diverse peoples on fresh and abundant land caused the French immigrant Michel-Guillaume
Jean de Crèvecoeur (who anglicized his name to J. Hector St. John Crèvecoeur) to
ask "What, then, is the American, this new man?"

The eighteenth century was filled with both adherence to tradition—the rights of
Englishmen and commonwealth ideals, for example—and a sense of change, of individuals and societies shaping themselves to bold new concepts of human aspiration. This second strand was part of something called the *Enlightenment*. The
Enlightenment was more a tendency or trend in the thinking of both Europeans and
Americans than an organized intellectual movement. In its most optimistic form, on
the eve of the American Revolution, the Enlightenment was characterized by faith in
progress and by a belief in humankind's ability to control its own fate.

Many Enlightenment thinkers, such as Benjamin Franklin, were Deists. They believed that God had created the world, but that He had left men and women alone
to work out their own destinies. There were natural moral laws, boundaries of good
and evil, but these had to be discovered and implemented by people acting on
their own behalf. Enlightenment thought tended toward the concrete and particular,
the empirical and experimental; it was a philosophy rooted in the day-to-day life of
the world, not in metaphysics. Science, technology, and progress were closely associated with the Enlightenment, and the discoveries of the natural world made by
men like Galileo in astronomy, Newton in physics, and Linnaeus in biology were
hallmarks of Enlightenment thought. Moreover, it was believed that the same scientific procedures that allowed clear-cut classification schemes in botany or zoology,
or that demonstrated the operation of natural physical laws, could yield equally rational plans for ordering human affairs.

Not all Americans subscribed to the tenets of the Enlightenment; indeed, those most influenced by such intellectual trends were a distinct minority, although a wealthy and powerful one by the last decades of the century. Even as Enlightenment ideals gained adherents, a great religious awakening was sweeping the land, causing growing numbers of people to monitor constantly the condition of their eternal souls and to find in sermons and the Bible their guides to living. But by the second half of the eighteenth century, many of the most influential Americans—in politics, commerce, and diplomacy—were inclined to hold religion at arm's length, and to dismiss the importance of church ritual, the Revealed Word, and specific ideas about heaven and Hell. They especially rejected the notion of an ever-present God who watched over and judged people according to some cosmic plan. Such individuals placed their faith in the human community and worked hard to build up institutions that promoted culture, learning, prosperity, and health.

In this chapter, we explore the writings of several Americans who lived just at the dawn of the Enlightenment. By the eighteenth century, the colonies from New England to the Carolinas were well established. All might still suffer economic setbacks, epidemics, and Indian uprisings, but there was no doubt they had become permanent settlements. And all of the colonies had well-developed social structures; tens of thousands of settlers and their descendants found themselves embedded in relatively stable relationships of power and dependence.

Large areas of British North America remained quite different from each other. The heirs of the Puritans still held considerable influence in New England, the cities of the middle colonies were growing rapidly from the profits of shipping and trading, and the southern colonies had developed their own plantation life based on chattel slavery. We must not draw these distinctions too sharply though; slavery existed throughout the colonies, trade out of Boston and Charleston rivaled that of New York and Philadelphia, and Protestantism was hegemonic everywhere. Still, patterns were emerging.

The historian David Hackett Fischer argues that the cultures of the northern, middle, and southern colonies differed from each other because migrants to those colonies came from different parts of England in the seventeenth century. New Englanders, for example, came mainly from East Anglia, the heart of religious reformation and political rebellion. Town meetings, large nuclear families, high levels of education, and bustling trade all were characteristic of England's eastern counties and, therefore, of New England. Settlers in the Chesapeake colonies, on the other hand, brought with them the ways of the south and west, an area of stronger royalist sentiment, families based more on extended kin networks, greater emphasis on social hierarchy, and a very strong patriarchal structure. The Quakers who settled New Jersey and Pennsylvania held strong feelings of ethnic pluralism, came predominantly from the middling ranks of society, practiced an ideal of good order that rested on social peace and harmony, and possessed a powerful work ethic and very positive attitudes toward business.

All of the colonies had developed social structures that gave great wealth, power, or prestige to some families and none of those advantages to others. The privileged people of the eighteenth century were almost invariably white, male, and Protestant. To be sure, most who fit that description were not wealthy or powerful, but the great majority who attained independent wealth and status were. To be propertyless, an African slave, Native American, a woman, or Catholic was to be (most likely) socially disadvantaged. Above all, the rich and powerful among the colonists thought of themselves as Englishmen. The three thousand miles of water that separated them from the mother country made them keen to maintain their Englishness. And even as they pushed Native Americans off the land, African slaves, and subordinated women, white men increasingly insisted on their freedom to define themselves.

As the colonies themselves evolved, leaders emerged who reflected local concerns, and who took advantage of local circumstances. William Byrd II, Jonathan Edwards, and Benjamin Franklin became very influential in the decades before the American Revolution. Despite the fact that all three were very different in how they acquired and exercised influence, all were sufficiently aware of their position in society that they wrote about their lives, either in a formal autobiography meant to be read by future generations or in the daily jottings of a diary. All were influenced by Enlightenment ideas, even if they would have mostly rejected Enlightenment assumptions. Byrd, who in many ways recreated an Old World patriarchal life like the landed gentry of England, began each day reading texts that included Greek and Latin secular works, foundation documents of Enlightenment thought. While attending Yale, Edwards, America's greatest religious thinker of the century, was greatly influenced by John Locke's *Essay Concerning Human Understanding*, which argued that human knowledge came to us through our senses, through our direct experience of the world, not through innate ideas implanted before birth. And of course Franklin became the leading figure in the American Enlightenment.

But there were other voices from the eighteenth century. The comfortable lives of men like Byrd were build on the backs of African slaves. Note how Byrd casually writes of "my people," assuming his right to their labor. Then read the passage from Olaudah Equiano's *Narrative*, which details the pain of enslavement and separation from loved ones in Africa, as well as the estrangement Equiano's people felt in the colonies. Or consider the Jonathan Edwards musings on his relationship to God, then read the words of Sarah Osborn, equally pious and writing in the same Protestant idiom, yet her words reflecting the fact that she is a woman, a mother, and a widow.

THE DOCUMENTS
Introduction to Documents 1 and 2

William Byrd II (1674–1744) of Westover, Virginia, was the oldest of this group. He was the son of William Byrd I, who built the family fortune on Indian trade and plantation agriculture. By the time young William inherited the estate in 1704, Virginia's seventeenth-century scramble for wealth that we read about in Chapter 2 had settled into a more stable pattern. Dominating that society was a small number of elite families like the Byrds, whose wealth was based on owning the most fertile lands. They farmed that land intensively with the use of African and African-American slaves to produce a profitable staple crop such as tobacco.

It was not just wealth but gentility that the southern elite craved. By the early eighteenth century the great families built large mansions and modeled their lives on the English rural gentry. At age ten, William Byrd was sent to England and then Holland for his education, since the colonies were not yet able to provide young men of good families with the polish of an old world gentleman. Byrd returned in 1692 at age eighteen and quickly became one of the leading lights of the landed aristocracy. Charming and learned, with powerful friends in England and America, Byrd quickly became one of the youngest members of the Virginia House of Burgesses (the colonial legislature) and a member of the Council of State. He served his colony as a colonel in the militia, as an agent in London, and he was elected a Fellow of the Royal Society, an elite scholarly organization of which he was very proud. His marriage to Lucy Parke in 1706 ratified his place among the cream of Virginia's cosmopolitan and sophisticated social elite.

Byrd's diary was not discovered, decoded, and published until 1941. He probably kept this journal from early in the century almost until he died in 1744. However, only a few selected years have been found. He kept the diary using a shorthand writing system. Byrd's daily entries are brief, roughly a paragraph long; they reveal little of his inner life, his emotions, and feelings. But in their sheer dailiness, they tell us much about how he lived his life, what he valued, and how he interacted with others. "I danced my dance" he wrote. His dance was a set of exercises to be done indoors when the weather was inclement, but that phrase can also be taken as a metaphor for Byrd's everyday transactions. Byrd often refers to "my people," meaning not only his family, but those who labored on his plantation, both Africans and whites. As you read these passages, think about in what sense Byrd could be called a patriarch.

After reading Byrd, consider the passage from *The Interesting Narrative of the Life of Olaudah Equiano,* who describes being captured as a slave in Africa, his separation from family and loved ones, and the alienation he felt in his strange new environment. Note Equiano's plea against slavery in the name of Christian ideals.

DOCUMENT 1   *The Diaries of William Byrd*

Nov. 2, 1709—I rose at 6 o'clock and read a chapter in Hebrew and some Greek in Lucian. I said my prayers and ate milk for breakfast, and settled some accounts, and then went to court where we made an end of the business. We went to dinner about 4 o'clock and I ate boiled beef again. In the evening I went to Dr. [Barret's] where my wife came this afternoon. Here I found Mrs. Chiswell, my sister Custis, and other ladies. We sat and talked till about 11 o'clock and then retired to our chambers. I played at [r-m] with Mrs. Chiswell and kissed her on the bed till she was angry and my wife also was uneasy about it, and cried as soon as the company was gone. I neglected to say my prayers, which I should not have done, because I ought to beg pardon for the lust I had for another man's wife. However I had good health, good thoughts, and good humor, thanks be to God Almighty. . . .

July 8, 1710—I rose at 6 o'clock and read a chapter in Hebrew and some Greek in Thucydides. I said my prayers and ate milk for breakfast. I settled several accounts. It rained gently all day. I sent away the sloop to Falling Creek. I was out of humor with Bannister and G-r-l for spoiling the curtains of the bed. I ate roast pork for dinner. Messrs. C-s and Chamberlayne dined with us. In the afternoon I unpacked several things in the afternoon [*sic*] and then gave my wife a flourish and then read in the *Tatler.* Two negroes of mine brought five of the cows that strayed away from hence and told me all was well above, but that Joe Wilkinson was very often absent from his business. It rained all the afternoon, that I could not walk. The negro woman was found and tied but ran away again in the night. I said my prayers but had good health, good thoughts, and indifferent good humor, thank God Almighty. . . .

William Byrd's Westover plantation on the James River. (Collection of Tazwell Ellett).

July 30, 1710—I rose at 5 o'clock and wrote a letter to Major Burwell about his boat which Captain Broadwater's people had brought round and sent Tom with it. I read two chapters in Hebrew and some Greek in Thucydides. I said my prayers and ate boiled milk for breakfast. I danced my dance. I read a sermon in Dr. Tillotson and then took a little [nap]. I ate fish for dinner. In the afternoon my wife and I had a little quarrel which I reconciled with a flourish. Then she read a sermon in Dr. Tillotson to me. It is to be observed that the flourish was performed on the billiard table. I read a little Latin. In the evening we took a walk about the plantation. I neglected to say my prayers but had good health, good thoughts, and good humor, thanks be to God. This month there were many people sick of fever and pain in their heads; perhaps this might be caused by the cold weather which we had this month, which was indeed the coldest that ever was known in July in this country. Several of my people have been sick, but none died, thank God. . . .

Oct. 9, 1710—I rose about 5 o'clock and got myself ready for my journey, and about 6 o'clock [I] recommended my wife and my family to God's protection, and after my people had set me over the creek, I got on horseback about 7 and proceeded to Williamsburg where I arrived about 12. About one I went to wait on the Governor, where I found Colonel Digges and several other gentlemen. My wife sent a present of blue wing which were kindly accepted. I ate some roast beef for dinner. In the afternoon we drank a bottle of claret and then we took leave of the Governor and went to the coffeehouse where after we had settled some accounts of the naval officers we played at cards till 11 o'clock. Then I went to my lodgings but my man was gone to bed and I was shut out. However I called him and beat him for it. I neglected to say my prayers but had good thoughts, good health, and good humor, thank God Almighty.

Nov. 4, 1710—I rose at 7 o'clock but read nothing because I prepared to go home this day. I said my prayers and ate boiled milk for breakfast. About 8 o'clock I went to court where I sat till 11 o'clock and took horses, which I borrowed of Mr. Clayton and Mr. Jackson, and rode home, where I came about 5 o'clock. I found all my family well except my daughter, who had a little fever but was much better than she had been. I found Mrs. Hamlin there to see the child. I ate some wild duck for supper and then examined how everything stood. I was very weary and so went to bed about 8 o'clock. I neglected to say my prayers in form but had good health, good thoughts, and good humor, thank God Almighty. I gave my wife a flourish in which she had a great deal of pleasure.

Nov. 13, 1710—I rose at 7 o'clock and said a short prayer. Then I took a little walk about the plantation. I ate toast and cider for breakfast. Colonel Digges sent for a white negro for us to see who except the color was featured like other negroes. She told us that in her country, which is called Aboh near Calabar there were many whites as well as blacks. We played at dice till about 12 o'clock and then we [went] to Williamsburg, but I was so dusted with dirt that I was forced to change my clothes. Yesterday Mr. Ingles had a child burnt to death by fire taking hold of its clothes. We went to the capitol and stayed there about two hours and then I went and dined with the Governor where I ate roast mutton. I had a letter from home which told me all was well except a negro woman who ran away and was found dead. I said my prayers and had good thoughts, good health, and good humor, thank God Almighty.

Dec. 22, 1710—I rose about 8 o'clock but read nothing because the sloop came and I was busy in loading her and in punishing Johnny and scolding at S-k-f-r for bringing goods for Mr. Tullitt contrary to my orders. About 10 o'clock I sent her away. It rained this morning. I ate boiled milk for breakfast. I neglected to say my prayers. I settled several things which took up all the morning. Some of the sick people grew better and some others fell sick. I ate raspberries for dinner. In the afternoon my wife and I played at billiards and I laid her down and rogered her on the [trestle]. About 4 o'clock Mr. Bland came on his way to Williamsburg but I persuaded him to stay all night. We sat and talked all the evening. I neglected to say my prayers but had good thoughts, good health, and good humor, thank God Almighty.

Dec. 29, 1710—I rose at 5 o'clock and read two chapters in Hebrew and four pages in Lucian. I said my prayers and ate boiled milk for breakfast. Then I danced my dance. Mr. Mumford ate some fried oysters for breakfast and then we went to play at billiards for the rest of the morning. I had two more sick people come down. These poor people suffer for my sins; God forgive me all my offenses and restore them to their health if it be consistent with His holy will. I ate wild turkey for dinner. In the afternoon Mr. Mumford went away. My poor child continued to have a fever, from which God of his excessive goodness deliver her. In the evening I took a walk about the plantation and was very melancholy on account of the unkindness of my wife. I read several leaves in the *Atlantis* and was much affected with it. I said my prayers and had good health, good thoughts, and good humor, thank God Almighty.

Dec. 31, 1710—I rose at 5 o'clock and read a chapter in Hebrew and four leaves in Lucian. I said my prayers and ate boiled milk for breakfast. My daughter was very sick all night and vomited a great deal but was a little better this morning. All my sick people were better, thank God, and I had another girl come down sick from the quarters. I danced my dance. Then I read a sermon in Dr. Tillotson and after that walked in the garden till dinner. I ate roast venison. In the afternoon I looked over my sick people and then took a walk about the plantation. The weather was very warm still. My wife walked with me and when she came back she was very much indisposed and went to bed. In the evening I read another sermon in Dr. Tillotson. About 8 o'clock the wind came to northwest and it began to be cold. I said my prayers and had good health, good thoughts, and good humor, thank God Almighty.

Some night this month I dreamed that I saw a flaming sword in the sky and called some company to see it but before they could come it was disappeared, and about a week after my wife and I were walking and we discovered in the clouds a shining cloud exactly in the shape of a dart and seemed to be over my plantation but it soon disappeared likewise. Both these appearances seemed to foretell some misfortune to me which afterwards came to pass in the death of several of my negroes after a very unusual manner. My wife about two months since dreamed she saw an angel in the shape of a big woman who told her the time was altered and the seasons were changed and that several calamities would follow that confusion. God avert his judgment from this poor country.

Feb. 6, 1711—I rose about 9 o'clock but was so bad I thought I should not have been in condition to go to Williamsburg, and my wife was so kind to [say] she would stay with me, but rather than keep her from going I resolved to go if possible. I was shaved with a very dull razor, and ate some boiled milk for breakfast but neglected to say my prayers. About 10 o'clock I went to Williamsburg without the ladies. As soon as I got there it began to rain, which hindered about [sic] the company from coming. I went to the President's where I drank tea and went with him to the Governor's and found him at home. Several gentlemen were there and about 12 o'clock several ladies came. My wife and her sister came about 2. We had a short Council but more for form than for business. There was no other appointed in the room of Colonel Digges. My cold was a little better so that I ventured among the ladies, and Colonel Carter's wife and daughter were among them. It was night before we went to supper, which was very fine and in good order. It rained so that several did not come that were expected. About 7 o'clock the company went in coaches from the Governor's house to the capitol where the Governor opened the ball with a French dance with my wife. Then I danced with Mrs. Russell and then several others and among the rest Colonel Smith's son, who made a sad freak. Then we danced country dances for an hour and the company was carried into another room where was a very fine collation of sweetmeats. The Governor was very gallant to the ladies and very courteous to the gentlemen. About 2 o'clock the company returned in the coaches and because the drive was dirty the Governor carried the ladies into their coaches. My wife and I lay at my lodgings. Colonel Carter's family and Mr. Blair were stopped by the unruliness of the horses and Daniel Wilkinson was so gallant as to lead the horses himself through all the dirt and rain to Mr. Blair's house. My cold continued bad. I neglected to say my prayers and had good thoughts, good humor, but indifferent health, thank God Almighty. It rained all day and all night. The President had the worst clothes of anybody there.

Feb. 15, 1711—I rose at 4 o'clock and read two chapters in Hebrew and six leaves in Lucian. I said my prayers and ate boiled milk for breakfast. I danced my dance. The weather was fair and warm. I wrote to the Falls to order a steer down. I heard news of another negro dead at the Falls. God's will be done. I granted rights to several people. I was out of humor and denied some men to catch their hogs on my land because they had bred them there. I read some English and took a walk in the garden. I ate roast mutton for dinner. In the afternoon I walked about the plantation till the evening and then my cousin Harrison came and when she had stayed here about an hour my wife and I walked home with her and did not return home till 8 o'clock. Then I ate some milk and wrote some rights that a man came for this evening. I neglected to say my prayers and had good thoughts, good humor, and good health, thank God Almighty. Colonel Eppes was taken very sick last night.

Feb. 27, 1711—I rose at 6 o'clock and read two chapters in Hebrew and some Greek in Lucian. I said my prayers and ate boiled milk for breakfast. I danced my dance and then went to the brick house to see my people pile the planks and found them all idle for which I threatened them soundly but did not whip them. The weather was cold and the wind at northeast. I wrote a letter to England. Then I read some English till 12 o'clock when Mr. Dunn and his wife came. I ate boiled beef for dinner. In the afternoon Mr. Dunn and I played at billiards. Then we took a long walk about the plantation and looked over all my business. In the evening my wife and little Jenny had a great quarrel in which my wife got the worst but at last by the help of the family Jenny was overcome and soundly whipped. At night I ate some bread and cheese. I said my prayers and had good health, good thoughts, and good humor, thank God Almighty.

March 4, 1711—I rose at 8 o'clock and read two chapters in Hebrew and some Greek in Lucian. I said my prayers and ate boiled milk for breakfast. I danced my dance. My [wife] continued still disordered in her back and belly. However she went to church with Mrs. Dunn in the coach and I walked there. Mr. Anderson gave us a good sermon. After church nobody came home with us. Little Peter came from above and brought news another negro died, which makes 17 this winter; God's will be done. Several others are sick. The Lord have mercy on them, and spare them if it be His will. I ate boiled beef for dinner. In the afternoon Mrs. Dunn went away and I was at the trouble to send John home with her, who did not come back till 8 o'clock. He had a great cold still. In the evening I took a walk about the plantation. In the evening I read a little English. I said my prayers and had good health, good thoughts, and indifferent humor, thank God Almighty.

April 30, 1711—I rose at 5 o'clock and said a short prayer and then drank two dishes of chocolate. Then I took my leave about 6 o'clock and found it very cold. I met with nothing extraordinary in my journey and got home about 11 o'clock and found all well, only my wife was melancholy. We took a walk in the garden and pasture. We discovered that by the contrivance of Nurse and Anaka Prue got in at the cellar window and stole some strong beer and cider and wine. I turned Nurse away upon it and punished Anaka. I ate some fish for dinner. In the afternoon I caused Jack and John to be whipped for drinking at John [Cross] all last Sunday. In the evening I took a walk about the plantation and found things in good order. At night I ate some bread and butter. I said my prayers and had good health, good thoughts, and good humor, thank God Almighty. The weather was very cold for the season. I gave my wife a powerful flourish and gave her great ecstasy and refreshment.

June 23, 1711—I rose about 7 o'clock and read two chapters in Hebrew and about 200 verses in Homer. I said my prayers and ate milk for breakfast. My wife was indisposed and was threatened with miscarriage. I again persuaded to bleed but she could not be persuaded to it. It rained again and I believe it was the rain that disposed my wife to that infirmity at this time. I settled several accounts till dinner. I ate some pig. In the afternoon I read some French till the evening and then the wind was northwest and it held up so that I took a walk about the plantation. I repeated my petition to my wife to be bled and at night she did try but could not suffer it. I drank some syllabub and gave my daughter some with me. I said my prayers and had good health, good thoughts, and good humor, thank God Almighty. I had a small quarrel with my wife because she would not be bled but neither good words nor bad could prevail against her fear which is very uncontrollable.

June 25, 1711—I rose about 5 o'clock and read two chapters in Hebrew and 200 verses in Homer. I said my prayers and ate milk for breakfast. I danced my dance. My wife grew worse and after much trial and persuasion was let blood when it was too late. Captain Stith came about some [n-l] he said he lent my father 20 years ago. Mr. Rogers came also about Mrs. Parker's business. My wife grew very ill which made [me] weep for her. I ate roast mutton for dinner. In the afternoon my wife grew worse and voided a prodigious quantity of blood. I settled some accounts till the evening and then took a walk about the plantation. Before I returned my wife sent for me because she was very weak and soon after I came she was delivered of a false conception and then grew better. I sent for Mrs. Hamlin who came presently. I said my prayers and had good health, good thoughts, and good humor, thank God Almighty.

June 26, 1711—I rose about 6 o'clock and read a chapter in Hebrew and 200 verses in Homer. I said my prayers and ate milk for breakfast. Mrs. Dunn went home and so did Mrs. Hamlin. I received a letter from the attorney general to send his accounts, which I did and wrote a letter to Mr. Bland by him. My wife was extremely mended and very cheerful, thank God. I settled some accounts till dinner. I ate some boiled mutton for dinner. In the afternoon I took a nap by my wife and then went and read some French. I lent my wife some pictures to divert her. Then I went and showed my people how to manage some hay they had mowed out of the swamp. In the evening I took a walk about the plantation and drank some warm milk from the cow. I said my prayers and had good health, good thoughts, and good humor, thank God Almighty.

July 8, 1711—I rose about 8 o'clock and was pretty well and ate some water gruel. I said a short prayer and sat up till 1 o'clock and then came my ague violently and Colonel Hill and Mr. Anderson came from church and found me very ill. I went to bed and had a very severe fit. I took more snakeroot and sweated very much with it, but it made my hot fit the worse and last the longer. I was not very dry nor did my head ache at all, or my back. I drank sage tea and some apple drink. At night came Dr. Cocke out of pure friendship and not as a doctor. He gave me some comfort but said little to me that night because he would not disturb me. Only he did not approve of the sweats that I took. I sweated all night and could not sleep but in the morning the fever went off and left me very weak.

July 9, 1711—This day I was so weak I could not rise but I was without a fever, but the Doctor would not give me the bark because there would not be time before next fit to take quantity enough to prevent the next fit and if it did not prevent it, it would make it worse. I could eat nothing and took little or nothing but sage tea. The Doctor told me he would stay with me till I was safe, notwithstanding he neglected a great deal of other business. Several came to see me but the Doctor would let nobody to me because when people are weak company do them mischief. The Doctor assured me I should have but one fit more which pleased me much in my weak condition. Everybody was concerned for my sickness and my people attended me very well and particularly Mrs. Dunn. The Doctor comforted my wife so that she was very easy, thank God Almighty. I slept very little all night, nor could I command my thoughts enough to pray but I addressed myself to heaven to be restored.

July 10, 1711—I was a little easy this morning but had nothing but sage tea. The weather was [. . .] but I was very hot notwithstanding. I had a good intermission, thank God, but I lived in fear of the next fit, which came about 11 o'clock with terrible violence. My cold fit lasted four hours and the hot fit [. . .]. It was much the most violent I ever had in my life. The Doctor said he had not seen such a one and if I had another he believed it would turn to the quartan fever. It is not possible to describe the uneasy condition I was in but God enabled me to bear it, thanks to His holy name. The fit did not go away till the evening and then the bark was prepared for me and I took it every three hours.

July 11, 1711—This morning about 6 o'clock I began to be easy and continued to take the bark every three hours, but at first it purged me and gave me four stools. This obliged the Doctor to give me laudanum with the bark and made me drink a drink made of burnt hartshorn. He also gave me barley cinnamon water to stop the purge and it succeeded very well. I swallowed the bark like milk and took two ounces. Mr. Rogers was here yesterday and paid off Mrs. Parker's mortgage and I surrendered it to him. I was very weak-kneed and could eat nothing but bark and drink [whey] drink made of burnt hartshorn. The Doctor was very merry with Mrs. Dunn. In the evening Mr. Clayton came to see me, which was very kind. He brought me no news. My mouth was very clammy and I washed it with water very often to cool it. In the evening I began to look very yellow which the Doctor took for a good sign that the medicine had taken effect. Mr. Clayton lay at Mrs. Harrison's.

July 12, 1711—I was a little better this morning and the bark had thrown the distemper into my skin and I had the yellow jaundice in a great degree for which the Doctor prescribed turmeric and [l-p of s-l-p-n-c] and saffron, and every night and morning I had my [p-s b-k]. This distemper made me very [unclean] and burdensome to myself. Captain Posford sent often to know how I did. Mr. Clayton came this morning, but the Doctor would not let him or anybody else come up to see me. Colonel Hill and Mr. Anderson came to the house and dined here but I saw them not. Blessed be God, I lost my fit this day. The Doctor ordered the bark to be mixed with the turmeric without my knowledge so that I took three ounces of bark in all. I was very weak and had a clammy mouth and no stomach. Nor could I sleep but distracted sleep but I was easy, thank God Almighty.

July 13, 1711—I found myself better this morning though my jaundice was full on me. The Doctor saw me in a good way and so took his leave but he took nothing for all his trouble, which amazed me. However the Doctor did not go till after dinner. I gave him a million of thanks since he would take nothing else and his man led a horse to Williamsburg for Tom who was perfectly recovered. My jaundice began to clear up and I grew better and ate some rice. I got up just to have my bed made and went to bed again. I was thirsty and drank sage tea. In the evening my wife sang to me but however I could not sleep well. I began to say my prayers in order again and to give God thanks for my recovery. . . .

The following passages are from Byrd's London Diary. Byrd lived in England for a few years after the death of his wife.

Oct. 4, 1718—I rose about 7 o'clock and read a chapter in Hebrew and some Greek. I said my prayers and had boiled milk for breakfast. The weather was cold and clear, the wind west. About 11 o'clock came Mrs. Wilkinson and brought me some linen. Then I went into the City and dined with old Mr. Perry who gave me several letters from Virginia. I ate some cold roast beef. After dinner I received a hundred pounds and then went to visit Dick Perry who was exceedingly bad of the gout. Here I drank tea and about 4 o'clock went to Molly Cole's and sat with her half an hour. Then I went home and wrote a letter into the country and then looked in at the play. Then I went to visit Mrs. A-l-n and committed uncleanness with the maid because the mistress was not at home. However, when the mistress came I rogered her and about 12 o'clock went home and ate a plum cake for supper. I neglected my prayers, for which God forgive me.

May 13, 1719—I rose about 8 o'clock and read a chapter in Hebrew and some Greek in Lucian. I said my prayers, and had milk for breakfast. The weather was cold and cloudy, the wind west, and it blew violently. I danced my dance and about 11 o'clock went to the Duke of Argyll's but he was from home. Then to Mrs. Southwell's where I sat about an hour. Then I returned home and wrote two letters to Virginia and put several things in order till 2 o'clock when I was angry with my man about my dinner. I ate some veal cutlets. After dinner I put several things in order till 5 o'clock and then I went to the widow Pierson's, where I stayed till 9 o'clock and then went to Will's where I had two dishes of chocolate. Then I went to my kind Mrs. Smith where I met a fine young woman, with whom I ate some rabbit fricassee and then we went to bed together and I rogered her three times and neglected my prayers.

June 13, 1719—I rose about 9 o'clock and read a chapter in Hebrew and some Greek in Lucian. I said my prayers, and had milk for breakfast. The weather was cold and cloudy, having rained abundance yesterday. I received a letter from Captain Ward which made me resolve not to go out of town to the Duke of Argyll's as I intended. About 12 o'clock came Mr. N-l-r and stayed about half an hour. I read some English till 1 o'clock and then I went to Colonel Blakiston's to dinner where was Colonel Lowther and Colonel [Folliot]. I ate some ham and chicken. After dinner came in young M-t-n-y and we drank a glass till 5 o'clock and then I went to the widow Pierson's but she was from home. Then to Lady Dunkellen's but she was from home. Then to Mrs. M-r-s but she was from home; then to Mrs. [Sands'] where I stayed two hours and then went to walk in the park where was abundance of company. About ten I walked home and endeavored to pick up a whore but could not. I said my prayers.

Nov. 11, 1719—I rose about 7 o'clock and read nothing because I prepared to go out about business. However, I said my prayers, and had boiled milk for breakfast. The weather was cold and foggy, the wind east. About 10 o'clock came Mr. B-r-n-t but I could not stay with him, being obliged to go to Colonel Blakiston's with whom I went to Mr. Aislabie about my account, who was very courteous to me. Then I went to my Lord Orkney, who promised to write to his lieutenant governor. Then I went to the Duke of Argyll's and stayed there about an hour and then to my Lord Orrery's who was from home; then to White's Chocolate House and then to Colonel Blakiston's to dinner and ate some wild duck. Here I stayed till 5 o'clock and then went to the park and walked and then to Will's where I stayed half an hour and then went with Lord Orrery to Mrs. B-r-t-n where we found two chambermaids that my Lord had ordered to be got for us and I rogered one of them and about 9 o'clock returned again to Will's where Betty S-t-r-d called on me in a coach and I went with her to the bagnio and rogered her twice, for which God forgive me.

DOCUMENT 2 *Narrative of the Life of Olaudah Equiano*

We were not many days in the merchant's custody, before we were sold after their usual manner, which is this: On a signal given (as the beat of a drum), the buyers rush at once into the yard where the slaves are confined, and make choice of that parcel they like best. The noise and clamor with which this is attended, and the eagerness visible in the countenances of the buyers, serve not a little to increase the apprehension of terrified Africans, who may well be supposed to consider them as the ministers of that destruction to which they think themselves devoted. In this manner, without scruple, are relations and friends separated, most of them never to see each other again. I remember, in the vessel in which I was brought over, in the men's apartment, there were several brothers, who, in the sale, were sold in different lots; and it was very moving on this occasion, to see and hear their cries at parting. O, ye nominal Christians! might not an African ask you— Learned you this from your God, who says unto you, Do unto all men as you would men should do unto you? It is not enough that we are torn from our country and friends, to toil for your luxury and lust of gain? Must every tender feeling be likewise sacrificed to your avarice? Are the dearest friends and relations, now rendered more dear by their separation from their kindred, still to be parted from each other, and thus prevented from cheering the gloom of slavery, with the small comfort of being together, and mingling their sufferings and sorrows? Why are parents to lose their children, brothers their sisters, and husbands their wives? Surely, this is a new refinement in cruelty, which, while it has no advantage to atone for it, thus aggravates distress, and adds fresh horrors even to the wretchedness of slavery.

. . . We were landed up a river a good way from the sea, about Virginia county, where we saw few or none of our native Africans, and not one soul who could talk to me. I was a few weeks weeding grass and gathering stones in a plantation; and at last all my companions were distributed different ways, and only myself was left. I was now exceedingly miserable, and thought myself worse off than any of the rest of my companions, for they could talk to each other, but I had no person to speak to that I could understand. In this state, I was constantly grieving and pining, and wishing for death rather than anything else. While I was in this plantation, the gentleman, to whom I suppose the estate belonged, being unwell, I was one day sent for to his dwelling-house to fan him; when I came into the room where he was I was very much affrighted at some things I saw, and the more so as I had seen a black woman slave as I came through the house, who was cooking the dinner, and the poor creature was cruelly loaded with various kinds of iron machines; she had one particularly on her head, which locked her mouth so fast that she could scarcely speak; and could not eat nor drink. I was much astonished and shocked at this contrivance, which I afterwards learned was called the iron muzzle. Soon after I had a fan put in my hand, to fan the gentleman while he slept; and so I did indeed with great fear. While he was fast asleep I indulged myself a great deal in looking about the room, which to me appeared very fine and curious. The first object that engaged my attention was a watch which hung on the chimney, and was going. I was quite surprised at the noise it made, and was afraid it would tell the gentleman anything I might do amiss; and when I immediately after observed a picture hanging in the room, which appeared constantly to look at me, I was still more affrighted, having never seen such things as these before. At one time I thought it was something relative to magic; and not seeing it move, I thought it might be some way the whites had to keep their great men when they died, and offer them libations as we used to do our friendly spirits. In this state of anxiety I remained till my master awoke, when I was dismissed out of the room, to my no small satisfaction and relief.

Introduction to Documents 3 and 4

Jonathan Edwards (1703–1758) was born in East Windsor, Connecticut, the son of pastor Timothy Edwards and grandson of the renowned Puritan minister Solomon Stoddard from Northampton, Massachusetts. When he was still twelve years old, in 1716, Jonathan entered the brand-new Yale College. His training, of course, was centered heavily in theology; he received his A.B. in 1720, an M.A. in 1723, and he became a tutor at the college the following year.

The following passage describes Edwards's conversion when he was about 18 years old. He had been religious as a child, but this memoir, written when Edwards was in his late thirties, looks back 20 years to describe that moment around age eighteen when he felt the presence of God in a deep emotional way. The description of Edwards's conversion is one of the great testaments of faith in the English language. More precisely, he here describes his surrender to the Calvinist concept of the absolute sovereignty of God. The untrammelled divine power to save or damned souls was but one aspect of the Lord's presence in every part of the Universe. For Edwards, the realization of God's infinitude, of His being everywhere in the cosmos, was an aesthetic and emotional experience; God's gift of salvation revealed the beauty of divine majesty. In 1727, a few years after the events described here, Edwards married Sarah Pierpont of New Haven, who became well known (some said notorious) for the emotional fervor of her faith. In the years after his conversion, Edwards's writings developed the connection between religious conviction and deep personal feeling as the touchstone of faith for his congregants.

Around the time that he wrote this memoir, Edwards had been ordained associate pastor of his grandfather's old congregation in Northampton. Between 1735 and 1737, Edwards's preaching ignited a local revival movement in his church that not only brought in vast numbers of new members but also attracted interest throughout the colonies. Edwards's preaching was an early local manifestation of what came to be called the Great Awakening. The outpouring of divine grace soon spread, especially as the Rev. George Whitefield of England began to preach in the colonies toward the end of the decade. Whitefield brought a new style to the pulpit: He preached in fields and in town squares, he told stories of real people saved and damned, he beat his breast while sinners cried out and groaned for salvation. Whitefield turned preaching into a theatrical performance. Many criticized his emotionalism, but for a few years, the Revival spread like wildfire across the colonies.

In the following excerpt from his memoirs, Edwards describes his own conversion experience. Why and for whom do you think this narrative was written? During the same Great Awakening that Edwards helped ignite, a young woman named Sarah Osborn pondered her own experience of God. Note how her personal troubles were interpreted as a sign of failure of piety, or of God's displeasure with her. Even as she writes in the same religious language as Edwards, Osborn provides a sharp contrast with her discussion of women's concerns.

DOCUMENT 3 *The Memoirs of Jonathan Edwards*

The first instance, that I remember, of that sort of inward, sweet delight in God and divine things, that I have lived much in since, was on reading those words. 1 Tim. i. 17. *Now unto the King eternal, immortal, invisible, the only wise God, be honour and glory for ever and ever. Amen.* As I read the words, there came into my soul, and was as it were diffused through it, a sense of the glory of the Divine Being; a new sense, quite different from any thing I ever experienced before. Never any words of Scripture seemed to me as these words did. I thought with myself, how excellent a Being that was, and how happy I should be, if I might enjoy that God, and be rapt up to him in heaven; and be as it were swallowed up in him for ever! I kept saying, and as it were singing, over these words of Scripture to myself; and went to pray to God that I might enjoy him; and prayed in a manner quite different from what I used to do, with a new sort of affection. But it never came into my thought, that there was any thing spiritual, or of a saying nature, in this.

From about that time I began to have a new kind of apprehensions and ideas of Christ, and the work of redemption, and the glorious way of salvation by him. An inward, sweet sense of these things, at times, came into my heart; and my soul was led away in pleasant views and contemplations of them. And my mind was greatly engaged to spend my time in reading and meditating on Christ, on the beauty and excellency of his person, and the lovely way of salvation by free grace in him. I found no books so delightful to me, as those that treated of these subjects. Those words Cant. ii. 1. used to be abundantly with me, *I am the rose of Sharon, and the lily of the valleys.* The words seemed to me sweetly to represent the loveliness and beauty of Jesus Christ. The whole book of Canticles used to be pleasant to me, and I used to be much in reading it, about that time; and found from time to time an inward sweetness, that would carry me away in my contemplations. This I know not how to express otherwise, than by a calm, sweet abstraction of soul from all the concerns of this world; and sometimes a kind of vision, or fixed ideas and imaginations, of being alone in the mountains, or some solitary wilderness, far from all mankind, sweetly conversing with Christ, and wrapt and swallowed up in God. The sense I had to divine things, would often of a sudden kindle up, as it were, a sweet burning in my heart, an ardour of soul, that I know not how to express.

Not long after I first began to experience these things, I gave an account to my father of some things that had passed in my mind. I was pretty much affected by the discourse we had together; and when the discourse was ended, I walked abroad alone, in a solitary place in my father's pasture, for contemplation. And as I was walking there, and looking upon the sky and clouds, there came into my mind so sweet a sense of the glorious *majesty* and *grace* of God, as I know not how to express—I seemed to see them both in a sweet conjunction; majesty and meekness joined together: it was a sweet, and gentle, and holy majesty; and also a majestic meekness; an awful sweetness; a high, and great, and holy gentleness.

After this my sense of divine things gradually increased, and became more and more lively, and had more of that inward sweetness. The appearance of every thing was altered; there seemed to be, as it were, a calm, sweet cast or appearance of divine glory, in almost every thing. God's excellency, his wisdom, his purity, and love, seemed to appear in every thing; in the sun, moon, and stars; in the clouds and blue sky; in the grass, flowers, trees; in the water and all nature; which used greatly to fix my mind. I often used to sit and view the moon for a long time; and in the day, spent much time in viewing the clouds and sky, to behold the sweet glory of God in these things: in the mean time singing forth, with a low voice, my contemplations of the Creator and Redeemer. And scarce any thing, among all the works of nature, was so sweet to me as thunder and lightning: formerly nothing had been so terrible to me. Before, I used to be uncommonly terrified with thunder, and to be struck with terror when I saw a thunder-storm rising; but now, on the contrary, it rejoiced me. I felt God, if I may so speak, at the first appearance of a thunder-storm; and used to take the opportunity, at such times, to fix myself in order to view the clouds, and see the lightnings play, and hear the majestic and awful voice of God's thunders, which oftentimes was exceedingly entertaining, leading me to sweet contemplations of my great and glorious God. While thus engaged, it always seemed natural for me to sing or chant forth my meditations; or, to speak my thoughts in soliloquies with a singing voice.

I felt then great satisfaction as to my good estate; but that did not content me. I had vehement longings of soul after God and Christ, and after more holiness, wherewith my heart seemed to be full, and ready to break; which often brought to my mind the words of the psalmist, Ps. cxix. 28. *My soul breaketh for the longing it hath*. I often felt a mourning and lamenting in my heart, that I had not turned to God sooner, that I might have had more time to grow in grace. My mind was greatly fixed on divine things; almost perpetually in the contemplation of them. I spent most of my time in thinking of divine things, year after year; often walking alone in the woods, and solitary places, for meditation, soliloquy, and prayer, and converse with God; and it was always my manner, at such times, to sing forth my contemplations. I was almost constantly in ejaculatory prayer, wherever I was. Prayer seemed to be natural to me, as the breath by which the inward burnings of my heart had vent. The delights which I now felt in the things of religion, were of an exceedingly different kind from those before mentioned, that I had when a boy; and what I had no more notion of, than one born blind has of pleasant and beautiful colours. They were of a more inward, pure, soul-animating, and refreshing nature. Those former delights never reached the heart; and did not arise from any sight of the divine excellency of the things of God; or any taste of the soul-satisfying and life-giving good there is in them.

My sense of divine things seemed gradually to increase, till I went to preach at New York; which was about a year and a half after they began: and while I was there I felt them very sensibly, in a much higher degree than I had done before. My longings after God and holiness were much increased. Pure and humble, holy and heavenly, Christianity appeared exceedingly amiable to me. I felt a burning desire to be, in every thing, a complete Christian; and conformed to the blessed image of Christ; and that I might live, in all things, according to the pure, sweet, and blessed rules of the gospel. . . .

While at New York, I sometimes was much affected with reflections on my past life, considering how late it was before I began to be truly religious; and how wickedly I had lived till then: and once so as to weep abundantly, and for a considerable time together.

On January 12, 1723, I made a solemn dedication of myself to God, and wrote it down; giving up myself, and all that I had, to God; to be for the future in no respect my own; to act as one that had no right to himself, in any respect. And solemnly vowed to take God for my whole portion and felicity, looking on nothing else as any part of my happiness, nor acting as it were; and his law for the constant rule of my obedience; engaging to fight with all my might against the world, the flesh, and the devil, to the end of my life. But I have reason to be infinitely humbled, when I consider how much I have failed of answering my obligation.

I had, then, abundance of sweet religious conversation, in the family where I lived, with Mr. John Smith, and his pious mother. My heart was knit in affection to those in whom were appearances of true piety; and I could bear the thoughts of no other companions, but such as were holy, and the disciples of the blessed Jesus. I had great longings for the advancement of Christ's kingdom in the world; and my secret prayers used to be, in great part, taken up in praying for it. If I heard the least hint of any thing that happened in any part of the world, that appeared, in some respect or other, to have a favourable aspect on the interests of Christ's kingdom, my soul eagerly catched at it, and it would much animate and refresh me. I used to be eager to read public news letters mainly for that end; to see if I could not find some news favourable to the interest of religion in the world.

I very frequently used to retire into a solitary place on the banks of Hudson's river, at some distance from the city, for contemplation on divine things and secret converse with God; and had many sweet hours there. Sometimes Mr. Smith and I walked there together, to converse on the things of God; and our conversation and to turn much on the advancement of Christ's kingdom is the world, and the glorious things that God would accomplish for his church in the latter days. I had then, and at other times, the greatest delight in the Holy Scriptures of any book whatsoever. Oftentimes in reading it every word seemed to touch my heart. I felt a harmony between something in my heart, and those sweet and powerful words. I seemed often to see so much light exhibited by every sentence, and such a refreshing food communicated, that I could not get along in reading; often dwelling long on one sentence, to see the wonders contained in it; and yet almost every sentence seemed to be full of wonders.

I came away from New York in the month of *April, 1723,* and had a most bitter parting with Madam Smith and her son. My heart seemed to sink within me, at leaving the family and city, where I had enjoyed so many sweet and pleasant days. I went from New York to Wethersfield by water; and as I sailed away, I kept sight of the city as long as I could. However, that night, after this sorrowful parting, I was greatly comforted in God at West Chester, where we went ashore to lodge: and had a pleasant time of it all the voyage to Saybrook. It was sweet to me to think of meeting dear Christians in heaven, where we should never part more. At Saybrook we went ashore to lodge on Saturday, and there kept the sabbath; where I had a sweet and refreshing season walking alone in the fields.

After I came home to Windsor, I remained much in a like frame of mind as when at New York; only sometimes I felt my heart ready to sink with the thoughts of my friends at New York. My support was in contemplations on the heavenly state; as I find in my diary of May 1, 1723. It was a comfort to think of that state, where there is fulness of joy; where reigns heavenly, calm and delightful love, without alloy; where there are continually the dearest expressions of this love; where is the enjoyment of the persons loved, without ever parting; where those persons who appear so lovely in this world, will really be inexpressibly more lovely, and full of love to us. And how secretly will the mutual lovers join together, to sing the praises of God and the Lamb! How will it fill us with joy to think, that this enjoyment, these sweet exercises, will never cease, but will last to all eternity! . . . "

DOCUMENT 4 *Memoirs of the Life of Mrs. Sarah Osborn*

In the process of time, I was married to Mr. Samuel Wheaten, being in my eighteenth year, October 21, 1731, and went with my husband, then next winter, to see his friends in the country; where I stayed almost five months; and was almost all the time under strong [religious] convictions. Oh, how I did sweat and tremble for fear my convictions should wear off again, and plead with God to set home strong convictions, and never, never suffer them to cease, till they ended in a sound and saving conversion. . . .

After I came home, I met with much affliction in many respects. It seemed to me that the whole world were in arms against me. I thought I was the most despised creature living upon the earth. I used to pray to God in secret to relieve me; but did not, as I ought, see his hand in permitting it so to be, as a just punishment for my vile sins: And therefore was not humbled under it as I ought; but let nature rise and acted very imprudently, in many respects. I was then with child, and often lamented that I was to bring a child into such a world of sorrow: But some times found a disposition to dedicate my babe to God, while in the womb; and did so, at all seasons of secret prayer. And after it was born, my husband being at sea, I could not rest till I had solemnly given it up to God in baptism. And I thought that I did indeed give up both myself and it to God.

I met with many trials in my lying in, it being an extreme cold season. My child was born on Oct. 27, 1732. The next spring, my husband returned home; but went to sea again, and died abroad in November 1733. I was then in my twentieth year. The news of my husband's death came to me on the first of the next of April . . . But God appeared wonderfully for my support. I saw his hand, and was enabled to submit with patience to his will. I daily looked round me, to see how much heavier the hand of God was laid on some others, than it was on me, where they were left with a large number of children, and much involved in debt. And I had but one to maintain; and though poor, yet not involved. Others, I saw, as well as myself, had their friends snatched from them by sudden accidents. The consideration of these things, together with the thoughts of what I deserved, stilled me so, that though the loss of my companion, whom I dearly loved, was great; yet the veins of mercy, which I saw running though all my afflictions, were so great likewise, that, with Job, I could say, "The Lord gave, and the Lord hath taken away, and blessed be the name of the Lord."

. . . As before this affliction every one seemed to be enemies to me, so from that time, all became friends. My parents treated me very tenderly; and God inclined every one who saw me to be kind to me. My brother was come into New England: And being a single man, we went to housekeeping together. But in three months after he married, and I soon found it would not do to live as before; and began to be thoughtful how I should do. I could see no way in which I could get a living. All doors seemed to be shut. But I verily believed that God would point out a way for me. And accordingly, the very day I came to a resolution to move as soon as I could, a stranger to my case, who kept a school a little way off, came to me, and told me that she only waited for a fair wind to go to Carolina; and, if it would suit me, I should have her chamber and scholars; which I joyfully accepted. Thus the widow's God remarkable provided for me. This was on Nov. 19, 1734. I was then placed in a family, who discovered a great deal of affection for me; and in all respects used me as tenderly as if I had been a near relation. . . .

These were happy days—But now how shall I speak! Oh, that I may do it with a heart truly broken for my sins! After all this, I began to grow more conformed to the world. Things which, when I was thus lively, appeared insipid, and indeed odious to me, began to grow more tolerable, and by degrees in a measure pleasant. And depraved nature and Satan together pleaded for them thus, "That there was a time for all things; and singing and dancing now and then, with a particular friend, was an innocent diversion.

. . . continued thus till March 1741. And then it pleased God to return Mr. Tennent to us again, and he preached twenty-one sermons here. But while he was here, I was more than ever distressed. I had lost the sensible manifestations of Christ's love. . . . And [Mr. Tennent] struck directly at those things, for which I had so foolishly and wickedly pleaded Christian example, such as singing songs, dancing and foolish jesting, which is not convenient. He said, he would not say there was no such thing as a dancing Christian, but he had a very mean opinion of such as could bear to spend their time so, when it is so short, and the work for eternity so great. Then, and not till then, was I fully convinced what prodigal wasters of precious time such things were. And, through grace, I have abhorred them all ever since.

Thus I sunk by degrees lower and lower, till I had at last almost lost all sense of my former experiences. I had only the bare remembrance of them, and they seemed like dreams or delusion; at some times. At others again, I had some revivals. . . . But I knew I was a dreadful backslider, and had dealt treacherously with God. . . .

In Sept. 1740, God in mercy sent his dear servant [George] Whitefield here, which in some measure stirred me up. But why Mr. [Gilbert] Tennent came soon after, it pleased

God to bless his preaching so to me, that it roused me. But I was all the winter after exercised with dreadful doubts and fears about my state. I questioned the truth of all I had experienced, and feared I had never yet passed through the pangs of the new birth, or ever had one spark of grace.

Introduction to Document 5

Benjamin Franklin became better known than Edwards or Byrd, and he was shaped by very different circumstances. He was much more clearly a child of the Enlightenment than the other two. Nonetheless, Franklin's ancestors were dissenting religious folk, devout like the Puritans, and he probably inherited more from them than he acknowledged. If he rejected their otherworldliness, he embraced their notion of stewardship. Calvinists believed that people should work hard not because they wanted money and goods, but because success could be a sign of God's grace, an indication that a heavenly future was in store. Franklin might not pin his hopes for salvation on worldly success, but he agreed with the old Puritans that mere wealth was not a worthy goal in life, that those who prospered were obliged to use their gifts to benefit others. Restraint, good temper, a sense of communal obligation, reason, rational discourse, and the spreading of wisdom—these were the real goals of life, and money's purpose was to serve those ends.

Franklin was born in Boston in 1706, the tenth and youngest son of Josiah Franklin, an English immigrant to Boston. At age ten, after a couple years of schooling, Benjamin was brought into his father's trade of tallow chandler. He hated the candle- and soap-making shop and soon was apprenticed to his half-brother James as a printer. Ben's rebelliousness emerged again; the brothers quarreled often, and in 1723, Franklin left for Philadelphia. His expertise was such that he easily found employment as a printer and by age twenty-three opened his own shop. Soon he entered a common-law marriage with Deborah Read, whose husband had deserted her. As Franklin's memoir reveals, he was very active in the affairs of his community. He experimented with electricity and produced one invention after another; he organized friends into a reading and debating society in Philadelphia; he joined others in founding a subscription library, a university, and a town fire department. When he retired from business a wealthy middle-aged man, he devoted even more time to public affairs, especially to the cause of American independence and the governance of the new nation.

Franklin embodied the spirit of success and optimism, accomplishment and energy that we like to think of as distinctly American. He was the consummate man of acts. But it is in the context of his own times, the eighteenth century, that he is best understood. Franklin composed his *Memoirs* as an older man looking back over his youth; these passages were written in 1771 and 1784 and then published in the early nineteenth century. Unlike Byrd, who recorded his impressions daily, the distance of several decades allowed Franklin to shape his story to fit the image he wanted. An autobiography is never just a retelling of events; authors have audiences in mind, and they try to persuade their readers, to impart some lesson or moral, to explain or justify or exonerate themselves. Why do you think Franklin wrote these memoirs?

DOCUMENT 5 *The Memoirs of Benjamin Franklin*

Before I enter upon my public appearance in business, it may be well to let you know the then state of my mind, with regard to my principles and morals, that you may see how far those influenced the future events of my life. My parents had early given me religious impressions, and brought me through my childhood piously in the dissenting way. But I was scarce fifteen, when, after doubting by turns several points, as I found them disputed in the different books I read, I began to doubt of the revelation itself. Some books against Deism fell into my hands. . . . It happened that they wrought an effect on me quite contrary to what was intended by them; for the arguments of the Deists which were quoted to be refuted appeared to me much stronger than the refutations; in short, I soon became a thorough Deist. . . .

I grew convinced that *truth, sincerity,* and *integrity,* in dealings between man and man, were of the utmost importance to the felicity of life; and I formed written resolutions (which still remain in my journal book) to practise them ever while I lived. Revelation had indeed no weight with me as such; but I entertained an opinion, that though certain actions might not be bad, *because* they were forbidden by it, or good *because* it commanded them; yet probably those actions might be forbidden *because* they were bad for us, or commanded *because* they were beneficial to us, in their own natures, all the circumstances of things considered. And this persuasion, with the kind hand of Providence, or some guardian angel, or accidental favourable circumstances and situations, or all together, preserved me through this dangerous time of youth and the hazardous situations I was sometimes in among strangers, remote from the eye and advice of my father; free from any *wilful* gross immorality or injustice, that might have been expected from my want of religion; I say *wilful,* because the instances I have mentioned had something of *necessity* in them, from my youth, inexperience, and the knavery of others: I had therefore a tolerable character to begin the world with; I valued it properly, and determined to preserve it.

I should have mentioned before, that in the autumn of the preceding year, I had formed most of my ingenious acquaintance into a club for mutual improvement, which we called the JUNTO; we met on Friday evenings. The rules that I drew up required that every member in his turn should produce one or more queries on any point of morals, politics, or natural philosophy, to be discussed by the company; and once in three months produce and read an essay of his own writing, on any subject he pleased. Our debates were to be under the direction of a president, and to be conducted in the sincere spirit of inquiry after truth, without fondness for dispute, or desire of victory; and to prevent warmth, all expressions of positiveness in opinions, or direct contradiction, were after some time made contraband, and prohibited under small pecuniary penalities.

The first members were Joseph Brientnal, a copyer of deeds for the scriveners. . . .

Nicholas Scull, a surveyor, afterwards surveyor general. . . .

William Parsons, bred a shoemaker, but loving reading, had acquired a considerable share of mathematics. . . .

William Maugridge, joiner, but a most exquisite mechanic, and a solid, sensible man. . . .

Robert Grace, a young gentlemen of some fortune. . . .

Lastly, William Coleman, then a merchant's clerk. . . .

About this time there was a cry among the people for more paper-money; only fifteen thousand pounds being extant in the province, and that soon to be sunk. The wealthy inhabitants opposed any addition; being against all paper currency, from the apprehension that it would depreciate, as it had done in New England, to the injury of all creditors. We had discussed this point in our junto, where I was on the side of an addition; being persuaded that the first small sum, struck in 1723, had done much good by increasing the trade, employment, and number of inhabitants in the province; since I now saw all the old houses inhabited, and many new ones building; whereas I remembered well when I first walked about the streets of Philadelphia, (eating my roll,) I saw many of the houses in Walnut street, between Second and Front streets, with bills on their doors "*to be let;*" and many likewise in Chestnut street, and other streets; which made me think the inhabitants of the city were one after another deserting it. Our debates possessed me so fully of the subject, that I wrote and printed an anonymous pamphlet on it, entitled "*The Nature and Necessity of a Paper Currency.*" It was well received by the common people in general; but the rich men disliked it, for it increased and strengthened the clamour for more money; and they happening to have no writers among them that were able to answer it, their opposition slackened, and the point was carried by a majority in the house. My friends there, who considered I had been of some service, thought fit to reward me, by employing me in printing the money; a very profitable job, and a great help to me: this was another advantage gained by my being able to write. . . .

I soon after obtained through my friend Hamilton, the printing of the Newcastle paper-money, another profitable job, as I then thought it; small things appearing great to those in small circumstances: and these to me were really great advantages, as they were great encouragements. Mr. Hamilton procured me also the printing of the laws and votes of that government; which continued in my hands as long as I followed the business.

I now opened a small stationer's shop: I had in it blanks of all kinds; the correctest that ever appeared among us. I was assisted in that by my friend Brientnal: I had also paper, parchment, chapmen's books, &c. One Whitemash, a compositor I had known in London, an excellent workman, now came to me, and worked with me constantly and diligently; and I took an apprentice, the son of Aquila Rose.

I began now gradually to pay off the debt I was under for the printing house. In order to secure my credit and character as a tradesman, I took care not only to be in *reality* industrious and frugal, but to avoid the appearances to the contrary. I dressed plain, and was seen at no places of idle diversion: I never went out a fishing or shooting: a book indeed sometimes debauched me from my work, but that was seldom, was private, and gave no scandal: and to show that I was not above my business, I sometimes brought home the paper I purchased at the stores, through the streets on a wheelbarrow. Thus being esteemed an industrious, thriving young man, and paying duly for what I bought, the merchants who imported stationery solicited my custom; others proposed supplying me with books, and I went on prosperously. . . .

There remained now no other printer in Philadelphia, but the old Bradford; but he was rich and easy, did a little in the business by straggling hands, but was not anxious about it: however as he held the post-office, it was imagined he had better opportunities of obtaining news, his paper was thought a better distributor of advertisements than mine, and therefore had many more; which was a profitable thing to him, and a disadvantage to me. For though I did indeed received and send papers by the post, yet the public opinion was otherwise; for what I did send was by bribing the riders, who took them privately; Bradford being unkind enough to forbid it, which occasioned some resentment on my part; and I thought so meanly of the practice, that when I afterwards came into his situation, I took care never to imitate it.

I had hitherto continued to board with [Thomas] Godfrey, who lived in part of my house with his wife and children, and had one side of the shop for his glazier's business; though he worked little, being always absorbed in his mathematics. Mrs. Godfrey projected a match for me, with a relation's daughter, took opportunities of bringing us often together, till a serious courtship on my part ensued; the girl being in herself very deserving. The old folks encouraged me by continual invitations to supper, and by leaving us together, till at length it was time to explain. Mrs. Godfrey managed our little treaty. I let her know that I expected as much money with their daughter as would pay off my remaining debt for the printing house; which I believe was not then above a hundred pounds. She brought me word they had no such sum to spare: I said they might mortgage their house in the loan-office. The answer to this after some days was, that they did not approve the match; that on inquiry of Bradford, they had been informed the printing business was not a profitable one, the types would soon be worn out and more wanted; that Keimer and David Harry had failed one after the other, and I should probably soon follow them; and therefore I was forbidden the house, and the daughter shut up. . . . But this affair having turned my thoughts to marriage, I looked round me and made overtures of acquaintance in other places; but soon found that the business of a printer being generally thought a poor one, I was not to expect money with a wife, unless with such an one, as I should not otherwise think agreeable. In the mean time that hard to be governed passion of youth, had hurried me frequently into intrigues with low women that fell in my way, which were attended with some expense and great inconvenience, besides a continual risk to my health by a distemper, which of all things I dreaded, though by great good luck I escaped it.

A friendly correspondence, as neighbours, had continued between me and Miss Reed's family, who all had a regard for me from the time of my first lodging in their house. I was often invited there and consulted in their affairs, wherein I sometimes was of service. I pitied poor Miss Reed's unfortunate situation, who was generally dejected, seldom cheerful, and avoided company: I considered my giddiness and inconstancy, when in London, as in a great degree the cause of her unhappiness; though the mother was good enough to think the fault more her own than mine, as she had prevented our marrying before I went thither, and persuaded the other match in my absence. Our mutual affection was revived, but there were now great objections to our union; that match was indeed looked upon as invalid, a preceding wife being said to be living in England; but this could not easily be proved, because of the distance, &c., and though there was a report of his death, it was not certain. Then, though it should be true, he had left many debts which his successor might be called upon to pay: we ventured, however, over all these difficulties, and I took her to wife, September 1, 1730. None of the inconveniences happened that we had apprehended; she proved a good and faithful helpmate, assisted me much by attending to the shop; we throve together, and ever mutually endeavored to make each other happy. Thus I corrected that great *erratum* as well as I could.

At the time I established myself in Pennsylvania, there was not a good bookseller's shop in any of the colonies to the southward of Boston. In New York and Philadelphia, the printers were indeed stationers, but they sold only paper, &c. almanacs, ballads, and a few common school-books. Those who loved reading were obliged to send for their books from England: the members of the junto had each a few. We had left the alehouse, where we first met, and hired a room to hold our club in. I proposed that we should all of us bring our books to that room; where they would not only be ready to consult in our conferences, but become a common benefit, each of us being at liberty to borrow such as he wished to read at home. This was accordingly done, and for some time contented us: finding the advantage of this little collection, I proposed to render the benefit from the books more common, by commencing a public subscription library. I drew a sketch of the plan and rules that would be necessary, and got a skilful conveyancer, Mr. Charles Brogden, to put the whole in form of articles of agreement to be subscribed; by which each subscriber engaged to pay a certain sum down for the first purchase of the books, and an annual contribution for increasing them. So few were the readers at that time in Philadelphia, and the majority of us so poor, that I was not able with great industry to find more than fifty persons, (mostly young tradesmen,) willing to pay down for this purpose forty shillings each, and ten shillings per annum; with this little fund we began. The books were imported; the library was open one day in the week for lending them to subscribers, on their promissory notes to pay double the value if not duly returned. The institution soon manifested its utility, was imitated by other towns, and in other provinces. The libraries were augmented by donations; reading became fashionable; and our people having no public amusements to divert their attention from study, became better acquainted with books, and in a few years were observed by strangers to be better instructed, and more intelligent than people of the same rank generally are in other countries. . . .

This library afforded me the means of improvement by constant study, for which I set apart an hour or two each day; and thus repaired in some degree the loss of the learned education my father once intended for me. Reading was the only amusement I allowed myself. I spent no time in taverns, games, or frolics of any kind; and my industry in my business continued as indefatigable as it was necessary. I was indebted for my printing house, I had a young family coming on to be educated, and I had two competitors to contend with for business, who were established in the place before me. My circumstances however grew daily easier. My original habits of frugality continuing, and my father having among his instructions to me when a boy, frequently repeated a Proverb of Solomon, *"seest thou a man diligent in his calling, he shall stand before kings, he shall not stand before mean men."* I thence considered industry as a means of obtaining wealth and distinction, which encouraged me; though I did not think that I should ever literally stand before kings, which however has since happened; for I have stood before five, and even had the honour of sitting down with one, (the king of Denmark,) to dinner.

We have an English proverb that says,

He that would thrive,
Must ask his wife;

it was lucky for me that I had one as much disposed to industry and frugality as myself. She assisted me cheerfully in my business, folding and stitching pamphlets, tending shop, purchasing old linen rags for the paper makers, &c. We kept no idle servants, our table was plain and simple, our furniture of the cheapest. For instance, my breakfast was for a long time bread and milk, (no tea) and I ate it out of a twopenny earthern porringer, with a pewter spoon: but mark how luxury will enter families, and make a progress in spite of principle; being called one morning to breakfast, I found it in a china bowl, with a spoon of silver. They had been bought for me without my knowledge by my wife, and had cost her the enormous sum of three and twenty shillings; for which she had no other excuse or apology to make, but that she thought *her* husband deserved a silver spoon and china bowl as well as any of his neighbours. This was the first appearance of plate and china in our house, which afterwards, in a course of years, as our wealth increased, augmented gradually to several hundred pounds in value.

I had been religiously educated as a Presbyterian; but though some of the dogmas of that persuasion, such as *the eternal decrees of God, election, reprobation, &c.* appeared to me unintelligible, and I early absented myself from the public assemblies of the sect, (Sunday being my studying day). I never was without some religious principles: I never doubted, for instance, the existence of a Deity, that he made the world, and governed it by his providence; that the most acceptable service of God was the doing good to man; that our souls are immortal; and that all crimes will be punished, and virtue rewarded, either here or hereafter; these I esteemed the essentials of every religion, and being to be found in all the religions we had in our country, I respected them all, though with different degrees of respect, as I found them more or less mixed with other articles, which, without any tendency to inspire, promote, or confirm morality, served principally to divide us, and make us unfriendly to one another. . . . I had some years before composed a little liturgy, or form of prayer, for my own private use, (viz. in 1728), entitled *Articles of Belief and Acts of Religion.* I returned to the use of this, and went no more to the public assemblies. My conduct might be blameable, but I leave it without attempting further to excuse it; my present purpose being to relate facts, and not to make apologies for them.

It was about this time I conceived the bold and arduous project of arriving at *moral perfection*; I wished to live without committing any fault at any time, and to conquer all that either natural inclination, custom, or company, might lead me into. As I knew, or thought I knew, what was right and wrong, I did not see why I might not *always* do the one and avoid the other. . . .

. . . I included under thirteen names of virtues, all that at that time occurred to me as necessary or desirable; and annexed to each a short precept, which fully expressed the extent I gave to its meaning.

These names of *virtues*, with their precepts, were,

1. *Temperance*.—Eat not to dulness: drink not to elevation.
2. *Silence*.—Speak not but what may benefit others or yourself: avoid trifling conversation.
3. *Order*.—Let all your things have their places: let each part of your business have its time.
4. *Resolution*.—Resolve to perform what you ought: perform without fail what you resolve.
5. *Frugality*.—Make no expense, but to do good to others or yourself: i.e. waste nothing.
6. *Industry*.—Lose no time: be always employed in something useful: cut off all unnecessary actions.
7. *Sincerity*.—Use no hurtful deceit: think innocently and justly: and, if you speak, speak accordingly.
8. *Justice*.—Wrong none by doing injuries, or omitting the benefits that are your duty.
9. *Moderation*.—Avoid extremes: forbear resenting injuries so much as you think they deserve.
10. *Cleanliness*.—Tolerate no uncleanliness in body, clothes, or habitation.
11. *Tranquillity*.—Be not disturbed at trifles, nor at accidents common or unavoidable.
12. *Chastity*.—Rarely use venery, but for health or offspring; never to dulness or weakness, or the injury of your own or another's peace or reputation.
13. *Humility*.—Imitate *Jesus* and *Socrates*. . . .

I made a little book, in which I allotted a page for each of the virtues. I ruled each page with red ink, so as to have seven columns, one for each day of the week, marking each column with a letter for the day. I crossed these columns with thirteen red lines, marking the beginning of each line with the first letter of one of the virtues; on which line, and in its proper column, I might mark by a little black spot, every fault I found upon examination to have been committed respecting that virtue, upon that day.

I determined to give a week's strict attention to each of the virtues successively. Thus in the first week, my great guard was to avoid every the least offence against *Temperance*; leaving the other virtues to their ordinary chance, only marking every evening the faults of the day. Thus, if in the first week I could keep my first line marked T. clear of spots, I supposed the habit of that virtue so much strengthened, and its opposite weakened, that I might venture extending my attention to include the next; and for the following week keep both lines clear of spots. Proceeding thus to the last, I could get through a course complete in thirteen weeks, and four courses in a year. . . .

And conceiving God to be the fountain of wisdom, I thought it right and necessary to solicit his assistance for obtaining it; to this end I formed the following little prayer, which was prefixed to my tables of examination, for daily use.

O powerful goodness! bountiful father! merciful guide! Increase in me that wisdom which discovers my truest interest: Strengthen my resolution to perform what that wisdom dictates: Accept my kind offices to thy other children, as the only return in my power for they continual favours to me.

The precept of *Order*, requiring that *every part of my business should have its allotted time*, one page in my little book contained the following scheme of employment for the twenty-four hours of a natural day.

I entered upon the execution of this plan for self-examination, and continued it with occasional intermissions for some time. I was surprised to find myself so much fuller of faults than I had imagined; but I had the satisfaction of seeing them diminish. . . .

It may be well my posterity should be informed, that to this little artifice with the blessing of God, their ancestor owed the constant felicity of his life down to his 79th year, in which this is written. What reverses may attend the remainder is in the hand of Providence: but if they arrive, the reflection on past happiness enjoyed, ought to help his bearing them with more resignation. To *Temperance* he ascribes his long continued health, and what is still left to him of a good constitution. To *Industry* and *Frugality*, the early easiness of his circumstances, and acquisition of his fortune, with all that knowledge that enabled him to be an useful citizen and obtained for him some degree of reputation among the learned. To *Sincerity* and *Justice*, the confidence of his country, and the honourable employs it conferred upon him: and to the joint influence of the whole mass of the virtues, even in the imperfect state he was able to acquire them, all that evenness of temper and that cheerfulness in conversation which makes his company still sought for, and agreeable even to his young acquaintance: I hope therefore that some of my descendants may follow the example and reap the benefit.

It will be remarked that, though my scheme was not wholly without religion, there was in it no mark of any of the distinguishing tenets of any particular sect; I had purposely avoided them; for being fully persuaded of the utility and excellency of my method, and that it might be serviceable to people in all religions, and intending some time or other to publish it, I would not have any thing in it, that should prejudice any one, of any sect, against it. I proposed writing a little comment on each virtue, in which I would have shown the advantages of possessing it, and the mischiefs attending its opposite vice; I should have called my book *The Art of Virtue*, because it would have shown the means and manner of obtaining virtue, which would have distinguished it from the mere exhortation to be good, that does not instruct and indicate the means; but is like the apostle's man of verbal charity, who without showing to the naked and hungry, how or where they might get clothes or victuals, only exhorted them to be fed and clothed. James ii. 15, 16. . . .

My list of virtues contained at first but twelve: but a quaker friend having kindly informed me that I was generally thought proud; that my pride showed itself frequently in conversation; that I was not content with being in the right when discussing any point, but was overbearing, and rather insolent; (of which he convinced me by mentioning several instances) I determined to endeavour to cure myself if I could of this vice or folly among the rest; and I added *Humility* to my list, giving an extensive meaning to the word. I cannot boast of much success in acquiring the *reality* of this virtue, but I had a good deal with regard to the appearance of it. I made it a rule to forbear all direct contradiction to the sentiments of others, and all positive assertion of mine own. I even forbid myself, agreeably to the old laws of our Junto, the use of every word or expression in the language that imported a fixed opinion; such as *certainly, undoubtedly, &c.* and I adopted instead of them, *I conceive, I apprehend,* or *I imagine,* a thing to be so, or so; or it so *appears to me at present.* When another asserted some thing that I thought an error, I denied myself the pleasure of contradicting him abruptly, and of showing immediately some absurdity in his proposition; and in answering I began by observing, that in certain cases or circumstances, his opinion would be right, but in the present case there *appeared*, or *seemed to*

Scheme

	Hours	
Morning The Quest. What good shall I do this day?	{ 5 6 7	Rise, wash, and address *Powerful Goodness!* contrive day's business, and take the resolution of the day; prosecute the present study, and breakfast.
	{ 8 9 10 11	Work.
Noon.	{ 12 1	Read, or look over my accounts and dine.
Afternoon.	{ 2 3 4 5	Work.
Evening. The Question, What good have I done to day?	{ 6 7 8 9	Put things in their places. Supper, music, or diversion, or conversation. Examination of the day.
Night	{ 10 11 12 1 2 3 4	Sleep.

me, some difference, &c. I soon found the advantage of this change in my manners; the conversations I engaged in went on more pleasantly. . . .

In reality there is perhaps no one of our natural passions so hard to subdue as *Pride;* disguise it, struggle with it, stifle it, mortify it as much as one pleases, it is still alive, and will every now and then peep out and show itself; you will see it perhaps often in this history. For even if I could conceive that I had completely overcome it, I should probably be *proud of my humility.*

QUESTIONS

Defining Terms

Identify in the context of the chapter each of the following:

the Enlightenment	Gilbert Tennent
"I danced my dance"	the thirteen virtues
landed aristocracy	Lucy Parke Byrd
Great Awakening	Deism
George Whitefield	Nominal Christians

Probing the Sources

1. How would you characterize the relationship between William Byrd and Lucy Parke Byrd? If Lucy had kept a diary, how do you think she might have characterized the same events?

2. What precisely did religious conversion mean to Jonathan Edwards? To Sarah Osborn?

3. Who were Franklin's friends? Was he completely a self-made man, or did he rely on connections—patrons, his peers, his wife—to get ahead?

4. How would you describe each individual's place in the colonial social structure?

5. If Equiano ever met Byrd, what might he say?

Interpreting the Sources

1. How did Byrd, Edwards, and Franklin differ in their religious outlooks?

2. What relationship did these men have with slaves, women, and working people? What did it mean to be a man for each of them?

3. Which of these five people seems most familiar to you today and which most different? Why?

4. Whom do you think Byrd, Edwards, Equiano, Osborn, and Franklin had in mind as they wrote about their lives? How do their different purposes for writing give their stories different meanings?

5. From these passages, what is your sense of the role of women in colonial society?

ADDITIONAL READING

On the origins of regional differences in American culture, read David Hackett Fischer's *Albion's Seed: Four British Folkways in America* (1989). Henry May's *The Enlightenment in America* (1976) is a classic work on the subject; for the southern colonies, see Allan Kulikoff, *Tobacco and Slaves: The Development of Southern Cultures in the Chesapeake, 1680–1800* (1986). On William Byrd, see Pierre Marambaud, *William Byrd of Westover, 1674–1744* (1971); for Jonathan Edwards, try Patricia J. Tracey, *Jonathan Edwards, Pastor: Religion and Society in Eighteenth Century Northampton* (1980); for Benjamin Franklin, see Ronald William Clark, *Benjamin Franklin: A Biography* (1983). On African Americans in the colonies, see Peter Wood, *Black Majority* (1974), and Michael Gomez, *Exchanging Our Country Marks* (1998); on women, see Laurel Thatcher Ulrich, *A Midwive's Tale* (1991), and Cornelia Dayton, *Women Before the Bar* (1995).

What Kind of Revolution?
Justifications for Rebellion

HISTORICAL CONTEXT

Independence movements today are everywhere. Many French-speaking Canadians seek independence for Quebec, while the majority of the country denounces separation. In Eastern Europe, Bosnians, Serbs, and Croats kill one another in the name of self-rule. The former Soviet Union no longer exists because its ethnic groups—Russians, Ukranians, Armenians, Lithuanians, and others—demanded independence. In Africa, competing ethnic factions vie for recognition. Muslims in India demand greater autonomy from the Hindu majority, while the movement to free Tibet from Chinese rule has gained international support.

Although calls for liberty and self-determination have wide appeal, the road to self-rule is often littered with the debris of internal strife, mob violence, and even civil war. Nevertheless, the desire of ethnic, national, and religious groups for autonomy—sometimes in opposition to powerful colonialist or imperialist nations—often becomes an irresistible force in the world.

One of the critical questions facing all humans in such crises is when and under what circumstances rebellions against established authorities are justified. This was the great question that confronted the English subjects who lived in America during the decade of the 1770s. After months of intense debate, during which many ideas were presented, considered, and rejected, the Americans declared the colonies to "be free and independent states." With this declaration, they launched the first national rebellion against colonial rule in modern times.

The American War of Independence began first in people's minds. Before a shot was fired, the colonists had to break the laws that governed them and to deny the right of those who had ruled them to do so any longer—in short, to reject what they had accepted for decades. Their *intellectual* work of justifying rebellion has inspired other people around the world for over two hundred years.

Years of controversy between the colonies and England divided the colonists into several schools of thought. On the one extreme were the militants, who vowed never to yield to British pretensions. In the middle were the moderates, who, while denouncing British encroachments on their liberties, saw benefits from their association with England and favored policies of conciliation. At the other extreme were the Tories, who desired to remain loyal to the Crown. These groups were roughly equal in numbers.

When the First Continental Congress opened in September 1774, the delegates debated and then rejected a plan of compromise proposed by Joseph Galloway of Pennsylvania. In its stead, the militants within the congress pushed through a Declaration of Rights and Grievances that attacked England's right to tax the colonists and demanded the repeal of several acts viewed by the delegates as "intolerable." The ensuing spring, the British Parliament considered the American question. In the end, it also rejected a plan of reconciliation and voted instead to send more troops to America.

With the militants in control on both sides of the Atlantic, the stage was set for confrontation. On April 18, 1775, General Thomas Gage dispatched 700 British troops from Boston to capture colonial leaders and supplies at Concord, Massachusetts. The Boston Committee of Correspondence immediately sent Paul Revere and two other patriots to warn the colonists of the British movements. At dawn the following morning, 70 "minutemen"—about half the adult males in Lexington—encountered the British regulars at a bridge along the road to Concord. Guns flashed, men fell, and a civil war began.

Three weeks later, colonial delegates to the Second Continental Congress gathered in Philadelphia. This body promptly resolved to undertake "the defense of American liberty." To secure this end, it created an army and appointed George Washington as commander-in-chief. These initial actions, however, did not include a demand for independence. Rather, for the next 15 months, the chief objective of the delegates to the congress was to secure the repeal of parliamentary legislation they considered oppressive. At first, they wanted not independence, but the constitutional liberties due all Englishmen, including those who lived in America.

As the rebellion continued, hopes for reconciliation evaporated. Late in the summer of 1775, British king George III issued a Proclamation for Suppressing Rebellion and Sedition and then hired mercenary soldiers to help crush the revolt. Meanwhile, Lord Dunmore, the Royal Governor of Virginia, placed his colony under martial law, issued a proclamation that offered freedom to slaves and indentured servants who joined the Loyalist army, and ordered the bombing of Norfolk. Early in 1776, another royal governor, Josiah Martin, also raised a force of 1,500 Scottish Highlanders in an attempt to seize control of North Carolina. Such actions by the king and his men provoked many planters from the South as well as patriots from the North to demand a final break with Great Britain.

Perhaps the individual most influential in arousing public sentiment for independence was Thomas Paine. As a recent British immigrant who had been in America scarcely a year, Paine was an unlikely person to assume this role. Born in 1737, the son of a poor Quaker father and an Anglican mother, Paine had known poverty and hardship from birth. In his youth, Paine had lived an unsettled life, finding temporary employment as a sailor, a teacher, a tobacconist, a grocer, and an exciseman. His two unhappy marriages were brief—the first ending with the death of his wife, the second in legal separation. Himself a working man with a lively intellectual curiosity, Paine often championed the causes of England's laboring classes. On occasions, his crusades got him into trouble. In the winter of 1772–1773, for instance, Paine lobbied Parliament for higher wages for underpaid excisemen. For leading this effort, Paine was dismissed from his governmental post and was forced to sell his possessions to escape imprisonment for debt.

In 1774, without work or money, Paine left England for the New World. Armed with a letter of introduction from Benjamin Franklin, Paine found employment with a Philadelphia printer and rapidly rose in prominence, securing in February 1775 the editorship of the *Pennsylvania Magazine*. During the ensuing months, Paine published several promising pieces, including "African Slavery in America," an article that compared slavery with "murder, robbery, lewdness and barbarity." Another essay, "A Serious Thought," included the bold prediction that "the Almighty will finally separate America from Britain." In these pieces, Paine flashed glimpses of his literary genius, a genius that became fully manifest in January 1776 with the publication of his electrifying masterpiece *Common Sense*.

The influence of this pamphlet can hardly be exaggerated. Written in a simple, plain, and direct style, easily read and understood by all, *Common Sense* became an instant hit, selling 120,000 copies in three months and more than half a million copies altogether. Newspapers across the colonies printed extended excerpts from *Common Sense* and summarized its arguments in favor of independence. Given the wide circulation of the tract and the low population of the period, it is probable that virtually everyone in the colonies either read *Common Sense* or heard it discussed in public forums.

The arguments in *Common Sense* appealed to Americans of varying stations. Common people applauded those passages that ridiculed hereditary monarchy and denounced the British ruling classes for exploiting the lower classes in America and in England. More-cautious Americans were persuaded by Paine's promise that an independent America would be better able to remain aloof from European conflicts. Similarly, Paine's optimistic forecasts of enormous European markets for American merchants and farmers freed from British mercantile policies convinced others to favor a final break with England. Like a catalytic agent, Paine's brilliant piece of propaganda helped transform reluctant rebels into republican revolutionaries inflamed with a passion for independence.

As Americans discussed *Common Sense* in town meetings and taverns, colonial assemblies debated the desirability of independence. In April 1776, North Carolina became the first colony to empower its delegates to the Second Continental Congress to support "independency." A month later, a Virginia convention passed a resolution instructing its delegates to introduce to the congress a motion declaring the colonies to be "free and independent States, absolved from all allegiance to, or dependence on, the Crown or Parliament of Great Britain." In early June, Richard Henry Lee presented the Virginia Resolution to the congress, and John Adams of Massachusetts seconded the motion. When moderate delegates questioned the wisdom of declaring independence before the people of the middle colonies demanded it, the congress decided to postpone debate on the resolution until July 1, hoping that a three-week delay would produce a more united front. In the interim, the congress appointed a committee, composed of Thomas Jefferson, John Adams, Benjamin Franklin, Robert Livingston, and Roger Sherman, to draft a document proposing a rationale for independence.

The Committee of Five selected the 33-year-old Jefferson to write the preliminary draft of the declaration. Despite his youth, Jefferson was the obvious choice. He was a Virginian, and according to protocol, it was proper for a delegate from the colony that had introduced the resolution to draft the formal declaration. Moreover,

This oil painting by Robert Edge Pine and Edward Savage (1785) depicts John Adams, Roger Sherman, Robert Livingston, and Thomas Jefferson presenting a draft of the Declaration of Independence to Congress. Benjamin Franklin, the fifth member of the draft committee, is seated in the center-left foreground. (Historical Society of Pennsylvania).

Jefferson was an eloquent writer. He labored for about two weeks on his preliminary draft, showing it privately to Adams and Franklin (who offered a few suggestions) before bringing it back to the committee for further revisions.

On July 1, as agreed upon, the congress reopened debate on the Virginia Resolution. When John Dickinson of Pennsylvania attempted to delay the decision—saying he did not oppose the action as much as the timing—John Adams responded with a lengthy rebuttal, recapitulating once again the arguments in favor of immediate action. Nine colonies expressed support for the resolution, and two (Pennsylvania and South Carolina) opposed the motion. Meanwhile, the delegation from Delaware was evenly split, and New York's delegation refused to vote until it received specific instructions on the matter from home. With only nine affirmative votes, the congress decided to defer the decision to another day.

By the next morning, however, circumstances had changed considerably. The South Carolina delegation agreed for the sake of unity to support independence. Similarly, two Pennsylvania delegates who had opposed the resolution agreed to stay away so that the majority of their colleagues could vote affirmatively. Finally, Caesar Rodney, an absent delegate from Delaware, rode 80 miles on horseback, night and day, and arrived in time to break the tie in his delegation. Thus, on July 2, 1776, the congress voted unanimously—12 colonies in favor, none opposed, with New York abstaining—to sever all ties with England and become free and independent states.

Having made the critical decision, the congress began debate on the wording of the formal declaration that would announce the birth of a nation. For two days the congress examined, line by line, the document originally drafted by Jefferson and revised by the Committee of Five. After making a number of modifications, on July 4 the congress officially approved the Declaration of Independence.

THE DOCUMENTS
Introduction to Documents 1, 2, and 3

By 1774, the British Parliament's power to regulate trade and tax goods had been challenged with boycotts, the destruction of property, and the intimidation of customs officials by organized mobs. When Bostonians threw chests of East India Company tea into the harbor rather than pay taxes on it, Parliament reacted by closing the port of Boston, sending soldiers to enforce order, exempting those soldiers from local civil laws, tightening colonial control over the Massachusetts legislature, banning town meetings, and installing a British general, Thomas Gage, as the new royal governor. In response to these Intolerable Acts, as some called them, the colonies sent delegates to what became known as the First Continental Congress. Rather suddenly, 13 separate disputes with England found a single, although extralegal, forum.

The issues that confronted the congress give us a good sense of how divided people were ideologically. The first document here is an excerpt from Joseph Galloway's "Plan of Union." Galloway was a moderate from Pennsylvania, and he sought some way to reconcile the colonists' desire to rule their own destinies with their status as British subjects. The congress rejected his plan of union, demanding instead the repeal of the Intolerable Acts.

Reverend Samuel Seabury reacted in January 1775 with his appeal to the New York legislature to resist the drift toward radical ideas and to become a bulwark of loyalism to the Crown and Parliament. On the other side, Benjamin Franklin wrote personally to Galloway from London in February 1775, explaining the limits of his own moderation. In all of these documents, note how charged the rhetoric had become, an indication of the emotional depth of the issues. Note especially how Franklin contrasted England's "extreme corruption" with America's "glorious public virtue."

 DOCUMENT 1   *"Plan of Union"*

Joseph Galloway

Resolved, That this Congress will apply to His Majesty for a redress of grievances, under which his faithful subjects in America labour, and assure him that the colonies hold in abhorrence the idea of being considered independent communities on the British Government, and most ardently desire the establishment of a political union, not only among themselves, but with the mother state, upon those principles of safety and freedom which are essential in the constitution of all free governments, and particularly that of the British Legislature. And as the colonies from their local circumstances cannot be represented in the Parliament of Great Britain, they will humbly propose to His Majesty, and his two Houses of Parliament, the following plan, under which the strength of the whole Empire may be drawn together on any emergency; the interests of both countries advanced; and the rights and liberties of America secured.

A Plan of a proposed Union between Great Britain and the Colonies . . .

That a British and American Legislature, for regulating the administration of the general affairs of America, be proposed and established in America, including all the said colonies; within and under which government, each colony shall retain its present constitution and powers of regulating and governing its own internal police in all cases whatsoever.

That the said government be administered by a President-General to be appointed by the King, and a Grand Council to be chosen by the representatives of the people of the several colonies in their respective Assemblies, once in every three years. . . .

That the Grand Council shall meet once in every year if they shall think it necessary, and oftener if occasions shall require, at such time and place as they shall adjourn to at the last preceding meeting, or as they shall be called to meet at, by the President-General on any emergency.

That the Grand Council shall have power to choose their Speaker, and shall hold and exercise all the like rights, liberties, and privileges as are held and exercised by and in the House of Commons of Great Britain.

That the President-General shall hold his office during the pleasure of the King, and his assent shall be requisite to all Acts of the Grand Council, and it shall be his office and duty to cause them to be carried into execution.

That the President-General, by and with the advice and consent of the Grand Council, hold and exercise all the legislative rights, powers, and authorities, necessary for regulating and administering all the general police and affairs of the colonies. . . .

That the said President-General and Grand Council be an inferior and distinct branch of the British Legislature, united and incorporated with it for the aforesaid general purposes; and that any of the said general regulations may originate, and be formed and digested, either in the Parliament of Great Britain or in the said Grand Council; and being prepared, transmitted to the other for their approbation or dissent; and that the assent of both shall be requisite to the validity of all such general Acts and Statutes. . . .

DOCUMENT 2 *"An Alarm to the Legislature"*

Samuel Seabury

Honourable Gentlemen,

When you reflect upon the present confused and distressed state of this, and the other colonies, I am persuaded, that you will think no apology necessary for the liberty I have taken, of addressing you on that subject. The unhappy contention we have entered into with our parent state, would inevitably be attended with many disagreeable circumstances, with many and great inconveniences to us, even were it conducted on our part, with *propriety* and *moderation*. What then must be the case, when all proper and moderate measures are *rejected*? When not even the *appearance* of decency is regarded? When nothing seems to be consulted, but how to perplex, irritate, and affront, the *British Ministry, Parliament, Nation and King*? When every scheme that tends to *peace*, is branded with *ignominy;* as being the machination of slavery! When nothing is called FREEDOM but SEDITION! Nothing LIBERTY but REBELLION! . . .

When the Delegates had met at Philadelphia, instead of settling a reasonable plan of accommodation with the parent country, they employed themselves in censuring acts of the British parliament, which were principally intended to prevent *smuggling*, and all *illicit trade*;—in writing addresses to the people of *Great-Britain*, to the inhabitants of the *colonies* in *general*, and to those of the *province of Quebec*, in *particular*; with the *evident design* of making them *dissatisfied with their present government*; and of *exciting clamours*, and raising *seditions* and *rebellions* against the *state*;—and in exercising a *legislative authority over all the colonies*. They had the insolence to proclaim themselves "A FULL AND FREE REPRESENTATION OF"—"HIS MAJESTY'S FAITHFUL SUBJECTS IN ALL THE COLONIES FROM NOVA-SCOTIA TO GEORGIA;" and, as such, have laid a *tax* on all those colonies, viz. the *profits* arising from the *sales of all goods* imported from Great-Britain, Ireland, &c. during the months of December and January: Which *tax* is to be employed for the *relief* of the Boston *poor*. . . .

I must beg leave to enumerate a few of the *effects* of the measures of the Congress.— The government of *Rhode-Island* have dismantled the fort in their harbour, and carried off the cannon, in order to employ them *against his Majesty's forces*. The inhabitants of *New-Hampshire* have, under the command of Major SULLIVAN, one of the *Delegates*, *attacked*, and by *force of arms taken* a FORT at *Portsmouth*, belonging to his Majesty, and carried off all the powder and small arms found in it. The people of *Maryland* have had a *provincial Congress* who have assessed that colony in the sum of £.10,000, to be expended in arming and disciplining the inhabitants, to *fight against the King*. The people in *New-England* are raising, arming and disciplining men, for the same *loyal* and *christian* purpose. . . .

The state to which the GRAND CONGRESS, and the *subordinate Committees*, have reduced the colonies, is *really deplorable*. They have introduced a *system* of the most *oppressive tyranny* that can possibly be imagined;—a *tyranny*, not only over the *actions*, but over the *words*, *thoughts*, and *wills*, of the *good people of this province*. People have been threatened with the *vengeance of a mob*, for speaking in support of *order* and *good government*. Every method has been used to intimidate the *printers* from publishing any thing, which tended to *peace*, or seem'd in favour of government; while the most *detestable libels* against the *King*, the *British parliament*, and *Ministry*, have been *eagerly read*, and *extravagantly commended*. . . .

Behold, Gentlemen, behold the wretched state to which we are reduced! A *foreign power* is brought in to *govern this province*. Laws made at *Philadelphia*, by factious men from *New-England*, *New-Jersey*, *Pennsylvania*, *Maryland*, *Virginia*, and the *Carolinas*, are imposed upon us by the most *imperious menaces*. Money is levied upon us without the *consent* of our *representatives*: which very *money*, under colour of relieving the *poor* people of Boston, it is too *probable* will be employed to *raise an army against the King*. Mobs and *riots* are encouraged, in order to *force* submission to the *tyranny of the Congress*. . . .

Act now, I beseech you, as you ever have done, as the faithful representatives of the people; as the real guardians of their Rights and Liberties. Give them deliverance from the tyranny of the *Congress* and *Committees*: Secure them against the horrid carnage of a *civil war*: And endeavour to obtain for them a FREE AND PERMANENT CONSTITUTION. . . .

Be assured, Gentlemen, that a very great majority of your constituents disapprove of the late violent proceedings, and will support you in the pursuit of more *moderate measures*, as soon as You have *delivered* Them from the *tyranny of Committees*, from the *fear of violence*, and the *dread of mobs*. Recur boldly to your good, old, legal and successful way of proceeding, by *petition* and *remonstrance*.

Address yourselves to the *King* and the *two Houses of Parliament*. Let your representations be *decent* and *firm*, and principally directed to obtain a *solid American Constitution*; such as *we* can *accept* with *safety*, and *Great-Britain* can *grant* with *dignity*. Try the experiment, and you will assuredly find that our most gracious Sovereign and both Houses of Parliament will readily *meet* you in the *paths of peace*. Only shew your *willingness* towards an accommodation, by *acknowledging the supreme legislative authority of Great-Britain*, and I dare confidently pronounce the attainment of whatever YOU with *propriety*, can *ask*, and the LEGISLATURE OF GREAT-BRITAIN with *honour concede*.

DOCUMENT 3   *Benjamin Franklin on the Galloway Plan and the North Resolution*

TO JOSEPH GALLOWAY

Dear Friend,—In my last I mentioned to you my showing your plan of union to Lords Chatham and Camden. I now hear that you had sent it to Lord Dartmouth. . . .

I have not heard what objections were made to the plan in the Congress, nor would I make more than this one, that, when I consider the extreme corruption prevalent among all orders of men in this old, rotten state, and the glorious public virtue so predominant in our rising country, I cannot but apprehend more mischief than benefit from a closer union. I fear they will drag us after them in all the plundering wars which their desperate circumstances, injustice, and rapacity may prompt them to undertake; and their wide-wasting prodigality and profusion is a gulf that will swallow up every aid we may distress ourselves to afford them.

Here numberless and needless places, enormous salaries, pensions, perquisites, bribes, groundless quarrels, foolish expeditions, false accounts or no accounts, contracts and jobs, devour all revenue, and produce continual necessity in the midst of natural plenty. I apprehend, therefore, that to unite us intimately will only be to corrupt and poison us also. . . .

. . . However, I would try anything, and bear anything that can be borne with safety to our just liberties, rather than engage in a war with such relations, unless compelled to it by dire necessity in our own defence.

But should that plan be again brought forward, I imagine that before establishing the union, it would be necessary to agree on the following preliminary articles.

(1) The Declaratory Act; (2) all Acts of Parliament, or parts of Acts laying duties on the colonies; (3) all Acts of Parliament altering the charters, or constitutions, or laws of any colony; (4) all Acts of Parliament restraining manufactures; to be repealed. (5) Those parts of the Navigation Acts, which are for the good of the whole Empire, such as require that ships in the trade should be British or Plantation built, and navigated by three-fourths British subjects, with the duties necessary for regulating commerce, to be re-enacted by both Parliaments. (6) Then, to induce the Americans to see the regulating Acts faithfully executed, it would be well to give the duties collected in each colony to the treasury of that colony, and let the Governor and Assembly appoint the officers to collect them, and proportion their salaries. Thus the business will be cheaper and better done, and the misunderstandings between the two countries, now created and fomented by the unprincipled wretches generally appointed from England, be entirely prevented.

These are hasty thoughts submitted to your consideration.

You will see the new proposal of Lord North, made on Monday last, which I have sent to the committee. Those in [the English] administration, who are for violent measures, are said to dislike it. The others rely upon it as a means of dividing, and by that means subduing us. But I cannot conceive that any colony will undertake to grant a revenue to a government that holds a sword over their heads with a threat to strike the moment they cease to give or do not give so much as it is pleased to expect. In such a situation, where is the right of giving our own property freely or the right to judge of our own ability to give? It seems to me the language of a highwayman who, with a pistol in your face, says: "Give me your purse, and then I will not put my hand into your pocket. But give me all your money, or I will shoot you through the head." With great and sincere esteem, I am, etc.,

B. Franklin.

Introduction to Document 4

The convening of the First Continental Congress in 1774 was an enormous step in the thinking of the colonists. If Patrick Henry went further than most in declaring himself an American more than a Virginian, he nonetheless captured the drift of events. The Continental Congress was only one quasi-governmental body among countless others throughout the colonies, all of which were completely unauthorized by British law. In 1775 and 1776, extralegal institutions raised money, passed legislation, and gathered armed militia. And the radicals had effectively ended trade with Britain. With the bloody day in Lexington and Concord, when scores of British and Colonial troops fell, and then with the convening of the Second Continental Congress, the die of rebellion was cast.

Yet what was the meaning of these events? Why were people fighting and dying? Thomas Paine helped provide some answers. The following is an excerpt from his *Common Sense*. In reading this document, consider how eighteenth-century men and women from various social groups would respond to his arguments. What were Paine's ideas about the origins of law, government, and community? How did the English monarchy deviate from these origins? Pay particular attention to the metaphors that Paine used to make his case.

DOCUMENT 4 *From* Common Sense

Thomas Paine

. . . Mankind being originally equals in the order of creation, the equality could only be destroyed by some subsequent circumstance: the distinctions of rich and poor may in a great measure be accounted for, and that without having recourse to the harsh ill-sounding names of oppression and avarice. Oppression is often the *consequence*, but seldom or never the *means* of riches; and though avarice will preserve a man from being necessitously poor, it generally makes him too timorous to be wealthy.

But there is another and greater distinction for which no truly natural or religious reason can be assigned, and that is the distinction of men into KINGS and SUBJECTS. Male and female are the distinctions of nature, good and bad the distinctions of heaven; but how a race of men came into the world so exalted above the rest, and distinguished like some new species, is worth inquiring into, and whether they are the means of happiness or of misery to mankind.

In the early ages of the world, according to the scripture chronology there were no kings; the consequence of which was, there were no wars; it is the pride of kings which throws mankind into confusion. . . .

In the following pages I offer nothing more than simple facts, plain arguments, and common sense: and have no other preliminaries to settle with the reader, than that he will divest himself of prejudice and prepossession, and suffer his reason and his feelings to determine for themselves: that he will put on, or rather that he will not put off, the true character of a man, and generously enlarge his views beyond the present day. . . .

The sun never shone on a cause of greater worth. 'Tis not the affair of a city, a country, a province, or a kingdom; but of a continent—of at least one eighth part of the habitable globe. 'Tis not the concern of a day, a year, or an age; posterity are virtually involved in the contest, and will be more or less affected even to the end of time, by the proceedings now. Now is the seed-time of continental union, faith and honor. The least fracture now will be like a name engraved with the point of a pin on the tender rind of a young oak; the wound would enlarge with the tree, and posterity read it in full grown characters. . . .

I have heard it asserted by some, that as America has flourished under her former connection with Great Britain, the same connection is necessary towards her future happiness, and will always have the same effect. Nothing can be more fallacious than this kind of argument. We may as well assert that because a child has thrived upon milk, that it is never to have meat, or that the first twenty years of our lives is to become a precedent for the next twenty. But even this is admitting more than is true; for I answer roundly, that America would have flourished as much, and probably much more, had no European power taken any notice of her. The commerce by which she hath enriched herself are the necessaries of life, and will always have a market while eating is the custom of Europe.

But she has protected us, say some. That she hath engrossed us is true, and defended the continent at our expense as well as her own, is admitted; and she would have defended Turkey from the same motive, *viz.* for the sake of trade and dominion.

Alas! we have been long led away by ancient prejudices and made large sacrifices to superstition. We have boasted the protection of Great Britain, without considering, that her motive was *interest* not *attachment*; and that she did not protect us from *our enemies* on *our account*; but from *her enemies* on *her own account*, from those who had no quarrel with us on any *other account*, and who will always be our enemies on the *same account*. Let Britain waive her pretensions to the continent, or the continent throw off the dependance, and we should be at peace with France and Spain, were they at war with Britain. The miseries of Hanover's last war ought to warn us against connections.

It hath lately been asserted in Parliament, that the colonies have no relation to each other but through the parent country, *i.e.*, that Pennsylvania and the Jerseys, and so on for the rest, are sister colonies by the way of England; this is certainly a very roundabout way of proving relationship, but it is the nearest and only true way of proving enmity (or enemyship, if I may so call it.). France and Spain never were, nor perhaps ever will be, our enemies as *Americans*, but as our being the *subjects of Great Britain*.

But Britain is the parent country, say some. Then the more shame upon her conduct. Even brutes do not devour their young, nor savages make war upon their families; wherefore, the assertion, if true, turns to her reproach; but it happens not to be true, or only partly so, and the phrase *parent* or *mother country* hath been jesuitically adopted by the king and his parasites, with a low papistical design of gaining an unfair bias on the credulous weakness of our minds. Europe, and not England, is the parent country of America. This new world hath been the asylum for the persecuted lovers of civil and religious liberty from *every part* of Europe. Hither have they fled, not from the tender embraces of the mother, but from the cruelty of the monster; and it is so far true of England, that the same tyranny which drove the first emigrants from home, pursues their descendants still. . . .

I challenge the warmest advocate for reconciliation to show a single advantage that this continent can reap by being connected with Great Britain. I repeat the challenge; not a single advantage is derived. Our corn will fetch its price in any market in Europe, and our imported goods must be paid for, buy them where we will.

But the injuries and disadvantages which we sustain by that connection, are without number; and our duty to mankind at large, as well as to ourselves, instruct us to renounce the alliance: because, any submission to, or dependance on, Great Britain, tends directly to involve this continent in European wars and quarrels, and set us at variance with nations who would otherwise seek our friendship, and against whom we have neither anger nor complaint. As Europe is our market for trade, we ought to form no partial connection with any part of it. It is the true interest of America to steer clear of European contentions, which she never can do, while, by her dependance on Britain, she is made the makeweight in the scale of British politics.

Europe is too thickly planted with kingdoms to be long at peace, and whenever a war breaks out between England and any foreign power, the trade of America goes to ruin, *because of her connection with Britain.* The next war may not turn out like the last, and should it not, the advocates for reconciliation now will be wishing for separation then, because neutrality in that case would be a safer convoy than a man of war. Every thing that is right or reasonable pleads for separation. The blood of the slain, the weeping voice of nature cries, 'TIS TIME TO PART. Even the distance at which the Almighty hath placed England and America is a strong and natural proof that the authority of the one over the other, was never the design of heaven. The time likewise at which the continent was discovered, adds weight to the argument, and the manner in which it was peopled, encreases the force of it. The Reformation was preceded by the discovery of America: As if the Almighty graciously meant to open a sanctuary to the persecuted in future years, when home should afford neither friendship nor safety. . . .

Though I would carefully avoid giving unnecessary offence, yet I am inclined to believe, that all those who espouse the doctrine of reconciliation, may be included within the following descriptions.

Interested men, who are not to be trusted, weak men who *cannot* see, prejudiced men who will not see, and a certain set of moderate men who think better of the European world than it deserves; and this last class, by an ill-judged deliberation, will be the cause of more calamities to this continent than all the other three. . . .

Men of passive tempers look somewhat lightly over the offences of Great Britain, and, still hoping for the best, are apt to call out, *Come, come, we shall be friends again for all this.* But examine the passions and feelings of mankind: bring the doctrine of reconciliation to the touchstone of nature, and then tell me whether you can hereafter love, honor, and faithfully serve the power that hath carried fire and sword into your land? If you cannot do all these, then are you only deceiving yourselves, and by your delay bringing ruin upon posterity. Your future connection with Britain, whom you can neither love nor honor, will be forced and unnatural, and being formed only on the plan of present convenience, will in a little time fall into a relapse more wretched than the first. But if you say, you can still pass the violations over, then I ask, hath your house been burnt? Hath your property been destroyed before your face? Are your wife and children destitute of a bed to lie on, or bread to live on? Have you lost a parent or a child by their hands, and yourself the ruined and wretched survivor? If you have not, then are you not a judge of those who have. But if you have, and can still shake hands with the murderers, then are you unworthy the name of husband, father, friend, or lover, and whatever may be your rank or title in life, you have the heart of a coward, and the spirit of a sycophant. . . .

'Tis repugnant to reason, to the universal order of things, to all examples from former ages, to suppose that this continent can long remain subject to any external power. The most sanguine in Britain doth not think so. The utmost stretch of human wisdom cannot, at this time, compass a plan, short of separation, which can promise the continent even a year's security. Reconciliation is *now* a fallacious dream. Nature has deserted the connection, and art cannot supply her place. For, as Milton wisely expresses, "never can true reconcilement grow where wounds of deadly hate have pierced so deep."

 . . . Small islands not capable of protecting themselves are the proper objects for government to take under their care; but there is something absurd, in supposing a Continent to be perpetually governed by an island. In no instance hath nature made the satellite larger than its primary planet; and as England and America, with respect to each other, reverse the common order of nature, it is evident that they belong to different systems. England to Europe: America to itself.

I am not induced by motives of pride, party or resentment to espouse the doctrine of separation and independence; I am clearly, positively, and conscientiously persuaded that it is the true interest of this continent to be so; that everything short of *that* is mere patchwork, that it can afford no lasting felicity,—that it is leaving the sword to our children, and shrinking back at a time when a little more, a little further, would have rendered this continent the glory of the earth.

As Britain hath not manifested the least inclination towards a compromise, we may be assured that no terms can be obtained worthy the acceptance of the continent, or any ways equal to the expence of blood and treasure we have been already put to. . . .

. . . As I have always considered the independency of this continent, as an event which sooner or later must arrive, so from the late rapid progress of the continent to maturity, the event cannot be far off. Wherefore, on the breaking out of hostilities, it was not worth the while to have disputed a matter which time would have finally redressed, unless we meant to be in earnest: otherwise it is like wasting an estate on a suit at law, to regulate the trespasses of a tenant whose lease is just expiring. No man was a warmer wisher for a reconciliation than myself, before the fatal nineteenth of April, 1775, but the moment the event of that day was made known, I rejected the hardened, sullen-tempered Pharaoh of England for ever; and disdain the wretch, that with the pretended title of FATHER OF HIS PEOPLE can unfeelingly hear of their slaughter, and composedly sleep with their blood upon his soul. . . .

. . . But where, say some, is the king of America? I'll tell you, friend, he reigns above, and doth not make havoc of mankind like the royal brute of Great Britain. Yet that we may not appear to be defective even in earthly honors, let a day be solemnly set apart for proclaiming the charter; let it be brought forth placed on the divine law, the Word of God; let a crown be placed thereon, by which the world may know, that so far as we approve of monarchy, that in America the law is king. For as in absolute governments the king is law, so in free countries the law ought to be king; and there ought to be no other. But lest any ill use should afterwards arise, let the crown at the conclusion of the ceremony be demolished, and scattered among the people whose right it is.

A government of our own is our natural right: and when a man seriously reflects on the precariousness of human affairs, he will become convinced, that it is infinitely wiser and safer, to form a Constitution of our own in a cool deliberate manner, while we have it in our power, than to trust such an interesting event to time and chance. . . . Ye that oppose independence now, ye know not what ye do: ye are opening a door to eternal tyranny, by keeping vacant the seat of government. There are thousands and tens of thousands, who would think it glorious to expel from the continent, that barbarous and hellish power, which hath stirred up the Indians and the Negroes to destroy us; the cruelty hath a double guilt, it is dealing brutally by us, and treacherously by them.

To talk of friendship with those in whom our reason forbids us to have faith, and our affections wounded through a thousand pores instruct us to detest, is madness and folly. Every day wears out the little remains of kindred between us and them; and can there be any reason to hope, that as the relationship expires, the affection will increase, or that we shall agree better when we have ten times more and greater concerns to quarrel over than ever?

Ye that tell us of harmony and reconciliation, can ye restore to us the time that is past? Can ye give to prostitution its former innocence? neither can ye reconcile Britain and America. The last cord now is broken, the people of England are presenting addresses against us. There are injuries which nature cannot forgive; she would cease to be nature if she did. As well can the lover forgive the ravisher of his mistress, as the continent forgive the murders of Britain. The Almighty hath implanted in us these unextinguishable feelings for good and wise purposes. They are the guardians of his image in our hearts. They distinguish us from the herd of common animals. The social compact would dissolve, and justice be extirpated from the earth, or have only a casual existence were we callous to the touches of affection. The robber and the murderer would often escape unpunished, did not the injuries which our tempers sustain, provoke us into justice.

O! ye that love mankind! Ye that dare oppose not only the tyranny but the tyrant, stand forth! Every spot of the old world is overrun with oppression. Freedom hath been hunted round the globe. Asia and Africa have long expelled her. Europe regards her like a stranger, and England hath given her warning to depart. O! receive the fugitive, and prepare in time an asylum for mankind.

Introduction to Document 5

Notwithstanding Paine's persuasive pen, not everyone agreed with his assertions. For American Loyalists, it was the so-called "patriots" and not the King who were waging war against basic English liberties. One Englishman who articulated this position was the Rev. John Wesley, an Anglican minister beloved both in England and the colonies by all who called themselves "Methodists." A lifelong Tory (according to Wesley, a Tory was "one who believes God, not the people, to be the origin of all civil power"), Wesley was an outspoken critic of the rebellion. When asked to deliver a "charity sermon" for the benefit of the widows and orphans of the early victims of the war, Wesley wrote and later published "National Sins and Miseries." Compare the argument and rhetoric of this sermon with Paine's *Common Sense*. What groups would have been more persuaded by Wesley than Paine? Which argument do you find to be the most compelling?

DOCUMENT 5 *From "A Sermon Preached at St. Matthew's, Bethnal Green, on Sunday, Nov. 12, 1775"*

John Wesley

Let not anyone think this is but a small calamity which is fallen upon our land. If you saw, as I have seen, in every county, city, town, men who were once of a calm, mild, friendly temper, mad with party zeal, foaming with rage against their quiet neighbours, ready to tear out one another's throats, and to plunge their swords into each other's bowels; if you had heard men who once feared God and honoured the king now breathing out the bitterest invectives against him, and just ripe, should any occasion offer, for treason and rebellion; you would not then judge this to be a little evil, a matter of small moment, but one of the heaviest judgments which God can permit to fall upon a guilty land.

Such is the condition of Englishmen at home. And is it any better abroad? I fear not. From those who are now upon the spot I learn that in our colonies, also, many are causing the people to drink largely of the same deadly wine; thousands of whom are there inflamed more and more, till their heads are utterly turned, and they are mad to all intents and purposes. Reason is lost in rage; its small still voice is drowned by popular clamour. Wisdom is fallen in the streets. And where is the place of understanding? It is hardly to be found in these provinces. Here is *slavery*, real slavery indeed, most properly so called. For the regular, legal, constitutional form of government is no more. Here is real, not imaginary, bondage; not the shadow of English liberty is left. Not only no *liberty of the press* is allowed—none dare print a page or a line unless it be exactly conformable to the sentiments of our lords, the people—but no *liberty of speech*. Their 'tongue' is not 'their own.' None must dare to utter one word either in favour of King George, or in disfavour of the idol they have set up—the new, illegal, unconstitutional government, utterly unknown to us and to our forefathers. Here is no *religious liberty*; no liberty of conscience from them that 'honour the King,' and whom consequently a sense of duty prompts them to defend from the vile calumnies continually vented against him. Here is no *civil liberty*; no enjoying the fruit of their labour any further than the populace pleases. A man has no security for his trade, his house, his property, unless he will swim with the stream. Nay, he has no security for his life if his popular neighbour has a mind to cut this throat. For there is no law, and no legal magistrate to take cognizance of offenses. There is the gulf of tyranny—of arbitrary power on one hand, and of anarchy on the other. And, as if all this were not misery enough, see likewise the fell monster, war! But who can describe the complicated misery which is contained in this? Hark! The cannons roar! A pitchy cloud covers the face of the sky. Noise, confusion, terror, reign over all! Dying groans are on every side. The bodies of men are pierced, torn, hewed in pieces; their blood is poured on the early like water! Their souls take their flight into the eternal world; perhaps into everlasting misery. The ministers of grace turn away from the horrid scene; the minister of vengeance triumph. Such already has been the face of things in that once happy land where peace and plenty, even while banished from great part of Europe, smiled for near a hundred years.

And what is it which drags on these poor victims into the field of blood? It is a great phantom which stalks before them, which they are taught to call, 'liberty'! It is this which breathes

. . . into their hearts stern love of war,
And thirst of vengeance, and contempt of death.

Real liberty, meantime, is trampled underfoot, and is lost in anarchy and confusion.

But which of these warriors all the while considered the wife of his youth, that is now left a disconsolate widow—perhaps with none that careth for her; perhaps deprived of her only comfort and support, and not having where to lay her head? Who considered his helpless children, now desolate orphans, it may be, crying for bread, while their mother has nothing left to give them but her sorrows and her tears?

Introduction to Documents 6, 7, and 8

Even as Paine and Wesley penned their tirades against the evils of tyranny, events in Virginia were forcing Patriots and Loyalists alike to reflect upon the condition of that group of Americans most robbed of human freedoms. On November 7, 1775, Lord Dunmore issued a proclamation for the colony of Virginia that offered freedom to any slave who agreed to join the fight for the British side. This proclamation caused a immediate stir, and in mid-December, the Virginia colonial assembly responded with its own proclamation threatening strict punishment for slaves deserting to the British. The following documents include Lord Dunmore's Proclamation, a published letter about the proclamation, and Virginia's official reaction to the proclamation. What insights about American and British attitudes toward slavery and liberty are contained in these documents? How do you think southern planters and African-American slaves would have responded to the arguments in this debate?

DOCUMENT 6 **By His Excellency the Right Honorable JOHN Earl of DUNMORE, His Majesty's Lieutenant and Governor General of the Colony and Dominion of VIRGINIA, and Vice Admiral of the same**

A Proclamation

As I have ever entertained Hopes, that an Accommodation might have taken Place between GREAT-BRITAIN and this Colony, without being compelled by my Duty to this most disagreeable but now absolutely necessary Step, rendered so by a Body of armed Men unlawfully assembled, firing on His MAJESTY'S Tenders, and the formation of an Army, and that Army now on their March to attack his MAJESTY'S Troops and destroy the well disposed subjects of the Colony. To defeat such treasonable Purposes, and that all such Traitors, and their Abettors, may be brought to Justice, and that the Peace, and good Order of this Colony may be again restored, which the ordinary Course of the Civil Law is unable to effect; I have thought fit to issue this my Proclamation, hereby declaring, that until the aforesaid good Purpose can be obtained, I do in Virtue of the Power and Authority to ME given, by His MAJESTY, determine to execute Martial Law, and cause the same to be executed throughout this Colony: and to ****** the Peace and good Order may the sooner be restored, I do require every Person capable of bearing Arms, to resort to His MAJESTY'S STANDARD, or be looked upon as Traitors to His MAJESTY'S Crown and Government, and thereby become liable to the Penalty the Law inflicts upon such Offenses; such as forfeiture of Life, confiscation of Lands, &. &. And I do hereby further declare all indented [sic] Servants, Negroes, or others, (appertaining to Rebels,) free that are able and willing to bear Arms, they joining His MAJESTY'S Troops as soon as may be, foe the more speedily reducing this Colony to a proper Sense of their Duty, to His MAJESTY'S Crown and Dignity. I do further order, and require, all His MAJESTY'S Liege Subjects, to retain their Quitrents, or any other Taxes due or that may become due, in their own Custody, till such a Time as Peace may be again restored to this at present most unhappy Country, or demanded of them for their former salutary Purposes, by Officers properly ***** to receive the same.

GIVEN *under my Hand on board the Ship WILLIAM by Norfolk, the 7th Day of November in the SIXTEENTH Year of His MAJESTY'S Reign.*
DUNMORE *(GOD save the KING.)*

DOCUMENT 7 **Letter Regarding Dunmore's Proclamation from the Virginia Gazette (Dixon and Hunter), November 5, 1775**

The second class of people, for whose sake a few remarks upon this proclamation seem necessary, is the Negroes. They have been flattered with their freedom, if they be able to bear arms, and will spedily join Lord Dunmore's troops. To none then is freedom promised but to such as are able to do Lord Dunmore service: The aged, the infirm, the women and children, are still to remain the property of their masters, masters who will be provoked to severity, should part of their slaves desert them. Lord Dunmore's declaration, therefore, is a cruel declaration to the Negroes. He does not even pretend to make it out of any tenderness to them, but solely on his own account; and should it meet with success, it leaves by far the greater number at the mercy of an enraged and injured people. But should there be any amongst the Negroes weak enough to believe that Dunmore intends to do them a kindness, and wicked enough to provoke the fury of the Americans against their defenceless fathers and mothers, their wives, their women and children, let them only consider the difficulty of effecting their escape, and what they must expect to suffer if they fall into the hands of the Americans. Let them farther consider what must be their fate, should the English prove conquerors in this dispute. If we can judge of the future from the past, it will not be much mended. Long have the Americans, moved by compassion, and actuated by sound policy, endeavoured to stop the progress of slavery. Our Assemblies have repeatedly passed acts laying heavy duties upon imported Negroes, by which they meant altogether to prevent the horrid traffick; but their humane intentions have been as often frustrated by the cruelty and covetousness of a set of English merchants, who prevailed upon the King to repeal our kind and merciful acts, little indeed to the credit of his humanity. Can it then be supposed that the Negroes will be better used by the English, who have always encouraged and upheld this slavery, than by their present masters, who pity their condition, who wish, in general, to make it as easy and comfortable as possible, and who would willingly, were it in their power, or were they permitted, not only prevent any more Negroes from losing their freedom, but restore it to such as have already unhappily lost it. No, the ends of Lord Dunmore and his party being answered, they will either give up the offending Negroes to the rigour of the laws they have broken, or sell them in the West Indies, where every year they sell many thousands of their miserable brethren, to perish either by the inclemency of the weather, or the cruelty of barbarous masters. Be not then, ye Negroes, tempted by this proclamation to ruin yourselves. I have given you a faithful view of what you are to expect; and I declare, before GOD, in doing it, I have considered your welfare, as well as that of the country. Whether you will profit by my advice I cannot tell; but this I know, that whether we suffer or not, if you desert us, you most certainly will.

DOCUMENT 8   *By the Representatives of the People of the Colony and Dominion of VIRGINIA, assembled in GENERAL CONVENTION*

A Declaration

WHEREAS lord Dunmore, by his proclamation, dated on board the ship William, off Norfolk, the 7th day of November 1775, hath offered freedom to such abled-bodied slaves as are willing to join him, and take up arms, against the good people of this colony, giving thereby encouragement to a general insurrection, which may induce a necessity of inflicting the severest punishments upon those unhappy people, already deluded by his base and insidious arts; and whereas, by an act of the General Assembly now in force in this colony, it is enacted, that all negro or other slaves, conspiring to rebel or make insurrection, shall suffer death, and be excluded all benefit of clergy: We think it proper to declare, that all slaves who have been, or shall be seduced, by his lordship's proclamation, or other arts, to desert their masters' service, and take up arms against the inhabitants of this colony, shall be liable to such punishment as shall hereafter be directed by the General Convention. And to that end all such, who have taken this unlawful and wicked step, may return in safety to their duty, and escape the punishment due to their crimes, we hereby promise pardon to them, they surrendering themselves to col. William Woodford, or any other commander of our troops, and not appearing in arms after the publication hereof. And we do farther earnestly recommend it to all humane and benevolent persons in this colony to explain and make known this our offer of mercy to those unfortunate people.

EDMUND PENDLETON, president.

Introduction to Documents 9 and 10

Just half a year after Paine published his stirring call for rebellion, the 13 colonies declared themselves free and independent states. The following documents are taken from this period of decision. Document 9 contains selections from the letters of John and Abigail Adams that were written during 1776 while John was a delegate to the Second Continental Congress. Consider the advice that Abigail gave to John in these letters, and John's response to her requests. Also note John's predictions about how future generations would celebrate July 2, 1776, the day that Congress first declared its independence from England. The spelling in the letters has been modernized.

Document 10 is the finalized draft of the Declaration of Independence, which was originally written by Thomas Jefferson in June 1776 and then edited and approved by Congress on July 4, 1776. This historic document consists of two parts: an introduction that justifies the abstract right of revolution and as much longer section listing specific grievances against George III that explains to the world why the colonists felt driven to exercise the inalienable rights outlined in the introduction. While the list of grievances was probably the section of greatest importance to the generation that fought the Revolution, the words contained in the preamble have provided timeless, inspiring oppressed peoples all across the world for more than two centuries.

 DOCUMENT 9 *Correspondence of Abigail and John Adams*

Braintree March 31 1776

Abigail Adams to John Adams

I long to hear that you have declared an independency—and by the way in the new Code of Laws which I suppose it will be necessary for you to make I desire you would Remember the Ladies, and be more generous and favorable to them than your ancestors. Do not put such unlimited power into the hands of the Husbands. Remember all Men would be tyrants if they could. If particular care and attention is not paid to the Ladies we are determined to foment a Rebellion, and will not hold ourselves bound by any Laws in which we have no voice, or Representation.

That your Sex are Naturally Tyrannical is a Truth so thoroughly established as to admit of no dispute, but such of you as wish to be happy willingly give up the harsh title of Master for the more tender and endearing one of Friend. Why then, not put it out of the power of the vicious and the Lawless to use us with cruelty and indignity with impunity. Men of Sense in all Ages abhor those customs which treat us only as the vassals of your Sex. Regard us then as Beings placed by providence under your protection and in imitation of the Supreme Being make use of that power only for our happiness.

[Philadelphia,] April 14 1776

John to Abigail

As to Declarations of Independency, be patient. Read our Privateering Laws, and our Commercial Laws. What signifies a Word.

As to your extraordinary Code of Laws, I cannot but laugh. We have been told that our Struggle has loosened the bands of Government every where. That Children and Apprentices were disobedient—that schools and Colleges were grown turbulent—that Indians slighted their Guardians and Negroes grew insolent to their Masters. But your Letter was the first Intimation that another Tribe more numerous and powerful than all the rest were grown discontended.—This is rather too coarse a Compliment but you are so saucy, I won't blot it out.

Depend upon it., We know better than to repeal our Masculine systems. Although they are in full Force, you know they are little more than Theory. We dare not exert our Power in its full Latitude. We are obliged to go fair, and softly, and in Practice you know We are the subjects. We have only the Name of Masters, and rather than give up this, which would completely subject Us to the Despotism of the Petticoat. I hope General Washington and all our brave Heroes would fight. I am sure every good Politician would plot, as long as he would against Despotism, empire, Monarchy, Aristocracy, Oligarchy, or Ochlocracy,—A fine Story indeed. I begin to think the Ministry as deep as they are wicked. After stirring up Tories, Landjobbers, Trimmers, Bigots, Canadians, Indians, Negroes, Hanoverians, Hessians, Russians, Irish Roman Catholics, Scotch Renegades, at last they have stimulated the to demand new Privileges and threaten to rebel.

B[raintre]e May 7 1776

Abigail to John

I can not say that I think you very generous to the Ladies, for while you are proclaiming peace and good will to Men, Emancipating all Nations, you insist upon retaining an absolute power over Wives. But you must remember that Arbitrary power is like most other things which are very hard, very liable to be broken—and notwithstanding all your wise Laws and Maxims we have it in our power not only to free ourselves but to subdue our Masters, and without violence throw both your natural and legal authority at our feet—

"Charm by accepting, by submitting sway
Yet have our Humor most when we obey."

Philadelphia, July 3 1776

John to Abigail

. . . The Hopes of Reconciliation, which were fondly entertained by Multitudes of honest and well meaning though weak and mistaken People, have been gradually and at last totally extinguished. . . . The Second of July 1776, will be the most memorable Epoch, in the History of America.—I am apt to believe that it will be celebrated, by succeeding Generations, as the great anniversary Festival. It ought to be commemorated, as the Day of Deliverance by solemn Acts of Devotion to God Almighty. It ought to be solemnized with Pomp and Parade, with Shows, Games, Sports, Guns, Bells, Bonfires and Illuminations from one End of this Continent to the other from this Time forward forever more.

You will think me transported with Enthusiasm but I am not.—I am well aware of the Toil and Blood and Treasure, that it will cost Us to maintain this Declaration, and support and defend these States.—yet through all the Gloom I can see the Rays of ravishing Light and Glory. I can see that the End is more than worth all the Means. And that Posterity will triumph in that Days Transaction, even although We should rue it, which I trust in God We shall not.

DOCUMENT 10 *The Declaration of Independence*

Text Approved by Congress, July 4, 1776
The Unanimous Declaration of the Thirteen United States of America

When, in the course of human events, it becomes necessary for one people to dissolve the political bands which have connected them with another, and to assume, among the powers of the earth, the separate and equal station to which the laws of nature and of nature's God entitle them, a decent respect to the opinions of mankind requires that they should declare the causes which impel them to the separation.

We hold these truths to be self-evident: That all men are created equal; that they are endowed by their Creator with certain unalienable rights; that among these are life, liberty, and the pursuit of happiness. That, to secure these rights, governments are instituted among men, deriving their just powers from the consent of the governed; that whenever any form of government becomes destructive of these ends, it is the right of the people to alter or to abolish it, and to institute new government, laying its foundation on such principles, and organizing its powers in such form, as to them shall seem most likely to effect their safety and happiness. Prudence, indeed, will dictate that governments long established should not be changed for light and transient causes; and accordingly all experience hath shown that mankind are more disposed to suffer, while evils are sufferable, than to right themselves by abolishing the forms to which they are accustomed. But when a long train of abuses and usurpations, pursuing invariably the same object, evinces a design to reduce them under absolute despotism, it is their right, it is their duty, to throw off such government, and to provide new guards for their future security. Such has been the patient sufferance of these colonies; and such is now the necessity which constrains them to alter their former systems of government. The history of the present King of Great Britain is a history of repeated injuries and usurpations, all having in direct object the establishment of an absolute tyranny over these states. To prove this, let facts be submitted to a candid world.

He has refused his assent to laws, the most wholesome and necessary for the public good.

He has forbidden his governors to pass laws of immediate and pressing importance, unless suspended in their operation till his assent should be obtained; and, when so suspended, he has utterly neglected to attend to them.

He has refused to pass other laws for the accommodation of large districts of people, unless those people would relinquish the right of representation in the legislature, a right inestimable to them, and formidable to tyrants only.

He has called together legislative bodies at places unusual, uncomfortable, and distant from the depository of their public records, for the sole purpose of fatiguing them into compliance with his measures.

He has dissolved representative houses repeatedly, for opposing, with manly firmness, his invasions on the rights of the people.

He has refused for a long time, after such dissolutions, to cause others to be elected; whereby the legislative powers, incapable of annihilation, have returned to the people at large for their exercise; the state remaining, in the mean time, exposed to all the dangers of invasions from without and convulsions within.

He has endeavored to prevent the population of these states; for that purpose obstructing the laws for naturalization of foreigners; refusing to pass others to encourage their migration hither, and raising the conditions of new appropriations of lands.

He has obstructed the administration of justice, by refusing his assent to laws for establishing judiciary powers.

He has made judges dependent on his will alone, for the tenure of their offices, and the amount and payment of their salaries.

He has erected a multitude of new offices, and sent hither swarms of officers to harass our people and eat out their substance.

He has kept among us, in times of peace, standing armies, without the consent of our legislatures.

He has affected to render the military independent of, and superior to, the civil power.

He has combined with others to subject us to a jurisdiction foreign to our constitution, and unacknowledged by our laws, giving his assent to their acts of pretended legislation:

For quartering large bodies of armed troops among us;

For protecting them, by a mock trial, from punishment for any murders which they should commit on the inhabitants of these states;

For cutting off our trade with all parts of the world;

For imposing taxes on us without our consent;

For depriving us, in many cases, of the benefits of trial by jury;

For transporting us beyond seas, to be tried for pretended offenses;

For abolishing the free system of English laws in a neighboring province, establishing therein an arbitrary government, and enlarging its boundaries, so as to render it at once an example and fit instrument for introducing the same absolute rule into these colonies;

For taking away our charters, abolishing our most valuable laws, and altering fundamentally the forms of our governments;

For suspending our own legislatures, and declaring themselves invested with power to legislate for us in all cases whatsoever.

He has abdicated government here, by declaring us out of his protection and waging war against us.

He has plundered our seas, ravaged our coasts, burned our towns, and destroyed the lives of our people.

He is at this time transporting large armies of foreign mercenaries to complete the works of death, desolation, and tyranny already begun with circumstances of cruelty and perfidy scarcely paralleled in the most barbarous ages, and totally unworthy the head of a civilized nation.

He has constrained our fellow-citizens, taken captive on the high seas, to bear arms against their country, to become the executioners of their friends and brethren, or to fall themselves by their hands.

He has excited domestic insurrection among us, and has endeavored to bring on the inhabitants of our frontiers the merciless Indian savages, whose known rule of warfare is an undistinguished destruction of all ages, sexes, and conditions.

In every stage of these oppressions we have petitioned for redress in the most humble terms; our repeated petitions have been answered only by repeated injury. A prince, whose character is thus marked by every act which may define a tyrant, is unfit to be the ruler of a free people.

Nor have we been wanting in attention to our British brethren. We have warned them, from time to time, of attempts by their legislature to extend an unwarrantable jurisdiction over us. We have reminded them of the circumstances of our emigration and settlement here. We have appealed to their native justice and magnanimity; and we have conjured them, by the ties of our common kindred, to disavow these usurpations, which would inevitably interrupt our connections and correspondence. They, too, have been deaf to the voice of justice and of consanguinity. We must, therefore, acquiesce in the necessity which denounces our separation, and hold them, as we hold the rest of mankind, enemies in war, in peace friends.

We, therefore, the representatives of the United States of America, in General Congress assembled, appealing to the Supreme Judge of the world for the rectitude of our intentions, do, in the name and by the authority of the good people of these colonies, solemnly publish and declare, that these United Colonies are, and of right ought to be, FREE AND INDEPENDENT STATES; that they are absolved from all allegiance to the British crown, and that all political connection between them and the state of Great Britain is, and ought to be, totally dissolved; and that, as free and independent states, they have full power to levy war, conclude peace, contract alliances, establish commerce, and to do all other acts and things which independent states may of right do. And for the support of this declaration, with a firm reliance on the protection of Divine Providence, we mutually pledge to each other our lives, our fortunes, and our sacred honor.

Introduction to Document 11

One of the changes that the Second Continental Congress made in Jefferson's draft of the Declaration was to delete a passage condemning King George for foisting slavery on the colonists: "He has waged cruel war against human nature itself, violating its most sacred rights of life and liberty in the persons of distant people who never offended him, captivating and carrying them into slavery in another hemisphere, or to incur miserable death in their transportation thither." Worse, Jefferson wrote, having forced colonists to buy and sell other human beings, the king had encouraged the slaves to rebel and kill their masters.

Historians have long noted the contradiction of the colonists' championing liberty while they practiced slavery. The northern colonies had fewer slaves and therefore less at stake; as states they assumed phased-out bondage. But in the South, the ideal of equality contrasted most sharply with slavery. The historian Edmund S. Morgan has argued that the contradiction was more apparent than real. Indeed, the two were dependent on each other during the Revolutionary era: "Aristocrats could more safely preach equality in a slave society than in a free one. Slaves did not become leveling mobs, because their owners would see to it that they had no chance to. The apostrophes to equality were not addressed to them. And because Virginia's labor force was composed mainly of slaves, who had been isolated by race and removed from the political equation, the remaining free laborers and tenant farmers were too few in number to constitute a serious threat to the superiority of the men who assured them of their equality. . . . Virginia's small farmers could perceive a common identity with the large. . . . Neither was a slave. And both were equal in not being slaves."

The revolutionary idea that human beings were equal by natural right allowed the colonists to ridicule a king and reject the rule of Parliament. But their devotion to equality had severe limits. In 1787, just four years after the victory over the British, Thomas Jefferson published his *Notes on the State of Virginia*. He lamented the fact that whites had not yet taken the opportunity to view blacks and Indians as "subjects of natural history." In Document 11, he offers observations on those of African lineage.

DOCUMENT 11 *From* Notes on the State of Virginia

Thomas Jefferson

. . . The first difference which strikes us is that of colour. Whether the black of the negro resides in the reticular membrane between the skin and scarf-skin, or in the scarf-skin itself; whether it proceeds from the colour of the blood, the colour of the bile, or from that of some other secretion, the difference is fixed in nature, and is as real as if its seat and cause were better known to us. And is this difference of no importance? Is it not the foundation of a greater or less share of beauty in the two races? Are not the fine mixtures of red and white, the expressions of every passion by greater or less suffusions of colour in the one, preferable to that eternal monotony, which reigns in the countenances, that immoveable veil of black which covers all the emotions of the other race? Add to these, flowing hair, a more elegant symmetry of form, their own judgment in favour of the whites, declared by their preference of them, as uniformly as is the preference of the Oran-ootan [orangutan] for the black women over those of his own species. The circumstance of superior beauty, is thought worthy of attention in the propagation of our horses, dogs, and other domestic animals; why not in that of man? Besides those of colour, figure, and hair, there are other physical distinctions proving a difference of race. They have less hair on the face and body. They secrete less by the kidnies, and more by the glands of the skin, which gives them a very strong and disagreeable odour. This greater degree of transpiration renders them more tolerant of heat, and less so of cold, than the whites. . . . A black, after hard labour through the day, will be induced by the slightest amusements to sit up till midnight, or later, though knowing he must be out with the first dawn of the morning. They are at least as brave, and more adventuresome. But this may perhaps proceed from a want of forethought, which prevents their seeing a danger till it be present. When present, they do not go through it with more coolness or steadiness than the whites. They are more ardent after their female: but love seems with them to be more an eager desire, than a tender delicate mixture of sentiment and sensation. Their griefs are transient. Those numberless afflictions, which render it doubtful whether heaven has given life to us in mercy or in wrath, are less felt, and sooner forgotten with them. In general, their existence appears to participate more of sensation than reflection. To this must be ascribed their disposition to sleep when abstracted from their diversions, and unemployed in labour. An animal whose body is at rest, and who does not reflect, must be disposed to sleep of course. Comparing them by their faculties of memory, reason, and imagination, it appears to me, that in memory they are equal to the whites; in reason much inferior, as I think one could scarcely be found capable of tracing and comprehending the investigations of Euclid; and that in imagination they are dull, tasteless, and anomalous. . . . Some have been liberally educated, and all have lived in countries where the arts and sciences are cultivated to a considerable degree, and have had before their eyes samples of the best works from abroad. The Indians, with no advantages of this kind, will often carve figures on their pipes not destitute of design and merit. They will crayon out an animal, a plant, or a country, so as to prove the existence of a germ in their minds which only wants cultivation. They astonish you with strokes of the most sublime oratory; such as prove their reason and sentiment strong, their imagination glowing and elevated. But never yet could I find that a black had uttered a thought above the level of plain narration; never see even an elementary trait of painting or sculpture. In music they are more generally gifted than the whites with accurate ears for tune and time, and they have been found capable of imagining a small catch. Whether they will be equal to the composition of a more extensive run of melody, or of complicated harmony, is yet to be proved. Misery is often the parent of the most affecting touches in poetry.—Among the blacks is misery enough, God knows, but no poetry. . . .

. . . I advance it therefore as a suspicion only, that the blacks, whether originally a distinct race, or made distinct by time and circumstances, are inferior to the whites in the endowments both of body and mind. It is not against experience to suppose, that different species of the same genus, or varieties of the same species, may possess different qualifications. Will not a lover of natural history then, one who views the gradations in all the races of animals with the eye of philosophy, excuse an effort to keep those in the department of man as distinct as nature has formed them? This unfortunate difference of colour, and perhaps of faculty, is a powerful obstacle to the emancipation of these people. Many of their advocates, while they wish to vindicate the liberty of human nature, are anxious also to preserve its dignity and beauty. . . .

Introduction to Documents 12 and 13

Benjamin Banneker was a free black living in Maryland. Although his early education was minimal, as an adult he taught himself trigonometry and calculus. In 1791 he served as assistant surveyor in laying out the boundaries for the newly created District of Columbia. That same year, he used his mathematical abilities to do the calculations for an astronomical almanac (people relied on such works to learn the timing of natural phenomena, such as tides, seasons, and lengths of days). Banneker's almanac went through twenty-nine editions and sold in cities throughout the Middle Atlantic states. Having read the *Notes on the State of Virginia*, Banneker sent a copy of his almanac to then secretary of state Thomas Jefferson, along with the following letter. Jefferson's reply to Banneker follows.

DOCUMENT 12 *Letter from Benjamin Banneker to Thomas Jefferson*

Maryland, Baltimore County, Near Ellicott's Lower Mills August 19th. 1791.

Thomas Jefferson Secretary of State.

Sir, I am fully sensible of the greatness of that freedom which I take with you on the present occasion; a liberty which Seemed to me Scarcely allowable, when I reflected on that distinguished, and dignifyed station in which you Stand; and the almost general prejudice and prepossession which is so previlent in the world against those of my complexion. . . .

Sir I freely and Chearfully acknowledge, that I am of the African race, and, in that colour which is natural to them of the deepest dye,* and it is under a Sense of the most profound gratitude to the Supreme Ruler of the universe, that I now confess to you, that I am not under that State of tyrannical thraldom, and inhuman captivity, to which too many of my brethren are doomed; but that I have abundantly tasted of the fruition of those blessings which proceed from that free and unequalled liberty with which you are favoured and which I hope you will willingly allow you have received from the immediate Hand of that Being from whom proceedeth every good and perfect gift.

Sir, Suffer me to recall to your mind that time in which the Arms and tyranny of the British Crown were exerted with every powerful effort, in order to reduce you to a State of Servitude; look back I intreat you on the variety of dangers to which you were exposed,

*My Father was brought here a Slave from Africa.

reflect on that time in which every human aid appeared unavailable, and in which even hope and fortitude wore the aspect of inability to the Conflict, and you cannot but be led to a Serious and grateful Sense of your miraculous and providential preservation; You cannot but acknowledge, that the present freedom and tranquillity which you enjoy you have mercifully received, and that it is the peculiar blessing of Heaven.

This, Sir, was a time in which you clearly saw into the injustice of a State of Slavery, and in which you had Just apprehensions of the horrors of its condition, it was now Sir, that your abhorrence thereof was so excited, that you publickly held forth this true and invaluable doctrine, which is worthy to be recorded and remembered in all Succeeding ages. "We hold these truths to be Self evident, that all men are created equal, and that they are endowed by their creator with certain inalienable rights, that amongst these are life, liberty, and the persuit of happiness."

Here, Sir, was a time in which your tender feelings for your selves engaged you thus to declare, you were then impressed with proper ideas of the great valuation of liberty, and the free possession of those blessings to which you were entitled by nature; but Sir how pitiable is it to reflect, that altho you were so fully convinced of the benevolence of the Father of mankind, and of his equal and impartial distribution of those rights and privileges which he had conferred upon them, that you should at the Same time counter-act his mercies, in detaining by fraud and violence so numerous a part of my brethren un-der groaning captivity and cruel oppression, that you should at the Same time be found guilty of that most criminal act, which you professedly detested in others, with respect to yourselves.

Sir, I suppose that your knowledge of the situation of my brethren is too extensive to need a recital here; neither shall I presume to prescribe methods by which they may be re-lieved, otherwise than by recommending to you, and all others, to wean yourselves from those narrow prejudices which you have imbibed with respect to them, and as Job pro-posed to his friends "Put your Souls in their Souls' stead," thus shall your hearts be en-larged with kindness and benevolence towards them, and thus shall you need neither the direction of myself or others in what manner to proceed herein.

And now, Sir, altho my Sympathy and affection for my brethren hath caused my en-largement thus far, I ardently hope that your candour and generosity will plead with you in my behalf, when I make known to you, that it was not originally my design; but that having taken up my pen in order to direct to you as a present, a copy of an Almanack which I have calculated for the Succeeding year, I was unexpectedly and unavoidably led thereto. . . .

And now Sir, I . . . Shall conclude and Subscribe my Self with the most profound respect,

Your most Obedient humble Servant

Benjamin Banneker.

📝 DOCUMENT 13 *Reply of Thomas Jefferson to Benjamin Banneker*

Philadelphia, Aug. 30. 1791.

SIR, I Thank you sincerely for your letter of the 19th instant and for the Almanac it contained. No body wishes more than I do to see such proofs as you exhibit, that nature has given to our black brethren, talents equal to those of the other colors of men, and that the appearance of a want of them is owing merely to the degraded condition of their exis-tence, both in Africa & America. I can add with truth, that no body wishes more ardently to see a good system commenced for raising the condition both of their body & mind to what it ought to be, as fast as the imbecility of their present existence, and other circumstances which cannot be neglected, will admit.

I have taken the liberty of sending your Almanac to Monsieur de Condorcet, Secretary of the Academy of Sciences at Paris, and member of the Philanthropic society, because I considered it as a document to which your whole colour had a right for their justification against the doubts which have been entertained of them.

I am with great esteem, Sir your most obed[t] humble serv[t].

Thomas Jefferson.

QUESTIONS

Defining Terms

Identify in the context of the chapter each of the following:

Continental Congress   Methodists
Lord Dunmore   July 2, 1776
Galloway's "Plan of Union"   "self-evident truths"
Samuel Seabury   John Wesley
Tory   Benjamin Banneker

Probing the Sources

1. Present arguments for and against Galloway's "Plan of Union."
2. Compare Seabury's arguments for cooperation with Britain with Paine's arguments for independence. Which do you find most persuasive? Why?
3. Compare Paine and Wesley's comments concerning slavery and liberty. Which do you find most persuasive? Why?
4. Compare the ideas and the rhetoric in Paine's *Common Sense* and Jefferson's Declaration of Independence? Account for the similarities and the differences.

Interpreting the Sources

1. Discuss the metaphors and rhetorical devices used by the various authors. How do you account for their language and tone?
2. What are the "self-evident truths" mentioned in the Declaration of Independence? Are these truths self-evident to you? Justify your response.
3. Can Jefferson's ideas in the Declaration be reconciled with his comment in *Notes on the State of Virginia?* Justify your answer.
4. Would you have supported the patriots or the Loyalists? Justify your response.

ADDITIONAL READING

Two of the better introductions to this period are Peter D. G. Thomas, *Tea Party to Independence: The Third Phase of the American Revolution, 1773–1776* (1991), and Benson Bobrick, *Angel in the Whirlwind: The Triumph of the American Revolution* (1997). An interesting account of the drafting of the Declaration of Independence is Pauline Maier's *American Scripture: Making the Declaration of Independence* (1997). John C. Dann, ed., *The Revolution Remembered: Eyewitness Accounts of the War for Independence* (1980), includes an interesting sample of primary materials from the Revolutionary era. For a stirring account of Paine's struggles for political equality, see Eric Foner, *Tom Paine and Revolutionary America* (1975). Edmund Morgan's *American Slavery, American Freedom* (1975) offers an interpretation that links black slavery to white equality. Among the more provocative interpretations of the period are Bernard Bailyn, *The Ideological Origins of the American Revolution* (1967), Gordon Wood, *The Radicalism of the American Revolution* (1992), and Ronald Hoffman and Peter J. Albert, ed., *The Transforming Hand of Revolution: Reconsidering the American Revolution as a Social Movement* (1996).

Forming a More Perfect Union: The Constitution of 1787 versus Friends, Foes, and the Disfranchised

HISTORICAL CONTEXT

Although Al Gore led George W. Bush in the popular vote by more than one-half million votes, owing to the closeness of the Election of 2000 in the Electoral College, the winner of the presidency was to be decided by the results in the state of Florida. The Secretary of State of Florida certified that Bush won the state by several hundred votes. The Gore camp, however, questioned the accuracy of how the machines had counted (or not counted) ballots in several counties and asked for a manual recount of the ballots in these areas. When the Florida Supreme Court allowed this recount to begin, the Bush supporters asked the U.S. Supreme Court to intervene and stop it. In a 5 to 4 decision, the U.S. Supreme Court decided that there was not time to conduct a recount that would be fair to both parties. In explaining this decision, the five judges who wrote the majority opinion reminded the nation that "the individual citizen has no federal constitutional right to vote for electors for the President of the United States unless and until the state legislature chooses a statewide election as a means to implement its power to appoint members of the Electoral College." The Court's intervention and decision settled the outcome of the election, but it confused many Americans who asked, "Can this be true? Do we not live in a democracy?"

Part of the national confusion over the Election of 2000 stemmed from public misconceptions regarding the content of the U.S. Constitution. Critics have suggested that the Constitution of 1787 is among the best known and least understood documents in American history. If this accusation contains even a glimmer of truth, it is only because we have forgotten one of the greatest arguments that was ever debated in this hemisphere. A central objective of this chapter is to review this great debate that resulted in the production and ratification of the Constitution of 1787.

The Constitution of 1787 was not the first constitution of the United States. During and immediately after the American Revolution, the supreme law of the land was known as the Articles of Confederation. Drafted in 1777 by the same body that produced the Declaration of Independence, the Articles established a "league of friendship" among the 13 former English colonies. Under this constitution, each state retained its sovereignty, but sent representatives to a unicameral national Congress that had powers to conduct foreign affairs, declare war, maintain an army and navy, create a post office, and arbitrate disputes between states. However, Congress under the Articles did not have the power to collect taxes or to regulate interstate trade. Moreover, at this time the United States had neither an independent executive branch nor a national court.

For over two hundred years scholars, pundits, journalists and politicians have argued over the ability of the U.S. government under the Articles to meet the needs of the people. All agreed that this was a difficult time economically. Some Americans, however, especially those who later would be known as Anti-Federalists, insisted that the hard times were understandable and temporary. They noted that for more than a century, almost all of the clients with whom the American colonials conducted business were British subjects. Since independence from England severed these business connections, it was not surprising that the American people would suffer through a period of economic hardship until other commercial relationships could be established. To these Anti-Federalists, however, the worst times had passed and the future of the infant nation under the Articles appeared bright.

Other Americans, including those who later would support the new constitution, were less optimistic about the ability of the republic to recover from the economic quagmire of the 1780s. Their concerns multiplied in 1786 when an armed rebellion against governmental authorities broke out in western Massachusetts. Led by the Revolutionary War veteran Captain Daniel Shays, a band of 1,500 discontented and indebted rebels stormed the jails in order to liberate imprisoned debtors and used physical force to prevent the courts from foreclosing on mortgages. These acts of resistance persuaded many that strong measures were needed in order to restore the social order. Frustrated at the lingering depression and fearful of the spread of mob violence, increasing numbers of Americans advocated strengthening the authority of the central government so that it would be able to deal with the growing national crises.

In September 1786, a group of concerned Americans from five states gathered in Annapolis to discuss ways to resolve the national troubles. From this convention came a call for each of the states to send delegates to another convention that would meet in Philadelphia the following May. According to this call, the purpose of the Philadelphia meeting was to "take into consideration the situation . . . [and] to devise such further provisions as shall appear to them necessary to render the constitution of the federal government adequate to the exigencies of the Union." Congress tacitly accepted the Annapolis proposal and asked the states to send delegates to the Philadelphia gathering. According to the instructions of Congress, however, this convention was being called "for the sole and express purpose of revising the Articles of Confederation." To legally amend the Articles, all thirteen states would have to accept the proposed changes. Twelve states responded to the call of Congress and sent delegates to Philadelphia. The state of Rhode Island, however, refused to participate.

THE DOCUMENTS
Introduction to Documents 1, 2, and 3

Selections from the Constitution of 1787

Between May 25 and September 17, 1787, the 55 delegates who arrived in Philadelphia presented several plans of governance, debated the merits of each plan, negotiated compromises, and drafted a new constitution that they announced would take effect when ratified by nine states. After nearly 17 weeks of work these "founding fathers" ultimately settled on a document that was both modest in size and ambitious in scope. Excluding the names of the signers, the Constitution of 1787 contained about 4,400 words. More than one-half of these words were included in Article I, the section that detailed the composition and powers of Congress. Article II, the next largest section with about one thousand words, specified the selection process and powers of the President. The remainder of the Constitution, Articles III, IV, V, VI, and VII together contained barely another one thousand words. In these sections, the founders defined the powers of the Judiciary, discussed the relationships between the national and the state governments, outlined the amendment and ratification processes, and established other miscellaneous guidelines for citizens and officeholders.

About one-half of the original Constitution of 1787 is included in the following documents. For your convenience, the selections are not presented in their traditional order. Instead, they are organized into three thematic categories. Document 1 includes those sections of the Constitution that present the eligibility, requirements and selection processes for members of Congress, for the president and vice president, and for members of the Court. Document 2 includes those sections that delineate the powers of the legislative and executive branches. The final selections in Document 3 provide the amendment and ratification rules established by the founders. (The sections of the constitution that have been amended and thus are no longer binding are written in italics. The spelling in all the documents in this chapter has been modernized).

As you read these pages, for each clause ask yourself two basic questions, (1) Why do you think this statement was included in the Constitution? (2) What groups would have supported or opposed this statement? Consider, for example, the varying perspectives of large states/small states, merchants/farmers, slaveholders/slaves and men/women as you reflect on these passages.

DOCUMENT 1   *The Constitution of 1787: Rules Regarding Eligibility and Election to Office*

For Members of Congress: selections from Article I, Sections 1, 2, 3, 4, and 5

Section. 1. All legislative Powers herein granted shall be vested in a Congress of the United States, which shall consist of a Senate and House of Representatives.

Section. 2. The House of Representatives shall be composed of Members chosen every second Year by the People of the several States, and the Electors in each State shall have the Qualifications requisite for Electors of the most, numerous Branch of the State Legislature.

No Person shall be a Representative who shall not have attained to the Age of twenty five Years, and been seven Years a Citizen of the United States, and who shall not, when elected, be an Inhabitant of that State in which he shall be chosen.

Representatives and direct Taxes shall be apportioned among the several States which may be included within this Union, according to their respective Numbers, which shall be determined by adding to the whole Number of free Persons, including those bound to Service for a Term of Years, and excluding Indians not taxed, three fifths of all other Persons. The actual Enumeration shall be made within three Years after the first Meeting of the Congress of the United States, and within every subsequent Term of ten Years, in such Manner as they shall by Law direct. The Number of Representatives shall not exceed one for every thirty Thousand, but each State shall have at Least one Representative; and until such enumeration shall be made, the State of New Hampshire shall be entitled to choose three, Massachusetts eight, Rhode-Island and Providence Plantations one, Connecticut five, New-York six, New Jersey four, Pennsylvania eight, Delaware one, Maryland six, Virginia ten, North Carolina five, South Carolina five, and Georgia three.

When vacancies happen in the Representation from any State, the Executive Authority thereof shall issue Writs of Election to fill such Vacancies.

The House of Representatives shall choose their Speaker and other Officers; and shall have the sole Power of Impeachment.

Section. 3. The Senate of the United States shall be composed of two Senators from each State, *chosen by the Legislature thereof* for six Years; and each Senator shall have one Vote. . . .

No Person shall be a Senator who shall not have attained to the Age of thirty Years, and been nine Years a Citizen of the United States, and who shall not, when elected, be an Inhabitant of that State for which he shall be chosen. . . .

Section. 4. The Times, Places and Manner of holding Elections for Senators and Representatives, shall be prescribed in each State by the Legislature thereof; but the Congress may at any time by Law make or alter such Regulations, except as to the Places of choosing Senators.

The Congress shall assemble at least once in every Year, *and such Meeting shall be on the first Monday in December,* unless they shall by Law appoint a different Day.

Section. 5. Each House shall be the Judge of the Elections, Returns and Qualifications of its own Members, and a Majority of each shall constitute a Quorum to do Business; but a smaller Number may adjourn from day to day, and may be authorized to compel the Attendance of absent Members, in such Manner, and under such Penalties as each House may provide.

Each House may determine the Rules of its Proceedings, punish its Members for disorderly Behavior, and, with the Concurrence of two thirds, expel a Member. . . .

For the President and Vice President—selections from Article II, Section 1:

Section. 1. The executive Power shall be vested in a President of the United States of America. He shall hold his Office during the Term of four Years, and, together with the Vice President, chosen for the same Term, be elected, as follows:

Each State shall appoint, in such Manner as the Legislature thereof may direct, a Number of Electors, equal to the whole Number of Senators and Representatives to which the State may be entitled in the Congress: but no Senator or Representative, or Person holding an Office of Trust or Profit under the United States, shall be appointed an Elector.

The Electors shall meet in their respective States, and vote by Ballot for two Persons, of whom one at least shall not be an Inhabitant of the same State with themselves. And they shall make a List of all the Persons voted for, and of the Number of Votes for each; which List they shall sign and certify, and transmit sealed to the Seat of the Government of the United States, directed to the President of the Senate. The President of the Senate shall, in the Presence of the

Senate and House of Representatives, open all the Certificates, and the Votes shall then be counted. The Person having the greatest Number of Votes shall be the President, if such Number be a Majority of the whole Number of Electors appointed; and if there be more than one who have such Majority, and have an equal Number of Votes, then the House of Representatives shall immediately choose by Ballot one of them for President; and if no Person have a Majority, then from the five highest on the List the said House shall in like Manner choose the President. But in choosing the President, the Votes shall be taken by States, the Representation from each State having one Vote: A quorum for this purpose shall consist of a Member or Members from two thirds of the States, and a Majority of all the States shall be necessary to a Choice. In every Case, after the Choice of the President, the Person having the greatest Number of Votes of the Electors shall be the Vice President. But if there should remain two or more who have equal Votes, the Senate shall choose from them by Ballot the Vice President.

The Congress may determine the Time of choosing the Electors, and the Day on which they shall give their Votes; which Day shall be the same throughout the United States.

No Person except a natural born Citizen, or a Citizen of the United States, at the time of the Adoption of this Constitution, shall be eligible to the Office of President; neither shall any Person be eligible to that Office who shall not have attained to the Age of thirty five Years, and been fourteen Years a Resident within the United States.

In Case of the Removal of the President from Office, or of his Death, Resignation, or Inability to discharge the Powers and Duties of the said Office, the Same shall devolve on the Vice President, and the Congress may by Law provide for the Case of Removal, Death, Resignation or Inability, both of the President and Vice President, declaring what Officer shall then act as President, and such Officer shall act accordingly, until the Disability be removed, or a President shall be elected.

For members of the Supreme Court—selections from Article III, Section 1:

Section. 1. The judicial Power of the United States shall be vested in one supreme Court, and in such inferior Courts as the Congress may from time to time ordain and establish. The Judges, both of the supreme and inferior Courts, shall hold their Offices during good Behavior, and shall, at stated Times, receive for their Services a Compensation, which shall not be diminished during their Continuance in Office.

Article IV includes one additional requirement that pertains to all officerholders:

The Senators and Representatives before mentioned, and the Members of the several State Legislatures, and all executive and judicial Officers, both of the United States and of the several States., shall be bound by Oath or Affirmation, to support this Constitution; but no religious Test shall ever be required as a Qualification to any Office or public Trust under the United States.

DOCUMENT 2   *The Constitution of 1787: The Delineated and Restricted Powers of Congress and of the President*

Powers of Congress—selections from Article I, Sections 8 and 9 and Article IV, Sections 1, 3, and 4:

Section. 8. The Congress shall have Power To lay and collect Taxes, Duties, Imposts and Excises, to pay the Debts and provide for the common Defense and general Welfare of the United States; but all Duties, Imposts and Excises shall be uniform throughout the United States:

To borrow Money on the credit of the United States;

To regulate Commerce with foreign Nations, and among the several States, and with the Indian Tribes;

To establish an uniform Rule of Naturalization, and uniform Laws on the subject of Bankruptcies throughout the United States;

To coin Money, regulate the Value thereof, and of foreign Coin, and fix the Standard of Weights and Measures;

To provide for the Punishment of counterfeiting the Securities and current Coin of the United States;

To establish Post Offices and post Roads;

To promote the Progress of Science and useful Arts, by securing for Limited Times to Authors and Inventors the exclusive Right to their respective Writings and Discoveries;

To constitute Tribunals inferior to the supreme Court;

To define and punish Piracies and Felonies committed on the high Seas, and Offences against the Law of Nations;

To declare War, grant Letters of Marque and Reprisal, and make Rules concerning Captures on Land and Water;

To raise and support Armies, but no Appropriation of Money to that Use shall be for a longer Term than two Years;

To provide and maintain a Navy;

To make Rules for the Government and Regulation of the land and naval Forces;

To provide for calling forth the Militia to execute the Laws of the Union, suppress Insurrections and repel Invasions;

To provide for organizing, arming, and disciplining, the Militia, and for governing such Part of them as may be employed in the Service of the United States, reserving to the States respectively, the Appointment of the Officers, and the Authority of training the Militia according to the discipline prescribed by Congress;

To exercise exclusive Legislation in all Cases whatsoever, over such District (not exceeding ten Miles square) as may, by Cession of particular States, and the Acceptance of Congress, become the Seat of the Government of the United States, and to exercise like Authority over all Places purchased by the Consent of the Legislature of the State in which the Same shall be, for the Erection of Forts, Magazines, Arsenals, dock-Yards, and other needful Buildings;—And

To make all Laws which shall be necessary and proper for carrying into Execution the foregoing Powers, and all other Powers vested by this Constitution in the Government of the United States, or in any Department or Officer thereof.

Section. 9. The Migration or Importation of such Persons as any of the States now existing shall think proper to admit, shall not be prohibited by the Congress prior to the Year one thousand eight hundred and eight, but a Tax or duty may be imposed on such Importation, not exceeding ten dollars for each Person.

The Privilege of the Writ of Habeas Corpus shall not be suspended, unless when in Cases of Rebellion or Invasion the public Safety may require it.

No Bill of Attainder or ex post facto Law shall be passed.

No Capitation, or other direct, Tax shall be laid, unless in Proportion to the Census or enumeration herein before directed to be taken.

No Tax or Duty shall be laid on Articles exported from any State.

No Preference shall be given by any Regulation of Commerce or Revenue to the Ports of one State over those of another, nor shall Vessels bound to, or from, one State, be obliged to enter, clear, or pay Duties in another.

No Money shall be drawn from the Treasury, but in Consequence of Appropriations made by Law; and a regular Statement and Account of the Receipts and Expenditures of all public Money shall be published from time to time.

No Title of Nobility shall be granted by the United States: And no Person holding any Office of Profit or Trust under them, shall, without the Consent of the Congress, accept of any present, Emolument, Office, or Title, of any kind whatever, from any King, Prince, or foreign State.

Article IV:

Section. 1. Full Faith and Credit shall be given in each State to the public Acts, Records, and judicial Proceedings of every other State. And the Congress may by general Laws prescribe the Manner in which such Acts, Records and Proceedings shall be proved, and the Effect thereof.

Section. 3. New States may be admitted by the Congress into this Union; but no new State shall be formed or erected within the Jurisdiction of any other State; nor any State be formed by the Junction of two or more States, or Parts of States, without the Consent of the Legislatures of the States concerned as well as of the Congress.

The Congress shall have Power to dispose of and make all needful Rules and Regulations respecting the Territory or other Property belonging to the United States; and nothing in this Constitution shall be so construed as to Prejudice any Claims of the United States, or of any particular State.

Section. 4. The United States shall guarantee to every State in this Union a Republican Form of Government, and shall protect each of them against Invasion; and on Application of the Legislature, or of the Executive (when the Legislature cannot be convened), against domestic Violence.

Powers of the president—selections from Article II, Sections 2 and 3:

Section. 2. The President shall be Commander in Chief of the Army and Navy of the United States, and of the Militia of the several States, when called into the actual Service of the United States; he may require the Opinion, in writing, of the principal Officer in each of the executive Departments, upon any Subject relating to the Duties of their respective Offices, and he shall have Power to grant Reprieves and Pardons for Offences against the United States, except in Cases of Impeachment.

He shall have Power, by and with the Advice and Consent of the Senate, to make Treaties, provided two thirds of the Senators present concur; and he shall nominate, and by and with the Advice and Consent of the Senate, shall appoint Ambassadors, other public Ministers and Consuls, Judges of the supreme Court, and all other Officers of the United States, whose Appointments are not herein otherwise provided for, and which shall be established by Law: but the Congress may by Law vest the Appointment of such inferior Officers, as they think proper, in the President alone, in the Courts of Law, or in the Heads of Departments.

The President shall have Power to fill up all Vacancies that may happen during the Recess of the Senate, by granting Commissions which shall expire at the End of their next Session.

Section. 3. He shall from time to time give to the Congress Information of the State of the Union, and recommend to their Consideration such Measures as he shall judge necessary and expedient; he may, on extraordinary Occasions, convene both Houses, or either of them, and in Case of Disagreement between them, with Respect to the Time of Adjournment, he may adjourn them to such Time as he shall think proper; he shall receive Ambassadors and other public Ministers; he shall take Care that the Laws be faithfully executed, and shall Commission all the Officers of the United States.

DOCUMENT 3 *The Constitution of 1787: Amendment and Ratification Rules—Selections from Article V and Article VII*

Article. V. The Congress, whenever two thirds of both Houses shall deem it necessary, shall propose Amendments to this Constitution, or, on the Application of the Legislatures of two thirds of the several States, shall call a Convention for proposing Amendments, which, in either Case, shall be valid to all Intents and Purposes, as Part of this Constitution, when ratified by the Legislatures of three fourths of the several States, or by

Conventions in three fourths thereof, as the one or the other Mode of Ratification may be proposed by the Congress; Provided that no Amendment which may be made prior to the Year One thousand eight hundred and eight shall in any Manner affect the first and fourth Clauses in the Ninth Section of the first Article; and that no State, without its Consent, shall be deprived of its equal Suffrage in the Senate.

Article. VII. The Ratification of the Conventions of nine States, shall be sufficient for the Establishment of this Constitution between the States so ratifying the Same.

Introduction to Documents 4 and 5

The Anti-Federalists: Arguments against Ratification

Between 1787 and 1789, the critics of the new government, known as "Anti-Federalists," waged a vigorous campaign against the ratification of the Constitution of 1787. Documents 4 and 5 include selections from two outspoken foes of the new constitution, Patrick Henry and Mercy Otis Warren. Both Henry and Warren had impeccable credentials as revolutionary patriots. Renowned for his flamboyant oratory, Henry had served Virginia as a member of the Continental Congress, and later as Governor. The excerpts printed below are taken from the speeches he delivered on June 4 and 5, 1788, at the Virginia State Ratifying Convention. Document 5 contains excerpts from Warren's political pamphlet entitled "Observations on the New Constitution and on the Federal and State Conventions by a Columbian Patriot." Like Henry, during the Revolution Warren was an unashamed patriot who used her literary skills to lampoon the British and undermine Loyalist sentiment. Later in life, she would write History of the Rise, Progress and Termination of the American Revolution (1805), an account that included some critical comments about President John Adams and provoked his retort: "History is not the province of the ladies."

According to Henry and Warren, what were the major problems with the Constitution of 1787? In your estimation, how valid were their arguments?

DOCUMENT 4 *From the Speeches of Patrick Henry in the Virginia State Ratifying Convention*

Mr. Chairman.—The public mind, as well as my own, is extremely uneasy at the proposed change of Government. . . . A year ago the minds of our citizens were at perfect repose. Before the meeting of the late Federal Convention at Philadelphia, a general peace, and an universal tranquility prevailed in this country;—but since that period [the people] are exceedingly uneasy and disquieted. . . . This proposal of altering our Federal Government is of a most alarming nature: . . . you ought to be extremely cautious, watchful, jealous of your liberty; for instead of securing your rights you may lose them forever. . . .

I would make this enquiry of those worthy characters who composed a part of the late Federal Convention. I am sure they were fully impressed with the necessity of forming a great consolidated Government, instead of a confederation. That this is a consolidated Government is demonstrably clear, and the danger of such a Government, is, to my mind, very striking. I have the highest veneration of those Gentlemen,—but, Sir, give me leave to demand, what right had they to say, We, the People. My political curiosity, exclusive of my anxious solicitude for the public welfare, leads me to ask who authorised them to speak the language of, We, the People, instead of We, the States? . . . That they exceeded their power is perfectly clear. . . . The Federal Convention ought to have amended the old system—for this purpose they were solely delegated: The object of their mission extended to no other consideration. You must therefore forgive the solicitation of one unworthy member, to know what danger could have arisen under the present confederation, and what are the causes of this proposal to change our Government. . . .

Is it necessary for your liberty, that you should abandon those great rights by the adoption of this system? Is the relinquishment of the trial by jury, and the liberty of the press, necessary for your liberty? Will the abandonment of your most sacred rights tend to the security of your liberty? Liberty [is] the greatest of all earthly blessings—give us that precious jewel, and you may take every thing else. . . .

In some parts of the plan before you, the great rights of freemen are endangered, in other parts absolutely taken away. How does your trial by jury stand? In civil cases gone—not sufficiently secured in criminal—this best privilege is gone: But we are told that we need not fear, because those in power being our Representatives, will not abuse the powers we put in their hands: I am not well versed in history, but I will submit to your recollection, whether liberty has been destroyed most often by the licentiousness of the people, or by the tyranny of rulers. . . . My great objection to this Government is, that it does not leave us the means of defending our rights; or, of waging war against tyrants: It is urged by some Gentlemen, that this new plan will bring us an acquisition of strength, an army, and the militia of the States: This is an idea extremely ridiculous: Gentlemen cannot be in earnest. This acquisition will trample on your fallen liberty: Let my beloved Americans guard against that fatal lethargy that has pervaded the universe: Have we the means of resisting disciplined armies? when our only defense, the militia is put into the hands of Congress? The Honorable Gentleman said, that great danger would ensue if the Convention rose without adopting this system: I ask, where is that danger? I see none: Other Gentlemen have told us within these walls, that the Union is gone—or, that the Union will be gone: Is not this trifling with the judgment of their fellow citizens? Till they tell us the ground of their fears, I will consider them as imaginary: I rose to make enquiry where those dangers were; they could make no answer: I believe I never shall have that answer: Is there a disposition in the people of this country to revolt against the dominion of laws? Has there been a single tumult in Virginia? . . .

To encourage us to adopt it, they tell us, that there is a plain easy way of getting amendments: When I come to contemplate this part, I suppose that I am mad, or, that my countrymen are so: The way to amendment, is, in my conception, shut. . . . For four of the smallest States, that do not collectively contain one-tenth part of the population of the United States, may obstruct the most salutary and necessary amendments: Nay, in these four States, six-tenths of the people may reject these amendments; and suppose, that amendments shall be opposed to amendments (which is highly probable) is it possible, that three-fourths can ever agree to the same amendments? A bare majority in these four small States may hinder the adoption of amendments; so that we may fairly and justly conclude, that one-twentieth part of the American people, may prevent the removal of the most grievous inconveniences and oppression, by refusing to accede to amendments. A trifling minority may reject the most salutary amendments. Is this an easy mode of securing the public liberty? It is, Sir, a most fearful situation, when the most contemptible minority can prevent the alteration of the most oppressive Government; for it may in many respects prove to be such: Is this the spirit of republicanism? . . .

If we admit this Consolidated Government it will be because we like a great splendid one. Some way or other we must be a great and mighty empire; we must have an army, and a navy, and a number of things: When the American spirit was in its youth, the language of America was different. Liberty, Sir, was then the primary object. We are descended from a people whose Government was founded on liberty. . . . But now, Sir, the American spirit, assisted by the ropes and chains of consolidation, is about to convert this country to a powerful and mighty empire: If you make the citizens of this country agree to become the subjects of one great consolidated empire of America, your Government will not have sufficient energy to keep them together: Such a Government is incompatible with the genius of republicanism: There will be no checks, no real balances, in this Government. . . . This Constitution is said to have beautiful features; but when I come to examine these features, Sir, they appear to me horridly frightful: Among other deformities, it has an awful squinting; it squints towards monarchy; And does not this raise indignation in the breast of every American? Your President may easily become King: Your Senate is so imperfectly constructed that your dearest rights may be sacrificed by what may be a small minority; and a very small minority may continue forever unchangeably this Government, although horridly defective: Where are your checks in this Government?

DOCUMENT 5   *Mercy Otis Warren, Observations on the New Constitution, and on the Federal and State Conventions by a Columbian Patriot*

. . . On these shores freedom has planted her standard, dipped in the purple tide that flowed from the veins of her martyred heroes; and here every uncorrupted American yet hopes to see it supported by the vigor, the justice, the wisdom and unanimity of the people, in spite of the deep-laid plots, the secret intrigues, or the bold effrontery of those interested and avaricious adventurers for place, who intoxicated with the ideas of distinction and preferment, have prostrated every worthy principle beneath the shrine of ambition. Yet these are the men who tell us republicanism is dwindled into theory—that we are incapable of enjoying our liberties—and that we must have a master. . . .

All writers on government agree, and the feelings of the human mind witness the truth of these political axioms, that man is born free and possessed of certain unalienable rights—that government is instituted for the protection, safety, and happiness of the people, and not for the profit, honor, or private interest of any man, family, or class of men—That the origin of all power is in the people, and that they have an incontestable right to check the creatures of their own creation, vested with certain powers to guard the life, liberty and property of the community . . . [Warren then gives her specific objections to the new constitution.]

1.   [A]nnual election is the basis of responsibility.—Man is not immediately corrupted, but power without limitation, or amenability, may endanger the brightest virtue—whereas a frequent return to the bar of their Constituents is the strongest check against the corruptions to which men are liable. . . .

2.   There is no security in the [new] system, either for the rights of conscience, or the liberty of the Press. . . .

3.   There are no well defined limits of the Judiciary Powers, they seem to be left as a boundless ocean. . . .

4.   The Executive and the Legislative are so dangerously blended as to give just cause of alarm. . . .

5.   The abolition of trial by jury in civil cases. . . .

6.   . . . Standing armies have been the nursery of vice and the bane of liberty from the Roman legions . . . to the planting of the British cohorts in the capitals of America:—By the edicts of authority vested in the sovereign power by the proposed constitution, the militia of the country, the bulwark of defense, and the security of national liberty is no longer under the control of civil authority; but at the prescript of the Monarch, or

the aristocracy, they may either be employed to extort the enormous sums tha necessary to support the civil list—to maintain the regalia of power—and the spl the most useless part of the community, or they may be sent into foreign countrie fulfillment of treaties, stipulated by the President and two thirds of the Senate.

7. Notwithstanding the delusory promise to guarantee a Republican form ernment to every State in the Union—If the most discerning eye could disco\ meaning at all in the engagement, there are no resources left for the support of ii..cinai government, or the liquidation of the debts of the State. Every source of revenue is in the monopoly of Congress, and if the several legislatures in their enfeebled state, should against their own feelings be necessitated to attempt a dry tax for the payment of their debts, and the support of internal police, even this may be required for the purposes of the general government.

8. As the new Congress are empowered to determine their own salaries, the requisitions for this purpose may not be very moderate, and the drain for public moneys will probably rise past all calculation. . . .

9. There is no provision for a rotation, nor any thing to prevent the perpetuity of office in the same hands for life; which by a little well timed bribery, will probably be done, to the exclusion of men of the best abilities from their share in the offices of government. . . .

10. The inhabitants of the United States, are liable to be dragged from the vicinity of their own county, or state, to answer to the litigious or unjust suit of an adversary, on the most distant borders of the Continent: in short the appellate jurisdiction of the Supreme Federal Court, includes an unwarrantable stretch of power over the liberty, life, and property of the subject, through the wide Continent of America.

11. One Representative to thirty thousand inhabitants is a very inadequate representation: and every man who is not lost to all sense of freedom to his country, must reprobate the idea of Congress altering by law, or on any pretence whatever, interfering with any regulations for the time, places, and manner of choosing our own Representatives.

12. If the sovereignty of America is designed to be elective, the circumscribing the votes to only ten electors in this State, and the same proportion in all the others, is nearly tantamount to the exclusion of the voice of the people in the choice of their first magistrate. It is vesting the choice solely in an aristocratic junto. . . .

13. A Senate chosen for six years will, in most instances, be an appointment for life, as the influence of such a body over the minds of the people will be coequal to the extensive powers with which they are vested, and they will not only forget, but be forgotten by their constituents—a branch of the Supreme Legislature thus set beyond all responsibility is totally repugnant to every principle of a free government.

14. There is no provision by a bill of rights to guard against the dangerous encroachments of power in too many instances to be named. . . .

15. The difficulty, if not impracticability, of exercising the equal and equitable powers of government by a single legislature over an extent of territory that reaches from the Mississippi to the Western lakes, and from them to the Atlantic ocean, is an insuperable objection to the adoption of the new system. . . .

16. It is an undisputed fact, that not one legislature in the United States had the most distant idea when they first appointed members for a convention, entirely commercial, or when they afterwards authorized them to consider on some amendments of the Federal union, that they would without any warrant from their constituents, presume on so bold and daring a stride, as ultimately to destroy the state governments. . . .

17. The first appearance of the article which declares the ratification of nine states sufficient for the establishment of the new system, wears the face of dissension,

is a subversion of the union of the Confederated States, and tends to the introduction of anarchy and civil convulsions, and may be a means of involving the whole country in blood.

18. The mode in which this constitution is recommended to the people to judge without either the advice of Congress, or the legislatures of the several states, is very reprehensible—it is an attempt to force it upon them before it could be thoroughly understood, and may leave us in that situation, that in the first moments of slavery the minds of the people agitated by the remembrance of their lost liberties, will be like the sea in a tempest, that sweeps down every mound of security.

. . . [I]t is to be feared we shall soon see this country rushing into the extremes of confusion and violence, in consequence of the proceedings of a set of gentlemen, who disregarding the purposes of their appointment, have assumed powers unauthorized by any commission, have unnecessarily rejected the confederation of the United States, and annihilated the sovereignty and independence of the individual governments. . . .

It has been observed by a zealous advocate for the new system, that most governments are the result of fraud or violence, and this with design to recommend its acceptance—but has not almost every step towards its fabrication been fraudulent in the extreme? Did not the prohibition strictly enjoined by the general Convention, that no member should make any communication to his Constituents, or to gentlemen of consideration and abilities in the other States, bear evident marks of fraudulent designs? . . . And the hurry with which it has been urged to the acceptance of the people, without giving time, by adjournments, for better information, and more unanimity has a deceptive appearance. . . .

[I]f after all, on a dispassionate and fair discussion, the people generally give their voice for a voluntary dereliction of their privileges, let every individual who chooses the active scenes of life, strive to support the peace and unanimity of his country, though every other blessing may expire—And while the statesman is plodding for power, and the courtier practicing arts of dissimulation without check—while the rapacious are growing rich by oppression, and fortune throwing her gifts into the lap of fools, let the sublimer characters, the philosophic lovers of freedom who have wept over her exit, retire to the calm shades of contemplation, there they may look down with pity on the inconsistency of human nature, the revolutions of states, the rise of kingdoms, and the fall of empires.

Introduction to Documents 6 and 7

The Federalists: Arguments for Ratification

The supporters of the new constitution responded to the discharges of the Anti-Federalists volley for volley. The following documents contain some of the arguments offered by three well-known delegates who attended the Philadelphia convention. Document 6 includes the views of George Washington, a statesman who lobbied for ratification not through the publication of political pamphlets, but though his personal correspondences. Document 7 includes selections from *The Federalist Papers,* a collection of 85 political pamphlets that were published in New York City newspapers under the pseudonym Publius. The strategy of *The Federalist Papers* was to persuade citizens that the Constitution was the best possible compromise given the divisions that beset Americans. The following selections were written by James Madison and Alexander Hamilton. Which of these arguments do you consider to be persuasive and which unconvincing?

DOCUMENT 6   *Selections from the Letters of George Washington*

George Washington to Henry Knox Oct 15 1787

Mount Vernon October 15th 1787

My *dear Sir* . . .

The Constitution is now before the judgment seat. It has, as was expected, its adversaries, and its supporters; which will preponderate is yet to be decided. The former, it is probable, will be most active because the Major part of them it is to be feared, will be governed by sinister and self important considerations on which no arguments will work conviction—the opposition from another class of them (if they are men of reflection, information and candor) may perhaps subside in the solution of the following plain, but important questions. 1. Is the Constitution which is submitted by the Convention preferable to the government (if it can be called one) under which we now live? 2. Is it probable that more confidence will, at this time, be placed in another Convention (should the experiment be tried) than was given to the last? and is it likely that there would be a better agreement in it? Is there not a Constitutional door open for alterations and amendments, & is it not probable that real defects will be as readily discovered after, as before, trial? and will not posterity be as ready to apply the remedy as ourselves, if there is occasion for it, when the mode is provided? To think otherwise will, in my judgment, be ascribing more of the amor patria—more wisdom—and more foresight to ourselves, than I conceive

Go: Washington

George Washington to Lafayette

Mount Vernon February 7th 1788

My *dear Marqs*,

. . . With regard to the two great points (the pivots on which the whole machine must move) my Creed is simply: 1st That the general Government is not invested with more Powers than are indispensably necessary to perform [the] functions of a good Government; and, consequently, that no objection ought to be made against the quantity of Power delegated to it. 2ly That these Powers (as the appointment of all Rulers will forever arise from, and, at short stated intervals, recur to the free suffrage of the People) are so distributed among the Legislative, Executive, and Judicial Branches, into which the general Government is arranged, that it can never be in danger of degenerating into a monarchy, an Oligarchy, an Aristocracy, or any other despotic or oppressive form; so long as there shall remain any virtue in the body of the People. . . .

We are not to expect perfection in this world: but mankind, in modern times, have apparently made some progress in the science of Government. Should that which is now offered to the People of America, be found an experiment less perfect than it can be made—a Constitutional door is left open for its amelioration. . . . So many . . . contradictory, and, in my opinion, unfounded objections have been urged against the System in contemplation; many of which would operate equally against every efficient Government that might be proposed. I will only add, as a farther opinion founded on the maturest deliberation, that there is no alternative—no hope of alteration—no intermediate resting place—between the adoption of this and a recurrence to an unqualified state of Anarchy, with all its deplorable consequences. . . .

Go. Washington

DOCUMENT 7 *Selections from* The Federalist Papers

From Number 39: Madison defends the terms, selection processes and "federal" structure on the government

The House of Representatives, like that of one branch at least of all the State legislatures, is elected immediately by the great body of the people. The Senate, like the present Congress, and the Senate of Maryland, derives its appointment indirectly from the people. The President is indirectly derived from the choice of the people, according to the example in most of the States. Even the judges, with all other officers of the Union, will, as in the several States, be the choice, though a remote choice, of the people themselves, the duration of the appointments is equally conformable to the republican standard, and to the model of State constitutions. The House of Representatives is periodically elective, as in all the States; and for the period of two years, as in the State of South Carolina. The Senate is elective, for the period of six years; which is but one year more than the period of the Senate of Maryland, and but two more than that of the Senates of New York and Virginia. The President is to continue in office for the period of four years; as in New York and Delaware, the chief magistrate is elected for three years, and in South Carolina for two years. In the other States the election is annual. In several of the States, however, no constitutional provision is made for the impeachment of the chief magistrate. And in Delaware and Virginia he is not impeachable till out of office. The President of the United States is impeachable at any time during his continuance in office. The tenure by which the judges are to hold their places, is, as it unquestionably ought to be, that of good behavior. The tenure of the ministerial offices generally, will be a subject of legal regulation, conformably to the reason of the case and the example of the State constitutions. . . .

The House of Representatives will derive its powers from the people of America; and the people will be represented in the same proportion, and on the same principle, as they are in the legislature of a particular State. So far the government is NATIONAL, not FEDERAL. The Senate, on the other hand, will derive its powers from the States, as political and coequal societies; and these will be represented on the principle of equality in the Senate, as they now are in the existing Congress. So far the government is FEDERAL, not NATIONAL. The executive power will be derived from a very compound source. The immediate election of the President is to be made by the States in their political characters. The votes allotted to them are in a compound ratio, which considers them partly as distinct and coequal societies, partly as unequal members of the same society. The eventual election, again, is to be made by that branch of the legislature which consists of the national representatives; but in this particular act they are to be thrown into the form of individual delegations, from so many distinct and coequal bodies politic. From this aspect of the government it appears to be of a mixed character, presenting at least as many FEDERAL as NATIONAL features. . . .

The proposed Constitution, therefore, is, in strictness, neither a national nor a federal Constitution, but a composition of both. In its foundation it is federal, not national; in the sources from which the ordinary powers of the government are drawn, it is partly federal and partly national; in the operation of these powers, it is national, not federal; in the extent of them, again, it is federal, not national; and, finally, in the authoritative mode of introducing amendments, it is neither wholly federal nor wholly national.

From Number 84: Hamilton defends the decision not to include a Bill of Rights

It has been several times truly remarked that bills of rights are, in their origin, stipulations between kings and their subjects, abridgments of prerogative in favor of privilege, reservations of rights not surrendered to the prince. Such was MAGNA CHARTA, obtained by the barons, sword in hand, from King John. Such were the subsequent confirmations of that charter by succeeding princes. Such was the PETITION OF RIGHT assented to by Charles the First in the beginning of his reign. Such, also, was the Declaration of Right presented by the Lords and Commons to the Prince of Orange in 1688, and afterwards thrown into the form of an act of parliament called the Bill of Rights. It is evident, therefore, that, according to their primitive signification, they have no application to constitutions professedly founded upon the power of the people, and executed by their immediate representatives and servants. Here, in strictness, the people surrender nothing; and as they retain every thing they have no need of particular reservations. "WE, THE PEOPLE of the United States, to secure the blessings of liberty to ourselves and our posterity, do ORDAIN and ESTABLISH this Constitution for the United States of America." Here is a better recognition of popular rights, than volumes of those aphorisms which make the principal figure in several of our State bills of rights, and which would sound much better in a treatise of ethics than in a constitution of government. . . .

I go further, and affirm that bills of rights, in the sense and to the extent in which they are contended for, are not only unnecessary in the proposed Constitution, but would even be dangerous. They would contain various exceptions to powers not granted; and, on this very account, would afford a colorable pretext to claim more than were granted. For why declare that things shall not be done which there is no power to do? Why, for instance, should it be said that the liberty of the press shall not be restrained, when no power is given by which restrictions may be imposed? . . . .On the subject of the liberty of the press, as much as has been said, I cannot forbear adding a remark or two: in the first place, I observe, that there is not a syllable concerning it in the constitution of this State; in the next, I contend, that whatever has been said about it in that of any other State, amounts to nothing. What signifies a declaration, that "the liberty of the press shall be inviolably preserved"? What is the liberty of the press? Who can give it any definition which would not leave the utmost latitude for evasion? I hold it to be impracticable; and from this I infer, that its security, whatever fine declarations may be inserted in any constitution respecting it, must altogether depend on public opinion, and on the general spirit of the people and of the government.

POSTSCRIPT

Although the Constitution of 1787 was ratified, the Anti-Federalist opposition forced some concessions from the Federalists. After the new government was formed, Congress sent to the states a proposal to add ten amendments to the original constitution. In 1791, these liberty-protecting amendments, which are known as the Bill of Rights, were ratified. Notwithstanding all the rhetoric about liberty and republicanism, the Constitution of 1787 made no attempt to protect the freedoms of all persons living in the United States. Although the constitution made no specific gender references (except the use of the pronoun *he* in reference to officeholders), throughout the nineteenth century it would be interpreted in ways that would define citizenship differently for men and women. Similarly, although on four occasions the writers of the Constitution of 1787 discussed issues pertaining to slavery, they intentionally omitted the words *slaves* or *slavery* in the final draft of the document, substituting on each occasion the euphemistic expressions *person* or *persons*. The word *slavery* did not appear in the Constitution until 1865, when it was mentioned in the Thirteenth Amendment. Another people specifically excluded in the Constitution of 1787 from membership in the nation were the Native Americans. One consequence of this exclusion is expressed in the following excerpt taken from a petition by two Native Americans, Henry Quaquaquid and Robert Ashpo, to the Connecticut State Assembly. This petition was delivered in May 1789, one month after George Washington was inaugurated as the first U.S. president.

"We beg leave to lay our concerns and burdens at your excellencies' feet. The times are exceedingly altered, yea the times are turned upside down, of rather we have changed the good times, chiefly by the help of the white people. For in times past our forefathers lived in peace, love and great harmony, and had everything in plenty. When they wanted meat, they would just run into the bush a little way, with their weapons, and would soon return, bringing home good venison, raccoon, bear and fowl. If they chose to have fish, they would only go to the river, or along the seashore; and they would presently fill their canoes with variety of fish, both scaled and shell-fish. And they had abundance of nuts, wild fruits, ground nuts and ground beans; and they planted but little corn and beans. They had no contention about their lands, for they lay in common; and they had but one large dish, and could all eat together in peace and love. But alas! it is not so now; all our hunting and fowling and fishing is entirely gone. And we have begun to work our land, keep horses and cattle and hogs; and we build houses and fence in lots. And now we plainly see that one dish and one fire will not do any longer for us. Some few there are that are stronger than others; and they will keep off the poor, weak, the halt and blind, and will take the dish to themselves. Yea, they will rather call the white people and the mulattoes to eat out of our dish; and poor widows and orphans must be pushed aside, and there they must sit, crying and starving, and die. And so we are now come to our good brethren of the Assembly, with hearts full of sorrow and grief, for immediate help. And therefore our most humble and earnest request is, that our dish of suckutash may be equally divided amongst us, so that every one may have his own little dish by himself, that he may eat quietly and do with his dish as he pleases, that every one may have his own fire."

QUESTIONS

Defining Terms

Identify in the context of the chapter each of the following:

Articles of Confederation

Electoral College

Mercy Otis Warren

"Republican form of government"

Magna Charta

Daniel Shays

Writ of Habeas Corpus

The Federalist Papers

"FEDERAL" and "NATIONAL"

Henry Quaquaquid and Robert Ashpo

Probing the Sources

1. What powers awarded to Congress in the Constitution of 1787 would an Anti-Federalist be most likely to oppose?

2. According to the Constitution of 1787, what are the eligibility prerequisites and selection processes for (a) members of the House of Representatives; (b) members of the Senate; and (c) the president and vice president.

3. Critique the provisions contained in the Constitution of 1787 from the point of view of each of the following groups: (a) states with large populations; (b) states with small populations; (c) Anglos who lived beyond the boundaries of the original 13 states; (d) African-Americans and (e) Native Americans.

4. Was the United States in a crisis under the Articles of Confederation, or was the alleged crisis simply an invention of the Federalists to justify their agendas? Explain your answer.

Interpreting the Sources

1. The preamble of the Constitution reads: "We the people of the United States, in Order to form a more perfect Union, establish Justice, insure domestic Tranquility, provide for the common defense, promote the general Welfare, and secure the Blessings of Liberty to ourselves and our Posterity, do ordain and establish This CONSTITUTION for the United States of America." In which of the six objectives designated in the preamble has the Constitution of 1787 lived up to its promises? In what areas has it not fully achieved its goals?

2. If you were a delegate to a state ratifying convention, would you have voted for or against the Constitution of 1787? Explain the reasons for your vote.

3. Did the writers of the Constitution of 1787 desire to create a democracy or an aristocracy?

ADDITIONAL READINGS

Much has been written on the Philadelphia convention and the new constitution. A classic piece that has had a great impact on twentieth-century American historiography is Charles Beard, *An Economic Interpretation of the Constitution of the United States* (1913). Other more recent publications of importance include Christopher Collier and James Collier, *Decision in Philadelphia* (1987); Forest McDonald, *Novus Ordo Seclorum; The Intellectual Origins of the Constitution* (1985); and Roger H. Brown, *Redeeming the Republic: Federalists, Taxation and the Origins of the Constitution* (1993). For the arguments of the Anti-Federalists, see Jackson Turner Main, *The Antifederalists: Critics of the Constitution* (1961).

7

Shouting for Glory
Camp Meeting Christianity Described, Decried, and Defended

HISTORICAL CONTEXT

The 1790s were troubling times for the dwindling remnant of Protestant churchgoers. For several decades, politics rather than religion had dominated the thoughts of most Americans. Normal church activities, interrupted during the years of the Revolution, continued to be undermined after the war by the incessant geographical mobility of the people. Meanwhile, Christian leaders—appalled that the newly ratified Constitution of 1787 made no reference to God—complained about the growing secularization of society and the religious apathy of the American people. Perhaps their complaints were justified. While about four in ten Americans during the 1790s attended religious worship intermittently, less than one in ten were official church members. Moreover, in almost every community, the most active church attenders were women—the least influential members of society. For many Christian ministers of the period, early national churches appeared to be weak, feminine institutions, a far cry from the once powerful and prestigious churches of colonial times.

It was during this era of religious pessimism that the camp meeting emerged and flourished. The camp meeting—an evangelistic outdoor gathering attended by families who camped together on the site of the meeting—originated on the western frontier around the turn of the nineteenth century. The first camp meeting erupted spontaneously during the summer of 1800 when a Presbyterian minister named James McGready invited nearby Protestants to a four-day meeting at his church in Gasper River, Kentucky. The response to his invitation was so great, however, that McGready found it necessary to move outdoors and to offer camping accommodations for the attenders.

News of the success of this outdoor meeting attended by members of several religious denominations spread rapidly across the frontier. The following summer a number of Protestants decided to hold an outdoor revival at Cane Ridge, Kentucky, a site closer to the population center of the region. The Cane Ridge revival, perhaps the largest and wildest of the early camp meetings, attracted some twenty-five thousand participants, an incredible crowd considering that the population of Lexington, the state's largest city, barely exceeded two thousand.

Consider the sights, sounds, and smells of twenty-five thousand rough-and-tumble backwoods people coming together in a recently cleared forest grove for a week of

135

religious instruction. Never before had any of them seen such a mass of humanity gathered in one spot at one time. By reputation, Kentuckians were known for expelling Indians and subduing the wilderness, not for their civility. But for one hot week in August, these rugged individuals ate, drank, and slept side by side in a densely packed communal village.

People came to Cane Ridge and the other early camps for a variety of reasons. After all, the community, fellowship, and excitement of the camp revivals provided a welcomed escape from the isolated drudgery of life on the frontier. Camp meeting times were festive occasions, times for boys to meet girls and for men and women to make and renew lasting friendships. For the organizers of the meetings, however, the camp revivals were fundamentally religious events. The daily schedule for most camps included morning, afternoon, and evening preaching services, interspersed with prayer and testimonial meetings. For those hungry and thirsty for spiritual nourishment, the meetings offered an almost intoxicating daily diet of 15 continuous hours of preaching, praying, and singing.

Inevitably, campers remembered most fondly the nightly services held around the flickering light of many campfires. For country folk accustomed to rising and retiring with the sun, these late-night meetings under the open air were extraordinary occasions that produced extraordinary effects. As multiple ministers and lay exhorters shouted fervent warnings of a coming day of judgment, thousands of trembling campers screamed for mercy and experienced an ecstatic assurance of divine forgiveness. Often physical manifestations such as falling, jerking, dancing, and barking accompanied these conversion moments. Ultimately, the emotionally charged meetings brought thousands of new converts into the evangelical churches that supported the camp meeting experience.

As rumors of the events at Cane Ridge circulated around the nation, evangelicals back east adopted the camp meeting model. Within a few years, camp meetings were as commonplace within a day's journey of the great eastern cities as they were on the western frontier. For some denominations, camp meetings and protracted indoor revivals led by professional evangelists became a primary mode of church recruitment. Not surprisingly, the churches that embraced these methods of evangelism also became the most rapidly growing churches of the period.

CLASS
BIAS

Of course, not everyone approved of camp meetings. Many Christians, especially those from among the "more respectable classes" and the more "dignified denominations," complained that the emotional excesses of the camp revivals were an embarrassment to the name of religion. Other critics insisted that camp attenders would be better off supporting their families at work than wasting their time and money in such frivolity. Still others condemned the moral laxity of the campers and insisted that more souls were begotten through sexual promiscuity at camps than were "saved" through religious conversion.

Camp organizers generally denied these accusations, but they also worked hard to remove the more excessive features from the meetings. As a consequence, camp meetings became more structured and orderly events, carefully organized and monitored by denominational authorities that scheduled formal activities for every hour of the day and that patrolled campsites, removing the disorderly from the grounds.

RELIGIOUS
BIAS

These precautions, however, did not still the opposition. Within a decade, most Presbyterians and Baptists joined the high church Episcopalians and the Catholics in rejecting the outdoor revivals. By the 1820s, the early ecumenical gatherings had become largely Methodist institutions.

By mid-century, even the Methodist camps had lost much of their early spontaneity. As cabins, residence houses, and dining halls replaced the primitive tents, the camp meeting became more of a Christian resort for vacationing families than a revival institution aimed at the unchurched. But during the early-nineteenth-century "harvest time," the camp meeting was both an engine of Methodist expansion and a forerunner of a coming age of mass revivalism.

As you read the following accounts of the early-nineteenth-century revivals, try to identify the major arguments both for and against the camp meeting experience. Why did some people passionately support the revival and others, equally passionately, oppose it? What social factors influenced their responses?

THE DOCUMENTS
Introduction to Documents 1 and 2

Camp meetings, while originating in Kentucky, were not confined to the western frontier. The following two pieces are eyewitness accounts of two early eastern camps. The first letter, which describes an 1803 meeting near Baltimore, was written by a female participant named Fanny Lewis and was addressed to her father. The second is an account of an 1804 meeting in New Haven described by the Methodist clergyman William Thacher.

DOCUMENT 1 *"Glory! Glory! This Is the Happiest Day I Ever Saw"*

Fanny Lewis - FEMALE

Baltimore, October 1803

I hasten to give you some account of our glorious camp-meeting; but alas! all description fails. It would take an Addison or a Pope to give you even an idea of the lovely grove, particularly in the night, when the moon glimmered through the trees, and all was love and harmony. The stand was placed at the bottom of several small hills, on which our tents and wagons were placed. The meeting began on Saturday; and was very lively.

On Sunday morning Mr. S——— called his family to prayer-meeting. At ten o'clock public preaching began, and great was the power of God. There was scarce any intermission day or night. It looked awful and solemn to see a number of fires burning before the tents, and the trees with lanterns and candles suspended to them. No sound was heard, except Glory to God in the highest! or mercy! mercy! Such was a night, my father, I never saw or felt before. Many souls were converted, and many witnessed that God was able to cleanse from all sin.

On Monday morning there was such a gust of the power of God, that it appeared to me, the very gates of hell would give way. All the people were filled with wonder, love, and praise. Mr. S——— came and threw himself in our tent, crying "Glory! glory! this is the happiest day I ever saw." He says he never knew such a continual power and increase of the love of God for three days and nights. We call it "the happy Monday." Yes, it was a happy, happy Monday! a day long to be remembered, and a night never to be forgotten. O! how I longed for you, that you might share in the happiness of your unworthy child.

Nor was our parting less glorious than our meeting; for several received perfect love after the congregation broke up. They were under the necessity of dismissing the people for want of preachers; all that were present were worn out. Truly the harvest was great, but the labourers were few.

Those who were absent, know not what they have lost; nor can they form any idea of what we enjoyed. It was none other than the gate of heaven.

Where! O! where shall we begin to praise redeeming love, for the peace and comfort and assurance our souls felt in realizing the promises of an unchangeable Jehovah. Camp-meeting! why the very name thrills through my every nerve! and almost makes me think I am in the charming woods. Every foot of ground seemed to me sacred. I saw nothing, heard nothing to molest my peace: Not one jarring string. Everything seemed to combine together to promote the glory of God, and his gospel.

Such indeed, my dear father, was our meetings; and I can but lament my inability to give you an account of it; but it was better felt than expressed. Sometimes you would see more than one hundred hands raised in triumphant praise with united voices, giving glory to God, for more than one hour together, with every mark of unfeigned humility and reverence.

The time between services was not taken up with "what shall we eat, or what shall we drink," but in weeping with those that wept, and rejoicing with those that rejoiced, and that had found their pearl of great price.

The preachers all seemed as men filled with new wine. Some standing crying, others prostrate on the ground, as insensible to every earthly object; while the Master of assemblies was speaking to the hearts of poor sinners, who stood trembling under a sense of the power and presence of a sin-avenging God. They seemed unwilling to move from the spot where they stood, with their eyes fixed on them that were rejoicing in God their Saviour.

After all was over, I walked over the ground by moon-light—the scene was solemn and delightful. When I left the place, I cannot describe the emotion I felt. It was something like parting with all that was dear to me. My foolish heart kept saying, adieu ye sacred grove, adieu—never, never shall I see you more.

I am your dutiful
And affectionate daughter,
Fanny Lewis

DOCUMENT 2   *"The Melting Power of God"*

William Thacher - MALE

New-Haven, December 7th, 1804

Friday the 14th of September, we, with six traveling preachers present, began our camp meeting. The melting power of God began with the exercises, which so overwhelmed the preacher that he could scarcely give out the hymn. After the first sermon and exhortation, we were joined by brother Snethen, and about fifty Yorkers with tents and baggage. Preaching again in the evening. Not a breeze to disturb the candles, the three nights we were on the ground. Evening exercises continued till after midnight. Numbers, deprived of their strength, fell to the ground, some awakened and some sanctified.

Saturday 15th, family prayer before 6 o'clock. General prayer-meeting at 8. Preaching at 10, followed by prayer and exhortations. Preaching again, &c. at 2. This day ten traveling preachers, and about two thousand five hundred people present; and what was infinitely better, the mighty power of God was present to wound, to heal and to cleanse. Such a work of awakening, conversion, sanctification, and falling to the ground, by the power of God, my eyes, my heart, my soul never witnessed. The exercises were regular and irregular; preaching was attempted in the evening, but in vain: the cries and shouts of the people drowned the preacher's voice. The exercises continued all night. On Sunday morning the people flocked from every direction; the computation of numbers that day was from seven to eight thousand. Prayer meeting at 8, preaching half past 9, by brother Snethen, with mighty energy; two or three more sermons and a number of prayers and exhortations were delivered from the stand, and then a short intermission, after which the worship continued in different groups till Monday 9 o'clock, when the sacrament was administered to numbers, who were overwhelmed with love divine. Then preaching with great clearness, freedom and power by brother Garrettson: a live pathetic exhortation by brother Moriarty, and a crowning discourse by brother Snethen, while tears of joy flowed down the animated faces of the saints, shouts of rapture filled the place, and convictions seemed to fasten on every auditor. After a very fervent prayer, and the accustomed benediction, the parting scene was truly affecting. The preachers first shook hands on the stand, then the people crowded up by scores and by hundreds, their hands extended, their eyes glowing with tears, and their bosoms heaving with big emotion, took a most affectionate leave of each other, reluctantly struck their tents, and dispersed.

Description sinks beneath the weight of facts. Such a scene I could not have conceived. The power increased during the whole meeting. Saints triumphing, penitents weeping, people falling, the voice of joy and sorrow mingling, prayer, praise, and shouting, shouting, shouting filled the groves around.

How many were awakened, converted, and sanctified at this meeting, could not be known by any of us. One man who was intoxicated, and came into the assembly to make disturbance, was struck to the ground by an invisible power, and is since soundly converted, and joined society. A work of God has since spread into the neighborhood of the meeting. The Methodists carried the fire home to their respective neighborhoods and families. The different love-feasts resounded with praises for camp-meetings: and in short, the whole district is eminently benefited by it. A general spring is given to the cause of the blessed Saviour, in every circuit and station in the scope of my travels. Glory to God in the highest, and on earth peace, and good will towards men!

Wm. Thacher

Introduction to Documents 3 and 4

Martin J. Spalding, a Kentucky-born Catholic priest who became the archbishop of Baltimore, viewed camp meetings far differently from Barton Stone, a Protestant clergyman who had helped organize the Cane Ridge revival. Both ministers, however, devoted considerable space in their memoirs to a description of the acrobatic "exercises" that accompanied the emotional services of the early camps. Printed below are excerpts from their respective writings. Note the similarities and differences in their accounts. How do you explain the differences?

DOCUMENT 3   *"The Smile of Heaven Shone"*

Barton Stone

The bodily agitations or exercises, attending the excitement in the beginning of this century, were various, and called by various names. . . . The falling exercise was very common among all classes, the saints and sinners of every age and of every grade, from the philosopher to the clown. The subject of this exercise would, generally, with a piercing scream, fall like a log on the floor, earth, or mud, and appear as dead. . . .

The jerks cannot be so easily described. Sometimes the subject of the jerks would be affected in some one member of the body, and sometimes the whole system. When the head alone was affected, it would be jerked backward and forward, or from side to side, so quickly that the features of the face could not be distinguished. When the whole system was affected, I have seen the person stand in one place, and jerk backward and forward in quick succession, their head nearly touching the floor behind and before. All classes, saints and sinners, the strong as well as the weak, were thus affected. . . .

The dancing exercise. This generally began with the jerks, and was peculiar to the professors of religion. The subject, after jerking awhile, began to dance, and then the jerks would cease. Such dancing was indeed heavenly to the spectators; there was nothing in it like levity, nor calculated to excite levity in the beholders. The smile of heaven shone on the countenance of the subject, and assimilated to angels appeared the whole person. Sometimes the motion was quick and sometimes slow. Thus they continued to move forward and backward in the same track or alley till nature seemed exhausted, and they would fall prostrate on the floor or earth, unless caught by those standing by. While thus exercised, I have heard their solemn praises and prayers ascending to God.

The barking exercise (as opposers contemptuously called it), was nothing but the jerks. A person affected with the jerks, especially in his head, would often make a grunt, or bark, if you please, from the suddenness of the jerk. . . .

The laughing exercise was frequent, confined solely with the religious. It was a loud, hearty laughter, but one *sui generis*; it excited laughter in none else. The subject appeared rapturously solemn, and his laughter excited solemnity in saints and sinners. It is truly indescribable.

The running exercise was nothing more than, that persons feeling something of these bodily agitations, through fear, attempted to run away, and thus escape from them; but it commonly happened that they ran not far, before they fell, or became so greatly agitated that they could proceed no further. . . .

I shall close this chapter with the singing exercise. This is more unaccountable than any thing else I ever saw. The subject in a very happy state of mind would sing most melodiously, not from the mouth or nose, but entirely in the breast, the sounds issuing from thence. Such music silenced every thing, and attracted the attention of all. It was most heavenly. None could ever be tired of hearing it.

DOCUMENT 4   *"A Fanaticism as Absurd as It Was Blasphemous"*

Martin J. Spalding

To understand more fully how very "precious and astonishing" this great revival was, we must further reflect: 1st, that it produced, not a mere momentary excitement, but one that lasted for several successive years. 2ndly, that it was not confined to one particular denomination, but, to a greater or less extent, prevaded all. 3rdly, that men of sense and good judgment in other matters were often carried away by the same fanaticism which swayed the mob. 4thly, that this fanaticism was as widespread as it was permanent—not being confined to Kentucky, but pervading most of the adjoining states and territories. And 5thly, that though some were found who had good sense enough to detect the impostor, yet they were comparatively few in number, and wholly unable to stay the rushing torrent of fanaticism, even if they had had the moral courage to attempt it.

Such are some of the leading features of a movement in religion (!) which is perhaps one of the most extraordinary recorded in history, and to which we know of but few parallels, except in some of the fanatical doings of the Anabaptists in Germany during the first years of their history. The whole matter furnishes one more conclusive evidence of the weakness of the human mind when left to itself; and one more sad commentary on the Protestant rule of faith.

Here we see whole masses of population, spread over a vast territory, boasting too of their enlightenment and Bible-learning, swayed for years by a fanaticism as absurd as it was blasphemous; and yet believing all this to be the work of the Holy Spirit! Let Protestants after this talk about Catholic ignorance and superstition! Had Catholics ever played the "fantastic tricks" which were played off by Protestants during these years, we would perhaps never hear the end of it. . . .

Besides the "exercises" [referred to earlier] there was also the jumping exercise. Spasmodic convulsions, which lasted sometimes for hours, were the usual sequel to the falling exercise. Then there were the "exercises" of screaming and shouting and crying. A camp meeting during that day exhibited the strangest bodily feats, accompanied with the most Babel-like sounds. An eyewitness of undoubted veracity stated to us that, in passing one of the campgrounds, he noticed a man in the "barking exercise," clasping a tree with his arms, and dashing his head against it until it was all besmeared with blood, shouting all the time that he had "treed his Saviour"! Another eyewitness stated that in casually passing by a camp in the night, while the exercises were at the highest, he witnessed scenes of too revolting a character even to be alluded to here.

One of the most remarkable features, perhaps, of these "exercises" is the apparently well-authenticated fact that many fell into them by a kind of sympathy, almost in spite of themselves, and some even positively against their own will! Some who visited the meetings to laugh at the proceedings, sometimes caught the contagion themselves. There seems to have then existed in Kentucky a kind of mental and moral epidemic—a sort of contagious frenzy—which spread rapidly from one to another.

Introduction to Documents 5 and 6

Catholics were not alone in condemning the excesses of the camp revivals. The following publications suggest the degree to which camp meetings stirred up controversy even among Protestant evangelicals. Document 5, which is taken from the Methodist Protestant periodical *Wesleyan Repository* (published in Philadelphia in 1820), attempts to discredit camp meetings by associating them with other events, such as fairs and horse races, that most evangelicals readily denounced.

Document 6 reveals in its defense of the revivals one of the most disturbing criticisms directed against camp meetings: the charge that camp meetings promoted sexual promiscuity. In reading these articles, attempt to identify the underlying values held by the authors. What, for instance, were their attitudes toward work and leisure? Toward the value and place of women in society? What fears did the writers express, and why did they share these concerns?

DOCUMENT 5 *"Camp-Meetings, and Agricultural Fairs"*

It has been for a long time a question of serious concern to many sober and considerate members of our Society, whether Camp Meetings did not involve such attendant evils *near large cities* and *in populous countries*, as to counterbalance much of their intended

This camp meeting scene was produced in 1839. What message does the artist wish to convey in this work? Do you think the artist was a critic or foe of the revivalistic practices of camp meeting religion? (Old Dartmouth Historical Society–New Bedford Whaling Museum)

good. On this subject, too, we may have been too partial to our own doings, to have duly attended to the voices or opinions of others; but we have now a chance to open our eyes to *facts* resulting from the *acts of others,* which bear sufficient analogy, in my opinion, to some of our Camp Meetings—and may, therefore, present us with a fair occasion, if we will consider it, of examining the reality of the alleged many evils, consequent on long continued night assemblages of indiscriminate masses of people. I allude to the recent "Agricultural Exhibitions and Fairs", [that] assemblage of riot, revel, and general vice, which lately assembled in the vicinity of Philadelphia for several continuous days and nights. . . .

Probably several may feel prompt to condemn the Fairs, (who see the vices of large promiscuous crowds) who, notwithstanding, will suppress or stifle their conviction of their obvious similarity to the ungovernable crowds which have surrounded some camp-meetings. Why camp-meetings alone should be exempt from the general objection, of being worse than useless, when and where they incidentally involve as much or more evil than good, is not made out a clear case to my mind. . . .

Some have said, if the gain of one converted soul at a camp meeting, be worth more than the whole world, they have achieved enough of good to justify its use. This argument is liable to several objections: First, we are bound to use the best means; and if better means are rejected, we are chargeable with neglect of duty to the souls of other men. 2nd, Although the world (the mundane sphere) be worth less than one soul, it is a solecism to say that that soul can surpass in value all the other souls which inhabit the world! And here recurs precisely the original question—whether the blessing effected for one soul is counterbalanced by the evil done at the same time to many souls! To impute, as we generally do, all the conversions which ensue to the special influence of the camp-meeting, is not, I think, conclusive reasoning, because the fact is, that almost all of such are composed of those who came with previous design and awakening, and determined to find their rest there. And who could say, that the same time and prayerfulness employed at some regular church, and for the same objects, would not produce an equal or greater proportion of good? . . .

If woods-meetings, in places where churches abound, do indeed far surpass in productive good the churches, why should we not, like the Druids, hold all our meetings in the open air, and give the value of our buildings in charities?

It may be questioned, too, whether the habit of leaving the ordinary churches to seek encampments in the woods, does not, in many cases, tend to draw us off unwarily from our principal design of worship, and engage our affections to the novelties of the scenes, the greetings of new faces, the hospitalities of reciprocal visits, the exemption from the usual labors and cares, the reports of the doings within and without the camp: All these things may give pleasing agitations to the mind; but are they certainly holy? And is it not possible that those who thus frequent them from choice, and not of necessity, (having left their churches to attend them) may and do acquire undue disrelish to the ordinary worship of the year to which they must however return. Take away the worship, and there would remain sufficient gratifications to allure the most of young people, and thousands if equally fed and freed from labor, would follow them perpetually. . . .

[As] to the loss of time, money and labor resulting to the general weal, from the assemblage of such crowds for sinister purposes, it might not be deemed irrelevant here to glance at the same facts attendant on large and protracted camp-meetings. If "time is money," and "labor is the wealth of the community," as is granted by all, it must be admitted that camp-meetings, in countries where churches for the ordinary congregation exist, is one of the most expensive measures to the community where they prevail, that could be devised. It could be easily demonstrated, that at any given camp-meeting, where the totality of persons, at any given time, was equal to 5,000 persons, with the horses and carriages, night and day, for one week, it is attended, at a moderate computation, with a loss of productive labor and expense for diet, drink, &c of 25,000 dollars—exclusive of cost of tents, furniture, congregation benches, and pulpits, and the time employed in preparation of camp, and for return. Whether we will heed it or not, it is nevertheless true, that as surely as a militia training, or horserace, near a great city, puts in requisition and motion, the idle and the profligate for ten to fifteen miles surrounding the centre of attraction, so true it also is, that the roads, inns and booths of the country which environ a camp-meeting, witness the same followers, with their revellings, profanity and idleness, and further departure from all that is good. These may be very unpopular sentiments to appear in your paper; but if some Methodists can and do entertain such sentiments, should you not thus expose their obliquity, that due measures may be taken to subdue such objections, and to save those who are thus out of the way? Let the evil be known, lest the remedy might not appear to be necessary to be applied.

Scrutator

📜 DOCUMENT 6 *From* An Apology for Camp Meetings

It has often been said that, "Camp-meetings are the cause of, or afford an opportunity for an illicit intercourse of the sexes; by which they have become a fruitful source of illegitimate children, and consequently great personal and social evils." That some few unmarried females, among many thousands who have attended those meetings, have afterwards become the mothers of such children, is no doubt true; and very probably would have been the case, if no such meeting had ever been held; for the circumstance of their having attended them, no more proves that the iniquitious conduct was committed at

[handwritten: MANY 1000's OF WOMEN.]

Camp-meeting, than at any other given place, where they were known to have been, just before or soon after; or even at their own place of residence, except it has the additional proof of their own confession; which I believe has seldom, if ever been the case. So that, we may fairly conclude, the voice of malignant rumors, and not facts, has propagated this objection.

But admitting the fact, what must have been the previous characters of those females? Certainly, not that of chastity, virtue, or even common modesty; but the reverse of all these: and a degree of depravity, which modesty forbids me to name in any other way, than by saying they must have been reduced to a level with the shameless nature of female brutes; for in no other state of mind, can it be imagined that a female, whose call for this life, especially, depends upon an unblemished character in this respect, should submit to such an act of self-degradation, in a place too, where she would be almost as much exposed to observation, either by day or night, as if in the most public highway, if she had no other cause of shame to fear, nor any other consequences to dread: for scarce an hour elapses, from the beginning to the close of a Camp-meeting, but the people are passing to, and from the place of worship, in every direction: and even in the adjacent groves it is extremely difficult at any hour, to find a place of such private retreat, as not to be observed. In addition to which, at night a vigilant watch, reconnoitre the place, and make frequent excursions in small parties, for the express purpose of preventing, or detecting such practices; especially where there are reasons for suspicion. And in the encampment itself (where even men and their wives are not suffered to lodge together) it could not escape notice and detection.

Under such circumstances as these, to suppose that a female of an unblemished character, should grant unwarrantable liberties, even to her most confidential friend, upon any consideration whatever, would be attaching an odium to the virtuous daughters of Columbia, of which they are not deserving; and to suppose that such characters should yield to the flatteries, be bought with the gold of strangers, would be doing them the most flagrant injustice, as well as not allowing our females to possess two grains of common sense above the most perfect idiot: although it is well known and acknowledged, that the American fair sex in general, are excelled by none for modesty, and for being tenacious of their own reputation; nor are any others their superiors for good sense, or mental abilities, considering their opportunities for improvement. From which it follows as a moral consequence, that those who have been guilty of the abominable conduct complained of on those solemn occasions, (let the result have been what it may) were mere prostitutes before; having followed the same practice, till hardened in the crime; naturalized to a brutal insensibility of unblushing shame, and completely at the command of the common debauchee. The evil therefore is not imputable to Camp-meetings, because it must have existed before, or it could never have been repeated there; at least it is contrary to reason to suppose it. Beside; matter of fact corroborates the foregoing remarks, for in those instances where persons have been detected (and some there have been) in this iniquity (and it is presumed, few have escaped notice) it has been ascertained, that, they were well known to be such characters as I have here supposed them.

That many of this character attend those meetings is unquestionable, (as well as every other description of sinners, among us) and numbers of them have been awakened and converted to God, who are now faithful, and worthy members of the church of Christ, who like Mary Magdalene, (once a Jewish harlot) now sit at the feet of Jesus, to hear his gracious works, and live upon his approbating smiles; while the less degraded and less penitent Martha's, are accosted by the Saviour in the reprehending language of, "Martha! Martha! thou art careful and troubled about many things; but one thing is needful: and Mary hath chosen that good part, which shall never be taken away from her."

So that Camp-meetings, instead of being the cause of female degeneracy, are the means of lessening the number of common prostitutes, and of restoring the self-degraded

daughters of our mother Eve, to the lost favour, both of God and man, to useful membership in society, and if faithful till death, to the eternal enjoyment of the virgin honours of
Paradise. To the self-righteous objectors then who stand aloof from this excellent institution, and would persuade all others to do the same, the words of Christ are truly applicable: "Publicans and harlots, go into the kingdom of God before you."

CLASS: LOWER-CLASS, PROSTITUTES

QUESTIONS   *SEX: FEMALE*

Defining Terms   *RELIGION: PROTESTANT*

Identify in the context of the chapter each of the following:

secularization   James McGready
Cane Ridge   religious denominations
Fanny Lewis   Martin Spalding
"bodily agitations   fanaticism
  or exercises"   Protestant evangelicals
Scrutator

Probing the Sources

1. Describe the setting and schedule of activities of a nineteenth-century camp meeting.
2. What class, sex, and religious biases do you find in the descriptions of the camp meetings?
3. What were the major arguments for and against the holding of camp meetings?
4. Identify the religious groups that supported and opposed the camp meetings. How do you think a group's support or opposition to the camps affected its growth during the early nineteenth century?

Interpreting the Sources

1. Compare the styles of piety of nineteenth-century Protestants with seventeenth-century Puritans and eighteenth-century Deists.
2. In the nineteenth century, more women than men attended church, but the size of the female majority was less in revivalistic churches than in nonrevivalistic ones. How do you explain these patterns of church involvement? Were the camp revivals primarily "masculine" or "feminine" institutions? Explain.
3. What similarities and differences do you see between camp-meeting religion and present-day television evangelism?

ADDITIONAL READING

Many historians view the early national era as a formative era that fundamentally reshaped the American religious environment. Two important monographs making this argument are Nathan Hatch's *Democratization of American Christianity* (1989) and Jon Butler's *Awash in a Sea of Faith* (1990). A classic overview of the revivals in upstate New York is Whitney Cross's *The Burned Over District* (1950). The standard introduction to the religious camp meeting experience itself is Charles Johnson's *The Frontier Camp Meeting: Religion's Harvest Time* (1955). Also of interest are Dickson Bruce, Jr.'s *And They All Sang Hallelujah: Plain Folk Camp-Meeting Religion, 1800–1845* (1974), which discusses the relationship between revivalism and frontier culture, and Terry D. Bilhartz, *Urban Religion and the Second Great Awakening* (1986), which documents the importance of camp revivals to urban churches. Other important works that discuss the social origins and implications of nineteenth-century revivalism include Mary P. Ryan, *Cradle of the Middle Class* (1981), and Paul Johnson, *A Shopkeepers' Millennium: Society and Revivals in Rochester, New York, 1815–1837* (1979). Students interested in exploring the linkage between religious practices and special social contexts will enjoy David D. Hall, ed., *Live Religion in America: Toward a History of Practice* (1997).

8

Living and Dying in Bondage
The Slave Conspiracy of 1822

HISTORICAL CONTEXT

Around the beginning of the nineteenth century, the English textile industry grew at an incredible pace. Work was reorganized so that a relatively small number of individuals controlled the buying of cotton and its spinning, weaving, and sale as cloth. Some of the new technologies were simple, others, complex, involving large factories. But the new industry was characterized by a heightened specialization of labor, the ability of some men to purchase the time of others as cheaply as possible, and the need of masses of people to sell their labor in order to make a living. The growth of the textile industry signaled the beginnings of a general reorganization of production under capitalism.

The freedom of individuals to buy and sell labor—of owners to hire and fire whomever they pleased and of workers to work for whomever they chose—was central to the system. But most of the individuals who produced the raw cotton that eventually became cloth were slaves, people without such freedom. First, long-staple cotton, which grew only in the coastal areas of the Carolinas and Georgia, fed the textile business. Short-staple cotton was hardy and could grow in varied climates, but the seeds stuck in the cotton bolls, making it unfit for spinning. Then, in 1793, an American inventor, Eli Whitney, developed his famous cotton gin, which easily separated fiber from seed. Now cloth could be produced from any kind of cotton.

Soon the cotton culture spread inland from the southern coast, overrunning Alabama and Mississippi by the 1830s, Texas and Louisiana slightly later. Textile mills opened in America and England, and despite ups and downs, the overall demand for cotton products in world markets seemed unlimited. The new industry spurred the expansion of other businesses, including banking, shipping, and insurance, as well as retailing, importing, and exporting. Thus, cotton was one of the most important ingredients in the development of modern capitalism, and where cotton spread, so did slavery. Here was an irony: The same product that had nurtured a free-labor capitalistic economy also was essential to the growth and extension of slavery, an ancient system antithetical to the free-labor marketplace. If cotton cloth production was the great engine of modern capitalism, enslaved men and women drove that engine. Freedom for some, then, depended on the bondage of others.

Before the great boom in cotton demand, the institution of slavery had been on the defensive. Especially in England, evangelical Christians, reformers, and advocates of free labor were beginning to push for outlawing the slave trade with Africa and, in some extreme cases, for the manumission of slaves in the Americas. The new American Constitution allowed Congress to prohibit the slave trade after 1808, and by 1820, the northern states had either outlawed servitude or were in the process of doing so. In the South, however, slavery had always been stronger, and if many whites justified it as a necessary evil, they nevertheless were not about to divest themselves of their most important form of productive property. Once the demand for short-staple cotton developed, slavery in the South became linked with opening up new western lands and providing economic opportunity for ambitious white men. By the early nineteenth century, bondage and a distinct southern way of life were joined, and before long, whites spoke of the enslavement of blacks as a positive good.

It was not a positive good for the slaves. When the importation of new Africans slowed early in the century, black culture began to change. Many African practices, customs, and beliefs remained, but large parts of the culture of whites became part of black ways. English—although in the form of a patois filled with African words and grammatical constructions—became the dominant language of African Americans. Many slaves were converted to Christianity, though in their own religious services, they incorporated African ideas about God and the spiritual world. Memories of an African homeland never disappeared, but increasingly these remembrances were secondhand, passed through the generations. Blacks forged a distinctive hybrid culture, including their own music, family structure, worship, humor, and social hierarchy.

African Americans needed all of their resources to survive a cruel system. At its worst, slavery meant the breakup of families on an owner's whim, whippings to enforce discipline, and even death for insubordination. Perhaps the daily grind was worse than the atrocities, for African Americans lived with being stigmatized as an inferior race, having no control over their work or the products of their labor, and having little hope that their lives would get better. Most masters provided roughly enough to eat, but the food was too often an unchanging regimen of corn meal, fat pork, molasses, and, for the lucky ones, the produce of their own small gardens. Sometimes work clothes barely kept them covered through the seasons, and housing often consisted of one-room dirt-floor slave cabins, places impossible to keep dry and disease-free. Slaves generally worked from sunrise to sunset, planting, hoeing, and harvesting, mostly in the brutal southern summers. Women labored alongside men except just before and after childbirth; the very elderly took care of the very young, though both groups were given their own tasks.

There was, of course, variation within slavery. Staple crops like rice, indigo, and sugarcane dictated rhythms of production different from those of cotton; slaves on large plantations had the most distance from the whites, meaning less personal kindness if there was any to be had, but also more independence. A minority of blacks worked as house servants or as skilled laborers, jobs with more diversity than field work, but with greater scrutiny by whites. Some sadistic masters worked their slaves nearly to death, but these were relatively rare. In most cases, a battle of wits was waged constantly, African Americans doing their best to preserve a bit of

It was a common sight in the Old South: slaves chained to each other enroute to being sold away from family and friends. (© Bettmann/Corbis)

autonomy, free time, or pleasure, masters trying to get as much labor out of their slaves as possible.

Most African Americans never openly rebelled against the system. Slave codes did not allow blacks to have weapons, use drums (important signaling devices in Africa), or congregate in large numbers. Whites were well armed, outnumbered blacks in most states, and had organized patrols to discourage insubordination. While slaves certainly would have preferred freedom to bondage, the risks of death or of being sold away from loved ones were overwhelming. If day-to-day life was harsh, it was usually stable enough to allow for the shared joys of conversation, play, and worship with kin and neighbors—humble pleasures, but not worth risking. Opposition to the slave system therefore took small and underground forms: resting as the overseer looked away, telling jokes about particular whites, stealing a hog for meat, running off for a few hours or days to get a bit of freedom, or in more extreme cases, secretly destroying tools and other white property, burning down a barn, and even poisoning individual masters.

Occasionally, too, there were organized rebellions. None of those in the United States were ever as massive or successful as those in Latin America. Both blacks and whites spoke in hushed tones of the revolution in Saint Domingue (Haiti) during the 1790s. There, Toussaint L'Ouverture led a long and bloody rebellion that resulted in the overthrow of French rule and freedom for the slaves. Southern states banned refugees from Saint Domingue, but the revolts in Latin America had become legendary events for many blacks. The largest attempt at rebellion in the United States was the conspiracy of 1800, in which preacher and blacksmith Gabriel Prosser organized hundreds of slaves in a plan to seize Richmond, Virginia, set fire to the city, and capture the governor. Heavy rain prevented the planned attack, after which the conspiracy was betrayed. Nat Turner, literate and charismatic, led the bloodiest rebellion on these shores. On August 22, 1831, this preacher and religious mystic led dozens of others on an attack through Southampton County, Virginia; sixty whites died before the rebellion was crushed, and as many as two hundred blacks were executed in the aftermath.

THE DOCUMENTS

The documents in this chapter come from the 1822 trial of Denmark Vesey, and from David Walker's 1829 *Appeal to the Coloured Citizens of the World.* Like Gabriel Prosser, Vesey was a free black, a man of unusual learning, skill, and independence. As in the Richmond plot of 1800, Vesey's rebellion was betrayed before it could begin, and it is therefore very difficult to know just how large it might have been. His lieutenants were able and persuasive men, though it is hard to credit claims that thousands had been enlisted for the rebellion. Particularly interesting, however, were the sorts of appeals made by the conspirators. One leader, Gullah Jack, offered magical invulnerability, and his legendary abilities as a conjurer embodied the slaves' African heritage. Vesey pitched his appeals on several levels: The Bible, he taught, sanctioned rebellion against bondage; the Constitution and the Declaration of Independence were antithetical to slavery; and the Caribbean revolts offered precedents for rebellion. Walker, too, justified black rebellion with the Bible and the Declaration of Independence. He also appealed to a glorious African past (but rejected colonization of American slaves back to Africa) and declared that the United States rightfully belonged to blacks as well as whites.

Introduction to Document 1

If open rebellions were not common in North America, they nonetheless revealed the desperation some slaves felt and the fears of whites that blacks longed to be free. When the Vesey conspiracy was over, thirty-five slaves were hanged and thirty-one banished from the United States. The following are excerpts from the published report of the June 1822 trial of Vesey and his lieutenants on the charge of inciting an insurrection. It was originally entitled *An Official Report of the Trials of Sundry Negroes, Charged with an Attempt to Raise an Insurrection* (Charleston, South Carolina, 1822). It was written by the two presiding magistrates, Lionel H. Kennedy and Thomas Parker, both local attorneys. While not a verbatim transcript of the proceedings, it summarized much of the case against the conspirators.

We must read this testimony carefully, always questioning the witnesses' motives, for both blacks and whites saw incidents through a veil of fear. Masters wanted to make an example of slaves, while slaves sought to protect each other and themselves. What is unmistakably clear, however, is that several blacks had thought long and hard about their plan, had worked out a sophisticated ideology of freedom, and had been quite persuasive in gaining converts, despite the desperate odds against them. As you read these selections, try to imagine how great the risks were that the slaves took. What sustained them as they gambled with their lives? And what kept other slaves from joining them?

DOCUMENT 1 *The Trials*

The Court organized for the trial of sundry Negroes apprehended and charged *with attempting to raise an Insurrection amongst the Blacks against the Whites*, and of such others as might be brought before them on the same charge, met on Wednesday, the 19th June, 1822. . . .

   THE TRIAL OF ROLLA, a Negro man, the slave of His Excellency, Governor Bennett—Jacob Axson, Esq., attending as counsel for his owner.

Evidence

Witness no. 1 A Negro man testified as follows: I know Rolla, belonging to Mr. Thomas Bennett, we are intimate friends; all that I know of the intended Insurrection I got from him. About three months ago he asked me to join with him in slaying the whites, I asked him to give me time to consider it; a week after he put the same question to me, and at the end of another week he again came to me on the same subject. I told him "take care, God says we must not kill"; you are a coward he said and laughed at me. He said he would tell me how it was to be done. There are said he, white men who have come from off, and who say that Santo Domingo and Africa will assist us to get our liberty if we will only make the motion first. I advised him to let it alone, and told him I would oppose them if they came to kill my owner, when he again laughed at me as a coward. He summoned me to go to their meetings where said he you will hear what is going on and be better informed; I told him yes, I would go. Friday night about three weeks ago he appointed to take me with him to their meeting; at that night he came to me and again summoned me to go to the meeting, I went away from him, I went out of his way. The next day he came to me and said the meeting had been expecting me and I must send my name to be put down as one of the band—this thing has been going on for four months. He told me that at the meeting it was said that *some white men said Congress had set us free, and that our white people here would not let us be so*, and that Santo Domingo and Africa would come over and cut up the white people if we only made the motion here first—that last Saturday night (the 15th June) might be the last he had to live, as they were determined to break open the thing on Sunday night (the 16th June). I told him it could not be done, it would not succeed, that our parents for generations back had been slaves, and we had better be contented. . . . I asked Rolla what was to be done with the women and children? he said, *"when we have done with the fellows, we know what to do with the wenches."* He said *there are a great many involved in it in the country;* that Mungo from James' Island was to come over to Charleston with 4,000 men, land on South Bay, march up and seize the Arsenal by the Guard House and kill all the City Guard; that another body was to seize upon the Powder Magazine, and another body to take the United States' Arsenal on the Neck, then march to town and destroy the inhabitants, who could only escape by jumping into the river. *My Army he said will first fix my old buck and then the Intendant.* I asked him if he could bind his master or kill him; he laughed at me again; I then told him I would have nothing to do with him. He said he was going to John's Island to hasten down the country Negroes, as he feared they would not come. I felt that it was a bad thing to disclose what a bosom friend had confided to me, and that it was wicked to betray him, and I suffered a great deal before I could bring myself to give information, but when I thought on the other hand that by doing so I would save so many lives *and prevent the horrible acts in contemplation,* 'twas overbalanced, and my duty was to inform. I refused to go to the meetings as Rolla wished, as I feared if I opposed them there, they might make away with me to prevent me from betraying them. . . . I know Denmark Vesey—I was one day on horse-back going to market when I met him on foot; he asked me if I was satisfied in my present situation; if I remembered the fable of Hercules and the Waggoner whose wagon was stalled, and he began to pray, and Hercules said, you fool put your shoulder to the wheel, whip up the horses and your waggon will be pulled out; that if we did not put our hand to the work and deliver ourselves, we should never come out of slavery; *that Congress had made us free.* . . .

Rolla's threats are that if any black person is found out giving information or evi-dence against them, they would be watched for day and night and be certainly killed. Even now the friends of those in prison are trying about the streets to find out who has given information—*If my name was known I would certainly be killed.* . . .

The voluntary confession of Rolla to the Court, made after all the evidence had been heard, but before his conviction: I know Denmark Vesey. On one occasion he asked me what news, I told him none; he replied we are free but the white people here won't let us be so, and the only way is to rise up and fight the whites. I went to his house one night to learn where the meetings were held. I never conversed on this subject with Batteau or Ned—Vesey told me he was the leader in this plot. I never conversed either with Peter or Mingo. Vesey induced me to join; when I went to Vesey's house there was a meeting there, the room was full of people, but none of them white. That night at Vesey's we de-termined to have arms made, and each man put in 12 1/2 cents towards that purpose. Though Vesey's room was full I did not know one individual there. At this meeting Vesey said we were to take the Guard House and Magazine to get arms; that we ought to rise up and fight against the whites for our liberties; he was the first to rise up and speak, and he read to us from the Bible, how the Children of Israel were delivered out of Egypt from bondage. He said that the rising would take place, last Sunday night week, (the 16th June). . . .

The court unanimously found Rolla guilty. After sentence of death had been passed upon him, he made a confession in prison to the Rev. Dr. Hall, who furnished the Court with it in writing, and in the following words: "I was invited by Denmark Vesey to his house, where I found Ned Bennett, Peter Poyas, and others, some were strangers to me, they said they were from the country. Denmark told us, it was high time we had our lib-erty, and he could show us how we might obtain it. He said, we must unite together as the Santo Domingo people did, never to betray one another, and to die before we would tell upon one another. He also said he expected the Santo Domingo people would send some troops to help us. The best way, said he, for us to conquer the whites, is to set the town on fire in several places, at the Governor's Mills, and near the Docks, and for every servant in the yards to be ready with axes, knives, and clubs, to kill every man as he came out when the bells began to ring. *He then read in the Bible where God commanded, that all should be cut off, both men, women and children, and said, he believed, it was no sin for us to do so, for the Lord had commanded us to do it.* But if I had read these Psalms, Doctor, which I have read, since I have been in this prison, they would never have got me to join them. At another meeting, some of the company were opposed to killing the Ministers, and the women and children, but Denmark said, it was not safe to keep one alive, but to destroy them totally, for you see, said he, the Lord has commanded it. When I heard this, master Hall, my heart pained me within, and I said to myself, I cannot kill my master and mistress, for they use me, more like a son, than a slave. I then concluded in my mind, that I would go into the country, on Saturday evening, before they were to commence on Sunday, that I might not see it. Some of the company asked, if they were to stay in Charleston; he said no, as soon as they could get the money from the banks, and the goods from the stores, they should hoist sail for Santo Domingo, for he expected some armed vessels would meet them to conduct and protect them." . . .

THE TRIAL OF DENMARK VESEY, a free black man—Col. G. W. Cross attending as his counsel. . . .

Evidence

Witness no. 1, gave the following testimony: I know Denmark Vesey. I was one day on horseback going to market when I met him on foot; he asked me if I was satisfied in my present situation; if I remembered the fable of Hercules and the Waggoner whose waggon was stalled, and he began to pray, and Hercules said, you fool put your shoulder to the wheel, whip up the horses and your waggon will be pulled out; that if we did not put our hand to the work and deliver ourselves, we should never come out of slavery; *that Congress had made us free.* I know that he is intimately acquainted with Rolla—Rolla told me that there had been a sort of disagreement and confusion at their place of meeting, and that they meant to meet at Vesey's. Vesey told me that a large army from Santo Domingo and Africa were coming to help us, and we must not stand with our hands in our pockets; he was bitter towards the whites.

Frank, Mrs. Ferguson's slave gave the following evidence: I know Denmark Vesey and have been to his house. I have heard him say that the Negro's situation was so bad he did not know how they could endure it, and was astonished they did not rise and fend for themselves, and he advised me to join and rise. He said he was going about to see different people, and mentioned the names of Ned Bennett and Peter Poyas as concerned with him—that he had spoken to Ned and Peter on this subject, and that they were to go about and tell the blacks that they were free, and must rise and *fight for themselves*—that they would take the Magazines and Guard Houses, and the city and be free—that he was going to send *into the country* to inform the people there too. He said he wanted me to join them— I said I could not answer—he said if I would not go into the country for him he could get others. He said himself, Ned Bennett, Peter Poyas, and Monday Gell were the principal men and himself the head man. He said they were the principal men to go about and inform the people and fix them,—that *one party would land on South Bay, one about Wappoo, and about the farms*—that the party which was to land on South Bay was to take the Guard House and get arms and then they would be able to go on—that the attack was to commence about twelve o'clock at night—*that great numbers would come from all about,* and it must succeed as so many were engaged in it—that they would kill all the whites. . . .

Benjamin Ford, a white lad, about 15 or 16 years of age, deposed as follows: Denmark Vesey frequently came into our shop which is near his house, and always complained of the hardships of the blacks. He said the laws were very rigid and strict and that the blacks had not their rights—that everyone had his time, and that his would come round too. *His general conversation was about religion which he would apply to slavery,* as for instance, he would speak of the creation of the world, in which he would say all men had equal rights, blacks as well as whites,—*all his religious remarks were mingled with slavery.* . . .

THE TRIAL OF MONDAY, a Negro man, the slave of Mr. John Gell,—Col. Wm. Rouse as his friend, and Jacob Axson, Esq., counsel for his owner attending.

Evidence

. . . [Monday's confession.] The Court conceiving it all important to obtain from Monday all the information he possessed (believing him to possess more information on this subject than any man then alive), offered to recommend him to the Governor for a conditional pardon, or commutation of his punishment to banishment, if he would reveal all he knew in relation to this plot. He promised to do so, and made this second confession:

. . . The plan was to break open all the stores where arms were deposited and seize them, after they had procured the five hundred muskets above-mentioned. Vesey said he would appoint his leaders, and places of meeting, about one week before the 16th of June, but the meeting for this purpose was prevented by the capture of some of the principals before that period. Vesey determined to kill both women and children, but I opposed him and offended him in doing so. Peter and the rest agreed to the opinion of Vesey in the murder of all. Sometime before any discoveries or apprehensions were made, myself and Peirault wished to drop the business, but thought we had gone too far to retreat. I knew personally of no arms, except six pikes, shown to me by Gullah Jack, which were made by Tom Russel. I knew of no lists except the one which I kept, containing about forty names, and which I destroyed after the first interruption and alarm. It was said that William Paul had a list, but I never saw it. William Garner told me that he was to command the dray-men, and that he had procured twelve or thirteen horses. . . .

. . . I do not recollect any person who refused when I applied to him. Some took time to consider, but they all finally agreed. Vesey was considered by the whole party, as a man of great capacity, and was also thought to possess a bloody disposition. He had, I am told, in the course of his life, seven wives, and had travelled through almost every part of the world, with his former master Captain Vesey, and spoke French with fluency. Morris Brown, Harry Drayton, and Charles Corr, and other influential leaders of the African Church, were never consulted on this subject, for fear they would betray us to the whites. Vesey had many years ago a pamphlet on the slave trade. Vesey said that his eldest stepson was engaged in this affair. . . .

THE TRIAL OF GULLAH JACK, a Negro man, belonging to Mr. Pritchard—his owner attending.

Evidence

Witness no. 10, testified as follows: Jack Pritchard also called on me about this business—he is sometimes called Gullah Jack, sometimes Cooter Jack. He gave me some dry food, consisting of parched corn and ground nuts, and said eat that and nothing else on the morning it breaks out, and when you join us as we pass put into your mouth this crab-claw and you can't then be wounded, and said he, I give the same to the rest of my troops—if you drop the large crab-claw out of your mouth, then put in the small one. Said I, when do you break out and have you got arms—he said a plenty, but they are over Boundary Street, we can't get at them now, but as soon as the Patrol was slack they could get them. . . . He said the white people were looking for him and he was afraid of being taken; that two men came to his master's wharf and asked him if he knew Gullah Jack, and that he told them no—*he said his charms would not protect him from the treachery of his own color.* He went away and I have not seen him since. . . .

George, Mr. Vanderhorst's slave, gave the testimony following: Gullah Jack is an enemy of the white people. I attended a meeting of several at his house, and he was the head man there. All present agreed to join & come against the whites. Jack was my leader—he is the head of the Gullah Company. I heard that among them they had charms. Jack said if any man betrayed them, they would injure him, and I was afraid to inform. The little man standing before me is Gullah Jack, who had large black whiskers, which he has cut since I saw him last. If I am accepted as a witness and my life spared, I must beg the Court to send me away from this place, *as I consider my life in great danger from having given testimony.* I have heard it said all about the streets, generally, I can't name anyone in particular, that whoever is the white man's friend, God help them; from which I understood they would be killed—I was afraid of Gullah Jack as a conjurer. . . .

The court unanimously found Gullah Jack guilty, and passed upon him the sentence of death.

Subsequently to his conviction, Harry Haig, who received sentence of death at the same time that he had, made the following confession:

. . . Until Jack was taken up and condemned to death, I felt as if I was bound up, and had not the power to speak one word about it. Jack charmed Julius and myself at last, and we then consented to join. Tom Russel the blacksmith and Jack are partners (in conjuring), Jack taught him to be a doctor. Tom talked to Jack about the fighting and agreed to join, and those two brought Julius and myself to agree to it. Jack said Tom was his second and "when you don't see me, and see Tom, you see me." Jack said Tom was making arms for the black people—Jack said he could not be killed, nor could a white man take him." . . .

SENTENCE ON DENMARK VESEY, a free black man—Denmark Vesey: the Court, on mature consideration, have pronounced you guilty. You have enjoyed the advantage of able Counsel, and were also heard in your own defence, in which you endeavored, with great art and plausibility, to impress a belief of your innocence. After the most patient deliberation, however, the Court were not only satisfied of your guilt, but that you were the author and original instigator of this diabolical plot. Your professed design was to trample on all laws, human and divine; to riot in blood, outrage, rapine, and conflagration, and to introduce anarchy and confusion in their most horrid forms. Your life has become, therefore, a just and necessary sacrifice, at the shrine of indignant justice. It is difficult to imagine what *infatuation* could have prompted you to attempt an enterprise so wild and visionary. You were a free man; were comparatively wealthy; and enjoyed every comfort compatible with your situation. You had, therefore, much to risk, and little to gain. From your age and experience, you *ought* to have known, that success was impracticable.

A moment's reflection must have convinced you, that the ruin of *your race,* would have been the probable result, and that years would have rolled away, before they could have recovered that confidence which they once enjoyed in this community. The only reparation in your power is a full disclosure of the truth. In addition to treason, you have committed the grossest impiety, in attempting to pervert the sacred words of God into a sanction for crimes of the blackest hue. It is evident, that you are totally insensible of the divine influence of that Gospel, "all whose paths are peace." It was to reconcile us to our destinies on earth, and to enable us to discharge with fidelity, all the duties of life, that those holy precepts were imparted by Heaven to fallen man.

If you had searched them with sincerity, you would have discovered instructions, immediately applicable to the deluded victims of your artful wiles—"Servants (says Saint Paul) obey in all things your masters, according to the flesh, not with eye-service, as men-pleasers, but in singleness of heart, fearing God." And again "Servants (says Saint Peter) be subject to your masters with all fear, not only to the good and gentle, but also to the froward." On such texts comment is unnecessary.

Your "lamp of life" is nearly extinguished; your race is run, and you must shortly pass "from time to eternity." Let me then conjure you to devote the remnant of your existence in solemn preparation for the awful doom that awaits you. Your situation is deplorable, but not destitute of spiritual consolation. To that Almighty Being alone, whose Holy Ordinances you have trampled in the dust, can you now look for mercy, and although "your sins be as scarlet," the tears of sincere penitence may obtain forgiveness at the "Throne of Grace." You cannot have forgotten the history of the malefactor on the Cross, who, like yourself, was the wretched and deluded victim of offended justice. His conscience was awakened in the pangs of dissolution, and yet there is reason to believe, that his spirit was received into the realms of bliss. May *you* imitate his example, and may *your* last moments prove like his!

SENTENCE ON JACK, a slave belonging to Paul Pritchard, commonly called Gullah Jack, and sometimes Cooter Jack—Gullah Jack: the Court after deliberately considering all the circumstances of your case, are perfectly satisfied of your guilt. In the prosecution of your wicked designs, you were not satisfied with resorting to natural and ordinary means, but endeavored to enlist on your behalf, all the powers of darkness, and employed for that purpose, the most disgusting mummery and superstition. You represented yourself as invulnerable; that you could neither be taken nor destroyed, and that all who fought under your banners would be invincible. While such wretched expedients are calculated to excite the confidence, or to alarm the fears of the ignorant and credulous, they produce no other emotion in the minds of the intelligent and enlightened, but contempt and disgust. Your boasted charms have not preserved yourself, and of course could not protect others. Your altars and your Gods have sunk together in the dust. The airy spectres, conjured by you, have been chased away by the superior light of Truth, and you stand exposed, the miserable and deluded victim of offended justice. Your days are literally numbered. You will shortly be consigned to the cold and silent grave; and all the Powers of Darkness cannot rescue you from your approaching Fate! Let me then, conjure you to devote the remnant of your miserable existence, in fleeing from the *wrath to come*. This can only be done by a full disclosure of the truth. The Court are willing to afford you all the aid in their power, and to permit any Minister of the Gospel, whom you may select to have free access to you. To him you may unburden your guilty conscience. Neglect not the opportunity, for there is no device nor art in the grave, to which you must shortly be consigned.

Introduction to Documents 2 and 3

White Americans reacted to the Vesey conspiracy with powerful emotions. Southerners often censored themselves for fear that merely discussing the matter openly would spread the seeds of rebellion. But what emerges from the surviving documents is a sense of fear that sometimes bordered on hysteria around Charleston. Anna Hayes Johnson, daughter of U.S. Supreme Court Justice William Johnson (who questioned the extent of the conspiracy and was widely condemned in South Carolina for counseling moderation), wrote several confidential letters to her cousin in Raleigh, North Carolina that expressed deep sexual fears about the rebels and also questioned the need for so many executions. John Potter, on the other hand, had no reservations about the draconian punishments being meted out. Potter, a financier, wrote to fellow South Carolinian Langdon Cheves, director of the Bank of the United States. As you read Johnson's and Potter's letters, consider in what ways their reactions to the plot were similar or different.

Document 2   *"Gracious Heaven When I Think What I Have Escaped"*

ANNA HAYES JOHNSON LETTERS TO HER COUSIN
Charleston, June 23, 1822

. . . *My Dear Betsy.* . . . ,

Gracious Heaven when I think what I have escaped & what I may yet suffer my blood curdles—Alas, Sterne too truly said that "Slavery was a bitter draught"—Our slaves have revolted and the plot was only found out by the noble interposition of a negro whom they invited to join them . . . he instantly with the subtlety of his class drew from his acquaintance the design plan time & ca and then with trembling anxiety inform'd his master who instantly informed the Intendant & my uncle who is fortunately Governour and by them every means was taken to protect the city—for the information was given only a few days before the insurrection was to have taken place—since which a court of enquiry has been instituted of the most impartial and honourable men of our city who have been sitting now more than a week and the number implicated is incredible—and I blush to own that it has been traced to the whites for this day one or two white men have been taken up and the proofs are so strong as to hang them—for some intelligent negro who acts as a spy for the court found where their nightly meetings were held and carried our Intendant and one or two others there who saw and heard scenes of rapine & murder talked of with the coolness of demons—Their plans were simply these—they were to have set fire to the town and while the whites were endeavouring to out it they were to have commenced their horrid depredations—It seems that the Governour Intendant and my poor father were to be the three first victims—the men & Black Women were to have been indiscriminately murdered—& we poor devils were to have been reserved to fill their Harams [sic]—horrible—I have a very beautiful cousin who was set apart for the wife or more properly the "light of the Haram" of one of their Chiefts—and the old and infirm women were to have shared the fate of our fathers—It is true that in our city the white & Black population are equal 16,000 each but about Georgetown the odds is fearful—16,000 B—to 150 W—I do not know the estimate of the black population thro' the state but I know that it is very great—I am told that the number in the plot is computed to be about 3000. . . .

God bless you

A. H. J.

Charleston, July 18th, 1822

My *dear Cousin,*

. . . I suppose that by this time you are anxious to hear more about the unhappy business which has filled with consternation all our city and nothing but the merciful interposition of our God has saved us from horror equal if not superior to the scenes acted in St Domingo—The catalogue is not filled up for we thought that it was ended and that the execution of six of the chiefs would suffice. The court had been dismissed and the town was again sinking into its wanted security when information was given that another attempt would be made at such a time, and the states witness gave information of such a nature as to induce the city council to recall the court, and since that period the alarm has spread most widely, and there are now between 50 & 60 of the leaders in our jail—It is said that twenty of them have been convicted & sentenced, and in all probability the execution will not end under 100, but I was told yesterday that the prisoners had been heard to say that even should there be 500 executed there would be still enough to carry the work into execution. Denmark Vesey one of those already executed and who was the instigator of the whole plot acknowledged that he had been nine years endeavouring to effect the diabolical scheme, how far the mischief has extended heaven only knows—I never heard in my life more deep laid plots or plots more likely to succeed, indeed "t'was a plot a good plot—an excellent plot."

But t'was a plot that had it succeeded would have told to after ages a most fearful tale—It would be absurd in me to attempt a detail of all the circumstances real or imaginary which I have heard—this much is all that I know of that bears the stamp of truth: that their intention was to take the city and keep it as long as possible and then carry *us* & the common negro's to St D there to be sold as slaves with as much plunder as they could find . . . it seems that this Vesey had been to St D and made an agreement that at such a time so many Vessels should be here to assist—it would have been a complete scene of desolation—as yet thank God none of our slaves have been found in the plot. . . .

. . . *Farewell God Bless you*
Anna

DOCUMENT 3 *"The Conspiracy Had Spread Wider and Wider"*

JOHN POTTER TO LANGDON CHEVES

(*private*)
Charleston 29th June 1822

My Dear Sir,

. . . A court of the most respectable individuals in the City have been patiently and laborously investigating this business, for 10 or 12 days past—and you will perceive by the news papers I send you that six wretches are to pay the forfeit of their worthless lives on tuesday—the plot was deeply laid, and a plan of insurrection (which a member of the court told me yesterday) was organized with an address & cunning, as he said would much surprise the community. At first Governor Bennett could not believe that his own negroes were implicated—but the subsequent investigation proved a scene of guilt, and murder, to be intended, unparallel'd even exceeding if possible, the *Demons,* of St. Domingo!!!

His excellency it is said was to be the first victim by his favorite servant Rolla—and his reward was to be Miss B. the Governor's daughter—the very thought makes my blood recoil in my veins. I believe the plan was that the white males were all to be cut off—!!

Their meetings commenced, and were held under the perfidious cover of religion—and I cannot doubt that they were aided by the black missionaries from your City! . . .

I am always Yrs truly
J: Potter

(*Confidential*)
Charleston 10th July 1822

My Dear Sir

. . . Since I last wrote you about this most diabolical plot which the mercy of God prevented on the very eve & very day of distruction—the public mind has been very much agitated—the first court resumed its labors, and every step they advanced it was found that the Conspiracy had spread wider and wider. . . . Indeed it is now well ascertained that most of the coachmen & favourite servants in the City knew of it even if they had not participated in the intentions & plans proposed. . . .

Alas a house newly built opposite Judge Johnson's, R. Cunningham's & several others most conspicuous, at the opposite corner—were to be fired on the night of the 16th ult. when as the white males were to appear—even before they could leave their own doors, the indiscriminate massacre was to take place—the females were to be reserved *for worse than death.* It is believed that Vesey's plans when this had been completed [were] to have forced the Banks and carried off as much plunder as he could to St. Domingo—and leave his blind agents behind (as all could not go) [to] perish for their crimes—

When your kind, and tender hearted Philadelphians, as well as Quakers preach up emancipation—let them *ponder* on the deeds of darkness & misery that would have taken place had this plot even in part succeeded—but such evils are disregarded if their favourite plan of *philanthropy* had been successful—God in his mercy reward them for it!!! this is the spot from whence our evils spring!! . . .

J: Potter

Charleston 20th July 1822

My Dear Sir

. . . This cunningly and deeply devised plot was much more extensive than you had any idea of, when you wrote on the 11th: nothing could be better arranged and would have done credit to a better cause & other means—

All the arms on the Neck were deposited in one place—to which a negro had access and was to deliver the key—700 stand of muskets would also [—?] been in their power—& there was enough powder ready at hand—and when the guard was overpowered—and arsenal taken, the torch was to give the signal of murder and blood—all those who were to go out on the cry of fire, which was to be multiplied, would meet their fate—the draymen, carters, and coachmen to act as Cavalry and secure the streets, when the confidential servants in the plot indoors were to murder every white male master of an adult age—many I hope were not implicated, I have no reason to suppose any of my house servants were guilty, but there were enough to commence with, and but anyway successfull even for a moment all, or nearly all, would have joined!

It is said by a fellow in his confession that when *Vesey* was inducing him to murder his master, he hesitated—but at length assented—then, what says he, will be done with the children? what says this *arch villain*, kill the *Lice* and let the *nitts* remain—no—no—never!!! Dr. Haig's Harry was pressed by Gulla Jack to poison his masters well—but he says he refused to do that deed, but assented to all the rest. . . .

J: Potter

Introduction to Document 4

Southern newspapers avoided covering the conspiracy for fear that literate slaves would spread word to their fellows. As northern newspapers learned of the trouble, however, they began to run stories on the rebellion, and the southern press responded. The following is an exchange that took place in the pages of the New York *Daily Advertiser* and the Charleston *Courier* in the summer of 1822. The *Advertiser's* position was an extreme one for the time, but it forced important local organs of public opinion to acknowledge the crisis openly. How do you think the *Advertiser's* editor would have responded to the remarks in the Charleston papers?

DOCUMENT 4   *"White Men, Too, Would Engender Plots"*

NEWSPAPERS REPORT THE VESEY CONSPIRACY

New York Daily Advertiser
INSURRECTION AMONG THE BLACKS JULY 31, 1822

. . . It ought to excite no astonishment with those who boast of freedom themselves, if they should occasionally hear of plots and desertion among those who are held in perpetual bondage. Human beings, who once breathed the air of freedom on their own mountains and in their own valleys, but who have been kidnapped by white men and dragged

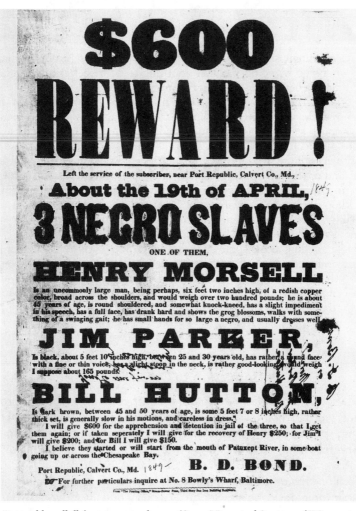

Reward handbill for runaway slaves. (State Historical Society of Wisconsin)

into endless slavery, cannot be expected to be contented with their situation. White men, too, would engender plots and escape from their imprisonment were they situated as are these miserable children of Africa.

INSURRECTION AT CHARLESTON AUGUST 6, 1822

. . . As yet nothing has appeared that has met our view to justify the great sacrifice of human lives that has taken place. . . . How many more of these miserable wretches are to pay the forfeit of their lives for an attempt to free themselves from bondage we are yet to learn. How far the destruction of so many lives as have already been taken can be justified in the eyes of a christian world, if it can be justified at all, must depend upon what is hereafter to be disclosed. Certain it is that neither the spirit nor letter of the law under which these executions have taken place, sanctions the enormous sacrifice.

Charleston Courier
AUGUST 12, 1822

. . . We have not been inattentive, in this distressing period, to the notice which might be taken of our situation by the journals in our sister states. It is grateful in the extreme to mark the tenderness and sympathy which, with the exception of one solitary print in New-York, have been universally manifested towards us. We are not in a state of mind to use language of acrimonious asperity. We regard with piety the individual who could deliberately sneer at our misfortunes—we leave him to the consolations of his conscience—his nightly dreams on his pillow—and hope he may always enjoy that security, which he so much rejoices that our city has been deprived of.

Yet, as an historical fact, worthy to be remembered, particularly at this time, and which Mr. STONE, of the N. York *Commercial Advertiser*, appears to have forgotten, we would remind him, as we had occasion once before to remind another editor of New-York, that in the year 1741, in the city of New-York, *thirteen Negroes were* BURNT ALIVE *for insurrectionary efforts.*

During the whole of this momentous inquiry, the utmost confidence has been felt in the State and City authorities, and in the two successive Courts organized to award justice, and acting under the most painful responsibilities. The Militia have with alacrity performed the unusual and laborious duties assigned them;—and now let us hope that the God of goodness and of mercy, who has guarded and protected us in the hour of peril, will continue to us his benevolent care, and frustrate always the evil designs of our enemies, and of those who conspire alike against our happiness and their own.

Introduction to Document 5

David Walker, a free black born in Wilmington, North Carolina, lived in Charleston on the eve of the Vesey plot, and he was probably a member of the African Methodist Episcopal church. Did the two men ever meet, did one influence the other, was Walker even part of the conspiracy? There is no way of knowing. Clearly, they shared many ideas about Africa, Haiti, the meanings of Christianity, and the necessity of freedom for all African Americans. Some time in the early 1820s, Walker moved to Boston, and he was soon a prominent member of the free black community, where he owned a used clothing store. And then in 1829 he wrote his *Appeal,* a clarion call to end slavery, peacefully if possible, violently if necessary. And once his words were on paper, Walker worked hard to distribute them into the South through ports like Wilmington and Charleston.

White people, Walker declared, "have always been an unjust, jealous, unmerciful, avaricious and blood-thirsty set of beings, always seeking after power and authority." Even within the nascent abolitionist movement (which was seen as very radical in the antebellum era) Walker's *Appeal* was controversial. Most antislavery people before the 1850s came to their convictions through pacifism, the belief that *all* violence was wrong. Walker's intimations of bloodshed offended many of those who otherwise agreed that slavery was evil, indeed sinful.

The *Appeal* reads like oratory more than finished prose. Walker's sentences are rough, even ungrammatical yet powerful. Despite circumlocutions and wordiness, the author's ability to address his audience directly (sometimes speaking to whites, sometimes to blacks), and to claim moral authority from sources like the Bible and the Declaration of Independence gave the work its power. From the following passages, on what grounds did Walker attack slavery? How did he justify an assault against a legally sanctioned institution?

DOCUMENT 5 *David Walker's* Appeal to the Coloured Citizens of the World

. . . When we take a retrospective view of the arts and sciences—the wise legislators—The Pyramids, and other magnificent buildings—the turning of the channel of the river Nile, by the sons of Africa or of Ham, among whom learning originated, and was carried thence into Greece, where it was improved upon and refined. Thence among the Romans, and all over the then enlightened parts of the world, and it has been enlightening the dark and benighted minds of men from then, down to this day. I say, when I view retrospectively, the renown of that once mighty people, the children of our great progenitor, I am indeed cheered. Yea further, when I view that mighty son of Africa, HANNIBAL, one of the greatest generals of antiquity, who defeated and cut off so many thousands of the white Romans or murderers, and who carried his victorious arms, to the very gate of Rome, and I give it as my candid opinion, that had Carthage been well united and had given him good support, he would have carried that cruel and barbarous city by storm. But they were disunited, as the colored people are now, in the United States of America, the reason our natural enemies are enabled to keep their feet on our throats.

Beloved brethren—here let me tell you, and believe it, that the Lord our God, as true as he sits on his throne in heaven, and as true as our Saviour died to redeem the world, will give you a Hannibal, and when the Lord shall have raised him up, and given him to you for your possession, O my suffering brethren! remember the divisions and consequent sufferings of *Carthage* and of *Hayti*, Read the history particularly of Hayti, and see how they were butchered by the whites, and do you take warning. The person whom God shall give you, give him your support and let him go his length, and behold in him the salvation of your God. . . .

I do declare it, that one good black man can put to death six white men; and I give it as a fact, let twelve black men get well armed for battle, and they will kill and put to flight fifty whites. The reason is, the blacks, once you get them started, they glory in death. The whites have had us under them for more than three centuries, murdering, and treating us like brutes; and, as Mr. Jefferson wisely said, they have never *found us out*—they do not know, indeed, that there is an unconquerable disposition in the breasts of the blacks, which when it is fully awakened and put in motion, will be subdued, only with the destruction of the animal existence. Get the blacks started, and if you do not have a gang of lions and tigers to deal with, I am a deceiver of the blacks and the whites. . . .

. . . Now, I ask you had you not rather be killed than to be a slave to a tyrant, who takes the life of your mother, wife, and dear little children? Look upon your mother, wife and children, and answer God Almighty; and believe this, that it is no more harm for you to kill a man, who is trying to kill you, than it is for you to take a drink of water when thirsty; in fact, the man who will stand still and let another murder him, is worse than an infidel, and if he has common sense, ought not to to be pitied. . . .

Will not those who were burnt up in Sodom and Gomorrah rise up in judgment against Christian Americans with the Bible in their hands, and condemn them? Will not the Scribes and Pharisees of Jerusalem, who had nothing but the laws of Moses and the Prophets to go by, rise up in judgment against Christian Americans, and condemn them who in addition to these have a revelation from Jesus Christ the son of the living God? In fine, will not the Antediluvians, together with the whole heathen world of antiquity, rise up in judgment against Christian Americans and condemn them? The Christians of Europe and America go to Africa, bring us away, and throw us into the seas, and in other ways murder us, as they would wild beasts. The Antediluvians and heathens never dreamed of such barbarities. . . .

How many vessel loads of human beings have the blacks thrown into the seas? How many thousand souls have the blacks murdered in cold blood to make them work in wretchedness and ignorance, to support them and their families . . . ? I say, from the beginning, I do not think that we were natural enemies to each other. But the whites having made us so wretched, by subjecting us to slavery, and having murdered so many millions of us in order to make us work for them, and out of devilishness—and they taking our wives, whom we love as we do ourselves—our mothers who bore the pains of death to give us birth—our fathers & dear little children, and ourselves, and strip and beat us one before the other—chain, handcuff and drag us about like rattle-snakes—shoot us down like wild bears, before each other's faces, to make us submissive to and work to support them and their families. . . .

Remember Americans, that we must and shall be free, and enlightened as you are, will you wait until we shall, under God, obtain our liberty by the crushing arm of power? Will it not be dreadful for you? I speak Americans for your good. We must and shall be free I say, in spite of you. You may do your best to keep us in wretchedness and misery, to enrich you and your children but God will deliver us from under you. And wo, wo, will be to you if we have to obtain our freedom by fighting. Throw away your fears and prejudices then, and enlighten us and treat us like men, and we will like you more than we do now hate you, and tell us now no more about colonization, for America is as much our country, as it is yours.—Treat us like men, and there is no danger but we will all live in peace and happiness together. For we are not like you, hard hearted, unmerciful, and unforgiving. What a happy country this will be, if the whites will listen. . . .

The Americans may say or do as they please, but they have to raise us from the condition of brutes to that of respectable men, and to make a national acknowledgement to us for the wrongs they have inflicted on us. As unexpected, strange, and wild as these propositions may to some appear, it is no less a fact, that unless they are complied with, the Americans of the United States, though they may for a little while escape, God will yet weigh them in a balance, and if they are not superior to other men, as they have represented themselves to be, he will give them wretchedness to their very heart's content. . . .

If any are anxious to ascertain who I am, know the world, that I am one of the oppressed, degraded and wretched sons of Africa, rendered so by the avaricious and unmerciful, among the whites.—If any wish to plunge me into the wretched incapacity of a slave, or murder me for the truth, know yet that I am in the hand of God, and at your disposal I count my life not dear unto me, but I am ready to be offered at any moment. For what is the use of living when in fact I am dead. But remember Americans, that as miserable, wretched, degraded and abject as you have made us in preceding, and in this generation, to support you and your families that some of you (whites) on the continent of America, will yet curse the day that you ever were born. You want slaves, and want us for your slaves!!! My colour will yet, root some of you out of the very face of the earth!!!!!! You may doubt it if you please. I know that thousands will doubt—they think they have us so well secured in wretchedness, to them and their children, that it is impossible for such things to occur. So did the antideluvians doubt Noah, until the day in which the flood came and swept them away. So did the Sodomites doubt, until Lot had got out of the City, and God rained down fire and brimstone from heaven, upon them and burnt them up. So did the king of Egypt doubt the very existence of a God, he said, "who is the Lord, that I should let Israel go?" Did he not find to his sorrow, who the Lord was, when he and all his mighty men of war, were smothered to death in the Red Sea?—So did the Romans doubt, many of them were really so ignorant, that they thought the world of mankind were made to be slaves to them; just as many of the Americans think now, of my colour. . . .

See the hundreds and thousands of us that are thrown into the seas by Christians, and murdered by them in other ways. They cram us into their vessel holds in chains and in hand-cuffs—men, women and children, all together!! O! save us, we pray thee, thou God of heaven and of earth, from the devouring hands of the white Christians!!!!!! . . .

I also ask the attention of the world of mankind to the declaration of these very American people, of the United States. . . .

> When in the course of human events it becomes necessary for one people to dissolve the political bands which have connected them with another, and to assume among the Powers of the earth, the separate and equal station to which the laws of nature and of nature's God entitle them, a decent respect for the opinions of mankind requires that they should declare the causes which impel them to the separation. We hold these truths to be self evident, that all men are created equal, that they are endowed by their Creator with certain unalienable rights; that among these are life, liberty, and the pursuit of happiness; that to secure these rights, governments are instituted among men, deriving their just powers from the consent of the governed; that whenever any form of government becomes destructive of these ends it is the right of the people to alter or to abolish it, and to institute a new government laying its foundation on such principles, and organizing its powers in such form as to them shall seem most likely to effect their safety and happiness. . . .

Compare your own language above, extracted from your Declaration of Independence, with your cruelties and murders inflicted by your cruel and unmerciful fathers on ourselves on our fathers and on us, men who have never given your fathers or you the least provocation!!! . . . Now, Americans! I ask you candidly, was your sufferings under Great Britain one hundredth part as cruel and tyrannical as you have rendered out under you? . . .

POSTSCRIPT

Walker's *Appeal* went through three editions, and much to the horror of masters, slaves were found with copies in their possession. Southerners demanded that the work be suppressed, bounties were offered on Walker, and in 1830, he was found dead on a Boston street. The cause of his demise was not determined. One year later, Nat Turner led the bloodiest slave rebellion in American history. There is no direct evidence linking Walker and Turner, only the coincidence of one man calling for rebellion and another fomenting it.

QUESTIONS

Defining Terms

Identify in the context of the chapter each of the following:

Eli Whitney	Gabriel Prosser
Santo Domingo	Rolla
Denmark Vesey	David Walker
Anna Hayes Johnson	"free-labor capitalistic economy"
staple crops	Toussaint L'Ouverture

Probing the Sources

1. How big was Vesey's conspiracy? What does the evidence indicate? Why is the size of the conspiracy important?
2. What was the role of religion in shaping or motivating the conspiracy and the white response? How did Vesey's understanding of Christianity differ from that of the court that sentenced him to death?
3. Why did the plot fail? What were the rebels up against, and why was it so hard to mount a successful rebellion?
4. How and why did Walker invoke the Declaration of Independence?

Interpreting the Sources

1. What was the white reaction to Vesey's plot? Why were some whites surprised by the "ingratitude" of their slaves? Why might previously loyal and relatively well-treated blacks become rebels?
2. How would you describe the motives and character of Vesey's lieutenants? How important was leadership and organizational ability to this incident?
3. Slavery was the law of the land: was rebellion justified?
4. Resolved. For the sake of public safety, Walker's *Appeal* must be banned. Discuss.

ADDITIONAL READING

On Denmark Vesey and the conspiracy itself, see Vincent Harding, *There Is a River: The Black Struggle for Freedom in America* (1981). For the daily life of slaves, including discussions of slave rebellions, see John Blassingame, *The Slave Community: Plantation Life in the Ante-Bellum South* (1979); Kenneth M. Stampp, *The Peculiar Institution: Slavery in the Ante-Bellum South* (1956); and Eugene Genovese, *Roll, Jordan, Roll: The World the Slaves Made* (1974). On African-American culture, including music, humor, and folktales, see Lawrence Levine, *Black Culture and Black Consciousness: Afro-American Folk Thought from Slavery to Freedom* (1977), and Charles Joyner, *Down by the Riverside: A South Carolina Slave Community* (1984). On women and slavery, see Elizabeth Fox Genovese, *Within the Plantation Household: Black and White Women of the Old South* (1988). For primary sources on day-to-day life, see the testimony of thousands of former slaves contained in George P. Rawick, ed., *The American Slave: A Composite Autobiography* (1972). On David Walker, see Peter P. Hinks, *To Awaken My Afflicted Bretheren: David Walker and the Problem of Antebellum Slave Resistance* (1997).

9

Remembering the Alamo

HISTORICAL CONTEXT

The story is a simple one. On March 6, 1836, 183 men, eight of them Mexicans and the rest Americans, were killed trying to defend the fortress Alamo in San Antonio de Béjar, Texas. They were overwhelmed shortly after dawn by hundreds of Mexican troops under General Antonio López de Santa Anna. The victors paid a high price; scaling the walls and taking the fortress cost the attacking army almost four times as many men as died defending it. The last half dozen or so Americans surrendered; they were immediately executed by order of Santa Anna.

But no good story is ever truly simple.

Seven-day-old Juan Nepomuceno Seguín was baptized in the parish church of San Antonio de Béjar on November 3, 1806. Seguín's father and grandfather had been baptized in the very same church in this outpost of the Spanish empire. Indeed, Seguín's great-great-grandfather had been a soldier, then a rancher and local leader in the region, and over the decades, the family had prospered and helped make the settlement of Spanish Texas permanent. Seguín's father, José Erasmo Seguín, controlled over fifteen thousand acres of land, and Juan, too, became part of the local elite.

The 1820s and 1830s, the years of Juan's young adulthood, were turbulent times. Early in the nineteenth century, Spain held more territory west of the Mississippi River than did the United States. Although a big chunk of the trans-Mississippi West had been acquired by the United States through the Louisiana Purchase of 1803, Spanish land still stretched from Louisiana and the Gulf Coast to the Pacific Ocean, and from the northern border of present-day California east to the Rocky Mountains and south through Mexico and beyond.

Yet rapidly, the Spanish empire fell apart. The contagion of colonial rebellion spread from North America, and soon new nations in the Southern Hemisphere defined and liberated themselves from Spanish rule. Independence came to Mexico in 1821, and that new nation claimed all of the land in the northernmost parts of the old Spanish empire, from the Yucatán peninsula north past Yerba Buena (later San Francisco) and Santa Fe.

The northeastern portion of the new Mexican nation was in a precarious position. These borderlands were quite underpopulated, and *Norteamericanos* alternately offered to buy or threatened to take them. The Mexican government decided that a stable population would help secure the region, so for a small amount of money and vague pledges to become Roman Catholics and Mexican citizens,

167

Americans were allowed to settle. Men such as Stephen F. Austin, who became a close friend of the Seguín family, made money leading hundreds of families into Texas. By 1835, nearly thirty thousand white Americans had settled in the area, outnumbering the Mexican population several times. The majority of these whites were southerners; many brought African slaves with them to Texas, where they hoped to grow rich on fresh land that was perfect for growing cotton.

But serious problems plagued the area. Under a new constitution, the Mexican government merged the provinces of Texas and Coahuila in 1824. Many Americans as well as Tejanos (Mexicans living in Texas) felt that the arrangement would not work, that they would be governed from afar and taxed for others' support. Additional issues arose. Would there really be an established church? Certainly, the Protestants were very secure in their private worship, but Catholicism was Mexico's official religion. Would slavery continue? Many Anglos came from the South—Sam Houston had been governor of Tennessee, for example—and were determined to secure their human property. Some in the Mexican congress were strongly opposed to servitude, and the Mexican government outlawed slavery in 1829, though enforcement of the law was all but nonexistent. Would open migration from the United States continue? As many of the immigrants grew hostile to their hosts (there was even an abortive uprising in 1826, which some Anglos fomented, but which others helped to put down), Mexico closed the border in 1830, although Americans continued to come in illegally.

Meanwhile, the U.S. government became increasingly belligerent as talk of the nation's future glory grew louder; southerners looked aggressively for new lands to farm with their slaves; and a strain of racism made many Anglos intolerant of their Mexican neighbors. In addition, Mexico's new leader, General Antonio López de Santa Anna seemed determined to rule in a manner that the Americans considered autocratic.

For a man like Juan Seguín, the situation was filled with tensions. His home, Béjar, was a terribly poor place, and some Tejanos—the Seguín family, for example—looked to immigration as a way to bring people, money, and therefore prosperity to the area. The Seguíns were wealthy and bilingual; they had good friends among the Americans and close commercial ties with them. The family even owned a slave, emblematic of their class identification with the more prosperous whites. Juan Seguín joined a small minority of Tejanos and supported Norteamericanos. He was commissioned as a captain, rode to the Alamo with that fortress's commander, Colonel William Travis, and escaped death there only because, a few nights before the attack, he had slipped out in order to bring reinforcements to the Americans.

So who was Juan Seguín? A freedom fighter? A traitor to his people? A defender of his class? And what of the American immigrants who died in the fort? Were they lovers of liberty or slave drivers, visionaries or racists, men who stood up to tyranny or men caught trying to take what belonged to others? Of course, no simple category can ever capture people or their times. Good answers are balanced and complex, but all answers depend on one's point of view. And when it comes to the Alamo, one's point of view is often shaped by emotion-laden legends.

Juan Seguín's story is a good example. Until the 1960s, the history of the Alamo and of Texas independence was written over and over again without his name's ever being mentioned. Historians kept the lines sharply drawn: Anglos versus Mexicans. But the political ferment of the 1960s gave a context for rethinking the past.

TEXAS
FOREVER!!

The usurper of the South has failed in his efforts to enslave the freemen of Texas.

The wives and daughters of Texas will be saved from the brutality of Mexican soldiers.

Now is the time to emigrate to the Garden of America.

A free passage, and all found, is offered at New Orleans to all applicants. Every settler receives a location of

EIGHT HUNDRED ACRES OF LAND.

On the 23d of February, a force of 1000 Mexicans came in sight of San Antonio, and on the 25th Gen. St. Anna arrived at that place with 2500 more men, and demanded a surrender of the fort held by 150 Texians, and on the refusal, he attempted to storm the fort, twice, with his whole force, but was repelled with the loss of 500 men, and the Americans lost none. Many of his troops, the liberals of Zacatecas, are brought on to Texas in irons and are urged forward with the promise of the women and plunder of Texas.

The Texian forces were marching to relieve St. Antonio, March the 2d. The Government of Texas is supplied with plenty of arms, ammunition, provisions, &c. &c.

A recruitment poster encouraging people to settle in Texas, "the garden of America," and to help "defend" it against Santa Anna's soldiers in exchange for land. The poster dates from the spring of 1836. (The University of Texas at Austin, Eugene C. Barker Texas History Center)

Some Mexican-Americans upheld Seguín as a hero, their people's contribution to the freedom of Texas. Schoolbooks and popular media quickly included him in a liberal gesture toward ethnic inclusiveness. Latinos on the political left, however, viewed Seguín not as a hero, but as an accommodationist—at best, a tragic figure in his mistaken identification with the Anglos and, at worst, complicit with the enemy in order to buttress his own privileged position. Conservatives now joined in, too. Seguín, for them, was proof that the struggle for Texas independence had had nothing to do with racism and imperialism; rather, the very participation of Latinos—a handful of them—on the Anglo side demonstrated that the real question was liberty versus tyranny, not Mexicans versus Americans.

Even an issue as simple as how Davy Crockett died at the Alamo became filled with emotion. During most of the nineteenth century, it was taken for granted that he was one of the six who surrendered and was then executed. The American press reported the event that way, and the story added credence to the image of Santa Anna as a tyrant. But in 1884, Edward S. Ellis published his fanciful *The Life of Colonel David Crockett*. According to Ellis (based on no evidence, for there was none to be had), when Santa Anna's order of execution was given, the exhausted Crockett pulled his bowie knife and attacked his enemies—and so went down fighting.

Then, in the mid–1950s, the Walt Disney Corporation televised a three-part saga on the life of Davy Crockett starring Fess Parker. Here, out of ammunition and surrounded by Mexican soldiers, Crockett is last seen swinging his rifle, "Old Betsy," like a club at his attackers. The image of the Disney Davy was reinforced by a half-year-long craze for Crockett toys marketed to children and by the sale of ten million copies of the record "The Ballad of Davy Crockett." Next, two feature-length films, *The Last Command* (1955) and *The Alamo* (1960), with John Wayne, depicted Davy dying by blowing up the Alamo's gunpowder magazine and, in the process, taking countless Mexican soldiers with him. (One American soldier, Robert Evans, actually tried to do this near the end of the siege, but he was killed in the attempt.)

Then, in 1975, Carmen Perry, former director of the Alamo Library for the Daughters of the Republic of Texas, brought out a translation of Lieutenent-Colonel José Enrique de la Peña's *With Santa Anna in Texas* (first published in 1836). De la Peña was a painstaking recorder of the events he saw, and his eyewitness account of the surrender and execution of Crockett was unimpeachable. But a generation of Disney Davy had done its work. Newspapers and popular magazines attacked the "new" interpretation. As Paul Hutton, a historian of the Alamo, noted, *People* magazine quoted Mrs. Charles Hall, then head of the Alamo committee of the Daughters of the Republic of Texas, as saying, "We don't believe Davy Crockett ever surrendered. We feel he went down fighting. And by 'we' I mean all Texans." What barely got reported was Mrs. Hall's denial of ever making that statement, the public support by the Daughters of the Republic of Texas for their former librarian, and the award given Perry's translation by the Sons of the Republic of Texas.

Three years later, in 1978, Dan Kilgore, president of the Texas State Historical Association, published a small book entitled *How Did Davy Die?* Weighing all of the evidence, Kilgore concluded that de la Peña was clearly right. But Kilgore's book, like Perry's, was both widely unread and bitterly attacked. Minds were already made up, and once again the bearer of unwelcome news was villified. Kilgore, it was implied, was an effete intellectual, or a communist, or both. By 1985, the media image of Davy Crockett was so entrenched, so much a part of the late-twentieth-century Texas mythology about itself, that the new president of the Daughters of the Republic of Texas repudiated Kilgore's work and returned to the idea that Davy died trying to blow up the powder magazine.

THE DOCUMENTS

The following documents tell the story of the Alamo from several perspectives. As you read through these pages, ask yourself how the different sources support or contradict each other and why. Who was each author's intended audience, and how did it affect what the authors said about the Alamo and how they said it? Do these documents support or contradict your own ideas about the Alamo?

DOCUMENT SET 1

Prelude

Years before the Texas revolution began, hostilities between Mexicans and Anglos had arisen. The following documents give a sense of the tensions in the borderlands. Note how each side characterized the other. What sort of differences did the authors seem to emphasize?

Introduction to Document 1

José María Sánchez was a military officer sent to the borderlands as part of a special investigative committee from Mexico City.

DOCUMENT 1 *"A Trip to Texas in 1828"*

José María Sánchez

The Americans from the north have taken possession of practically all the eastern part of Texas, in most cases without the permission of the authorities. They immigrate constantly, finding no one to prevent them, and take possession of the *sitio* [location] that best suits them without either asking leave or going through any formality other than that of building their homes. Thus the majority of inhabitants in the Department are North Americans, the Mexican population being reduced to only Bejar, Nacogdoches, and La Bahía del Espíritu Santo, wretched settlements that between them do not number three thousand inhabitants, and the new village of Guadalupe Victoria that has scarcely more than seventy settlers. The government of the state, with its seat at Saltillo, that should watch over the preservation of its most precious and interesting department, taking measures to prevent its being stolen by foreign hands, is the one that knows the least not only about actual conditions, but even about its territory. . . .

The Mexicans that live here are very humble people, and perhaps their intentions are good, but because of their education and environment they are ignorant not only of the customs of our great cities, but even of the occurrences of our Revolution, excepting a few persons who have heard about them. Accustomed to the continued trade with the North Americans, they have adopted their customs and habits, and one may say truly that they are not Mexicans except by birth, for they even speak Spanish with marked incorrectness.

[*Sánchez went on to describe the town of San Felipe de Austin.*]

This village has been settled by Mr. Stephen Austin, a native of the United States of the North. It consists, at present, of forty or fifty wooden houses on the western bank of the large river known as *Rio de los Brazos de Dios*, but the houses are not arranged systematically so as to form streets, but on the contrary, lie in an irregular and desultory manner. Its population is nearly two hundred persons, of which only ten are Mexicans, for the balance are all Americans from the North with an occasional European. Two wretched little stores supply the inhabitants of the colony: one sells only whiskey, rum, sugar, and coffee; the other, rice, flour, lard, and cheap cloth. It may seem that these items are too few for the needs of the inhabitants, but they are not because the Americans from the North, at least the greater part of those I have seen, eat only salted meat, bread made by themselves out of corn meal, coffee, and home-made cheese. To these the greater part of those who live in the village add strong liquor, for they are in general, in my opinion, lazy people of vicious character. Some of them cultivate their small farms by planting corn; but this task they usually entrust to their negro slaves, whom they treat with considerable harshness. Beyond the village in an immense stretch of land formed by rolling hills are scattered the families brought by Stephen Austin, which today number more than two thousand persons. The diplomatic policy of this empresario, evident in all his actions, has, as one may say, lulled the authorities into a sense of security, while he works diligently for his own ends. In my judgment, the spark that will start the conflagration that will deprive us of

Texas, will start from this colony. All because the government does not take vigorous measures to prevent it. Perhaps it does not realize the value of what it is about to lose.

Introduction to Document 2

General Manuel Mier y Terán was a hero of the Mexican War of Independence. He headed a special commission to investigate the boundary between Mexico and the United States in 1827.

DOCUMENT 2   *A Mexican General Describes the Borderlands, 1828 and 1829*

Manuel Mier y Terán

. . . As one covers the distance from Béjar to this town [Nacogdoches] he will note that Mexican influence is proportionately diminished until on arriving in this place he will see that it is almost nothing. And indeed, whence could such influence come? Hardly from superior numbers in population, since the ratio of Mexicans to foreigners is one to ten; certainly not from the superior character of the Mexican population, for exactly the opposite is true, the Mexicans of this town comprising what in all countries is called the lowest class— the very poor and very ignorant. The naturalized North Americans in the town maintain an English school, and send their children north for further education; the poor Mexicans not only do not have sufficient means to establish schools, but they are not of the type that take any thought for the improvement of its public institutions or the betterment of its degraded condition. . . . Thus, I tell myself that it could not be otherwise than that from such a state of affairs should arise an antagonism between the Mexicans and foreigners, which is not the least of the smoldering fires which I have discovered. Therefore, I am warning you to take timely measures. Texas could throw the whole nation into revolution.

The colonists murmur against the political disorganization of the frontier, and the Mexicans complain of the superiority and better education of the colonists; the colonists find it unendurable that they must go three hundred leagues to lodge a complaint against the petty pickpocketing that they suffer from a venal and ignorant *alcalde* [magistrate]; and the Mexicans with no knowledge of the laws of their own country, nor those regulating colonization, set themselves against the foreigners, deliberately setting nets to deprive them of the right of franchise and to exclude them from the *ayuntamiento* [city council]. Meanwhile, the incoming stream of new settlers is unceasing; the first news of these comes by discovering them on land already under cultivation, where they have been located for many months; the old inhabitants set up a claim to the property, basing their titles of doubtful priority, and for which there are no records, on a law of the Spanish government; and thus arises a lawsuit in which the *alcalde* has a chance to come out with some money. In this state of affairs, the town where there are no magistrates is the one in which lawsuits abound, and it is at once evident that in Nacogdoches and its vicinity, being most distant from the seat of the general government, the primitive order of things should take its course, which is to say that this section is being settled up without the consent of anybody. . . .

[One year later, Mier y Terán wrote the following to Mexico's Minister of War.]

. . . The North Americans have conquered whatever territory adjoins them. In less than half a century, they have become masters of extensive colonies which formerly belonged to Spain and France, and of even more spacious territories from which have disappeared the former owners, the Indian tribes. There is no Power like that to the north, which by silent means, has made conquests of momentous importance. Such dexterity, such constancy in their designs, such uniformity of means of execution which always are completely successful, arouses admiration. Instead of armies, battles, or invasions, which make a great noise and for the most part are unsuccessful, these men lay hands on means, which, if considered one by one, would be rejected as slow, ineffective, and at times palpably absurd. They begin by assuming rights, as in Texas, which it is impossible to sustain in a serious discussion, making ridiculous pretensions based on historical incidents which no one admits—such as the voyage of La Salle, which was an absurd fiasco, but serves as a basis for their claim to Texas. Such extravagant claims as these are now being presented for the first time to the public by dissembling writers; the efforts that others make to submit proofs and reasons are by these men employed in reiterations and in enlarging upon matters of administration in order to attract the attention of their fellow-countrymen, not to the justice of the claim, but to the profit to be gained from admitting it. At this stage it is alleged that there is a national demand for the step which the government meditates. In the meantime, the territory against which these machinations are directed, and which has usually remained unsettled, begins to be visited by adventurers and *empresarios*; some of these take up their residence in the country, pretending that their location has no bearing upon the question of their government's claim or the boundary disputes; shortly, some of these forerunners develop an interest which complicates the political administration of the coveted territory; complaints, even threats, begin to be heard, working on the loyalty of the legitimate settlers, discrediting the efficiency of the existing authority and administration; and the matter having arrived at this stage—which is precisely that of Texas at this moment—diplomatic maneuvers begin: They incite uprisings in the territory in question and usually manifest a deep concern for the rights of the inhabitants.

Introduction to Document 3

Copying the pattern set by American cities like Boston in the 1770s, Anglos in towns such as San Augustin formed committees of safety and correspondence. Note how unwavering the following excerpts from this document are in declaring the cultural and political incompatibility of Anglos and Mexicans.

DOCUMENT 3   *Petition from the Committee of Vigilance and Public Safety for the Municipality of San Augustin, 1835*

. . . In the year of eighteen hundred and twenty-one, Texas was an uninhabited wilderness, infested by hostile Indians, from the Sabine river to San Antonio; not excepting Nacogdoches itself. Encouraged by the invitation of the colonization laws, the settlement of the wilderness was commenced, and continued by individual enterprises, entirely unaided by succors of any kind from the government; the settlement of the country has not cost the government one cent. The emigrants dared to settle an unreclaimed wilderness, the haunt of wild beasts, and the home of the daring and hostile savages; and in so doing, poured out their blood like water. . . . In the successful progress of the settlement of the country, and in the midst of the enactment of the flood of laws proffering protection to the persons and property of the emigrants, General [Vicente] Guerrero came to the office of the presidency of the republic. He and his friends spoke of liberty as a goddess, before whose shrine they were wont to worship; and the inviolable sacredness of person and property; friendship to the emigrants, &c.

Among the first acts of his administration, was one to free all the negroes: this he said, was to give splendor to his official career, and make an epoch in the history of the republic. . . .

To Guerrero, succeeded [Anastacio] Bustamente, the vice-president. The latter was considered the antipode of the former. Under his rule was enacted the law of the sixth of April, 1830, the eleventh section of which prohibited the emigration of natives of the United States of the north [into Texas], but none other: this totally separated many of the first emigrants from their relatives and friends, who intended to have removed to the country, and had disposed of their property to do so. Families, and the nearest ties of kindred and friendship were thus severed.

Bustamente was displaced by Santa Anna, who was extolled as the great apostle of equal rights. He was represented as standing in the portico of the temple of Mexican liberty, with his brows bound with a patriot's wreath, unrolling and vindicating the constitution and laws of his country.

Him, the first Convention memorialised, petitioned, we will not say supplicated: he answered all their prayers with the silence of contempt. . . .

The Anglo-Americans and the Mexicans, if not primitively a different people, habit, education and religion, have made them essentially so. The two people cannot mingle together. The strong prejudices that existed at the first emigrations, so far from having become softened and neutralised contact, having increased many fold. And as long as the people of Texas belong to the Mexican nation, their interests will be jeopardised, and their prosperity cramped. And they will always be more or less affected by the excitements of that revolutionary people.

Of all the times for Texas to declare herself independent, the present is perhaps the most exquisitely appropriate. The causes will fully justify the act before the enlightened world, and win its approbation. . . . Then, fellow-citizens, let us instruct our delegates to the next convention to pass a *Declaration of Independence* with one loud and unanimous voice. . . .

DOCUMENT SET 2

The Battle

The spark that ignited the tinder for the battle at the Alamo was a skirmish between colonial militia and Mexican troops. Anglos began raising an army, and Mexico sent six thousand soldiers north under general Antonio López de Santa Anna. The following documents come from the period just weeks before and after the hostilities at the Alamo. Note how perspectives varied, depending not only on who was writing or speaking, but also according to the intended audience. Pay special attention to the use of rhetorical strategies to persuade or motivate individuals. Are there facts about the Alamo on which we can all agree? What sorts of issues did people differ about, and do some people still disagree over questions of the meaning and interpretation of events?

DOCUMENT 4   *Sam Houston to His Soldiers, January 15, 1836*

Comrades, Citizens of Texas!

Another time I am appearing before you, and it is with the most fervent desire that this time, at least, my words will find general approval.

Our proclamations to the other states of the Mexican Confederation, asking them to support us in our struggle for the restoration of our former rights, and for the protection of the Constitution of 1824, have, as you all know, been without results. Even many of the

Mexicans who live between the Sabine and the Rio Grande have disdainfully forsaken the cause of freedom, and have not only denied us their support but united themselves with the troops of Santa Anna and as enemies waged war against the land. Others have gone beyond the Rio Grande in order to smother us in conjunction with the next invasion. Still others have gone to their plantations on the banks of the forested rivers apparently to idly observe the war. These, comrades, are for us the most dangerous, because he who is not with us is against us. Also, from the otherwise liberal inhabitants of Zacatecas we have observed no movement in our favor. No other help remains for us now than our strength and the consciousness that we have seized our arms for a just cause. Since it is impossible to call forth any sympathy from our fellow Mexican citizens and no support is to be expected from this side, and as they let us, the smallest of all the provinces, struggle without any aid, let us then, comrades, sever that link that binds us to that rusty chain of the Mexican Confederation; let us break off the live slab from the dying cactus that it may not dry up with the remainder; let us plant it anew that it may spring luxuriantly out of the fruitful savannah. Nor will the vigor of the descendents of the sturdy north ever mix with the phlegm of the indolent Mexicans, no matter how long we may live among them. Two different tribes on the same hunting ground will never get along together. The tomahawk will ever fly and the scalping knife will never rest until the last of either one tribe or the other is either destroyed or is a slave. And I ask, comrades, will we ever bend our necks as slaves, ever quietly watch the destruction of our property and the annihilation of our guaranteed rights? NO!! Never! Too well I know my people. The last drop of our blood would flow before we would bow under the yoke of these half-Indians. On my journey through the province, I have had opportunities enough to learn the wishes of our countrymen. All of Texas is for separation. Even some prominent Mexicans, who are living among us, are preaching loudly that we should sever the bond that binds us to Mexico. "Texas must be a free and independent state," is the general word. . . .

DOCUMENT 5 *Proclamation of Acting Governor James W. Robinson, January 19, 1836*

Freemen of Texas,—Yesterday an express arrived from San Antonio de Bejar, bringing despatches from J. C. Neill, lieutenant-colonel commandant of that post, communicating the important intelligence that a force of two thousand five hundred men were a short time since at Laredo, and one thousand five hundred of them had advanced as far as the Rio Frio, eighty miles from San Antonio, and that an immediate attack was expected: and also communicating the alarming fact, that only seventy-five men were in the Alamo under his command, and that provisions were scarce. Under these circumstances they ask for your aid, to defend the fortress against the enemy. Will you go? I regret to call upon you at this time of the year, when your domestic affairs demand your care and attention; but I am constrained by the imminent danger that threatens your brethren in arms, and by the danger to which the frontier inhabitants would be exposed, by neglecting to defend them, and by the disgrace and ruin of the country, consequent upon delay.

Rally then my brave countrymen, to the standard of constitutional liberty, and join your united energies, and spread the mantle of your courage over your defenseless country. Your homes, your families, your country call, and who can refuse to obey? Your homes and your friends are assailed; will you refuse to defend them? The unprotected orphan makes the silent, but irresistable appeal: the prattling child, unconscious of its danger, makes its holy invocation: the tender mother, the kind sister, and the beloved wife, cling to you with a fond hope and unshaken confidence in your patriotism and unshaken bravery. March then, with the blessing of your household Gods, to the western frontier, where you will be organized for a short, but glorious campaign. March, then, where victory awaits you, and the genius of freedom spreads her banner, and will crown her sons with imperishable laurels. Roll back the crimson stream of war to its source, and make the tyrant feel the fiery sun of blazing, burning, consuming war; and since he has driven you to take up arms in your defence, give him "war to the knife, and the knife to the hilt." Let him know how freemen can die, and how free men will live—that one day of virtuous liberty is worth an eternity of slavery. That if there is a boon, an offering held dead in heaven, "'Tis the last libation liberty draws from the heart that breaks and bleeds in its cause."

March, then, united, and without delay, and you will erect a monument in the affection of your admiring countrymen, and of the world, that will stand as firm on the pyramids of Egypt 'mid surrounding ruins, that shall continue while time shall last, and only perish "amid the war of elements, the wreck of matter, and the crush of worlds."

The God of war guide you to victory, honor, and peace.

DOCUMENT 6 *William Barret Travis to Governor Henry Smith, February 13, 1836, From the Alamo*

To His Excellency Henry Smith.

. . . My situation is truly awkward & delicate—Col Neil left me in the command—but wishing to give satisfaction to the volunteers here & not wishing to assume any command over them I issued an order for the election of an officer to command them with the exception of one company of volunteers that had previously engaged to serve under me. Bowie was elected by two small company's; & since his election he has been roaring drunk all the time; has assumed all command—& is proceeding in a most disorderly & irregular manner—interfering with private property, releasing prisoners sentenced by court martial & by the civil court & turning every thing topsy turvey—If I did not feel my honor & that of my country compromitted I would leave here instantly for some other point with the troops under my immediate command—as I am unwilling to be responsible for the drunken irregularities of any man. . . . Our spies have just returned from Rio Grande—the enemy is there one thousand strong & is making every preperation to invade us. By the 15th of March I think Texas will be invaded & every preperation should be made to receive them. . . .

In conclusion, allow me to beg that you will give me definite orders—immediately.

DOCUMENT 7 *General Antonio López de Santa Anna to the Army, February 17, 1836*

Companions in arms!—Our most sacred duties have conducted us to these plains, and urged us forward to combat with the mob of ungrateful adventurers, on whom our authorities have incautiously lavished favors, which they have failed to bestow on Mexicans. They have appropriated to themselves our territories, and have raised the standard of rebellion in order that this fertile and expanded department may be detached from our republic—persuading themselves that our unfortunate dissensions have incapacitated us for defence of our native land. Wretches! they will soon see their folly.

Soldiers—Your comrades have been treacherously sacrificed at Anahuac, Goliad and Bejar; and you are the men chosen to chastise the assassins.

My friends!—We will march to the spot whither we are called by the interest of the nation in whose services we are engaged. The candidates for "acres" of land in Texas will learn to their sorrow that their auxiliaries from New Orleans, Mobile, Boston, New York and other northern ports, from whence no aid ought to proceed, are insignificant, and that Mexicans, though naturally generous, will not suffer outrages with impunity—injurious and dishonorable to their country—let the perpetrators be whom they may.

DOCUMENT 8   *William Travis to the Public, February 24, 1836*

To the People of Texas & all Americans in the world—Fellow Citizens & Compatriots—I am besieged by a thousand or more of the Mexicans under Santa Anna. I have sustained a continual Bombardment & cannonade for 24 hours & have not lost a man. The enemy has demanded a surrender at discretion, otherwise, the garrison are to be put to the sword, if the fort is taken. I have answered the demand with a cannon shot, & our flag still waves proudly from the walls. *I shall never surrender or retreat.* Then, I call on you in the name of Liberty, of patriotism & every thing dear to the American character, to come to our aid with all dispatch. The enemy is receiving reinforcements daily & will no doubt increase to three or four thousand in four or five days. If this call is neglected, I am determined to sustain myself as long as possible & die like a soldier who never forgets what is due his own honor & that of his country. VICTORY or DEATH.

William Barret Travis
Lt. Col. Comdt.

P.S.
    The Lord is on our side. When the enemy appeared in sight we had not three bushels of corn. We have since found in deserted houses 80 to 90 bushels and got into the walls 20 or 30 head of Beeves [cattle].

Travis

DOCUMENT 9   *William Travis to Sam Houston, February 25, 1836*

Sir: On the 23rd of Feb. the enemy in large force entered the city of Bexar, which could not be prevented, as I had not sufficient force to occupy both positions. Col. Batres, the Adjutant-Major of the President-General Santa Anna, demanded a surrender at discretion, calling us *foreign rebels*. I answered them with a cannon shot, upon which the enemy commenced a bombardment with a five-inch howitzer, which together with a heavy cannonade, has been kept up incessantly ever since. I instantly sent express to Col. Fannin, at Goliad, and to the people of Gonzales and San Felipe. Today at 10 o'clock A.M. some two or three hundred Mexicans crossed the river below and came up under cover of the houses until they arrived within point blank shot, when we opened a heavy discharge of grape and canister on them, together with a well directed fire from small arms which forced them to halt and take shelter in the houses about 90 or 100 yards from our batteries. The action continued to rage about two hours, when the enemy retreated in confusion, dragging off many of their dead and wounded.

    . . . The Hon. David Crockett was seen at all points, animating the men to do their duty. Our numbers are few and the enemy still continues to approximate his works to ours. I have every reason to apprehend an attack from his whole force very soon: but I shall hold out to the last extremity, hoping to secure reinforcements in a day or two. Do hasten on aid to me as rapidly as possible, as from the superior number of the enemy, it will be impossible for us to keep them out much longer. If they overpower us, we fall a sacrifice at the shrine of our country, and we hope posterity and our country will do our memory justice. Give me help, oh my Country! Victory or Death!

DOCUMENT 10 *Texas Declaration of Independence, March 2, 1836*

. . . The Mexican government, by its colonization laws, invited and induced the Anglo American population of Texas to colonize its wilderness under the pledged faith of a written constitution, that they should continue to enjoy that constitutional liberty and republican government to which they had been habituated in the land of their birth, the United States of America.

In this expectation they have been cruelly disappointed, inasmuch as the Mexican nation has acquiesced to the late changes made in the government by General Antonio Lopez de Santa Anna, who, having overturned the constitution of his country, now offers, as the cruel alternative, either to abandon our homes, acquired by so many privations, or submit to the most intolerable of all tyranny, the combined despotism of the sword and the priesthood.

It hath sacrificed our welfare to the state of Coahuila, by which our interests have been continually depressed through a jealous and partial course of legislation, carried on at a far distant seat of government, by a hostile majority, in an unknown tongue. . . .

It incarcerated in a dungeon, for a long time, one of our citizens [Stephen Austin] for no other cause but a zealous endeavour to procure the acceptance of our constitution, and the establishment of a state government.

It has failed and refused to secure, on a firm basis, the right of trial by jury. . . .

It has failed to establish any public system of education. . . .

It has suffered the military commandants, stationed among us, to exercise arbitrary acts of oppression and tyranny. . . .

It has dissolved, by force of arms, the state congress of Coahuila and Texas. . . .

It has demanded the surrender of a number of our citizens, and ordered military detachments to seize and carry them into the interior for trial, in contempt of the civil authorities, and in defiance of the laws and the constitution.

It has made piratical attacks upon our commerce, by commissioning foreign desperadoes, and authorizing them to seize our vessels, and convey the property of our citizens to far distant ports for confiscation.

It denies us the right of worshipping the Almighty according to the dictates of our own conscience, by the support of a national religion, calculated to promote the temporal interest of its human functionaries, rather than the glory of the true and living God.

It has demanded us to deliver up our arms, which are essential to our defence—the rightful property of freemen—and formidable only to tyrannical governments.

It has invaded our country both by sea and by land, with the intent to lay waste our territory, and drive us from our homes: and has now a large mercenary army advancing to carry on against us a war of extermination.

It has through its emissaries, incited the merciless savage, with the tomahawk and scalping knife, to massacre the inhabitants of our defenseless frontiers.

It has been, during the whole time of our connection with it, the contemptible sport and victim of successive military revolutions, and hath continually exhibited every characteristic of a weak, corrupt, and tyrannical government. . . .

The necessity of self-preservation, therefore, now decrees our eternal political separation.

We, therefore, the delegates, with plenary powers, of the people of Texas, in solemn convention assembled, appealing to a candid world for the necessities of our condition, do hereby resolve and declare, that our political connection with the Mexican nation has forever ended, and that the people of Texas do now constitute a free, sovereign, and independent republic, and are fully invested with all the rights and attributes which properly belong to independent nations; and, conscious of the rectitude of our intentions, we fearlessly and confidently commit the issue to the supreme Arbiter of the destinies of nations.

DOCUMENT 11   *General Santa Anna to General Urrea, March 3, 1836*

[Official.] In respect to the prisoners of whom you speak in your last communication, you must not fail to bear in mind the circular of the supreme government, in which it is decreed, that "foreigners invading the republic, and taken with arms in their hands, shall be judged and treated as pirates:" and as, in my view of the matter, every Mexican guilty of the crime of joining these adventurers loses the rights of a citizen by his unnatural conduct, the five Mexican prisoners whom you have taken ought also to suffer as traitors.

[Unofficial.] In regard to foreigners who make war, and those unnatural Mexicans who have joined their cause, you will remark that what I have stated to you officially is in accordance with the former provisions of the supreme government. An example is necessary, in order that those adventurers may be duly warned, and the nation be delivered from the ills she is daily doomed to suffer.

DOCUMENT 12   *William Travis to David Ayers, March 3, 1836*

Take care of my little boy. If the country should be saved, I may make him a splendid fortune; but if the country should be lost and I should perish, he will have nothing but the proud recollection that he is the son of a man who died for his country.

DOCUMENT 13   *William Travis to Jesse Grimes, March 3, 1836*

. . . I am still here, in fine spirits and well to do, with 145 men. I have held this place 10 days against a force variously estimated from 1,500 to 6,000, and shall continue to hold it till I get relief from my countrymen, or I will perish in its defense. We have had a shower of bombs and cannon balls continually falling among us the whole time, yet none of us has fallen. We have been miraculously preserved. You have no doubt seen my official report of the action of the 25th ult in which we repulsed the enemy with considerable loss; on the night of the 25th they made another attempt to charge us in the rear of the fort, but we received them gallantly by a discharge of grape shot and musquetry, and they took to their scrapers immediately. They are now encamped in entrenchments on all sides of us.

. . . Let the Convention go on and make a declaration of independence, and we will then understand, and the world will understand, what we are fighting for. If independence is not declared, I shall lay down my arms, and so will the men under my command. But under the flag of independence, we are ready to peril our lives a hundred times a day, and to drive away the monster who is fighting us under a blood-red flag, threatening to murder all prisoners and make Texas a waste desert. I shall have to fight the enemy on his own terms, yet I am ready to do it, and if my countrymen do not rally to my relief, I am determined to perish in the defense of this place, and my bones shall reproach my country for her neglect. With 500 men more, I will drive [Mexican general] Sesma beyond the Rio Grande, and I will visit vengeance on the enemy of Texas whether invaders or resident Mexican enemies. All the citizens of this place that have not joined us are with the enemy fighting against us. Let the government declare them public enemies, otherwise she is acting a suicidal part. I shall treat them as such, unless I have superior orders to the contrary. My respects to all friends, confusion to all enemies. God bless you.

DOCUMENT 14 *General Santa Anna to his Staff, March 5, 1836*

The time has come to strike a decisive blow upon the enemy occupying the Fortress of the Alamo. Consequently, His Excellency, the General in chief, has decided that, tomorrow, at 4 o'clock A.M., the columns of attack shall be stationed at musket-shot distance from the first entrenchments, reach for the charge, which shall commence, at a signal to be given with the bugle, from the Northern Battery. . . .

The honor of the nation being interested in this engagement against bold and lawless foreigners who are opposing us, His Excellency expects that every man will do his duty, and exert himself to give a day of glory to the country, and of gratification to the Supreme Government, who will know how to reward the distinguished deeds of the brave soldiers of the Army of Operations.

DOCUMENT 15 *General Santa Anna to Secretary of War José Maria Tornel y Mendivil, March 6, 1836*

Most Excellent Sir—Victory belongs to the army, which, at this very moment, 8 o'clock A.M., achieved a complete and glorious triumph that will render its memory imperishable. . . .

The Fortress is now in our power, with its artillery, stores, &c. More than 600 corpses of foreigners were buried in the ditches and intrenchments, and a great many who had escaped the bayonet of the infantry, fell in the vicinity under the sabres of the cavalry. I can assure Your Excellency that few are those who bore to their associates the tidings of their disaster.

Among the corpses are those of Bowie and Travis, who styled themselves Colonels, and also that of Crockett, and several leading men, who had entered the Fortress with dispatches from their Convention. We lost about 70 men killed and 300 wounded, among whom are 25 officers. The cause for which they fell renders their loss less painful, as it is the duty of the Mexican soldier to die for the defence of the rights of the nation; and all of us were ready for any sacrifice to promote this fond object; nor will we, hereafter, suffer any foreigners, whatever their origin may be, to insult our country and to pollute its soils. . . .

The bearer takes with him one of the flags of the enemy's Battalions, captured today. The inspection of it will show plainly the true intentions of the treacherous colonist, and of their abettors, who came from parts of the United States of the North.

God and Liberty!

DOCUMENT 16 *General Santa Anna to the Citizens of Texas, March 7, 1836*

Citizens! The causes which have conducted to this frontier a part of the Mexican army are not unknown to you: a parcel of audacious adventurers, maliciously protected by some inhabitants of a neighboring republic, dared to invade our territory, with an intention of

dividing amongst themselves the fertile lands that are contained in the spacious department of Texas. . . . I am pained to find amongst those adventurers the names of some
colonists, to whom had been granted repeated benefits, and who had no just motive of
complaint against the government of their adopted country.—These ungrateful men
must also necessarily suffer the just punishment that the laws and the public vengeance
demand. . . .

Bexarians! Return to your homes and to dedicate yourselves to your domestic duties.
Your city and the fortress of the Alamo are already in possession of the Mexican army,
composed of your own fellow citizens; and rest assured that no mass of foreigners will ever
interrupt your repose, and much less, attack your lives and plunder your property. The
supreme government has taken you under its protection, and will seek for your good.

Inhabitants of Texas! I have related to you the orders that the army of operations I
have the honor to command comes to execute; and therefore the good will have nothing
to fear. Fulfill always your duties as Mexican citizens, and you may expect the protection
and benefit of the laws; and rest assured that you will never have reason to report yourselves of having observed such conduct, for I pledge you in the name of the supreme authorities of the nation, and as your fellow citizen and friend, that what has been promised
you will be faithfully performed.

DOCUMENT 17   *Sam Houston to Colonel H. Raguet, March 13, 1836*

My dear Friend, . . .

. . . The awful news the fall of the Alamo reached us. . . . Our friend Bowie, as is
now understood, unable to get out of bed, shot himself as the soldiers approached it.
Despalier, Parker, and others, when all hope was lossed [*sic*] followed his example. Travis,
'tis said, rather than fall into the hands of the enemy, stabbed himself. . . .

Colonel Fannin should have relieved our Brave men in the Alamo. He had 430 men
with artillery under his command, and had taken up the line of march with a full knowledge of the situation of those in the alamo, and owing to the breaking down of a waggon
abandoned the march, returned to Goliad and left our Spartans to their fate!

. . . The enemy at the Alamo are said to have lossed 521 killed and an equal number wounded. Murdered Americans, 187. . . . Three negroes and Mrs Dickinson were
all in the fort who escaped Massacre as reported! Several Mexicans in the fort were also
murdered, and all killed in the fort were burned: The Mexicans killed in the assault were
burried—This is the report of the matter in substance! . . .

Salute affectionately your family with Dr. Porter's and all friends. . . .

DOCUMENT 18   *Benjamin Goodrich to Edmund Goodrich, March 15, 1836*

Dear Edmund,

Texas is in mourning, and it becomes my painful duty to inform my relations in Tennessee of the massacre of my poor brother John. He was murdered in the Texas fortress of
San Antonio de Bexar (known as the Alamo) on the night of the 6th of this month, together with one hundred and eighty of our brave countrymen, gallantly defending that
place against an invading army of Mexicans, eight thousand strong; not one escaped to
tell the dreadful tale. . . .

Seven of our brave men, being all that were left alive, called for quarter and to see Santa Anna, but were instantly shot by the order of the fiendish tyrant. . . . Santa Anna is now in Texas with an invading army of eight or ten thousand men strong—determined to carry on a war of extermination. We will meet him and teach the unprincipled scoundrel that freemen can never be conquered by the hirling soldiery of a military despot.

. . . The blood of a Goodrich has already crimsoned the soil of Texas and another victim shall be added to the list or I see Texas free and Independent.—Give my love to my dear mother, sisters, and brothers, and friends generally—

Benj. Briggs Goodrich

Introduction to Document 19

José Enrique de la Peña's account is the fullest and most balanced we have of the battle itself. (Note that his criticisms of Santa Anna came after the general's defeat at San Jacinto.)

DOCUMENT 19 *Eyewitness to the Alamo, 1836*

José Enrique de la Peña

Light began to appear on the horizon, the beautiful dawn would soon let herself be seen behind her golden curtain; a bugle call to attention was the agreed signal and we soon heard that terrible bugle call of death, which stirred our hearts. . . .

The columns advanced with as much speed as possible. . . . Travis, to compensate for the reduced number of the defenders, had placed three or four rifles by the side of each man, so that the initial fire was very rapid and deadly. Our columns left along their path a wide trail of blood, of wounded, and of dead. The bands from all the corps, gathered around our commander, sounded the charge; with a most vivid ardor and enthusiasm, we answered that call which electrifies the heart, elevates the soul, and makes others tremble. The second column, seized by this spirit, burst out in acclamations for the Republic and for the president-general. The officers were unable to repress this act of folly, which was paid for dearly. His attention drawn by this act, the enemy seized the opportunity, at the moment that light was beginning to make objects discernible around us, to redouble the fire on this column, making it suffer the greatest blows. It could be observed that a single cannon volley did away with half the company of chasseurs from Toluca, which was advancing a few paces from the column. . . .

The first to climb were thrown down by bayonets already waiting for them behind the parapet, or by pistol fire, but the courage of our soldiers was not diminished as they saw their comrades falling dead or wounded, and they hurried to occupy their places and to avenge them, climbing over their bleeding bodies. The sharp reports of the rifles, the whistling of bullets, the groans of the wounded, the cursing of the men, the sighs and anguished cries of the dying, the arrogant harangues of the officers, the noise of the instruments of war, and the inordinate shouts of the attackers, who climbed vigorously, bewildered all and made of this moment a tremendous and critical one. The shouting of those being attacked was no less loud and from the beginning had pierced our ears with desperate, terrible cries of alarm in a language we did not understand.

. . . The terrified defenders withdrew . . . into quarters placed to the right and the left of the small area that constituted their second line of defense. They had bolted and reinforced the doors, but in order to form trenches they had excavated some places inside

"Dawn at the Alamo" by H. A. McArdle on display at the state capitol building in Austin, Texas. How does this painting compare with the documents describing the siege? (Texas State Library and Archives Commission)

that were now a hindrance to them. Not all of them took refuge, for some remained in the open, looking at us before firing, as if dumbfounded at our daring. Travis was seen to hesitate, but not about the death that he would choose. He would take a few steps and stop, turning his proud face toward to discharge his shots; he fought like a true soldier. Finally he died, but he died after having traded his life very dearly. None of his men died with greater heroism, and they all died. Travis behaved as a hero; one must do him justice, for with a handful of men without discipline, he resolved to face men used to war and much superior in numbers, without supplies, with scarce munitions, and against the will of his subordinates. He was a handsome blond, with a physique as robust as his spirit was strong. . . .

Our soldiers, some stimulated by courage and others by fury, burst into the quarters where the enemy had entrenched themselves, from which issued an infernal fire. Behind these came others, who, nearing the doors and blind with fury and smoke, fired their shots against friends and enemies alike, and in this way our losses were most grievous. On the other hand, they turned the enemy's own cannon to bring down the doors to the rooms or the rooms themselves; a horrible carnage took place, and some were trampled to death. The tumult was great, the disorder frightful; it seemed as if the furies had descended upon us; different groups of soldiers were firing in all directions, on their comrades and on their officers, so that one was as likely to die by a friendly hand as by an enemy's. In the midst of this thundering din, there was such confusion that orders could not be understood, although those in command would raise their voices when the opportunity occurred. Some may believe that this narrative is exaggerated, but those who were witnesses will confess that this is exact, and in truth, any moderation in relating it would fall short. . . .

This scene of extermination went on for an hour before the curtain of death covered and ended it: shortly after six in the morning it was all finished; the corps were beginning to reassemble and to identify themselves, their sorrowful countenances revealing the losses in the thinned ranks of their officers and comrades, when the commander in chief appeared. He could see for himself the desolation among his battalions and that devastated area littered with corpses, with scattered limbs and bullets, with weapons and torn uniforms. Some of these were burning together with the corpses, which produced an unbearable and nauseating odor. The bodies, with their blackened and bloody faces disfigured by a desperate death, their hair and uniforms burning at once, presented a dreadful and truly hellish sight. What trophies—those of the battlefield! Quite soon some of the bodies were left naked by fire, others by disgraceful rapacity, especially among our men. The enemy could be identified by their whiteness, by their robust and bulky shapes. What a sad spectacle, that of the dead and dying! What a horror, to inspect the area and find the remains of friends—! With what anxiety did some seek others and with what ecstasy did they embrace each other! Questions followed one after the other, even while the bullets were still whistling around, in the midst of the groans of the wounded and the last breaths of the dying. . . .

. . . Some seven men had survived the general carnage and, under the protection of General Castrillón, they were brought before Santa Anna. Among them was one of great stature, well proportioned, with regular features, in whose face there was the imprint of adversity, but in whom one also noticed a degree of resignation and nobility that did him honor. He was the naturalist David Crockett, well known in North America for his unusual adventures, who had undertaken to explore the country and who, finding himself in Béjar at the very moment of surprise, had taken refuge in the Alamo, fearing that his status as a foreigner might not be respected. Santa Anna answered Castrillón's intervention in Crockett's behalf with a gesture of indignation and, addressing himself to the sappers, the troops closest to him, ordered his execution. The commanders and officers were outraged at this action and did not support the order, hoping that once the fury of the moment had blown over these men would be spared; but several officers who were around the president and who, perhaps, had not been present during the moment of danger, became noteworthy by an infamous deed, surpassing the soldiers in cruelty. They thrust themselves forward, in order to flatter their commander, and with swords in hand, fell upon these unfortunate, defenseless men just as a tiger leaps upon his prey. Though tortured before they were killed, these unfortunates died without complaining and without humiliating themselves before their torturers. . . .

DOCUMENT SET 3

The Aftermath

Great tragedies and dramatic events usually find people scrambling to give shape to the chaos through which they have passed. In the weeks and months following the battle, men tried to create meaning of the slaughter, to interpret events and build what might be called a "usable Alamo." Without being fully conscious of it, they sought to answer the question: "Whose Alamo?"

DOCUMENT 20   ***President David G. Burnet, Proclamation on Being Sworn in as President, Republic of Texas, March 17, 1836***

Fellow Citizens.

Your country demands your aid! The enemy is pressing upon us. Families, the wives and children of your neighbours, are driven from their firesides, and compelled to take shelter in woods and forests, while the enemy gathers confidence and audacity from every disaster we encounter. Under these painful circumstances, equally reproachful to our national character, and dangerous to our national existence, too many citizens are lingering in idleness and lethargy at home or ingloriously flying before our enemy, whom we have heretofore affected to despise. Is it possible that the free citizens of Texas, the descendants of the heroes of 76 can take panic at the approach of the paltry minions of a despot, who threatens to desolate our beautiful country? Let us rather "rush to the rescue." Let every man able to poise a rifle or wield a sabre fly to the army, and soon, very soon your families will be safe. Our country cleansed from the pollution of every hostile fort, and the "bond of promise" will smile benignly over the land. Fellow citizens! The Blood of the martyrs of freedom, the heroes of the "Alamo" call aloud for vengeance. The minions of despotism, the panders of priestly ambition are waging a merciless and extermination war upon us. . . .

The gallant Houston will lead you to victory. The stake is glorious, let it be gloriously won. If any man prove recreant, in this hour of his country's peril, let that man be marked, and the indignation of the people, the "slow unmoving finger of scorn" will hold him in perpetual derision. The laws of the land will be rigidly enforced. The times call for decision, for action. Those who are not for us are against us. . . .

DOCUMENT 21 *Governor Joaquín Muñoz y Muñoz to the Citizens of Veracruz, March 23, 1836*

The Governor of the State of Veracruz to Its Residents

Citizens: The invincible eagles of the republic have settled themselves again on the fortress of the Alamo; and the glorious national colors wave triumphantly over the ramparts that were once the goal of the colonial rebels. With sincerest happiness . . . and joy, we announce a victory which celebrates our patriotism and the highest honor for the Mexican nation.

The rebels, persecutors and desperados have suffered the fate which they provoked. The decisive triumph assures a quick end to this painful but brilliant journey. This achievement has cost patriotic blood, and bitterness on the part of the nation. But the unwithering glory of the valiant fighters who perished in defense of the most just of causes is to be rewarded with posterity's gratitude for heroes. . . .

Veracruzans: the greatest pleasure of my life is to share so fitting an illustration of our success with you; and to address you with effusions of affection of the highest order, to ardently invite you to seize the sweet fruit of victory which now embellishes the annals of our nation's history.

Your citizen and best friend.

DOCUMENT 22 *General Thomas Rusk to President Burnet, April 22, 1836*

War Department. Headquarters. Army of Texas. San Jacinto River. . . .

Sir: I have the honor to communicate to your excellency a brief account of a general engagement with the army of Santa Anna, at this place on the 21st instant.

Our army, under the command of General Houston, arrived here on the 20th instant. The enemy, a few miles off at New Washington, apprised of our arrival, committed some depredations upon private property, and commenced their line of march to this point.

They were unconscious of our approach until our standard was planted on the banks of the San Jacinto. Our position was a favorable one for battle. . . .

Early next morning, about nine o'clock, the enemy received a reinforcement of five hundred men, under the command of General Martin Prefecto do Cos, which increased their strength to fourteen or fifteen hundred men. It was supposed that an attack upon our encampment would now be made; and, having a good position, we stationed our artillery, and disposed of the forces, so as to receive the enemy to the best advantage. At three o'clock, however, the foe, instead of showing signs of attack, was evidently engaged in fortifying. We determined, therefore, immediately to assail him. . . . On arriving within reach of the enemy a heavy fire was opened, first with their artillery on our cavalry. A general conflict now ensued. Orders were given to charge. Colonel Sherman's division moved up, and drove the enemy from the woods occupied by them on their right wing. At the same moment, Colonel Burleson's division, together with the regulars, charged upon and mounted the breastwork of the enemy, and drove them from their cannon: our artillery, the meanwhile, charging up and firing upon them with great effect. The cavalry, under Colonel Lamar, at the same time fell on them with great fury and great slaughter, Major-General Houston acted with great gallantry, encouraging his men to the attack, and heroically charged, in front of the infantry, within a few yards of the enemy, receiving at the same time a wound in his leg. The enemy soon took to flight, officers and all, some on foot and some on horseback. In ten minutes after the firing of the first gun, we were charging through the camp, and driving them before us. They fled in confusion and dismay down the river, followed closely by our troops for four miles. Some of them took the prairie, and were pursued by our cavalry; others were shot in attempting to swim the river; and in a short period the sanguinary conflict was terminated by the surrender of nearly all who were not slain in the combat. One half of their army perished: the other half are prisoners, among whom are General Santa Anna himself, Colonel Almonte, and many other prominent officers of their army. The loss of the enemy is computed at over six hundred slain, and above six hundred prisoners; together with a caballada of several hundred mules taken, with much valuable baggage. Our loss, in point of numbers, is small, it being seven slain and fifteen wounded.

This glorious achievement is attributed, not to superior force, but to the valor of our soldiers and the sanctity of our cause. . . . There was a general cry which pervaded the ranks—"Remember the Alamo. remember La Bahia!" These words electrified all. "Onward!" was the cry. The unerring aim and irresistible energy of the Texan army could not be withstood. It was freemen fighting against the minions of tyranny, and the result proved the inequality of such a contest. . . .

DOCUMENT 23 *Public Meeting in Nashville, Tennessee, May 11, 1836*

In pursuance of public notice previously given, by a call signed by a large number of highly respectable citizens of Nashville and Davidson county, a numerously attended public meeting of the citizens of this city and county convened at the court-house in Nashville, on Saturday, the 11th instant. . . .

Every man in the Union has the undoubted right to emigrate to Texas if he chooses. This is lawful. Our citizens may vest a hundred millions in Texas cotton and sugar lands— far superior to any other on this continent. Who, or what is to prevent them? To do so is lawful. That is not all. There are cases where laws and treaties are as cobwebs in the way of the torrent of popular passion and will. Such a case the Mexican Government had the wickedness to present by the cold-blooded and inhuman slaughter of the defenders of the Alamo, and the treacherous butchery and burning of Colonel Fanning's men, prisoners of war on capitulation. Before these acts of savage cruelty, many, perhaps most of our orderly citizens stood, not indifferent, but inactive spectators of the contest; but afterwards, it is useless to pretend that men, money, and arms, were not almost openly furnished, as if the war had been our own. The laws of God, of man, and of all civilized nations, had been outraged—our people felt all legal and moral obligations cancelled, and viewed the Mexicans as they did pirates on the seas—enemies to all mankind. This was equally true in every part of the United States. Few inquired for the law, and fewer still regarded it, as there were none to enforce obedience. So the matter now stands, and so it must continue.

With a restless and migratory population of young men, whose physical prowess and romantic and chivalrous daring have even excelled the trained Indian warrior, when tested hand-to-hand, of whom the valley of the Mississippi can furnish, perhaps, one hundred thousand, ready to embark in any enterprise promising to be fraught with stirring adventures, what but peace is to prevent an army from Texas marching on Mexico—a city which is now, more than in a former age, possessed of those fatal charms that once tempted the Spaniard to her ruin?

The project has in it more of romantic attractions to daring ambition than any presented since the days of Pizarro and Cortes. Who fears successful resistance? The European Spaniards have been cut off or driven from the country by the Mexican revolution. The Mexican native never could fight, nor has he a motive: he of the mixed blood is no soldier, and the creole a most indifferent one. Before an army made up of the *material* supposed, Mexico would fall without a struggle. This it is the business of the United States to prevent; and it can only be prevented by recognizing the claim of Texas to be severed from Mexico, and an interference to end the war. . . .

1. *Resolved, therefore,* That, in the opinion of this meeting, the Republic of Texas is severed from Mexico; that she has a Government, in fact, in successful operation, republican in its character, and which she has abundant means to maintain; that no good reason exists why the Congress and Executive Government of the United States should not immediately recognise the independence of the Republic of Texas.

2. *Resolved,* That, in the opinion of this meeting, the present session of Congress should not be permitted to close until the independence of Texas is fully recognised, and every arrangement made with the new government consistent with the best interests of the United States. And this meeting hereby petitions the Executive and the Congress of the United States to give effect to these our wishes; and especially in recognising, in the most unequivocal terms, Texas as severed from Mexico, and that she is a free, sovereign, and independent state.

3. *Resolved,* That the Executive of the United States, and our Senators and Representatives in Congress from the State of Tennessee, are most respectfully requested to use their best exertions to give effect to our petition and wishes as expressed in these proceedings. . . .

DOCUMENT 24 *Mexican Secretary of War José Maria Tornel y Mendivil, 1837*

Everywhere meetings have been held, presided over, as in New York, by public officials of the government, to collect money, buy ships, enlist men, and fan that spirit of animosity that characterizes all the acts of the United States with regard to Mexico. The newspapers, paid by the land speculators, without excepting the *Globe* of Washington, which is doubtless an official organ, have sponsored the insurrection of Texas with the same ardor they would have supported the uprising of 1776. Our character, our customs, our very rights have been painted in the darkest hues, while the crimes of the Texans have been applauded in the house of the President, in the halls of the capitol, in the marts of trade, in public meetings, in small towns, and even in the fields. The President of the Mexican

republic was publicly executed in effigy in Philadelphia in an insulting and shameful bur-
lesque. The world has witnessed all these incidents, of which we have become aware
through the shameful accounts in the newspapers of the United States. Could greater insults, outrages, or indignities be offered us by an open declaration of war? Let national indignation answer the question.

. . . The loss of Texas will inevitably result in the loss of New Mexico and the Cali-
fornias. Little by little our territory will be absorbed, until only an insignificant part is left
to us. Our destiny will be similar to the sad lot of Poland. Our national existence, acquired at the cost of so much blood, recognized after so many difficulties, would end like
those weak meteors which, from time to time, shine fitfully in the firmament and disap-
pear. It is for this reason that General Terán wrote the government, "Whoever consents
to and refuses to oppose the loss of Texas is a despicable traitor, worthy of being punished
with a thousand deaths."

. . . Five thousand infantry and 500 cavalry would be enough, more than enough,
to put an end to the high hopes of the Texans, to drive them to the banks of the Sabine,
and to reconquer the favors of destiny. The superiority of the Mexican soldier over the
mountaineers of Kentucky and the hunters of Missouri are well known. He knows how to
endure all privations with serene calmness, and how to overcome hunger and conquer
death herself. Veterans, seasoned by twenty years of wars, cannot be intimidated by the
presence of an enemy, ignorant of the art of war, incapable of discipline, and renowned
for insubordination. . . .

The fear that we will find ourselves involved in a war against the United States if we
refuse to subscribe to the terms demanded is not without foundation. If their diplomacy
has been dictated by a preconceived plan,—and this cannot be doubted by those who
have observed the skill with which the cabinet in Washington directs its affairs—it is obvious that their aim has been to acquire possession of the disputed territory by force if
necessary. This will involve us in more serious difficulties than even those presented by
the Texas question itself. War with the United States, however, need not be feared, for
our final salvation may depend upon it.

📜 DOCUMENT 25 *Juan Seguín's Eulogy for the Defenders of the Alamo, February 25, 1837*

Companions in Arms!! These remains which we have the honor of carrying on our shoulders are those of the valiant heroes who died in the Alamo. Yes, my friends, they preferred
to die a thousand times rather than submit themselves to the tyrant's yoke. What a brilliant example! Deserving of being noted in the pages of history. The spirit of liberty appears to be looking out from its elevated throne with its pleasing mien and pointing to us,
saying: "There are your brothers, Travis, Bowie, Crockett, and others whose valor places
them in the rank of my heroes." Yes, soldiers and fellow citizens, these are the worthy beings who, by the twists of fate, during the present campaign delivered their bodies to the
ferocity of their enemies; who, barbarously treated as beasts, were bound by their feet and
dragged to this spot, where they were reduced to ashes. The venerable remains of our worthy companions as witnesses, I invite you to declare to the entire world, "Texas shall be
free and independent, or we shall perish in glorious combat."

Introduction to Documents 26 and 27

Long after the fall of the Alamo, two women, who claimed to have been inside the
Alamo during the attack, told their tales. Susanna Dickinson, wife of defender Al-

maron Dickinson, was certainly at the Alamo, and her account does not always agree with de la Pena. Andrea Gastanon Villanueva, better known as Madam Candelaria, may or may not have been inside the Alamo at the end, but she certainly knew Bowie.

DOCUMENT 26 *Susanna Hannig (Dickinson), 1875*

On February 23d, 1836, Santa Anna, having captured the pickets sent out by Col. Travis to guard the post from surprise, charged into San Antonio with his troops, variously estimated at from six to ten thousand, only a few moments after the bells of the city rang the alarm.

Capt. Dickinson galloped up to our dwelling and hurriedly exclaimed: "The Mexicans are upon us, give me the babe, and jump up behind me." I did so, and as the Mexicans already occupied Commerce street, we galloped across the river at the ford south of it, and entered the fort at the southern gate, when the enemy commenced firing shot and shell into the fort, but with little or no effect, only wounding one horse.

There were eighteen guns mounted on the fortifications, and these, with our riflemen, repulsed with great slaughter two assaults made upon them before the final one.

I knew Colonels Crockett, Bowie and Travis well. Col. Crockett was a performer on the violin, and often during the siege took it up and played his favorite tunes.

I heard him say several times during the eleven days of the siege: "I think we had better march out and die in the open air. I don't like to be hemmed up."

There were provisions and forage enough in the fort to have subsisted men and horses for a month longer.

A few days before the final assault three Texans entered the fort during the night and inspired us with sanguine hopes of speedy relief, and thus animated the men to contend to the last.

A Mexican woman deserted us one night, and going over to the enemy informed them of our very inferior numbers, which Col. Travis said made them confident of success and emboldened them to make the final assault, which they did at early dawn on the morning of the 6th of March.

Under the cover of darkness they approached the fortifications, and planting their scaling ladders against our walls just as light was approaching, they climbed up to the tops of our walls and jumped down within, many of them to immediate death.

As fast as the front ranks were slain, they were filled up again by fresh troops.

The Mexicans numbered several thousands while there were only one hundred and eighty-two Texans.

The struggle lasted more than two hours when my husband rushed into the church where I was with my child, and exclaimed: "Great God, Sue, the Mexicans are inside our walls! All is lost! If they spare you, save my child."

Then, with a parting kiss, he drew his sword and plunged into the strife, then raging in different portions of the fortifications.

Soon after he left me, three unarmed gunners who abandoned their then useless guns came into the church where I was, and were shot down by my side. One of them was from Nacogdoches and named Walker. He spoke to me several times during the siege about his wife and four children with anxious tenderness. I saw four Mexicans toss him up in the air (as you would a bundle of fodder) with their bayonets, and then shoot him. At this moment a Mexican officer came into the room, and, addressing me in English, asked: "Are you Mrs. Dickinson?" I answered: "Yes." The said he, "If you wish to save your life, follow me." I followed him, and although shot at and wounded, was spared.

As we passed through the enclosed ground in front of the church, I saw heaps of dead and dying. The Texans on an average killed between eight and nine Mexicans each—182 Texans and 1,600 Mexicans were killed.

I recognized Col. Crockett lying dead and mutilated between the church and the two story barrack building, and even remember seeing his peculiar cap lying by his side.

Col. Bowie was sick in bed and not expected to live, but as the victorious Mexicans entered his room, he killed two of them with his pistols before they pierced him through with their sabres.

Cols. Travis and Bonham were killed while working the cannon, the body of the former lay on top of the church. In the evening the Mexicans brought wood from the neighboring forest and burned the bodies of all the Texans, but their own dead they buried in the city cemetery across the San Pedro.

📜 DOCUMENT 27 *Historical Reminiscences of the Aged Madam Candelaria*

The name of Madam Candelaria is a household word in San Antonio. She is without doubt the oldest living native of Texas, being 107[88] years of age as is shown by the certificate of the priest who administered to her spiritual wants in her childhood. This certificate is in Spanish and its authenticity cannot be disputed. The aged heroine lives in a typical Mexican house on South Laredo Street, where she is visited by hundreds of tourists and old friends in the course of a year. On this day, the anniversary of the fall of the Alamo, it is befitting that a sketch of Madam Candelaria, who was in the midst of that stirring historical affair, be given. In order to secure a statement from her own lips a reporter for the *Express* in company with an interpreter visited her yesterday.

When the unpretentious dwelling of the centenarian [sic] was entered she rose from her comfortable chair and extended a cordial greeting to the visitors. The more than one hundred years [sic] that have passed over her head have not affected her voice in the least and she speaks the soft, musical Spanish language with a force and warmth that is entertaining and faultless in expression. In response to an inquiry of the reporter she stated that she was born on November 30, 1785 [1803] at Laredo, Texas and the priest's certificate bears out her statement.

"My father said he was the tailor of Ferdinand VII and after my birth I lived several years at Laredo with my parents. There were only a few houses there at that time and they were mere *jacales* [huts] covered with hides. I was first taken by my father to Rio Grande City and then to Zaragosa. After living there a few years I lived in various places in what is now the state of Coahuila, but which was at that time embraced in the state of Texas. I afterward lived in Nacogdoches and in 1820 came to San Antonio. This was a mere village at that time and was occupied by General [Anastacio?] Bustamante and his troops."

In relating her reminiscences of the fall of the Alamo Madam Candelaria stated that she was called upon a few days before the fatal attack was made [in order] to nurse Colonel Bowie, who was very sick of typhoid fever.

"Santa Anna made the attack," she continued, "on March 6. The Alamo was filled with Texans, a number of women being among them. Colonel Bowie died in my arms only a few minutes before the entrance to the Alamo by the soldiers. I was holding his head in my lap when Santa Anna's men swarmed into the room where I was sitting. One of them thrust a bayonet into the lifeless head of Colonel Bowie and lifted his body from my lap. As he did so the point of the weapon slipped and struck me in the jaw," and here the aged heroine showed the scar of the wound which she had received.

During her recital of this exciting experience she made numerous expressive gesticulations, swaying her body to and fro in a highly dramatic style.

POSTSCRIPT

It was almost a decade after Sam Houston's troops routed the unsuspecting Mexican army and won independence that Texas became a state. Many northerners rejected the repeated bids by Texas for statehood because its presence in the Union would destabilize the balance of thirteen free and thirteen slave states. By the 1840s, however, the fevers of territorial expansion had grown so hot that politicians were able to persuade most Americans that the "reannexation" of Texas would help expand the national "empire of liberty." While Americans grew intoxicated with the heady ideals of "Manifest Destiny," Mexicans viewed Texas statehood as proof that their northern neighbor had planned all along to steal territory.

Mexico severed diplomatic relations with the United States. Americans claimed that the Rio Grande constituted the southern border of the new state and sent troops. Mexico insisted on the Nueces River as the northern frontier. Soon soldiers clashed in the disputed territory, and President Polk used the hostilities as a pretext for asking Congress for a declaration of war, claiming that Mexico had violated American territory. When the Mexican-American War ended and the peace treaty of Guadalupe Hidalgo was signed, Mexico had lost one-third of its territory, and the United States had gained over 500,000 square miles, including lands that became the Rocky Mountain states, the Southwest, and California.

The chain of events that began with the Texas rebellion, however, divided Americans in important respects. A minority, including Congressman Abraham Lincoln, considered the Mexican-American War immoral and accused President Polk of lying about the circumstances that had led to hostilities. Even more important, Manifest Destiny exacerbated sectional tensions. Slavery reemerged in the 1850s as the issue that menaced the union. If America was becoming an Empire for Liberty, some people insisted that liberty meant the freedom to bring slaves into new lands, while others argued that liberty required the eventual end of slavery. It was the issue of slavery in the new territories that embittered northerners and southerners against each other and inflamed emotions in the sectional conflict.

QUESTIONS

Defining Terms

Identify in the context of the chapter each of the following:

Santa Anna	Juan Sequín
Stephen Austin	Daughters of the Republic of Texas
alcalde	Sam Houston
William Travis	"Remember the Alamo"
Mrs. Dickinson	Manifest Destiny

Probing the Sources

1. What sorts of tensions can you find between Anglo immigrants and Mexicans before the actual fighting began?

2. Reconstruct the military circumstances of the battle at the Alamo.

③ On what grounds did Anglos justify their actions on the Mexican borderlands? How did the Mexicans respond? Which side do you find more convincing?

4. How do you think Davy Crockett died, and why is it important?

Interpreting the Sources

1. How did the Alamo become an emotional symbol? How was the symbol invoked?

2. In what sense did the Texas revolution repeat some of the same issues already to be found in American society?

3. Why do you think the Alamo remains so important to people today?

4. Was the Texas revolution a fight for freedom or a land grab?

ADDITIONAL READING

For the story of the defense of the Alamo and how it has been remembered, see Randy Roberts and James S. Olson, *A Line in the Sand: The Alamo in Blood and Memory* (2001). The classic study of American expansion during this era is Frederick Merk, *Manifest Destiny and Mission in American History* (1963). For a fine collection of primary sources on Texas, some of them from Mexican archives, see John H. Jenkins's ten-volume work *Papers of the Texas Revolution, 1835–1836* (1973). The Mexican-American War is the subject of Robert Johanssen's *The Mexican War in the American Imagination* (1985). On the era during which Mexico controlled these lands, see David J. Weber, *The Mexican Frontier, 1821–1846* (1982). For iconography, see Susan Prendergast Schoelwer, *Alamo Images: Changing Perceptions of a Texas Experience* (1985). For background, see David J. Weber, *The Mexican Frontier, 1821–1846* (1982); and Sanford Wexler, ed., *Westward Expansion, an Eyewitness History* (1991).

Women in Antebellum America

HISTORICAL CONTEXT

Looking back over her girlhood in New England in the 1840s, Lucy Larcom declared,

> It was seldom said to little girls, as it always has been said to boys, that they ought to have some definite plan while they were children, what to be and do when they were grown up. There was usually but one path open before them, to become good wives and housekeepers. And the ambition of most girls was to follow their mothers' footsteps in this direction; a natural and laudable ambition.

By the early nineteenth century, the role of the wife and housekeeper was indeed being upheld as the ideal one for middle-class women. Yet ideals and realities are not the same things. Larcom's mother ran a boardinghouse for young women who worked in textile mills, so Lucy knew firsthand many women who did not live within the domestic ideal.

Equally important, Lucy Larcom questioned the desirability of what some have called the *cult of true womanhood,* that cluster of beliefs that places a woman in the home not only for domestic duties, but also as the moral center and spiritual font of family values. Larcom recalled that she had sometimes been encouraged to develop her talents and learn to be a useful citizen: "Girls, as well as boys must often have been conscious of their own peculiar capabilities—must have desired to cultivate and make use of their individual powers."

Larcom's thoughts on her own girlhood addressed problems that many American women were feeling. The nineteenth century was an era of changing identities, and the "proper" roles of men and women were not always clear. Gender identity— how we define what it means to be a man or a woman—was very much influenced by the economy. By the 1830s and 1840s, farms in the soil-poor Northeast had failed, as new markets for agricultural goods opened up and as the vast lands of the South and the Midwest produced unprecedented quantities of staple crops. Moreover, in the eastern cities, the old artisan method of manufacture—a household-based economy that gave a productive role to women and children— was being replaced. The increased division of labor under capitalism brought new factories and the wage-labor system. While farms and artisanal shops were highly patriarchal (that is, men were given the dominant role as authority figures and decision makers), they did make labor a family-centered activity. The new, more specialized system that gradually replaced the old tended to disperse family members: children at school, men at the job, women in the home. Production became divorced from the household. In other words, the old economic function of the family declined, and the middle-class family became more the center for fulfilling emotional and domestic needs, such as cooking, education, spiritual uplift, and religious instruction.

This new division of roles within the family presented dilemmas for the middle-class American woman. She could simply accept the domestic tasks of homemaker, mother, spiritual guide, and uplifter of the race. Certainly, it was flattering to be told that work in the home was the most godly of occupations, the most elevating for humankind. Ironically, the women who wrote in this vein, women like writer-reformer Catherine Beecher, were themselves stepping out of the private household to enter the public realm, the world of work. After all, it was fine to argue that raising good children and providing a haven for one's husband were the noblest of tasks, but money, power, and status were all to be found outside the home.

For other women, however, the cult of domesticity was a luxury. Some continued to work on farms, where the sheer labor of milking, harvesting, preserving, churning, and sewing, not to mention the usual cooking, cleaning, and nursing, left little time for pure moral uplift. Other women—young, unmarried, widowed, immigrant, some abandoned by their husbands, some with elderly parents—needed to earn a living, and many of these worked either as domestic servants in others' homes or as operatives in new factories like the Lowell textile mills in Massachusetts. Perhaps some of these women would have enjoyed the luxury of staying home as a wife and mother, but many clearly welcomed the chance to go out into the world. Nevertheless, domestic labor was demeaning, and work in the mills required long hours at low pay. Both were subject to the vagaries of the marketplace, including wage cuts and unemployment, and both quickly became stigmatized as lower-class occupations. The domestic ideal could be suffocating, but as a middle-class role, it promised higher social status than that afforded to working-class women.

Other middle-class women, a small but articulate group, rejected the domestic ideal outright. Some of them went so far as to draw parallels between the condition of slaves and their own. Sarah and Angelina Grimké, for example, noted that neither women nor slaves could vote, neither could hold property, both had virtually no public voice, and both were restricted from positions of power and prestige. For white women like Lucy Larcom who were given at least a rudimentary education and who were encouraged to lead useful lives, the cult of domesticity could be a trap. But at its most extreme, African-American women experienced how the oppression of both slavery and gender reinforced each other.

Many American women hated the lack of occupational outlets for their talents and loathed appearing submissive to men in public; home, the moral center of the universe, suffocated them. But the alleged moral superiority of women—an idea supported by the evangelical religion so popular in the antebellum era—cut two ways, becoming a bulwark of activism. Women's spirituality could be expressed not just at home or in church, but in organizations that went out into the world to change it and spread benevolence. Thus, in the powerful reform movements of the antebellum era—antislavery, temperance, missionary work, education, and others—women founded organizations, proselytized, and assumed active public roles.

During these years, middle-class women gained a bit more control of their lives in another way. Throughout the nineteenth century, the birthrate declined, and it is clear that, by the 1840s, this decline was due in part to the deliberate practice of birth control. Smaller families gave women some freedom from the drudgery of daily home life. This was also an era that saw the decline of arranged marriages (in which parents worked out nuptial agreements for their children, often for economic motives) and the growing presence of the idea of romantic love, of choosing one's mate solely on the basis of personal attraction and emotional compatibility. Once again, this new way of arranging marriages gave women far more control of their lives than they had had under the older, more purely patriarchal ways.

THE DOCUMENTS

The following documents capture much of the variety in women's identities around the middle of the nineteenth century, ranging from ringing endorsements of the cult of true womanhood through a feminist declaration of independence. However, it is probably best not think of antebellum women as fitting into one or another category, such as worker, mother, or activist. There was considerable ambivalence in roles and ideals: Some young mill workers probably longed for a cottage and a family as far from factories as possible; overburdened mothers fantasized about leaving home behind to seek their independence; promoters of the domestic ideal sought public acclaim; and feminists sometimes made demands for women's empowerment based on inherent female moral superiority. This was, then, an era of new possibilities and also one of confusing goals and expectations. As you read the documents, try to think of these women as engaged in a great dialogue. What were they saying to each other, and where were they agreeing and disagreeing?

Introduction to Document 1

The 1840s witnessed a growing consciousness of women's place in American society. Document 1 is excerpted from A. J. Graves's *Women in America* (1843). She argued vigorously from Scripture that a woman's place was in the home. Compare Graves's ideas about religion with how the Bible was cited by the court in the Vesey conspiracy (Chapter 8).

DOCUMENT 1   *"Religious Women"*

A. J. Graves

Our chief aim throughout these pages is to prove that [women's] domestic duties have a paramount claim over everything else upon her attention—that *home* is her appropriate sphere of action; and that whenever she neglects these duties, or goes out of this sphere of action to mingle in any of the great public movements of the day, she is deserting the station which God and nature have assigned to her. She can operate far more efficiently in promoting the great interests of humanity by supervising her own household than in any other way. Home, if we may so speak, is the cradle of the human race; and it is here the human character is fashioned either for good or for evil. It is the "nursery of the future man and of the undying spirit"; and woman is the nurse and the educator. Over infancy she has almost unlimited sway; and in maturer years she may powerfully counteract the evil influences of the world by the talisman of her strong, enduring love, by her devotedness to those intrusted to her charge, and by those lessons of virtue and of wisdom which are not of the world. . . .

That woman should regard home as her appropriate domain is not only the dictate of religion, but of enlightened human reason. Well-ordered families are the chief security for the permanent peace and prosperity of the state, and such families must be trained up by enlightened female influence acting within its legitimate sphere. . . .

Let man, then, retain his proud supremacy in the world's dominion; let him inscribe his name upon its high places, and be the leader of the congregated masses of his fellow-men, with all their excitements, their agitations, and their powerful concentration of effort; but these things belong not to woman. She best consults her happiness, best maintains her dignity, and best fulfils the great object of her being, by keeping alive the sacred flame of piety, patriotism, and universal love to man, upon the domestic altar; and by drawing worshippers around it, to send them forth from thence better citizens, and purer and holier men. . . .

. . . Then, when our husbands and our sons go forth into the busy and turbulent world, we may feel secure that they will walk unhurt amid its snares and temptations. Their hearts will be at home, where their treasure is; and they will rejoice to return to its sanctuary of rest, there to refresh their wearied spirits, and renew their strength for the toils and conflicts of life.

Introduction to Document 2

Catharine Beecher, in her *Treatise on Domestic Economy for Young Ladies at Home and at School* (1847), made her case for the importance of the domestic ideal, declaring that woman's subordination to man in the world of politics and work sheltered her and enabled her to perform the task of moral uplift. Document 2 is taken from Chapter 1 of this treatise, "The Peculiar Responsibilities of American Women." Catharine Beecher was a member of one of the most influential families of the nineteenth century, which included her father, the Reverend Lyman Beecher; her brother, the Reverend Henry Ward Beecher; and her sister, Harriet Beecher (Stowe), author of *Uncle Tom's Cabin*.

DOCUMENT 2   *"The Peculiar Responsibilities of American Women"*

Catharine Beecher

. . . There must be the magistrate and the subject, one of whom is the superior, and the other the inferior. There must be the relations of husband and wife, parent and child, teacher and pupil, employer and employed, each involving the relative duties of subordination. The superior, in certain particulars, is to direct, and the inferior is to yield obedience. Society could never go forward, harmoniously, nor could any craft or profession be successfully pursued, unless these superior and subordinate relations be instituted and sustained.

But who shall take the higher, and who the subordinate, stations in social and civil life? This matter, in the case of parents and children, is decided by the Creator. He has given children to the control of parents, as their superiors, and to them they remain subordinate, to a certain age, or so long as they are members of their household. And parents can delegate such a portion of their authority to teachers and employers, as the interests of their children require.

In most other cases, in a truly democratic state, each individual is allowed to choose for himself, who shall take the position of his superior. No woman is forced to obey any husband but the one she chooses for herself; nor is she obliged to take a husband, if she prefers to remain single. So every domestic, and every artisan or laborer, after passing from parental control, can choose the employer to whom he is to accord obedience, or, if he prefers to relinquish certain advantages, he can remain without taking a subordinate place to any employer.

And the various privileges that wealth secures, are equally open to all classes. Every man may aim at riches, unimpeded by any law or institution which secures peculiar privileges to a favored class, at the expense of another. Every law, and every institution, is tested by examining whether it secures equal advantages to all; and, if the people become convinced that any regulation sacrifices the good of the majority to the interests of the smaller number, they have power to abolish it. . . .

It appears, then, that it is in America, alone, that women are raised to an equality with the other sex; and that, both in theory and practice, their interests are regarded as of equal value. They are made subordinate in station, only where a regard to their best interests demands it, while, as if in compensation for this, by custom and courtesy, they are always treated as superiors. Universally, in this Country, through every class of society, precedence is given to woman, in all the comforts, conveniences, and courtesies, of life.

In civil and political affairs, American women take no interest or concern, except so far as they sympathize with their family and personal friends; but in all cases, in which they do feel a concern, their opinions and feelings have a consideration, equal, or even superior, to that of the other sex.

In matters pertaining to the education of their children, in the selection and support of a clergyman, in all benevolent enterprises, and in all questions relating to morals or manners, they have a superior influence. In such concerns, it would be impossible to carry a point, contrary to their judgement and feelings; while an enterprise, sustained by them, will seldom fail of success.

If those who are bewailing themselves over the fancied wrongs and injuries of women in this Nation, could only see things as they are, they would know, that, whatever remnants of a barbarous or aristocratic age may remain in our civil institutions, in reference to the interests of women, it is only because they are ignorant of them, or do not use their influence to have them rectified; for it is very certain that there is nothing reasonable, which American women would unite in asking, that would not readily be bestowed. . . .

. . . The flow of wealth, among all classes, is constantly increasing the number of those who live in a style demanding much hired service, while the number of those, who are compelled to go to service, is constantly diminishing. Our manufactories, also, are making increased demands for female labor, and offering larger compensation. In consequence of these things, there is such a disproportion between those who wish to hire, and those who are willing to go to domestic service, that, in the non-slaveholding States were it not for the supply of poverty-stricken foreigners there would not be a domestic for each family who demands one. And this resort to foreigners, poor as it is, scarcely meets the demand: while the disproportion must every year increase, especially if our prosperity increases. For, just in proportion as wealth rolls in upon us, the number of those, who will give up their own independent homes to serve strangers, will be diminished.

The difficulties and sufferings, which have accrued to American women, from this cause, are almost incalculable. There is nothing, which so much demands system and regularity, as the affairs of a housekeeper, made up, as they are, of ten thousand desultory and minute items; and yet, this perpetually fluctuating state of society seems forever to bar any such system and regularity. The anxieties, vexations, perplexities, and even hard labor, which come upon American women, from this state of domestic service, are endless; and many a woman has, in consequence, been disheartened, discouraged, and ruined in health. The only wonder is, that, amid so many real difficulties, American women are still able to maintain such a character for energy, fortitude, and amiableness, as is universally allowed to be their due.

Introduction to Document 3

Among middle-class women, the views of Graves and Beecher quickly gained adherents; indeed, such women expressed ideas that others had felt earlier, even if they could not fully articulate them. But there were powerful alternative views. Sarah Grimké was the daughter of a South Carolina slaveholder. Like Graves, she relied on the Bible as her authority, but she reached very different conclusions. For women, as for African slaves, the main question was one of freedom, according to Grimké. In this letter to her sister Angelina, she examined a range of issues from unequal pay through the nature of housekeeping duties.

DOCUMENT 3 *"On the Condition of Women in the United States"*

Sarah M. Grimké

Brookline, 1837

My Dear Sister,

During the early part of my life, my lot was cast among the butterflies of the *fashionable* world; and of this class of women, I am constrained to say, both from experience and observation, that their education is miserably deficient; that they are taught to regard marriage as the one thing needful, the only avenue to distinction; hence to attract the notice and win the attentions of men, by their external charms, is the chief business of fashionable girls. They seldom think that men will be allured by intellectual acquirements, because they find, that where any mental superiority exists, a woman is generally shunned and regarded as stepping out of her "appropriate sphere," which, in their view, is to dress, to dance, to set out to the best possible advantage her person, to read the novels which inundate the press, and which do more to destroy her character as a rational creature, then any thing else. Fashionable women regard themselves, and are regarded by men, as pretty toys or as mere instruments of pleasure; and the vacuity of mind, the heartlessness, the frivolity which is the necessary result of this false and debasing estimate of women, can only be fully understood by those who have mingled in the folly and wickedness of fashionable life; and who have been called from such pursuits by the voice of the Lord Jesus, inviting their weary and heavy laden souls to come unto Him and learn of Him, that they may find something worthy of their immortal spirit, and their intellectual powers; that they may learn the high and holy purposes of their creation, and consecrate themselves unto the service of God; and not, as is now the case, to the pleasure of man.

There is another and much more numerous class in this country, who are withdrawn by education or circumstances from the circle of fashionable amusements, but who are brought up with the dangerous and absurd idea, that *marriage* is a kind of preferment; and that to be able to keep their husband's house, and render his situation comfortable, is the end of her being. Much that she does and says and thinks is done in reference to this situation; and to be married is too often held up to the view of girls as the sine qua non of human happiness and human existence. For this purpose more than for any other, I verily believe the majority of girls are trained. This is demonstrated by the imperfect education which is bestowed upon them, and the little pains taken to cultivate their minds, after they leave school, by the little time allowed them for reading, and by the idea being constantly inculcated, that although all household concerns should be attended to with scrupulous punctuality at particular seasons, the improvement of their intellectual capacities is only a secondary consideration, and may serve as an occupation to fill up the odds and ends of time. In most families, it is considered a matter of far more consequence to call a girl off from making a pie, or a pudding, than to interrupt her whilst engaged in her studies. This mode of training necessarily exalts, in their view, the animal above the intellectual and spiritual nature, and teaches women to regard themselves as a kind of machinery, necessary to keep the domestic engine in order, but of little value as the *intelligent* companions of men.

Let no one think, from these remarks, that I regard a knowledge of housewifery as beneath the acquisition of women. Far from it: I believe that a complete knowledge of household affairs is an indispensable requisite in a woman's education,—that by the mistress of a family, whether married or single, doing her duty thoroughly and *understandingly*, the happiness of the family is increased to an incalculable degree, as well as a vast amount of time and money saved. All I complain of is, that our education consists so almost exclusively in culinary and other manual operations. I do long to see the time, when it will no longer be necessary for women to expend so many precious hours in furnishing "a well spread table," but that their husbands will forego some of their accustomed indulgences in this way, and encourage their wives to devote some portion of their time to mental cultivation, even at the expense of having to dine sometimes on baked potatoes, or bread and butter. . . .

There is another way in which the general opinion, that women are inferior to men, is manifested, that bears with tremendous effect on the laboring class, and indeed on almost all who are obliged to earn a subsistence, whether it be by mental or physical exertion—I allude to the disproportionate value set on the time and labor of men and of women. A man who is engaged in teaching, can always, I believe, command a higher price for tuition than a woman—even when he teaches the same branches, and is not in any respect superior to the women. This I know is the case in boarding and other schools with which I have been acquainted, and it is so in every occupation in which the sexes engage indiscriminately. As for example, in tailoring, a man has twice, or three times as much for making a waistcoat or pantaloons as a woman, although the work done by each may be equally good. In those employments which are peculiar to women, their time is estimated at only half the value of that of men. A woman who goes out to wash, works as hard in proportion as a wood sawyer, or a coal heaver, but she is not generally able to make more than half as much by a day's work. The low remuneration which women receive for their work, has claimed the attention of a few philanthropists, and I hope it will continue to do so until some remedy is applied for this enormous evil. I have known a widow, left with four or five children, to provide for, unable to leave home because her helpless babes demand her attention, compelled to earn a scanty subsistence, by making coarse shirts at 12 1/2 cents a piece, or by taking in washing, for which she was paid by some wealthy persons 12 1/2 cents per dozen. All these things evince the low estimation in which woman is held. There is yet another and more disastrous consequence arising from this unscriptural notion—women being educated, from earliest childhood, to regard themselves as inferior creatures, have not that self-respect which conscious equality would engender, and hence when their virtue is assailed, they yield to temptation with facility, under the idea that it rather exalts than debases them, to be connected with a superior being.

There is another class of women in this country, to whom I cannot refer, without feelings of the deepest shame and sorrow. I allude to our female slaves. Our southern cities are whelmed beneath a tide of pollution; the virtue of female slaves is wholly at the mercy of irresponsible tyrants, and women are bought and sold in our slave markets, to gratify the brutal lust of those who bear the name of Christians. In our slave States, if amid all her degradation and ignorance, a woman desires to preserve her virtue unsullied, she is either bribed or whipped into compliance, or if she dares resist her seducer, her life by the laws of some of the slave States may be, and has actually been sacrificed to the fury of disappointed passion. Where such laws do not exist, the power which is necessarily vested in the master over his property, leaves the defenceless slave entirely at his mercy, and the sufferings of some females on this account, both physical and mental, are intense. Mr. Gholson, in the House of Delegates of Virginia, in 1832, said, "He really had been under the impression that he owned his slaves. He had lately purchased four women and ten children, in whom he thought he had obtained a great bargain; for he supposed they were his own property, *as were his brood mares.*" But even if any laws existed in the United States, as in Athens formerly, for the protection of female slaves, they would be null and void, because the evidence of a colored person is not admitted against a white, in any of our Courts of Justice in the slave States. "In Athens, if a female slave had cause to complain of any want of respect to the laws of modesty, she could seek the protection of the temple, and demand a change of owners; and such appeals were never discountenanced, or neglected by the magistrate." In Christian America, the slave has no refuge from unbridled cruelty and lust.

S. A. Forrall, speaking of the state of morals at the South, says, "Negresses when young and likely, are often employed by the planter, or his friends, to administer to their sensual desires. This frequently is a matter of speculation, for if the offspring, a mulatto, be a handsome female, 800 or 1000 dollars may be obtained for her in the New Orleans market. It is an occurrence of no uncommon nature to see a Christian father sell his own daughter, and the brother his own sister." The following is copied by the N.Y. Evening Star from the Picayune, a paper published in New Orleans. "A very beautiful girl, belonging to the estate of John French, a deceased gambler at New Orleans, was sold a few days since for the round sum of $7,000. An ugly-looking bachelor named Gouch, a member of the Council of one of the Principalities, was the purchaser. The girl is a brunette; remarkable for her beauty and intelligence, and there was considerable contention, who should be the purchaser. She was, however, persuaded to accept Gouch, he having made her princely promises. . . . That such a state of society should exist in a Christian nation, claiming to be the most enlightened upon earth, without calling forth any *particular attention* to its existence, though ever before our eyes and *in our* families, is a moral phenomenon at once unaccountable and disgraceful." Nor does the colored woman suffer alone: the moral purity of the white woman is deeply contaminated. In the daily habit of seeing the virtue of her enslaved sister sacrificed without hesitancy or remorse, she looks upon the crimes of seduction and illicit intercourse without horror, and although not personally involved in the guilt, she loses that value for innocence in her own, as well as the other sex, which is one of the strongest safeguards to virtue. She lives in habitual intercourse with men, whom she knows to be polluted by licentiousness, and often is she compelled to witness in her own domestic circle, those disgusting and heart-sickening jealousies and strifes which disgraced and distracted the family of Abraham. In addition to all this, the female slaves suffer every species of degradation and cruelty, which the most wanton barbarity can inflict; they are indecently divested of their clothing, sometimes tied up and severely whipped, sometimes prostrated on the earth, while their naked bodies are torn by the scorpion lash.

> The whip on woman's shrinking flesh!
> Our soil yet reddening with the stains
> Caught from her scourging warm and fresh.

Can any American woman look at these scenes of shocking licentiousness and cruelty, and fold her hands in apathy, and say, "I have nothing to do with slavery"? *She cannot and be guiltless.*

I cannot close this letter, without saying a few words on the benefits to be derived by men, as well as women, from the opinions I advocate relative to the equality of the sexes. Many women are now supported, in idleness and extravagance, by the industry of their husbands, fathers, or brothers, who are compelled to toil out their existence, at the counting house, or in the printing office, or some other laborious occupation, while the wife and daughters and sisters take no part in the support of the family, and appear to think that their sole business is to spend the hard bought earnings of their male friends. I deeply regret such a state of things, because I believe that if women felt their responsibility, for the support of themselves, or their families it would add strength and dignity to their characters, and teach them more true sympathy for their husbands, than is now generally manifested,—a sympathy which would be exhibited by actions as well as words. Our brethren may reject my doctrine, because it runs counter to common opinions, and because it wounds their pride; but I believe they would be "partakers of the benefit" resulting from the Equality of the Sexes, and would find that woman, as their equal, was unspeakably more valuable than woman as their inferior, both as a moral and an intellectual being.

> *Thine in the bonds of womanhood,*
> *Sarah M. Grimké*

Introduction to Document 4

Harriet Jacobs was born a slave in Edenton, North Carolina, in 1813. The events described in this passage took place around 1830, though her story was not published, as *Incidents in the Life of a Slave Girl,* until 1861. Jacobs's life was filled with drama. Unrelenting sexual exploitation finally drove her into hiding. For seven years a black family sheltered her in a tiny crawl space of their home, until Harriet was able to escape to New York City in 1842. Finally, she was reunited with her two children. Note how Jacobs's story underscores some of Grimké's main themes. Jacobs was caught between the powerlessness of enslavement and a set of sexual mores that offered few alternatives. But if the roles of slave and woman gave Jacobs few choices, they never completely destroyed her ability to act in her own behalf.

DOCUMENT 4 *From* Incidents in the Life of a Slave Girl

Harriet Jacobs

. . . I now entered on my fifteenth year—a sad epoch in the life of a slave girl. My master began to whisper foul words in my ear. Young as I was, I could not remain ignorant of their import. I tried to treat them with indifference or contempt. The master's age, my extreme youth, and the fear that his conduct would be reported to my grandmother, made him bear this treatment for many months. He was a crafty man, and resorted to many means to accomplish his purposes. Sometimes he had stormy, terrific ways, that made his victims tremble; sometimes he assumed a gentleness that he thought must surely subdue. Of the two, I preferred his stormy moods, although they left me trembling. He tried his utmost to corrupt the pure principles my grandmother had instilled. He peopled my young mind with unclean images, such as only a vile monster could think of. I turned from him with disgust and hatred. But he was my master. I was compelled to live under the same roof with him—where I saw a man forty years my senior daily violating the most sacred commandments of nature. He told me I was his property; that I must be subject to his will in all things. My soul revolted against the mean tyranny. But where could I turn for protection? No matter whether the slave girl be as black as ebony or as fair as her mistress. In either case, there is no shadow of law to protect her from insult, from violence, or even from death; all these are inflicted by fiends who bear the shape of men. The mistress, who ought to protect the helpless victim, has no other feelings towards her but those of jealousy and rage. . . .

I had entered my sixteenth year, and every day it became more apparent that my presence was intolerable to Mrs. Flint [the wife of Harriet Jacobs's owner]. Angry words frequently passed between her and her husband. He had never punished me himself, and he would not allow anybody else to punish me. In that respect, she was never satisfied; but, in her angry moods, no terms were too vile for her to bestow upon me. Yet I, whom she detested so bitterly, had far more pity for her than he had, whose duty it was to make her life happy. I never wronged her, or wished to wrong her; and one word of kindness from her would have brought me to her feet.

After repeated quarrels between the doctor and his wife, he announced his intention to take his youngest daughter, then four years old, to sleep in his apartment. It was necessary that a servant should sleep in the same room, to be on hand if the child stirred. I was selected for that office, and informed for what purpose that arrangement had been made. By managing to keep within sight of people, as much as possible, during the day time, I had hitherto succeeded in eluding my master, though a razor was often held to my throat to force me to change this line of policy. At night I slept by the side of my great aunt, where I felt safe. He was too prudent to come into her room. She was an old woman, and had been in the family many years. Moreover, as a married man, and a professional man [a doctor], he deemed it necessary to save appearances in some degree. But he resolved to remove the obstacle in the way of his scheme; and he thought he had planned it so that he should evade suspicion. He was well aware how much I prized my refuge by the side of my old aunt, and he determined to dispossess me of it. The first night the doctor had the little child in his room alone. The next morning, I was ordered to take my station as nurse the following night. A kind Providence interposed in my favor. During the day Mrs. Flint heard of this new arrangement and a storm followed. I rejoiced to hear it rage. . . .

The secrets of slavery are concealed like those of the Inquisition. My master was, to my knowledge, the father of eleven slaves. But did the mothers dare to tell who was the father of their children? Did the other slaves dare to allude to it, except in whispers among themselves? No, indeed! They knew too well the terrible consequences. . . .

. . . Dr. Flint contrived a new plan. He seemed to have an idea that my fear of my mistress was his greatest obstacle. In the blandest tones, he told me that he was going to build a small house for me, in a secluded place, four miles away from the town. I shuddered; but I was constrained to listen, while he talked of his intention to give me a home of my own, and to make a lady of me. Hitherto, I had escaped my dreaded fate, by being in the midst of people. My grandmother had already had high words with my master about me. She had told him pretty plainly what she thought of his character, and there was considerable gossip in the neighborhood about our affairs, to which the open-mouthed jealousy of Mrs. Flint contributed not a little. When my master said he was going to build a house for me, and that he could do it with little trouble and expense, I was in hopes something would happen to frustrate his scheme; but I soon heard that the house was actually begun. I vowed before my Maker that I would never enter it. I had rather toil on the plantation from dawn till dark; I had rather live and die in jail, than drag on, from day to day, through such a living death. I was determined that the master, whom I so hated and loathed, who had blighted the prospects of my youth, and made my life a desert, should not, after my long struggle with him, succeed at last in trampling his victim under his feet. I would do any thing, every thing, for the sake of defeating him. What *could* I do? I thought and thought, till I became desperate, and made a plunge into the abyss.

And now, reader, I come to a period in my unhappy life, which I would gladly forget if I could. The remembrance fills me with sorrow and shame. It pains me to tell you of it; but I have promised to tell you the truth, and I will do it honestly, let it cost me what it may. I will not try to screen myself behind the plea of compulsion from a master; for it was not so. Neither can I plead ignorance or thoughtlessness. For years, my master had done his utmost to pollute my mind with foul images, and to destroy the pure principles inculcated by my grandmother, and the good mistress of my childhood. The influences of slavery had had the same effect on me that they had on other young girls; they had made me prematurely knowing, concerning the evil ways of the world. I knew what I did, and I did it with deliberate calculation.

But, O, ye happy women, whose purity has been sheltered from childhood, who have been free to choose the objects of your affection, whose homes are protected by law, do not judge the poor desolate slave girl too severely! If slavery had been abolished, I also, could have married the man of my choice; I could have had a home shielded by the laws; and I should have been spared the painful task of confessing what I am now about to relate; but all my prospects had been blighted by slavery. I wanted to keep myself pure; and, under the most adverse circumstances, I tried hard to preserve my self-respect; but I was struggling alone in the powerful grasp of the demon Slavery; and the monster proved too strong for me. I felt as if I was forsaken by God and man; as if all my efforts must be frustrated; and I became reckless in my despair.

I have told you that Dr. Flint's persecutions and his wife's jealousy had given rise to some gossip in the neighborhood. Among others, it chanced that a white unmarried gentleman had obtained some knowledge of the circumstances in which I was placed. He knew my grandmother, and often spoke to me in the street. He became interested for me, and asked questions about my master, which I answered in part. He expressed a great deal of sympathy, and a wish to aid me. He constantly sought opportunities to see me, and wrote to me frequently. I was a poor slave girl, only fifteen years old.

So much attention from a superior person was, of course, flattering; for human nature is the same in all. I also felt grateful for his sympathy, and encouraged by his kind words. It seemed to me a great thing to have such a friend. By degrees, a more tender feeling crept into my heart. He was an educated and eloquent gentleman; too eloquent, alas, for the poor slave girl who trusted in him. Of course I saw whither all this was tending. I knew the impassable gulf between us; but to be an object of interest to a man who is not married, and who is not her master, is agreeable to the pride and feelings of a slave, if her miserable situation has left her any pride or sentiment. It seems less degrading to give one's self, than to submit to compulsion. There is something akin to freedom in having a lover who has no control over you, except that which he gains by kindness and attachment. A master may treat you as rudely as he pleases, and you dare not speak; moreover, the wrong does not seem so great with an unmarried man, as with one who has a wife to be made unhappy. There may be sophistry in all this; but the condition of a slave confuses all principles of morality, and, in fact, renders the practice of them impossible. . . .

As for Dr. Flint, I had a feeling of satisfaction and triumph in the thought of telling *him*. From time to time he told me of his intended arrangements, and I was silent. At last, he came and told me the cottage was completed, and ordered me to go to it. I told him I would never enter it. He said, "I have heard enough of such talk as that. You shall go, if you are carried by force; and you shall remain there."

I replied, "I will never go there. In a few months I shall be a mother."

He stood and looked at me in dumb amazement, and left the house without a word. I thought I should be happy in my triumph over him. But now that the truth was out, and my relatives would hear of it, I felt wretched. Humble as were their circumstances, they had pride in my good character. Now, how could I look them in the face? My self-respect was gone! I had resolved that I would be virtuous, though I was a slave. I had said, "Let the storm beat! I will brave it till I die." And now, how humiliated I felt!

Introduction to Document 5

In 1848, ten years after Grimké's letter, several women and a few men met in Seneca Falls, New York, and drew up their Declaration of Sentiments, a women's Declaration of Independence addressing a whole range of legal and customary inequalities that they wanted changed.

Document 5　*Declaration of Sentiments*

When, in the course of human events, it becomes necessary for one portion of the family of man to assume among the people of the earth a position different from that which they have hitherto occupied, but one to which the laws of nature and of nature's God entitle them, a decent respect to the opinions of mankind requires that they should declare the causes that impel them to such a course.

We hold these truths to be self-evident: that all men and women are created equal; that they are endowed by their Creator with certain inalienable rights; that among these are life, liberty, and the pursuit of happiness; that to secure these rights governments are instituted, deriving their just powers from the consent of the governed. Whenever any form of government becomes destructive of these ends, it is the right of those who suffer from it to refuse allegiance to it, and to insist upon the institution of a new government, laying its foundation on such principles, and organizing its powers in such form, as to them shall seem most likely to effect their safety and happiness. Prudence, indeed, will dictate that governments long established should not be changed for light and transient causes; and accordingly all experience hath shown that mankind are more disposed to suffer, while evils are sufferable, than to right themselves by abolishing the forms to which they were accustomed. But when a long train of abuses and usurpations, pursuing invariably the same object evinces a design to reduce them under absolute despotism, it is their duty to throw off such government, and to provide new guards for their future security. Such has been the patient sufferance of the women under this government, and such is now the necessity which constrains them to demand the equal station to which they are entitled.

The history of mankind is a history of repeated injuries and usurpations on the part of man toward woman, having in direct object the establishment of an absolute tyranny over her. To prove this, let facts be submitted to a candid world.

He has never permitted her to exercise her inalienable right to the elective franchise.

He has compelled her to submit to laws, in the formation of which she had no voice.

He has withheld from her rights which are given to the most ignorant and degraded men—both natives and foreigners.

Having deprived her of this first right of a citizen, the elective franchise, thereby leaving her without representation in the halls of legislation, he has oppressed her on all sides.

He has made her, if married, in the eye of the law, civilly dead.

He has made her, morally, an irresponsible being, as she can commit many crimes with impunity, provided they be done in the presence of her husband. In the covenant of marriage, she is compelled to promise obedience to her husband, he becoming, to all intents and purposes, her master—the law giving him power to deprive her of her liberty, and to administer chastisement.

He has so framed the laws of divorce, as to what shall be the proper causes, and in case of separation, to whom the guardianship of the children shall be given, as to be wholly regardless of the happiness of women—the law, in all cases, going upon a false supposition of the supremacy of man, and giving all power into his hands.

After depriving her of all rights as a married woman, if single, and the owner of property, he has taxed her to support a government which recognizes her only when her property can be made profitable to it.

He has monopolized nearly all the profitable employments, and from those she is permitted to follow, she receives but a scanty remuneration. He closes against her all the avenues to wealth and distinction which he considers most honorable to himself. As a teacher of theology, medicine, or law, she is not known.

He has denied her the facilities for obtaining a thorough education, all colleges being closed against her.

He allows her in Church, as well as State, but a subordinate position, claiming Apostolic authority for her exclusion from the ministry, and, with some exceptions, from any public participation in the affairs of the Church.

He has created a false public sentiment by giving to the world a different code of morals for men and women, by which moral delinquencies which exclude women from society, are not only tolerated, but deemed of little account in man.

He has usurped the prerogative of Jehovah himself, claiming it as his right to assign for her a sphere of action, when that belongs to her conscience and to her God.

He has endeavored, in every way that he could, to destroy her confidence in her own powers, to lessen her self-respect, and to make her willing to lead a dependent and abject life.

Now, in view of this entire disfranchisement of one-half the people of this country, their social and religious degradation—in view of the unjust laws above mentioned, and because women do feel themselves aggrieved, oppressed, and fraudulently deprived of their most sacred rights, we insist that they have immediate admission to all the rights and privileges which belong to them as citizens of the United States.

In entering upon the great work before us, we anticipate no small amount of misconception, misrepresentation, and ridicule; but we shall use every instrumentality within our power to effect our object. We shall employ agents, circulate tracts, petition the State and National legislatures, and endeavor to enlist the pulpit and the press in our behalf. We hope this Convention will be followed by a series of Conventions embracing every part of the country.

Introduction to Document 6

Lucy Larcom's life changed dramatically when her father passed away. Financial pressure caused her mother to open up a boardinghouse for "girls" (many were in their twenties and thirties) who worked in the textile mills. Young Lucy alternated between school and the mills, but her intelligence and curiosity made her long for something more, a longing that most working-class people rarely got the chance to fulfill. Document 6 is an excerpt from her memoirs, in which she recalls her youth—*A New England Girlhood* (1889).

DOCUMENT 6   *From* A New England Girlhood

Lucy Larcom

During my father's life, a few years before my birth, his thoughts had been turned towards the new manufacturing town growing up on the banks of the Merrimack. He had once taken a journey there, with the possibility in his mind of making the place his home, his limited income furnishing no adequate promise of a maintenance for his large family of daughters. From the beginning, Lowell had a high reputation for good order, morality, piety, and all that was dear to the old-fashioned New Englander's heart.

After his death, my mother's thoughts naturally followed the direction his had taken; and seeing no other opening for herself, she sold her small estate, and moved to Lowell, with the intention of taking a corporation-house for mill-girl boarders. Some of the family objected, for the Old World traditions about factory life were anything but attractive; and they were current in New England until the experiment at Lowell had shown that independent and intelligent workers invariably give their own character to their occupation. My mother had visited Lowell, and she was willing and glad, knowing all about the place, to make it our home.

The change involved a great deal of work. "Boarders" signified a large house, many beds, and an indefinite number of people. Such piles of sewing accumulated before us! A sewing-bee, volunteered by the neighbors, reduced the quantity a little, and our child-fingers had to take their part. But the seams of those sheets did look to me as if they were miles long! . . .

Our house was quickly filled with a large feminine family. As a child, the gulf between little girlhood and young womanhood had always looked to me very wide. I supposed we should get across it by some sudden jump, by and by. But among these new companions of all ages, from fifteen to thirty years, we slipped into womanhood without knowing when or how.

Most of my mother's boarders were from New Hampshire and Vermont, and there was a fresh, breezy sociability about them which made them seem almost like a different race of beings from any we children had hitherto known.

We helped a little about the housework, before and after school, making beds, trimming lamps, and washing dishes. The heaviest work was done by a strong Irish girl, my mother always attending to the cooking herself. She was, however, a better caterer than the circumstances required or permitted. She liked to make nice things for the table, and, having been accustomed to an abundant supply, could never learn to economize. At a dollar and a quarter a week for board (the price allowed for mill-girls by the corporations), great care in expenditure was necessary. It was not in my mother's nature closely to calculate costs, and in this way there came to be a continually increasing leak in the family purse. The older members of the family did everything they could, but it was not enough. I heard it said one day, in a distressed tone, "The children will have to leave school and go into the mill."

There were many pros and cons between my mother and sisters before this was positively decided. The mill-agent did not want to take us two little girls, but consented on condition we should be sure to attend school the full number of months prescribed each year. I, the younger one, was then between eleven and twelve years old.

I listened to all that was said about it, very much fearing that I should not be permitted to do the coveted work. For the feeling had already frequently come to me, that I was the one too many in the overcrowded family nest. Once, before we left our old home, I had heard a neighbor condoling with my mother because there were so many of us, and her emphatic reply had been a great relief to my mind:—

"There isn't one more than I want. I could not spare a single one of my children."

But her difficulties were increasing, and I thought it would be a pleasure to feel that I was not a trouble or burden or expense to anybody. So I went to my first day's work in the mill with a light heart. The novelty of it made it seem easy, and it really was not hard, just to change the bobbins on the spinning-frames every three quarters of an hour or so, with half a dozen other little girls who were doing the same thing. When I came back at night, the family began to pity me for my long, tiresome day's work, but I laughed and said,—

"Why, it is nothing but fun. It is just like play."

And for a little while it was only a new amusement; I liked it better than going to school and "making believe" I was learning when I was not. And there was a great deal of play mixed with it. We were not occupied more than half the time. The intervals were spent frolicking around among the spinning-frames, teasing and talking to the older girls, or entertaining ourselves with games and stories in a corner, or exploring, with the overseer's permission, the mysteries of the carding-room, the dressing-room, and the weaving-room.

I never cared much for machinery. The buzzing and hissing and whizzing of pulleys and rollers and spindles and flyers around me often grew tiresome. I could not see into their complications, or feel interested in them. But in a room below us we were sometimes allowed to peer in through a sort of blind door at the great waterwheel that carried the works of the whole mill. It was so huge that we could only watch a few of its spokes at a time, and part of its dripping rim, moving with a slow, measured strength through the darkness that shut it in. It impressed me with something of the awe which comes to us in thinking of the great Power which keeps the mechanism of the universe in motion. Even now, the remembrance of its large, mysterious movement, in which every little motion of every noisy little wheel was involved, brings back to me a verse from one of my favorite hymns:—

Our lives through various scenes are drawn,
And vexed by trifling cares,
While Thine eternal thought moves on
Thy undisturbed affairs.

There were compensations for being shut in to daily toil so early. The mill itself had its lessons for us. But it was not, and could not be, the right sort of life for a child, and we were happy in the knowledge that, at the longest, our employment was only to be temporary.

When I took my next three months at the grammar school, everything there was changed, and I too was changed. The teachers were kind, and thorough in their instruction; and my mind seemed to have been ploughed up during that year of work, so that knowledge took root in it easily. It was a great delight to me to study, and at the end of the three months the master told me that I was prepared for the high school.

But alas! I could not go. The little money I could earn—one dollar a week, besides the price of my board—was needed in the family, and I must return to the mill. It was a severe disappointment to me, though I did not say so at home. I did not at all accept the conclusion of a neighbor whom I heard talking about it with my mother. His daughter was going to the high school, and my mother was telling him how sorry she was that I could not.

"Oh," he said, in a soothing tone, "my girl hasn't got any such head-piece as yours has. Your girl doesn't need to go."

Of course I knew that whatever sort of a "head-piece" I had, I did need and want just that very opportunity to study. I think the resolution was then formed, inwardly, that I *would* go to school again, some time, whatever happened. I went back to my work, but now without enthusiasm. I had looked through an open door that I was not willing to see shut upon me.

I began to reflect upon life rather seriously for a girl of twelve or thirteen. What was I here for? What could I make of myself? Must I submit to be carried along with the current, and do just what everybody else did? No: I knew should not do that, for there was a certain Myself who was always starting up with here own original plan or aspiration before me, and who was quite indifferent as to what people generally thought.

Well, I would find out what this Myself was good for, and that she should be!

Introduction to Document 7

The letters of Malenda Edwards to Sabrina Bennett and of Mary Paul to her father give us insight into the life and labor of American women. Mill workers usually worked from 11 to 13 hours per day, beginning around sunrise; they received very short breaks for meals, and their pay was not only low but unstable, as mills often cut wages in response to oversupply, slack demand, or a quest for greater profits. Such letters reveal that many mill workers considered their labor temporary and that

Timetable of the Lowell Mills, 1853. (Merrimack Valley Textile Museum)

they expected to marry or return to their old farms or small towns. This sense of transiency blunted the efforts of workers to organize. Nevertheless, in 1845, hundreds of mill workers petitioned the Massachusetts legislature for a ten-hour day. They complained that poor sanitary conditions and long hours were destroying their health. Their request was not granted.

DOCUMENT 7   *Malenda Edwards and Mary Paul Letters*

[April 4, 1839]

Dear Sabrina,

. . . You have been informed I suppose that I am a factory girl and that I am at Nashua and I have wished you were here too but I suppose your mother would think it far beneith your dignity to be a factory girl. Their are very many young Ladies at work in the factories that have given up milinary d[r]essmaking & s[c]hool keeping for to work in the mill. But I would not advise any one to do it for I was so sick of it at first I wished a factory had never been thought of. But the longer I stay the better I like and I think if nothing unforesene calls me away I shall stay here till fall. . . . If you should have any idea of working in the factory I will do the best I can to get you a place with us. We have an excelent boarding place. We board with a family with whome I was acquainted with when I lived at Haverhill. Pleas to write us soon and believe your affectionate Aunt

M[alenda] M. Edwards

Bristol [N.H.] Aug 18, 1845

Dear Sabrina,

We received your letter sent by Mr Wells and I embrace the first opportunity to answer it and will now confess that I am a tremendous lazy corespondent at the best—and between my house work and da[i]ry spining weaving and raking hay I find but little time to write so I think I have appologised sifficiently for not writing you before this. I am very glad indeed you have been so kind to write us so often this summer for I am always glad to hear from absent friends if I cannot see them. I think it was a kind providence that directed my steps to Haverhill last winter for it is not likely that I shall visit you again so long as father and mother live if I should live for so long for they fail fast especially father. He has had quite a number of ill turns this summer and I have been physician and nurse too. Dont you think Sabrina it is well I have taken some lessons in the line of phisick? Mother is able to do but little this sumer [compared] to what she has been sumers past. The warm wether overcomes her very much but we get a long first rate. I have got the most of my wool spun and two webs wove and at the mill and have been out and raked hay almost every afternoon whilst they were haying. Father did not have but two days extra help about his haying and we have not had a moments help in the House. Mother commenced spinning this summer with great speed and thought she should do wonders but she only spun 17 skeins and gave it up as a bad bargain. We received a letter from Brother and Sister Colby about 3 weeks ago. They are well and prospering nicely. They have a young son born in May last. Thay call his name Allen James for his two uncles. They bought a half lot of land and built them a house four good rooms on the ground and paid for it. Then they bought the other half lot with a good brick house on it and Mary says if we will just step in we may see Elias and Molly with thare two pretty babies in thare own brick house almost as grand as Lawyer Bryants folks. O Sabrina how my western fever rages. Were it not for my father and mother

I would be in the far west ere this summer closes but I shall not leave them for friends nor foes! Mary and Elias say Liz dont get married for you must come out here. I shall take up with thare advice unles I can find some kind hearted youth that want a wife and mother, one that is good looking and can hold up his head up. Then when all that comes to pass I am off in a fit of matrimony like a broken jug handle but till I find such an one I glory in being an old maid, ha ha ha! . . .

M. M. Edwards

Lowell Dec 21st 1845

Dear Father

I received your letter on Thursday the 14th with much pleasure. I am well which is one comfort. My life and health are spared while others are cut off. Last Thursday one girl fell down and broke her neck which caused instant death. She was coming in or coming out of the mill and slipped down it being very icy. The same day a man was killed by the cars. Another had nearly all of his ribs broken. Another was nearly killed by falling down and having a bale of cotton fall on him. Last Tuesday we were paid. In all I had six dollars and sixty cents paid $4.68 for board. With the rest I got me a pair of rubbers and a pair of 50.cts shoes. Next payment I am to have a dollar a week beside my board. . . . Perhaps you would like something about our regulations about going in and coming out of the mill. At 5 o'clock in the morning the bell rings for the folks to get up and get breakfast. At half past six it rings for the girls to get up and at seven they are called into the mill. At half past 12 we have dinner are called back again at one and stay till half past seven. I get along very well with my work. . . . I think that the factory is the best place for me and if any girl wants employment I advise them to come to Lowell. Tell Harriet that though she does not hear from me she is not forgotten. I have little time to devote to writing that I cannot write all I want to. There are half a dozen letters which I ought to write to day but I have not time. Tell Harriet I send my love to her and all of the girls. Give my love to Mrs. Clement. Tell Henry this will answer for him and you too for this time.

This from
Mary S. Paul

Lowell Nov 5th 1848

Dear Father

Doubtless you have been looking for a letter from me all the week past. I would have written but wished to find whether I should be able to stand it—to do the work that I am now doing. I was unable to get my old place in the cloth room on the Suffolk or on any other corporation. I next tried the dressrooms on the Lawrence Cor[poration], but did not succe[e]d in getting a place. I almost concluded to give up and go back to Claremont, but thought I would try once more. So I went to my old overseer on the Tremont Cor. I had no idea that he would want one, but he *did*, and I went to work last Tuesday—warping—the same work I used to do.

It is *very* hard indeed and sometimes I think I shall not be able to endure it. I never worked so hard in my life but perhaps I shall get used to it. I shall try hard to do so for there is no other work that I can do unless I spin and that I shall not undertake on any account. I presume you have heard before this that the wages are to be reduced on the 20th of this month. It is *true* and there seems to be a good deal of excitement on the subject but I can not tell what will be the consequence. The companies pretend they are losing immense sums every *day* and therefore they are obliged to lessen the wages, but this seems perfectly absurd to me for they are constantly making *repairs* and it seems to me that this would not be if there were really any danger of their being obliged to *stop* the mills.

It is very difficult for any one to get into the mill on any corporation. All seem to be very full of help. I expect to be paid about two dollars a week but it will be dearly earned. . . .

Write soon. Yours affectionately
Mary S. Paul

QUESTIONS

Defining Terms

Identify in the context of the chapter each of the following:

"cult of true womanhood"   feminists
Lucy Larcom   "a woman's place is in the home"
Sarah Grimké   *Incidents in the Life of a Slave Girl*
Seneca Falls   Declaration of Sentiments
textile mills   Lowell, Massachusetts

Probing the Sources

1. What was daily life like for the women who worked in mills or on farms?
2. What did Beecher and Graves say was the proper role for women? What did Grimké say? What about the writers of the Declaration of Sentiments?
3. How did the ideals of middle-class domestic life and working-class realities compare?
4. What tensions and conflicts did Lucy Larcom describe in the account of her life?
5. What did it mean to be not only a woman, but also black and a slave?

Interpreting the Sources

1. Why did women who upheld the domestic ideal and those who wrote against it both argue on the basis of religious ideals? Why and how did both sides claim to be upholders of American equality?
2. What do you think family life—as daughters, mothers, and wives—was like for women in this era?
3. Why do you think the writers of the Declaration of Sentiments used the Declaration of Independence as their model?
4. Sarah Grimké compared the condition of women with that of black slaves. How do you think their situations were similar or different?

ADDITIONAL READING

Katherine Kish Sklar's *Catharine Beecher: A Study in Domesticity* (1973) is a fine biography of that very influential woman. *The Bonds of Womanhood: Woman's Sphere in New England, 1780–1835* (1977) by Nancy F. Cott is an important discussion of women's culture during the era. Carol Smith Rosenberg's *Disorderly Conduct: Visions of Gender in Victorian America* (1985) provides brilliant interpretive essays on women's experiences.

Christine Stansell, *City of Women: Sex and Class in New York, 1789–1869* (1986), and Thomas Dublin, *Transforming Women's Work: New England Lives in the Industial Revolution* (1994), describe the lives of working-class women. Mary P. Ryan's *Cradle of the Middle Class* (1981) offers insight into the origins of women's roles in middle-class culture. Harriet A. Jacobs's *Incidents in the Life of a Slave Girl* is available in an edited version by Jean Fagan Yellin (1987). Jeanne Boydston's *Home and Work: Housework, Wages, and the Ideology of Labor in the Early Republic* (1990) offers insight into the relationship between work inside and outside the home.

11

A House Divided
Free Labor, Slave Labor

HISTORICAL CONTEXT

The American Civil War was fought, in Abraham Lincoln's words, because the Union could no longer exist "half slave and half free." Four million Americans in the southern states were held in bondage. Many northerners believed that slave owners wanted to extend this system, while southerners felt that northerners were out to destroy the source of their wealth, their "peculiar institution" of black chattel slavery. The issues involved were not only about race; they were also about work.

As Americans, we long have taken it for granted that men and women should be free to learn the trade, craft, or profession they choose or to start a business making, buying, or selling goods. Whether or not individuals really do have an equal opportunity to succeed, most people in this country assume that equal opportunity is a good thing, that individuals should be free to do the best they can for themselves and their families, and that they should be enabled to seek economic success. By the middle of the nineteenth century, however, many Americans believed that southern slavery threatened these assumptions.

The ideal of equality is often referred to as liberalism. For our purposes, we use the term *liberalism* to mean maximum civil liberty and economic opportunity for each individual. A liberal society is one where individuals seek their own betterment, unobstructed by inherited traits like race, gender, religion, or caste. Liberalism assumes that humans are born equal and that no one deserves more or less than another because of ascribed status (for example, being born a prince or a peasant, a duke or a slave). Ideally, a liberal society enhances the freedom of each individual to maximize his or her economic opportunity and to compete against others on equal terms.

Liberalism in this sense is so much a part of American ideology and seems so common to us that it is hard to imagine alternatives. Yet the liberal ideal is rather new. When Adam Smith wrote his *Wealth of Nations* just two centuries ago, his argument that unobstructed individual freedom to compete in open markets rendered the greatest good to both individuals and societies was quite new. Open markets meant that neither prices of goods nor wages for labor should be fixed by custom; one could sell one's muscle power, skills, ideas, inventions, and goods for the maximum amount someone else was willing to pay. Before Smith's time, various forms of servitude were the predominant forms of labor: Serfs and peasants were obligated to work particular lands for particular individuals; African and Indian slaves in the Americas were bought and sold; and even apprentices and indentured servants in the American colonies were not able to render their labor freely to the highest bidder but instead owed it to others for years at a time. The *ideal* of a liberal society grew increasingly compelling throughout Europe and its colonial dependencies during the nineteenth century, though the reality of true equal opportunity remained elusive.

In his classic study entitled *Democracy in America,* published in the 1830s, the French traveler Alexis de Tocqueville marveled at how completely Americans accepted the ideology of equality; unlike in his country, no tradition of respect for kings and aristocrats called into question maximum equality as a social ideal. Perhaps better than anyone else, Abraham Lincoln articulated the liberal creed. Indeed, his ability to give almost poetic expression to it precisely when these cherished beliefs were being threatened by the breakup of the Union made him a compelling political figure. Lincoln declared on the eve of his race for the presidency against Steven A. Douglas:

> The prudent, penniless beginner in the world labors for wages awhile, saves a surplus with which to buy tools or land for himself, then labors on his own account another while, and at length hires another new beginner to help him. This, say its advocates, is free labor—the just, and generous, and prosperous system, which opens the way for all, gives hope to all, and energy, and progress, and improvement of condition to all.

Such a system, it was argued, gave wealth, happiness, and autonomy to the greatest number of people, each individual seeking his own good maximized society's benefits.

Lincoln added that a person who continued through life as a hired laborer did so not because of any fault in the system, but "because of either a dependent nature which prefers it, or improvidence, folly, or singular misfortune." Even on the eve of the Civil War, this was an overly optimistic assessment of opportunity in America. The trend was toward consolidation, and while the numbers of small businesses did grow, an ever-increasing proportion of Americans were working as employees, and the great majority of these would be employees for life. The division of labor grew always finer, factories and shops grew ever larger, and, even in the country, farms became places where hired hands worked for others. Yet the ideals that Lincoln espoused were so attractive to Americans that they would continue to be taken as descriptions of reality long after a minority of citizens owned productive property (farms, businesses, factories, and so on) and the vast majority worked for them.

The very belief that employees had every expectation of someday becoming employers muted potential conflict between the two classes. After all, both shared the values of hard work, productivity, self-improvement, and autonomy, and both believed they were part of a system that could fulfill those values. The problem, of course, was that individuals who were free to acquire productive property were also free to take charge of more and more resources, to monopolize markets, to keep others out of the system, and to control prices and wages. A truly open and egalitarian society is one that is easily threatened because when wealth and power do accumulate, there are few institutions or individuals strong enough to check their influence.

Karl Marx viewed this problem as inherent in capitalist economies. Marx wrote his critique of liberal society during the middle of the nineteenth century. He argued that capitalism—whether in his native Germany, in England, where he was writing, or in America, which he studied—inevitably concentrated power and wealth in fewer and fewer hands and that, before long, a small number of individuals monopolized goods and services and exploited the masses for their own private benefit. For Marx, the fact that individuals were equal in the eyes of the law and free to enter economic markets was a cruel sham; power rested with the ownership of productive property, liberal ideology notwithstanding.

But one did not have to be a follower of Marx to be a critic of capitalism. In the following documents, we see how the central liberal ideal of autonomy—of individual independence from oppressive concentrations of power—seemed threatened on the eve of the Civil War.

THE DOCUMENTS
Introduction to Documents 1 and 2

Hinton Rowan Helper's *Impending Crisis of the South* and George Fitzhugh's *Cannibals All! or Slaves Without Masters* were extreme books in their day. Both were published in 1857, just as the fragile compromises that had kept the union together were coming apart. Helper went much further than most northerners in his vituperation against the slaveholders. Similarly, Fitzhugh's argument that slavery should not be confined to blacks but was the appropriate condition for most people was an extremist stance that was rejected by his fellow slaveholders. But by taking radical positions, each man sharpened the debate. Southerners suspected that most northerners secretly agreed with Helper but were unwilling to admit it; northerners feared that Fitzhugh actually spoke for a power-hungry "slavepower" conspiracy that wanted to enslave most free white men in the North as well as in the South.

Note that Helper's hatred of slavery did not arise from sympathy for African Americans. On the contrary, he believed they were, whether slave or free, an "undesirable population" and that, once emancipated, they should be colonized in Africa, though nearly all had been born and raised in America. Rather, it was the alleged contrast of what free labor did for the North and slave labor for the South that he dwelled on: "In the former, wealth, intelligence, power, progress, and prosperity are the prominent characteristics; In the latter, poverty, ignorance, imbecility, inertia, and extravagance, are the distinguishing features." Slavery's impact on poor whites most concerned Helper, for by concentrating wealth (land and slaves) in the hands of the few, he argued, the system degraded the majority.

George Fitzhugh, on the other hand, argued that so-called free society made cannibals of all and rendered humans selfish and heartless. The solution was not, as many northern reformers would have it, to tinker with society to make it more humane. "To secure true progress," Fitzhugh declared, "we must unfetter genius and chain down mediocrity. Liberty for the few—Slavery, in every form, for the mass." Or, even more pithily: " 'Some were born with saddles on their backs, and others booted and spurred to ride them'—and the riding does them good."

Fitzhugh explicitly rejected race as the basis for enslavement; racism, he felt, hardened masters' hearts toward their slaves. He was a true conservative in the classical sense of the word. He argued that humans, white or black, were not born with equal inheritances of money or talent, so that, for most, liberty meant merely the chance to be exploited by those more rich, powerful, or intelligent. Freedom,

"After the sale: Slaves going south from Richmond." (Chicago Historical Society)

progress, equality of opportunity, and autonomous individualism were all pipe dreams. Human beings, Fitzhugh believed, were predators, and only systems of bondage recognized this fact, but they mollified it by imposing mutual rights and obligations on masters and slaves. The ideology of equal opportunity, of capitalism, he argued, was merely a ruse by which the strong exploited the weak. The world, he concluded, was too little governed; most people needed masters to tell them what to do.

If the following passages are extreme, they give a good sense of the clash of northern and southern economic systems and the underlying values that would soon explode in civil war.

DOCUMENT 1 *From Cannibals All!*

George Fitzhugh

The Universal Trade

We are all, North and South, engaged in the White Slave Trade, and he who succeeds best is esteemed most respectable. It is far more cruel than the Black Slave Trade, because it exacts more of its slaves, and neither protects nor governs them. We boast that it exacts more when we say, "that the *profits* made from employing free labor are greater than those from slave labor." The profits, made from free labor are the amount of the products of such labor, which the employer, by means of the command which capital or skill gives him, takes away, exacts, or "exploitates" from the free laborer. The profits of slave labor are that portion of the products of such labor which the power of the master enables him to appropriate. These profits are less, because the master allows the slave to retain a larger share of the results of his own labor than do the employers of free labor. But we not only boast that the White Slave Trade is more exacting and fraudulent (in fact, though not in intention) than Black Slavery; but we also boast that it is more cruel, in leaving the laborer to take care of himself and family out of the pittance which skill or capital have allowed him to retain. When the day's labor is ended, he is free, but is overburdened with the cares of family and household, which make his freedom an empty and delusive mockery. But his employer is really free, and may enjoy the profits made by others' labor, without a care, or a trouble, as to their well-being. The negro slave is free, too, when the labors of the day are over, and free in mind as well as body; for the master provides food, raiment, house, fuel, and everything else necessary to the physical well-being of himself and family. The master's labors commence just when the slave's end. No wonder men should prefer white slavery to capital, to negro slavery, since it is more profitable, and is free from all the cares and labors of black slave-holding. . . .

The negro slaves of the South are the happiest, and, in some sense, the freest people in the world. The children and the aged and infirm work not at all, and yet have all the comforts and necessaries of life provided for them. They enjoy liberty, because they are oppressed neither by care nor labor. The women do little hard work, and are protected from the despotism of their husbands by their masters. The negro men and stout boys work, on the average, in good weather, not more than nine hours a day. The balance of their time is spent in perfect abandon. Besides, they have their Sabbaths and holidays. White men, with so much of license and liberty, would die of ennui; but negroes luxuriate in corporeal and mental repose. With their faces upturned to the sun, they can sleep at any hour; and quiet sleep is the greatest of human enjoyments. "Blessed be the man who invented sleep." 'Tis happiness in itself—and results from contentment with the present, and confident assurance of the future. We do not know whether free laborers ever sleep. They are fools to do so; for, whilst they sleep, the wily and watchful capitalist is devising means to ensnare and exploitate them. The free laborer must work or starve. He is more of a slave than the negro, because he works longer and harder for less allowance than the slave, and has no holiday, because the cares of life with him begin when its labors end. He has no liberty, and not a single right. . . .

We agree with Mr. Jefferson that all men have natural and inalienable rights. To violate or disregard such rights, is to oppose the designs and plans of Providence, and cannot "come to good." The order and subordination observable in the physical, animal, and human world show that some are formed for higher, others for lower stations—the few to command, the many to obey. We conclude that about nineteen out of every twenty individuals have "a natural and inalienable right" to be taken care of and protected, to have guardians, trustees, husbands, or masters; in other words, they have a natural and inalienable right to be slaves. The one in twenty are as clearly born or educated or some way fitted for command and liberty. Not to make them rulers or masters is as great a violation of natural right as not to make slaves of the mass. A very little individuality is useful and necessary to society—much of it begets discord, chaos and anarchy. . . .

Liberty and Slavery

. . . What is falsely called Free Society is a very recent invention. It proposes to make the weak, ignorant, and poor, free, by turning them loose in a world owned exclusively by the few (whom nature and education have made strong, and whom property has made stronger) to get a living. In the fanciful state of nature, where property is unappropriated, the strong have no weapons but superior physical and mental power with which to oppress the weak. Their power of oppression is increased a thousand fold when they become the exclusive owners of the earth and all the things thereon. They are masters without the obligations of masters, and the poor are slaves without the rights of slaves.

It is generally conceded, even by abolitionists, that the serfs of Europe were liberated because the multitude of laborers and their competition as freemen to get employment, had rendered free labor cheaper than slave labor. But, strange to say, few seem to have seen that this is in fact asserting that they were less free after emancipation than before. Their obligation to labor was increased; for they were compelled to labor more than before to obtain a livelihood, else their free labor would not have been cheaper than their labor as slaves. They lost something in liberty, and everything in rights—for emancipation liberated or released the masters from all their burdens, cares, and liabilities, whilst it increased both the labors and the cares of the liberated serf. . . .

The Family

All modern philosophy converges to a single point—the overthrow of all government, the substitution of the untrammelled "Sovereignty of the Individual" for the Sovereignty of Society, and the inauguration of anarchy. First domestic slavery, next religious institutions, then separate property, then political government, and, finally, family government and family relations, are to be swept away. This is the distinctly avowed programme of all able abolitionists and socialists; and towards this end the doctrines and the practices of the weakest and most timid among them tend. . . .

It is pleasing, however, to turn from the world of political economy, in which "might makes right," and strength of mind and of body are employed to oppress and exact from the weak, to that other and better, and far more numerous world, in which weakness rules, clad in the armor of affection and benevolence. . . . The infant, in its capricious dominion over mother, father, brothers and sisters, exhibits, in strongest colors, the "strength of weakness," the power of affection. The wife and daughters are more carefully attended by the father, than the sons, because they are weaker and elicit more of his affection. . . .

But, besides wife and children, brothers and sister, dogs, horses, birds and flowers—slaves, also, belong to the family circle. Does their common humanity, their abject weakness and dependence, their great value, their ministering to our wants in childhood, manhood, sickness and old age, cut them off from that affection which everything else in the family elicits? No; the interests of master and slave are bound up together, and each in his appropriate sphere naturally endeavors to promote the happiness of the other.

The humble and obedient slave exercises more or less control over the most brutal and hard-hearted master. It is an invariable law of nature, that weakness and dependence are elements of strength, and generally sufficiently limit that universal despotism, observable throughout human and animal nature. The moral and physical world is but a series of subordinations, and the more perfect the subordination, the greater the harmony and the happiness. . . .

Government a Thing of Force, Not of Consent

We do not agree with the authors of the Declaration of Independence, that governments "derive their just powers from the consent of the governed." The women, the children, the negroes, and but few of the non-property holders were consulted, or consented to the Revolution, or the governments that ensued from its success. As to these, the new governments were self-elected despotisms, and the governing class self-elected despots. Those governments originated in force, and have been continued by force. All governments must originate in force, and be continued by force. The very term, government, implies that it is carried on against the consent of the governed. Fathers do not derive their authority, as heads of families, from the consent of wife and children, nor do they govern their families by their consent. They never take the vote of the family as to the labors to be performed, the moneys to be expended, or as to anything else. Masters dare not take the vote of slaves as to their government. If they did, constant holiday, dissipation, and extravagance would be the result. Captains of ships are not appointed by the consent of the crew, and never take their vote, even in "doubling Cape Horn." If they did, the crew would generally vote to get drunk, and the ship would never weather the cape. Not even in the most democratic countries are soldiers governed by their consent, nor is their vote taken on the eve of battle. They have some how lost (or never had) the "inalienable rights of life, liberty, and the pursuit of happiness," and, whether Americans or Russians, are forced into battle without and often against their consent. Riots, mobs, strikes, and revolutions are daily occurring. The mass of mankind cannot be governed by Law. More of despotic discretion, and less of Law, is what the world wants. We take our leave by saying *"There is too much of Law and too little of Government in this world."*

. . . The negro sees the driver's lash, becomes accustomed to obedient cheerful industry, and is not aware that the lash is the force that impels him. The free citizen fulfills *con amore*, his round of social, political, and domestic duties, and never dreams that the Law, with its fines and jails, penitentiaries and halters, or Public Opinion, with its ostracism, its mobs, and its tar and feathers, help to keep him revolving in his orbit. Yet, remove these physical forces, and how many good citizens would shoot, like firey comets, from their spheres, and disturb society with their eccentricities and their crimes.

📜 DOCUMENT 2 *From* The Impending Crisis of the South

Hinton Rowan Helper

It is a fact well known to every intelligent Southerner that we are compelled to go to the North for almost every article of utility and adornment, from matches, shoepegs and paintings up to cotton-mills, steamships and statuary; that we have no foreign trade, no princely merchants, nor respectable artists; that, in comparison with the free states, we contribute nothing to the literature, polite arts and inventions of the age . . . that almost everything produced at the North meets with ready sale, while, at the same time, there is no demand, even among our own citizens, for the productions of Southern industry; that, owing to the absence of a proper system of business amongst us, the North becomes, in one way or another, the proprietor and dispenser of all our floating wealth, and that we are dependent on Northern capitalists for the means necessary to build our railroads, canals and other public improvements . . . and that nearly all the profits arising from the exchange of commodities, from insurance and shipping offices, and from the thousand and one industrial pursuits of the country, accrue to the North, and are there invested in the erection of those magnificent cities and stupendous works of art which dazzle the eyes of the South, and attest the superiority of free institutions! . . .

In our opinion, an opinion which has been formed from data obtained by assiduous researches, and comparisons, from laborious investigation, logical reasoning, and earnest reflection, the causes which have impeded the progress and prosperity of the South, which have dwindled our commerce, and other similar pursuits, into the most contemptible insignificance; sunk a large majority of our people in galling poverty and ignorance, rendered a small minority conceited and tyrannical, and driven the rest away from their homes; entailed upon us a humiliating dependence on the Free States; disgraced us in the recesses of our own souls, and brought us under reproach in the eyes of all civilized and enlightened nations—may all be traced to one common source, and there find solution in the most hateful and horrible word, that was ever incorporated into the vocabulary of human economy—*Slavery!*

Reared amidst the institution of slavery, believing it to be wrong both in principle and in practice, and having seen and felt its evil influences upon individuals, communities and states, we deem it a duty, no less than a privilege, to enter our protest against it, and to use our most strenuous efforts to overturn and abolish it! Then we are an abolitionist? Yes! not merely a freesoiler, but an abolitionist, in the fullest sense of the term. We are not only in favor of keeping slavery out of the territories, but, carrying our opposition to the institution a step further, we here unhesitatingly declare ourself in favor of its immediate and unconditional abolition, in every state in this confederacy, where it now exists! Patriotism makes us a freesoiler; state pride makes us an emancipationist; a profound sense of duty to the South makes us an abolitionist; a reasonable degree of fellow feeling for the negro, makes us a colonizationist. . . .

In the South, unfortunately, no kind of labor is either free or respectable. Every white man who is under the necessity of earning his bread, by the sweat of his brow, or by manual labor, in any capacity, no matter how unassuming in deportment, or exemplary in morals, is treated as if he was a loathsome beast, and shunned with the utmost disdain. His soul may be the very seat of honor and integrity, yet without slaves—himself a slave—he is accounted as nobody, and would be deemed intolerably presumptuous, if he dared to open his mouth, even so wide as to give faint utterance to a three-lettered monosyllable, like yea or nay, in the presence of an august knight of the whip and the lash. . . .

Notwithstanding the fact that the white non-slaveholders of the South, are in the majority, as five to one, they have never yet had any part or lot in framing the laws under which they live. There is no legislation except for the benefit of slavery, and slaveholders. As a general rule, poor white persons are regarded with less esteem and attention than negroes, and though the condition of the latter is wretched beyond description, vast numbers of the former are infinitely worse off. A cunningly devised mockery of freedom is guaranteed to them, and that is all. To all intents and purposes they are disfranchised, and outlawed, and the only privilege extended to them, is a shallow and circumscribed participation in the political movements that usher slaveholders into office. . . .

Non-slaveholders of the South! farmers, mechanics and workingmen, we take this occasion to assure you that the slaveholders, the arrogant demagogues whom you have elected to offices of honor and profit, have hoodwinked you, trifled with you, and used you as mere tools for the consummation of their wicked designs. They have purposely kept you in ignorance, and have, by moulding your passions and prejudices to suit themselves, induced you to act in direct opposition to your dearest rights and interests. . . . Not at the persecution of a few thousand slaveholders, but at the restitution of natural rights and prerogatives to several millions of non-slaveholders, do we aim.

Henceforth, let it be distinctly understood that ownership of slaves constitutes ineligibility—that it is a crime, as we verily believe it is, to vote for a slavocrat for any office whatever. Indeed, it is our honest conviction that all the proslavery slaveholders, who are alone responsible for the continuance of the baneful institution among us, deserve to be at once reduced to a parallel with the basest criminals that lie fettered within the cells of our public prisons. Beyond the power of computation is the extent of the moral, social, civil, and political evils which they have brought, and are still bringing, on the country. Were it possible that the whole number could be gathered together and transformed into four equal gangs of licensed robbers, ruffians, thieves, and murderers, society, we feel assured, would suffer less from their atrocities then than it does now. . . .

And, then, there is the Presidency of the United States, which office has been held *forty-eight* years by slaveholders from the South, and only *twenty* years by non-slaveholders from the North. Nor is this the full record of oligarchal obtrusion. On an average, the offices of Secretary of State, Secretary of the Treasury, Secretary of the Interior, Secretary of the Navy, Secretary of War, Postmaster-General and Attorney-General, have been under the control of slavedrivers nearly two-thirds of the time. The Chief Justices and the Associate Justices of the Supreme Court of the United States, the Presidents pro tem. of the Senate, and the Speakers of the House of Representatives, have, in a large majority of instances, been slave-breeders from the Southern side of the Potomac. . . .

With all our heart, we hope and believe it is the full and fixed determination of a majority of the more intelligent and patriotic citizens of this Republic, that the Presidential chair shall never again be filled by a slavocrat. Safely may we conclude that the doom of the oligarchy is already sealed with respect to that important and dignified station. . . .

Some few years ago, when certain ethnographical oligarchs proved to their own satisfaction that the negro was an inferior "type of mankind," they chuckled wonderfully, and avowed, in substance, that it was right for the stronger race to kidnap and enslave the weaker—that because Nature had been pleased to do a trifle more for the Caucasian race than for the African, the former, by virtue of its superiority, was perfectly justifiable in holding the latter in absolute and perpetual bondage! No system of logic could be more antagonistic to the spirit of true democracy. It is probable that the world does not contain two persons who are exactly alike in all respects; yet "*all* men are endowed by their Creator with certain *inalienable* rights, among which are life, *liberty*, and the pursuit of happiness." All mankind may or may not be the descendants of Adam and Eve. In our own humble way of thinking, we are frank to confess, we do not believe in the unity of the races. This is a matter, however, which has little or nothing to do with the great question at issue. Aside from any theory concerning the original parentage of the different races of men, facts, material and immaterial, palpable and impalpable—facts of the eyes and facts of the conscience—crowd around us on every hand, heaping proof upon proof, that slavery is a shame, a crime, and a curse—a great moral, social, civil, and political evil—an oppressive burden to the blacks, and an incalculable injury to the whites—a stumbling-block to the nation, an impediment to progress, a damper on all the nobler instincts, principles, aspirations and enterprises of man, and a dire enemy to every true interest.

Introduction to Document 3

If Fitzhugh and Helper were extremists, Abraham Lincoln and Steven A. Douglas spoke for the great majority of moderate Americans. Yet their famous debates—stretching across Illinois through the summer and fall of 1858, and resulting in Douglas's reelection to the U.S. Senate—signaled just how intractable the issue of slavery had become.

For years, the territories, those lands that eventually would become states, had been a source of trouble. Not only did new states have the potential to tip the balance of power, North versus South, in the federal government, but the vast western lands also had great emotional significance. The West was a lightning rod for the ideals of rural self-sufficiency, republican virtue, democratic government, and equality of opportunity. Compromises had been reached, notably in 1820 and 1850, but the issue of slavery in the territories kept threatening to explode, and in the late 1850s, Stephen Douglas's support for popular sovereignty relit the fuse.

Douglas insisted that the West must be kept open for new white men to succeed and prosper, to create the local institutions that best served their interests. Lincoln countered that the western territories should become free states in order to confine slavery and put it on the road to eventual extinction.

Fitzhugh and Helper argued about slavery as a labor system; for both men, the key issues were how work was organized, how goods were distributed, and how power was exercised. Douglas, on the other hand, was much more explicit in arguing on grounds of race. He invoked white fears of black economic and even sexual preda- tions. Lincoln defended himself against Douglas's attacks by making clear his belief in blacks' inferiority—intellectual, physical, and social—yet insisted that this in no way should stand in the way of their natural rights. Above all, he insisted that all men possessed a God-given claim to the fruit of their labor. What set America apart from other nations was the right of all to better themselves to the extent that their ini- tiative and hard work allowed. So long as men might secure economic autonomy, Lincoln believed, freedom could survive.

DOCUMENT 3 *The Lincoln-Douglas Debates*

First Debate, August 21, 1858, Ottawa, Illinois

Douglas:

. . . I ask you, are you in favor of conferring upon the negro the rights and privileges of citizenship? Do you desire to strike out of our State constitution that clause which keeps slaves and free negroes out of the State, and allow the free negroes to flow in, and cover your prairies with black settlements? Do you desire to turn this beautiful State into a free negro colony, in order that when Missouri abolishes slavery she can send one hun- dred thousand emancipated slaves into Illinois, to become citizens and voters, on an equality with yourselves? If you desire negro citizenship, if you desire to allow them to come into the State and settle with the white man, if you desire them to vote on an equality with yourselves, and to make them eligible to office, to serve on juries, and to ad- judge your rights, then support Mr. Lincoln and the Black Republican party, who are in favor of the citizenship of the negro. For one, I am opposed to negro citizenship in any and every form. I believe this government was made on the white basis. I believe it was made by white men, for the benefit of white men and their posterity forever, and I am in favor of confining citizenship to white men, men of European birth and descent, instead of conferring it upon negroes, Indians, and other inferior races. . . .

Lincoln:

. . . I have no purpose to introduce political and social equality between the white and the black races. There is a physical difference between the two, which, in my judg- ment, will probably forever forbid their living together upon the footing of perfect equal- ity; and inasmuch as it becomes a necessity that there must be a difference, I, as well as Judge Douglas, am in favor of the race to which I belong having the superior position. I have never said anything to the contrary, but I hold that, notwithstanding all this, there is no reason in the world why the negro is not entitled to all the natural rights enumer- ated in the Declaration of Independence—the right to life, liberty, and the pursuit of hap- piness. I hold that he is as much entitled to these as the white man. I agree with Judge Douglas he is not my equal in many respects—certainly not in color, perhaps not in moral or intellectual endowment. But in the right to eat the bread, without the leave of any- body else, which his own hand earns, he is my equal and the equal of Judge Douglas, and the equal of every living man. . . .

Second Debate, August 27, 1858, Freeport, Illinois

Douglas:

. . . The last time I came here to make a speech, while talking from the stand to you, people of Freeport, as I am doing today, I saw a carriage, and a magnificent one it was, drive up and take a position on the outside of the crowd; a beautiful young lady was sitting on the box-seat, whilst Fred Douglass and her mother reclined inside, and the owner of the carriage acted as driver. I saw this in your own town. . . . All I have to say of it is this, that if you Black Republicans think that the negro ought to be on a social equality with your wives and daughters, and ride in a carriage with your wife, whilst you drive the team, you have perfect right to do so. I am told that one of Fred Douglass's kinsmen, another rich black negro, is now traveling in this part of the State making speeches for his friend Lincoln as the champion of black men. . . . All I have to say on that subject is, that those of you who believe that the negro is your equal and ought to be on an equality with you socially, politically, and legally, have a right to entertain those opinions, and of course will vote for Mr. Lincoln.

Fourth Debate, September 18, 1858, Charleston, Illinois

Lincoln:

    . . . I am not, nor ever have been, in favor of making voters or jurors of negroes, nor of qualifying them to hold office, nor to intermarry with white people; and I will say in addition to this that there is a physical difference between the white and black races which I believe will forever forbid the two races living together on terms of social and political equality. And inasmuch as they cannot so live, while they do remain together there must be the position of superior and inferior, and I as much as any other man am in favor of having the superior position assigned to the white race. I say upon this occasion I do not perceive that because the white man is to have the superior position the negro should be denied everything. I do not understand that because I do not want a negro woman for a slave I must necessarily want her for a wife. My understanding is that I can just let her alone. I am now in my fiftieth year, and I certainly never have had a black woman for either a slave or a wife. So it seems to me quite possible for us to get along without making either slaves or wives of negroes. . . . I have never had the least apprehension that I or my friends would marry negroes if there was no law to keep them from it; but as Judge Douglas and his friends seem to be in great apprehension that they might, if there was no law to keep them from it, I give him the most solemn pledge that I will to the very last stand by the law of this State, which forbids the marrying of white people with negroes. . . .

Fifth Debate, October 7, 1858, Galesburg, Illinois

Douglas:

    . . . The signers of the Declaration of Independence never dreamed of the negro when they were writing that document. They referred to white men, to men of European birth and European descent, when they declared the equality of all men. I see a gentleman there in the crowd shaking his head. Let me remind him that when Thomas Jefferson wrote that document he was the owner, and so continued until his death, of a large number of slaves. Did he intend to say in that Declaration that his negro slaves, which he held and treated as property, were created his equals by divine law, and that he was violating the law of God every day of his life by holding them as slaves? It must be borne in mind that when that Declaration was put forth, every one of the thirteen colonies were slave-holding colonies, and every man who signed that instrument represented a slave-holding constituency. Recollect, also, that no one of them emancipated his slaves, much less put them on an equality with himself, after he signed the Declaration. On the contrary, they all continued to hold their negroes as slaves during the Revolutionary War. Now, do you believe—are you willing to have it said—that every man who signed the

Declaration of Independence declared the negro his equal, and then was hypocrite enough to hold him as a slave, in violation of what he believed to be the divine law? And yet when you say that the Declaration of Independence includes the negro, you charge the signers of it with hypocrisy.

I say to you frankly, that in my opinion this government was made by our fathers on the white basis. It was made by white men for the benefit of white men and their posterity forever, and was intended to be administered by white men in all time to come. But while I hold that under our Constitution and political system the negro is not a citizen, cannot be a citizen, and ought not to be a citizen, it does not follow by any means that he should be a slave. On the contrary, it does follow that the negro as an inferior race ought to possess every right, every privilege, every immunity which he can safely exercise consistent with the safety of the society in which he lives. Humanity requires, and Christianity commands, that you shall extend to every inferior being, and every dependent being, all the privileges, immunities, and advantages which can be granted to them consistent with the safety of society. If you ask me the nature and extent of these privileges, I answer that that is a question which the people of each State must decide for themselves. Illinois has decided that question for herself. We have said that in this State the negro shall not be a slave, nor shall he be a citizen. Kentucky holds a different doctrine. . . . Illinois had as much right to adopt the policy which we have on that subject as Kentucky had to adopt a different policy. The great principle of this government is that each State has the right to do as it pleases on all these questions, and no other State or power on earth has the right to interfere with us, or complain of us merely because our system differs from theirs. In the compromise measures of 1850, Mr. Clay declared that this great principle ought to exist in the Territories as well as in the States, and I reasserted his doctrine in the Kansas and Nebraska bill in 1854. . . .

Seventh Debate, October 15, 1858, Alton, Illinois

Lincoln:

. . . The real issue in this controversy—the one pressing upon every mind—is the sentiment on the part of one class that looks upon the institution of slavery as a wrong, and of another class that does not look upon it as a wrong. The sentiment that contemplates the institution of slavery in this country as a wrong is the sentiment of the Republican party. It is the sentiment around which all their actions, all their arguments, circle; from which all their propositions radiate. They look upon it as being a moral, social, and political wrong; and while they contemplate it as such, they nevertheless have due regard for its actual existence among us, and the difficulties of getting rid of it in any satisfactory way, and to all the constitutional obligations thrown about it. Yet having a due regard for these, they desire a policy in regard to it that looks to its not creating any more danger. . . .

. . . [Douglas] contends that whatever community wants slaves has a right to have them. So they have if it is not a wrong. But if it is a wrong, he cannot say people have a right to do wrong. . . .

That is the real issue. That is the issue that will continue in this country when these poor tongues of Judge Douglas and myself shall be silent. It is the eternal struggle between these two principles—right and wrong—throughout the world. They are the two principles that have stood face to face from the beginning of time; and will ever continue to struggle. The one is the common right of humanity, and the other the divine right of kings. It is the same principle in whatever shape it develops itself. It is the same spirit that says, "You toil and work and earn bread, and I'll eat it." No matter in what shape it comes, whether from the mouth of a king who seeks to bestride the people of his own nation and live by the fruit of their labor, or from one race of men as an apology for enslaving another race, it is the same tyrannical principle. . . .

Introduction to Document 4

Harriet Beecher Stowe's *Uncle Tom's Cabin* was probably the best-known book in America during the nineteenth century, the Bible excepted. The work set off a firestorm of controversy when first published in 1851–1852. Stowe's story drew on the conventions of melodrama: exciting scenes of escape and rescue, of cruelty and forebearance, of suffering and redemption, of pure good and evil. Stowe used this dramatic form to write an impassioned condemnation of slavery. This passage is taken from the end of the book. Here, Stowe finished her narrative and now told the reader in the didactic style of the day how the curse of slavery might be ended. Note how she brought together the themes of economic opportunity, virtuous hard work, sacred motherhood, and evangelical religion in her indictment of slavery.

Abraham Lincoln allegedly called Stowe "the little woman who started the big war." He exaggerated, of course, but the debate over slave labor versus free labor eventually consumed the nation.

DOCUMENT 4 *From* Uncle Tom's Cabin; or Life Among the Lowly

Harriet Beecher Stowe

The writer has given only a faint shadow, a dim picture, of the anguish and despair that are, at this very moment, riving thousands of hearts, shattering thousands of families, and driving a helpless and sensitive race to frenzy and despair. There are those living who know the mothers whom this accursed traffic has driven to the murder of their children; and themselves seeking in death a shelter from woes more dreaded than death. Nothing of tragedy can be written, can be spoken, can be conceived, that equals the frightful reality of scenes daily and hourly acting on our shores, beneath the shadow of American law, and the shadow of the cross of Christ. . . .

But, what can any individual do? Of that, every individual can judge. There is one thing that every individual can do,—They can see to it that *they feel right*. An atmosphere of sympathetic influence encircles every human being; and the man or woman who *feels* strongly, healthily, and justly on the great interests of humanity, is a constant benefactor to the human race. See, then, to your sympathies in this matter! Are they in harmony with the sympathies of Christ? or are they swayed and perverted by the sophistries of worldly policy?

Christian men and women of the north! still further,—you have another power; you can *pray!* Do you believe in prayer? or has it become an indistinct apostolic tradition? You pray for the heathen abroad; pray also for the heathen at home. And pray for those distressed Christians whose whole chance of religious improvement is an accident of trade and sale: from whom any adherence to the morals of Christianity is, in many cases, an impossibility, unless they have given them, from above the courage and grace of martyrdom.

But, still more. On the shores of our free states are emerging the poor, shattered, broken remnants of families,—men and women, escaped, by miraculous providences, from the surges of slavery,—feeble in knowledge, and, in many cases, infirm in moral constitution, from a system which confounds and confuses every principle of Christianity and morality. They come to seek a refuge among you; they come to seek education, knowledge, Christianity. . . .

Do you say, "We don't want them here; let them go to Africa?"

That the providence of God has provided a refuge in Africa, is, indeed, a great and noticeable fact; but that is no reason why the Church of Christ should throw off that responsibility to this outcast race which her profession demands of her.

Harriet Beecher Stowe's Uncle Tom's Cabin *enjoyed astonishing success from the first year it was published. For millions of Americans, the book summed up the evils of slavery. (The Granger Collection)*

To fill up Liberia with an ignorant, inexperienced, half-barbarized race, just escaped from the chains of slavery, would be only to prolong, for ages, the period of struggle and conflict which attends the inception of new enterprises. Let the Church of the north receive these poor sufferers in the spirit of Christ; receive them to the educating advantages of Christian republican society and schools, until they have attained to somewhat of a moral and intellectual maturity, and then assist them in their passage to those shores, where they may put in practice the lessons they have learned in America. . . .

The first desire of the emancipated slave, generally, is for *education*. There is nothing that they are not willing to give or do to have their children instructed; and, so far as the writer has observed herself, or taken the testimony of teachers among them, they are remarkably intelligent and quick to learn. The results of schools, founded for them by benevolent individuals in Cincinnati, fully establish this.

The author gives the following statement of facts, on the authority of Professor C. E. Stowe, then of Lane Seminary, Ohio, with regard to emancipated slaves, now resident in Cincinnati; given to show the capability of the race, even without any very particular assistance or encouragement.

The initial letters alone are given. They are all residents of Cincinnati.

"B—. Furniture-maker; twenty years in the city; worth ten thousand dollars, all his own earnings; a Baptist.

"C—. Full black; stolen from Africa; sold in New Orleans; been free fifteen years; paid for himself six hundred dollars; a farmer; owns several farms in Indiana; Presbyterian; probably worth fifteen or twenty thousand dollars, all earned by himself.

"K—. Full black; dealer in real estate; worth thirty thousand dollars; about forty years old; free six years; paid eighteen hundred dollars for his family; member of the Baptist Church; received a legacy from his master, which he has taken good care of, and increased.

"G—. Full black; coal-dealer; about thirty years old; worth eighteen thousand dollars; paid for himself twice, being once defrauded to the amount of sixteen hundred dollars; made all his money by his own efforts,—much of it while a slave, hiring his time of his master, and doing business for himself; a fine, gentlemanly fellow.

"W—. Three fourths black; barber and waiter; from Kentucky; nineteen years free; paid for self and family over three thousand dollars; worth twenty thousand dollars, all his own earnings; deacon in the Baptist Church.

"G. D—. Three fourths black; whitewasher; from Kentucky; nine years free; paid fifteen hundred dollars for self and family; recently died, aged sixty; worth six thousand dollars." . . .

If this persecuted race, with every discouragement and disadvantage, have done thus much, how much more they might do if the Christian Church would act towards them in the spirit of her Lord! . . .

A day of grace is yet held out to us. Both North and South have been guilty before God; and the *Christian Church* has a heavy account to answer. Not by combining together, to protect injustice and cruelty, and making a common capital of sin is this Union to be saved,—but by repentance, justice and mercy; for, not surer is the eternal law by which the millstone sinks in the ocean, than that stronger law by which injustice and cruelty shall bring on nations the wrath of Almighty God!

Introduction to Document 5

While whites debated the merits of slavery as a labor system, as a method of racial control, and as means of producing and distributing wealth, blacks felt the lash on their backs.

For all of the agony of that era, the ideal of freedom remained intoxicating stuff. Frederick Douglass was born a slave in Maryland, but as he reached his twenty-first year, he resolved to risk all and flee north. From then on, he dedicated himself to the abolitionist cause, and after the war, to the goal of freedmen's rights. Douglass was in no sense naive about the racism that pervaded America, nor about the difficult time that blacks had in the capitalist economy.

In the following open letter to his former master, written on the tenth anniversary of his flight from bondage, Douglass described the breakup of his family and thereby invoked the sanctity of that institution to reveal slavery in terms deeply offensive to all that northerners held dear. Douglass's strategy was to paint slavery as antithetical to the most sacred American values.

Document 5 *Open Letter to Thomas Auld*

Frederick Douglass

September 3d, 1848

Sir: . . .

I have selected this day on which to address you, because it is the anniversary of my emancipation; and knowing of no better way, I am led to this as the best mode of celebrating that truly important event. . . .

I have often thought I should like to explain to you the grounds upon which I have justified myself in running away from you. . . . When yet but a child about six years old, I imbibed the determination to run away. The very first mental effort that I now remember on my part, was an attempt to solve the mystery, Why am I a slave? and with this question my youthful mind was troubled for many days, pressing upon me more heavily at times than others. When I saw the slave-driver whip a slave woman, cut the blood out of her neck, and heard her piteous cries, I went away into the corner of the fence, wept and pondered over the mystery. I had, though some medium, I know not what, got some idea of God, the Creator of all mankind, the black and the white, and that he had made the blacks to serve the whites as slaves. How he could do this and be *good*, I could not tell. I was not satisfied with this theory, which made God responsible for slavery, for it pained me greatly, and I have wept over it long and often. At one time, your first wife, Mrs. Lucretia, heard me singing and saw me shedding tears, and asked of me the matter, but I was afraid to tell her. I was puzzled with this question, till one night, while sitting in the kitchen, I heard some of the old slaves talking of their parents having been stolen from Africa by white men, and were sold here as slaves. The whole mystery was solved at once. Very soon after this my aunt Jinny and uncle Noah ran away, and the great noise made about it by your father-in-law, made me for the first time acquainted with the fact, that there were free States as well as slaves States. From that time, I resolved that I would some day run away. The morality of the act, I dispose as follows: I am myself; you are yourself; we are two distinct persons, equal persons. What you are, I am. You are a man, and so am I. God created both, and made us separate beings. I am not by nature bound to you, or you to me. . . .

Since I left you, I have had a rich experience. I have occupied stations which I never dreamed of when a slave. Three out of the ten years since I left you, I spent as a common laborer on the wharves of New Bedford, Massachusetts. It was there I earned my first free dollar. It was mine. I could spend it as I pleased. I could buy hams or herring with it, without asking any odds of any body. That was a precious dollar to me. You remember when I used to make seven or eight, or even nine dollars a week in Baltimore, you would take every cent of it from me every Saturday night, saying that I belonged to you, and my earnings also. I never liked this conduct on your part—to say the best, I thought it a little mean. . . .

. . . I married soon after leaving you: in fact, I was engaged to be married before I left you; and instead of finding my companion a burden, she was truly a helpmeet. She went to live at service, and I to work on the wharf, and though we toiled hard the first winter, we never lived more happily. After remaining in New Bedford for three years, I met with Wm. Lloyd Garrison, a person of whom you have *possibly* heard, as he is pretty generally known among slaveholders. He put it into my head that I might make myself serviceable to the cause of the slave by devoting a portion of my time to telling my own sorrows, and those of other slaves which had come under my observation. This was the commencement of a higher state of existence than any to which I had ever aspired. I was thrown into society the most pure, enlightened and benevolent that the country affords. Among these I have never forgotten you, but have invariably made you the topic of conversation—thus giving you all the notoriety I could do. I need not tell you that the opinion formed of you in these circles, is far from being favorable. They have little respect for your honesty, and less for your religion.

. . . So far as my domestic affairs are concerned, I can boast of as comfortable a dwelling as your own. I have an industrious and neat companion and four dear children— the oldest a girl of nine years, and three fine boys, the oldest eight, the next six, and the youngest four years old. The three oldest are now going regularly to school—two can read and write, and the other can spell with tolerable correctness words of two syllables: Dear fellows! they are all in comfortable beds, and are sound asleep, perfectly secure under my own roof. There are no slaveholders here to rend my heart by snatching them from my arms, or blast a mother's dearest hopes by tearing them from her bosom. . . . Oh! sir, a slaveholder never appears to me so completely an agent of hell, as when I think of and look upon my dear children. It is then that my feelings rise above my control. I meant to have said more with respect to my own prosperity and happiness, but thoughts and feelings which this recital has quickened unfits me to proceed further in that direction. The grim horrors of slavery rise in all their ghastly terror before me, the wails of millions pierce my heart, and chill my blood. I remember the chain, the gag, the bloody whip, the death-like gloom overshadowing the broken spirit of the fettered bondman, the appalling liability of his being torn away from wife and children, and sold like a beast in the market. Say not that this is a picture of fancy. You well know that I wear stripes on my back inflicted by your direction; and that you, while we were brothers in the same church, caused this right hand, with which I am now penning this letter, to be closely tied to my left, and my person dragged at the pistol's mouth, fifteen miles, from the Bay side to Easton to be sold like a beast in the market, for the alleged crime of intending to escape from your possession. All this and more you remember, and know to be perfectly true, not only of yourself, but of nearly all of the slaveholders around you.

At this moment, you are probably the guilty holder of at least three of my own dear sisters, and my only brother in bondage. These you regard as your property. They are recorded on your ledger, or perhaps have been sold to human flesh mongers, with a view to filling your own ever-hungry purse. Sir, I desire to know how and where these dear sisters are. Have you sold them? or are they still in your possession? What has become of them? are they living or dead? And my dear old grand-mother, whom you turned out like an old horse, to die in the woods—is she still alive? Write and let me know all about them. If my grandmother be still alive, she is of no service to you, for by this time she must be nearly eighty years old—too old to be cared for by one to whom she has ceased to be of service, send her to me at Rochester, or bring her to Philadelphia, and it shall be the crowning happiness of my life to take care of her in her old age. Oh! she was to me a mother, and a father, so far as hard toil for my comfort could make her such. Send me my grandmother! that I may watch over and take care of her in her old age. And my sisters, let me know all about them. I would write to them, and learn all I want to know of them, without disturbing you in any way, but that, through your unrighteous conduct, they have been entirely deprived of the power to read and write. You have kept them in utter ignorance, and have therefore robbed them of the sweet enjoyments of writing or receiving letters from absent friends and relatives. Your wickedness and cruelty committed in this respect on your fellow-creatures, are greater than all the stripes you have laid upon my back, or theirs. It is an outrage upon the soul—a war upon the immortal spirit, and one for which you must give account at the bar of our common Father and Creator.

. . . How, let me ask, would you look upon me, were I some dark night in company with a band of hardened villains, to enter the precincts of your elegant dwelling and seize the person of your own lovely daughter Amanda, and carry her off from your family, friends and all the loved ones of her youth—make her my slave—compel her to work, and I take her wages—place her name on my ledger as property—disregard her personal rights—fetter the powers of her immortal soul by denying her the right and privilege of learning to read and write—feed her coarsely—clothe her scantily, and whip her on the naked back occasionally; more and still more horrible, leave her unprotected—a degraded victim to the brutal lust of fiendish overseers, who would pollute, blight, and blast her fair soul—rob her of all dignity—destroy her virtue, and annihilate all in her person the graces that adorn the character of virtuous womanhood? I ask how would you regard me, if such were my conduct? Oh! the vocabulary of the damned would not afford a word sufficiently infernal, to express your idea of my God-provoking wickedness. Yet sir, your treatment of my beloved sisters is in all essential points, precisely like the case I have now supposed. Damning as would be such a deed on my part, it would be no more so than that which you have committed against me and my sisters.

I will now bring this letter to a close, you shall hear from me again unless you let me hear from you. I intend to make use of you as a weapon with which to assail the system of slavery—as a means of concentrating public attention on the system, and deepening their horror of trafficking in the souls and bodies of men. I shall make use of you as a means of exposing the character of the American church and clergy—and as a means of bringing this guilty nation with yourself to repentance. In doing this I entertain no malice towards you personally. There is no roof under which you would be more safe than mine, and there is nothing in my house which you might need for your comfort, which I would not readily grant. Indeed, I should esteem it a privilege, to set you an example as to how mankind ought to treat each other.

I am your fellow man, but not your slave,

Frederick Douglass

QUESTIONS

Defining Terms

Identify in the context of the chapter each of the following:

liberalism

Alexis de Tocqueville

George Fitzhugh

Lincoln-Douglas debates

Frederick Douglass

Wealth of Nations

"we must unfetter genius and chain-down mediocrity"

Hinton Helper

"the little woman who started the big war"

"free labor, slave labor"

Probing the Sources

1. What were Hinton Helper's and George Fitzhugh's views on black people? Lincoln's and Douglas's? Were they racists?

2. Why did George Fitzhugh oppose "free" society and free labor?

3. Why did Helper oppose slavery? Why did Lincoln?

4. What persuasive strategies did the different participants in the slavery debate use to make their points?

Interpreting the Sources

1. Since both Fitzhugh and Helper were extremists—since neither of them was "typical" in his thinking—can their writings be valuable for understanding the free labor-slave labor conflict?

2. What were the fundamental conflicts of values, beliefs, and ideologies between the various individuals in this chapter?

3. In what sense was it true that the debate over slavery was not really about black people, but about whites?

4. What was at stake in the debate over slavery?

ADDITIONAL READING

To understand the ideology of the North and the South, see Eric Foner, *Free Soil, Free Labor, Free Men: The Ideology of the Republican Party Before the Civil War* (1970); Foner, *Politics and Ideology in the Age of the Civil War* (1980); and Eugene Genovese, *The World the Slaveholders Made: Two Essays in Interpretation* (1969). For background on the sectional conflict, see David M. Potter, *The Impending Crisis: 1848–1861* (1971); C. Vann Woodward, *American Counterpoint: Slavery and Racism in the North-South Dialogue* (1964); and James M. McPherson, *Battle Cry of Freedom* (1988). For the ideological conflicts undergirding the era, see Bruce Levine, *Half Slave and Half Free* (1992); and Tyler Anbinder, *Nativism and Slavery: The Northern Know Nothings and the Politics of the 1850's* (1992). On the public discourse, see David Zarefsky, *Lincoln, Douglass, and Slavery: In the Crucible of Public Debate* (1990).

A War within A War
The New York City Draft Riots

HISTORICAL CONTEXT

During three days of mid-July 1863, white workers, mostly Irish-Americans, terrorized much of New York City. They attacked the rich, the police, and those who supported Republican policies. Above all, they attacked free African Americans. They torched an asylum for black orphans, tarred and feathered blacks who happened to get in their way, and dismembered, mutilated, burned, and drowned their victims. Hanging, however, was the punishment of choice. For example, Abraham Franklin, a handicapped black coachman, was pulled from his room, beaten, and strung up on a lamppost. The military intervened to disperse the crowd and cut down Franklin's corpse. But after the officials left, the lifeless body was hanged anew, taken down, and then dragged through the streets by its genitals as the crowd applauded.

The North's commitment to the Civil War was never absolute. Throughout the region there were pockets of Americans who resisted President Abraham Lincoln's efforts to preserve the Union and end slavery. Northern Democrats, dubbed Copperheads, sympathized with the South and opposed the war. Many Irish-American Catholics in the coal-fields of eastern Pennyslvania and German-American Catholics throughout Wisconsin also opposed the war. In the southern portions of Ohio, Indiana, and Illinois, pro-Confederate sympathies were particularly strong. Southerners had settled the region, and its corn-hog-whiskey economy tied it to the Ohio-Mississippi river network and the South. Called Butternuts because they dyed their homespun clothes with walnut or butternut oil, these northerners opposed almost every objective of Lincoln and the Republicans. "We won't fight to free the nigger," became their battle cry, and its echo was heard throughout Democratic centers in the North.

Among the most vocal opponents of the war and emancipation were the Irish-Americans. Most had come from Ireland during the late 1840s and the early 1850s in the wake of the Great Famine. When the potato crops failed, many poverty-stricken Irish Catholics had faced a grim decision: emigrate or starve. Roughly one million Irish died. By 1860, two million more came to the United States. There they found employment in unskilled jobs. They cleaned stables, carried bricks and mortar in hods, loaded and unloaded ships, dug canals, drained swamps, drove horses, mined coal, and worked as maids. They worked long and hard for meager wages, and they were barred from most avenues of economic and social mobility. Native-born Americans despised the Irish for their religion and their poverty, ridiculing them in print and caricaturing them as half ape, half human in cartoons. For many native-born Americans, and particularly for Republicans, the Irish represented alien invaders, distinct threats to Protestantism and Anglo-American culture and institutions.

Faced by American prejudices, the Irish displayed prejudices of their own. They tended to view Americans as a joyless, sober, and overworked people with souls as cold as a New England winter. If Irish-Americans were able to control their disdain for Anglo-Americans, they seldom tried to hide their hostility toward African Americans. In the North, Irish and blacks competed for the same unskilled jobs, and often employers used black longshoremen to destroy Irish unions. During the mid-1850s, the Irish Longshoremen's Society waged a violent, bitter struggle against black strikebreakers. They demanded an all-white waterfront, which the Longshoremen's United Benevolent Society—an Irish organization—interpreted as all-Irish. Confronted by this economic competition from African Americans, the Irish opposed any political move to improve the lot of blacks in the South as well as in the North.

The outbreak of the Civil War in 1861 presented the Irish-Americans with a thorny question of loyalty. Those who took an interest in the conflict viewed it in particularly Irish terms. Some supported the North and expressed shock at their fellow Irish who sided with the South. How, they asked, could an Irish person oppose the Union whose liberty had been won from the hated British? Confederate sympathizers responded that the South was fighting for its independence, an ambition that any Irish person should support. In either case, those Irish who joined the Union or the Confederate army often wore sprigs of green on their caps when they marched into battle. They proudly displayed their ethnic loyalties.

Most Irish, however, were less enmeshed in the Civil War than other Americans. It was not their war; the issues—Union and slavery—were not their issues. Patriotism for their adopted land did not always run deep in their veins. Of all ethnic groups in the United States, the Irish were the most underrepresented group in uniform in proportion to their population. While other immigrant groups enlisted in rough proportion to their numbers in the population, Irish Catholics—followed closely by German Catholics—did not. And if they did enlist or were drafted into the army, they were more likely to desert. Irish, Catholic, and Democrat, they felt no strong bonds to the Anglo-American, Protestant governments in Washington and Richmond.

For many Irish, the Civil War was a rich man's war. In support of this contention, they pointed to the Union's March 1863 conscription act, the Enrollment Act of 1863. It provided that any draftee who hired a substitute or paid a $300 commutation fee was exempt from military service. Of the 207,000 men who were drafted, 87,000 paid the commutation fee, and 74,000 furnished substitutes. From the point of view of the Irish, the draft was a clear example of class legislation. Rich men paid poor men to fight their battles. Three hundred dollars was a year's wages for an unskilled laborer. As one Iowa editor noted, "Did you ever know aristocratic legislation to so directly point out the poor man as inferior to the rich?"

But was the draft a piece of class legislation? The idea of paying for a substitute was hardly novel. It was both an American tradition and a European tradition, practiced in the American Revolution, the French Revolution, and other wars. And the $300 commutation fee was specified in the bill to hold down the price of a substitute. Poor as well as rich men paid the commutation fee. To be sure, the poor did not pay the $300 out of their own pockets. City and county governments, ward committees and political machines, and draft insurance societies and private companies paid sometimes to exempt those who did not have the money.

Nevertheless Democrats criticized the conscription act as class legislation. Along with Lincoln's Emancipation Proclamation, the conscription act was overwhelmingly opposed by Democrats in Congress. Democratic orators and journalists condemned both in the most vitriolic language. A midwestern convention resolved that "we will not render support to the present Administration in its wicked Abolitionist cause [and] we will *resist* to the *death* all attempts to draft any of our citizens into the army." An editor of a New York Catholic newspaper agreed and urged men at a mass meeting: "When the President called upon them to go and carry on the war for the nigger, he would be d—d if he believed they would go."

To New York Irish-Americans, the wording of the conscription act was particularly ominous. The law was directed to all "able-bodied male citizens of the United States." Since blacks were not citizens, this meant that only whites were subject to the draft. Orators inflamed the emotions of unskilled Irish-American workers by raising two specters: (1) hardworking Irish men would be drafted into the army, and (2) hordes of emancipated African Americans would swarm to New York to fill their unskilled jobs. By July 1863 the orators' speeches had accomplished their task. Fear and violence, palpable as the summer heat, surfaced. Describing the mood of the day, historian James M. McPherson observed:

> Crowded into noisome tenements in a city with the worst disease mortality and highest crime rate in the Western world, working in low-skill jobs for marginal wages, fearful of competition from black workers, hostile toward the Protestant middle and upper classes who often disdained and exploited them, the Irish were ripe for revolt against this war waged by Yankee Protestants for black freedom.

All that was needed was a spark to set ablaze the tinder of resentments, hostilities, and fear. That event came in the second week of July 1863, only a week after the great Union victories at Gettysburg and Vicksburg. On July 11, draft officers started drawing names, and New York laborers began to grumble, complain, and threaten. The next day the threats turned to violence. Rioters burned draft offices, tore up railroad tracks and telegraph lines, smashed into homes and businesses, and attacked innocent bystanders. Shouting, "Down with the rich," they assaulted well-dressed men—but they saved their most vicious onslaughts for blacks. They burned the Colored Orphan Asylum to the ground and beat or lynched scores of blacks. For five days the class and racial violence continued. To suppress the rioters, Lincoln ordered five Union Army regiments from Gettysburg to New York. By July 17, the ruthless application of firepower restored an uneasy quiet to New York. The riot had ended. At least 105 people had been killed. Order had been restored. But the rioters—about two-thirds of whom were Irish—had made their point. Through the politics of street violence, they had expressed their opinion of the conscription act and the Emancipation Proclamation.

The riot underscored the divisions between rich and poor, white and black, and local and national power. In the following sources, consider these divisions. How did the economic or racial attitudes of the observers influence their attitude toward the riot and the rioters? Also, what class, racial, and political factors shaped the conscription act?

THE DOCUMENTS

Introduction to Document 1

Printed below are excerpts from the Enrollment Act of 1863. Many Northerners considered the act a wartime necessity. Others condemned it as un-American and unconstitutional. Do you believe that the act treated all citizens equally?

 DOCUMENT 1   *Enrollment Act of 1863*

MARCH 3, 1863

Be it enacted . . . , That all able-bodied male citizens of the United States, and persons of foreign birth who shall have declared on oath their intention to become citizens under and in pursuance of the laws thereof, between the ages of twenty and forty-five years, except as hereinafter excepted, are hereby declared to constitute the national forces, and shall be liable to perform military duty in the service of the United States when called out by the President for that purpose.

SEC. 2. *And be it further enacted,* That the following persons be . . . exempt from the provisions of this act, and shall not be liable to military duty under the same, to wit: Such as are rejected as physically or mentally unfit for the service; also, First the Vice-President of the United States, the judges of the various courts of the United States, the heads of the various executive departments of the government, and the governors of the several States. Second, the only son liable to military duty of a widow dependent upon his labor for support. Third, the only son of aged or infirm parent or parents dependent upon his labor for support. Fourth, where there are two or more sons of aged or infirm parents subject to draft, the father, or, if he be dead, the mother, may elect which son shall be exempt. Fifth, the only brother of children not twelve years old, having neither father nor mother dependent upon his labor for support. Sixth, the father of motherless children under twelve years of age dependent upon his labor for support. Seventh, where there are a father and sons in the same family and household, and two of them are in the military service of the United States as non-commissioned officers, musicians, or privates, the residue of such family and household, not exceeding two, shall be exempt. And no persons but such as are herein excepted shall be exempt: *Provided, however,* That no person who has been convicted of any felony shall be enrolled or permitted to serve in said forces. . . .

SEC. 13. *And be it further enacted,* That any person drafted and notified to appear as aforesaid, may, on or before the day fixed for his appearance, furnish an acceptable substitute to take his place in the draft; or he may pay to such person as the Secretary of War may authorize to receive it, such sum, not exceeding three hundred dollars, as the Secretary may determine, for the procuration of each substitute; which sum shall be fixed at a uniform rate by a general order made at the time of ordering a draft for any state or territory; and thereupon such person so furnishing the substitute, or paying the money, shall be discharged from further liability under that draft. . . .

Introduction to Document 2

Ellen Leonard, a visitor to New York in July 1863, was trapped in the city during the turbulent days of the draft riots. This eyewitness account was published in *Harper's Magazine* in January 1867. What biases, if any, do you find in the report? To what degree do you think Leonard was a credible witness?

DOCUMENT 2 *"Three Days of Terror"*

Ellen Leonard

On the tenth of July, 1863, my mother and myself arrived in the city of New York. We had set out on a grand tour of visitation. After vegetating year after year in a New England village, we had sallied forth in genuine country fashion to hunt up our kinsfolk in various parts of the land. We were in no hurry. We had the whole summer before us. We wished to avoid crowds, noise, and excitement, to stop whenever we pleased, as long as we chose, and have a slow, old-fashioned, sociable, sensible journey. Thus far our tranquil visions had been more than realized. For three weeks we had been loitering placidly along our way, and nothing had occurred to mar our tranquillity. We hoped now to spend a few days quietly with my brother J., call on various friends and relatives, visit Central Park and a lion or so, shop a little, and move onward at our leisure.

But man proposes and Fate *disposes*, and nothing in New York turned out as we expected. . . .

. . . I could see nothing attractive. Every thing looked hot, glaring, and artificial, and every body looked shabby, jaded, and careworn. An overworked horse dropped dead in the street before me, and I was glad to take refuge for a time in the Astor Library.

Returning [to my brother's house] at mid-day I first saw signs of disturbance. A squad of policemen passed before me into Third Avenue, clerks were looking eagerly from the doors, and men whispering in knots all up and down the street; but I was too much a stranger to be certain that these appearances were unusual, though they annoyed me so much that I crossed at once to Second Avenue, along which I pursued my way peacefully, and once at home thought no more of it. We were indulging ourselves in siestas after our noonday lunch, when a great roaring suddenly burst upon our ears—a howling as of thousands of wild Indians let loose at once; and before we could look out or collect our thoughts at all the cry arose from every quarter, "The mob! the mob!" "The Irish have risen to resist the draft!"

In a second my head was out the window, and I saw it with my own eyes. We were on a cross-street between First and Second avenues. First Avenue was crowded as far as we could see it with thousands of infuriated creatures, yelling, screaming, and swearing in the most frantic manner; while crowds of women, equally ferocious, were leaning from every door and window, swinging aprons and handkerchiefs, and cheering and urging them onward. The rush and roar grew every moment more terrific. Up came fresh hordes faster and more furious; bareheaded men, with red, swollen faces, brandishing sticks and clubs, or carrying heavy poles and beams; and boys, women, and children hurrying on and joining with them in this mad chase up the avenue like a company of raging fiends. In the hurry and tumult it was impossible to distinguish individuals, but all seemed possessed alike with savage hate and fury. The most dreadful rumors flew through the street, and we heard from various sources the events of the morning. The draft had been

Destruction of provost marshal's office during the New York City draft riots. (Frank Leslie's Illustrated Newspaper, 1863)

resisted, buildings burned, twenty policemen killed, and the remainder utterly routed and discomfited; the soldiers were absent, and the mob triumphant and increasing in numbers and violence every moment.

Our neighborhood was in the greatest excitement. The whole population turned out at once, gazing with terror and consternation on the living stream passing before them, surging in countless numbers through the avenue, and hurrying up town to join those already in action. Fresh yells and shouts announced the union of forces, and bursting flames their accelerated strength and fury. The armory on Twenty-second Street was broken open, sacked, and fired, and the smoke and flames rolled up directly behind us.

With breathless interest we watched their rapid progress till diverted by a new terror. Our own household had been invaded. My brother's wife was gone; no one knew whither. Above and below we looked in vain for her. We could only learn that a note had been brought to her just before her disappearance. What could have happened? At such times imagination is swift and mystery unsupportable. We were falling into a terrible panic, and devising all manner of desperate expedients, when the wanderer appeared, looking very heroic, accompanied by J., all bloody and wounded. He had been attacked by the mob while passing a little too near them, knocked down, terribly beaten, and robbed of watch and pocket-book. Reality for once had outstripped imagination. For a time all our attention was absorbed in him. The wounds, though numerous, were happily not of a dangerous character. The gang which attacked him, attracted by his little tri-colored badge of loyalty, were fortunately only armed with light fence-pickets; so that, though weak from loss of blood, and badly cut and bruised in head, limbs, and body, no serious consequences seemed likely to result from his injuries.

Outdoors, meanwhile, all was clamor and tumult. Bells were tolling in every quarter. The rioters were still howling in Twenty-second Street, and driving the firemen from the burning armory. The building fell and the flames sunk, and then darkness came all at once and shut out every thing. We gathered gloomily around my brother in the back-parlor. An evening paper was procured, but brought no comfort. It only showed more clearly the nature and extent of this fearful outbreak. It only told us that the whole city was as helpless and anxious as ourselves. Many were in far greater danger, for obscurity is sometimes safety; but the black, lowering night, and the disabled condition of our only male protector, oppressed us heavily. Our neighborhood was all alive. Men tramped incessantly through the street, and women chatted and scolded in the windows; children cried and cats squalled; a crazy man in the rear raved fiercely for Jeff Davis and the Southern Confederacy; but over every other sound every few moments the bells rang out the alarm of some new fire. . . .

Thus passed the eve, till at last we separated and tried to compose ourselves to rest; but who could sleep with such terrors around them? . . .

At break of day it roused again. . . . Our household meanwhile bestirred itself slowly. J. had rested little, but was free from fever or any alarming symptoms. Much time was spent in dressing his wounds, and some in preparing breakfast. There was no milk, no ice to be had, and meat and bread were on the wane; and so I ventured out with my sister H. for supplies. We found our street full of people, excitement, and rumors. Men and boys ran past us with muskets in their hands. We heard that a fight was in progress above Twenty-second Street. The mob had seized a gun-factory and many muskets; but the police had driven them off and taken back part of their plunder. It was cheering to find that the police were still alive. Second Avenue was densely thronged, but no cars were running. A great crowd surrounded the ruins of the Armory and blackened the Twenty-second Street crossing. Men talked in low, excited tones, and seemed afraid of each other. The stores were mostly closed and business suspended. With difficulty we procured supplies of provisions and a newspaper; but percussion caps and ammunition were stoutly denied us. No one dared to admit that they kept any such articles lest the rioters should take them away by force. A friendly bookseller at last supplied us. He had been out in disguise, he said, and heard the rioters boasting among themselves. One said he had made a hundred dollars already, and now he had arms and meant to use them. All the shops on the avenue had been threatened. The mob were gathering in great force in our vicinity, and things looked every moment more threatening; so we hurried home as fast as possible, and I took my post again at the window. . . .

The sun set clear, and a beautiful night came on; a radiant midsummer night, but darker to us than the preceding. Dark skies seemed more in harmony with the scenes around us, and the contrast only deepened the gloom. The papers brought no encouragement. Fearful deeds of atrocity were recorded. The mob were increasing in power and audacity, and the city was still paralyzed and panic-stuck. The small military force available could only protect a few important positions, leaving the greater part defenseless. Our inflammable neighborhood was wholly at the mercy of the mob. . . . The tramping, scolding, screaming, squalling, and raving of the preceding night were repeated and intensified. Cats and dogs squalled and howled, bells rang incessantly, and mingled with all these sounds came at intervals the most mournful of all, the long-drawn piercing wails of Irishwomen bemoaning their dead.

Worn out with listening we resolved at last to try to rest. I made up a bundle, put my clothes in running order, read the most comforting Psalms I could find, and laid myself down to sleep. Scarcely had my head touched the pillow when a new alarm of fire sounded. Lights streamed through the door of my room and illumined the houses opposite. "Another fire in Twenty-second Street!" was the cry. The police station had been set on fire, and volumes of smoke and flame were rising again very near us. From the rear windows we saw it all with the utmost distinctness; heard the roaring and crackling, and felt the heat of the flames. Soon they wrapped the house and caught the adjacent fire-tower, whose bell was clamoring even now for aid. The mob yelled with delight, and drove off the eager firemen. The flames soon wreathed the tower and rose in majestic columns. The whole neighborhood was flooded with light. Thousands of spectators gazed upon the scene, crowning the housetops as with statues of living fire. Would the night ever end, or any thing be left should morning come? Once only the welcome report of musketry reached my ears. At last the glimmering of dawn appeared. The mist dissolved; the wandering houses came back to position; the street resumed its old familiar look, and men and boys their ceaseless tramp, tramp, tramp.

One of these men stopped across the way, and said, in a low, scared tone to some one in the house: "They hung a Massachusetts———over there last night." One word was lost to me—what it was I can only conjecture; but whether citizen, soldier, or negro, I do not doubt that some poor fellow very near us met the fate of so many others in those days of terror; and though his name and story may never be known on earth, his cries for help will surely rise up in judgment against his murderers.

But another day had come, Wednesday, July 15th. A long, bright, blazing midsummer day was before us. There was little change in the aspect of affairs without. The city was not all burned down, we found. The newspapers were still alive, and insisting that more troops were on hand and the mob checked; but we saw no signs of it. . . .

It was most humiliating, it was almost incredible, that such a state of things should exist in the heart of a civilized and Christian community. "Was this your joyous city, whose merchants were princes, whose traffickers were among the honorable of the earth?" Could it be that this great city, the pride and boast of the nation, was trampled down and held under the feet of these mad rioters? She seemed utterly prostrate and helpless. Her vast treasures, her immense store-houses, her long lines of palaces, her great multitudes of citizens, were bound and offered up for sacrifice. The whole nation was trembling and terror-struck. No one could see when and where it would terminate. . . .

. . . As night approached we heard drums beating, and gangs of rioters marched up their favorite avenue. The whole population bestirred itself at once. Men, women, and children rushed out cheering and clamoring, some hurrying on with the crowd, some hanging around the corner. Many soon returned, laden with spoil—bedding, clothing, and furniture. The crowd increased rapidly in the street and around the liquor store. Great excitement prevailed. There was loud talking with fierce gestures. Some ran thither with fire-arms, some with poles and boards. Then some one shouted, "They are coming!" and a small band of soldiers appeared marching up our street. The mob seemed to swell into vast dimensions, and densely filled the whole street before them. Hundreds hurried out on the house-tops, tore up brickbats, and hurled them with savage howls at the approaching soldiers. Shots were fired from secret ambushes, and soldiers fell before they had fired. Then they charged bravely into the mob, but their force was wholly inadequate. One small howitzer and a company of extemporized militia could do little against those raging thousands. A fierce conflict raged before our eyes. With breathless interest we watched them from door and windows. We feared the soldiers would be swallowed up and annihilated. Some now appeared in sight with a wounded officer and several wounded men, looking from side to side for shelter. Their eyes met ours with mute appeal. There was no time to be lost; the mob might any moment be upon them. There was a moment's consulation, a hasty reference to J., an unhesitating response: "Yes, by all means"; we beckoned them in, and in they came. Doors and windows were at once closed, and the house became a hospital, and seemed filled with armed men. The wounded men were carried into my brother's room; the Colonel was laid on the bed, and the others propped up with pillows. There were a few moments of great commotion and confusion. We flew for fans, ice water, and bandages. Some of the soldiers went out into the fight again, and some remained with the wounded. A surgeon, who had volunteered as a private under his old commander, dressed the wounds of the sufferers. The Colonel was severely wounded in the thigh by a slug made of a piece of lead pipe, producing a compound fracture. The wounds of two others, though less dangerous, were severe and painful. . . .

The Colonel was conveyed to the cellar and placed on a mattress. The young soldier, next to him most severely wounded, was assisted up to the rear apartment on the upper floor and placed in charge of my mother and myself. The soldiers who had remained were then ordered to make their escape from the house as they best could, and to hasten to head-quarters with an urgent request that a force might be sent to our relief. The surgeon was also requested to go, but would not listen to the suggestion. He had been regimental surgeon for two years under the Colonel, and insisted on remaining by his side, to take care of him, and to share his fate whatever it might be. . . .

In front the demonstrations were still more alarming. The rioters had taken possession of the street, stationed a guard on both avenues, and were chasing up and down for the soldiers. Then they were seen searching from house to house; beginning, fortunately for us and ours, on the opposite side, proceeding toward Second Avenue, then crossing the street and coming back gradually toward us. At last they reached the house next to ours. A few moments we waited in breathless silence. Then came a rush up the steps, and the bell rang violently. Not a sound was heard through the house. Again and yet again the bell rang, more and more furiously. Heart throbbed, nerves quivered, but no one stirred. Then came knocks, blows, kicks, threats, attempts to force the door. Come in they must and would; nothing could stay them.

Having gained for the retreating party all the time she could, Mrs. P—[J.'s sister-in-law] at length unlocked the door, opened it, passed out, and closing it behind her, stood face to face with the mob, which crowded the steps and swarmed on the sidewalk and the adjacent street. What could she do? She knew that they would come in, that they would search the house, that they would find the men; but she was determined not to give them up without an effort to save them. Possibly, in parleying with them, she might at least calm somewhat the fury of the passion that swayed that howling mob; possibly in that brutal and maddened throng there might be a few with human hearts in their bosoms to which she might find a way, win them to her side, and enlist their aid in saving the lives of the intended victims. That was her only hope.

"What do you want?" she asked, while the air was yet ringing with the cry that came up from the crowd, "The soldiers! the soldiers!" "Bring out the soldiers!" One who stood near and seemed to be a leader replied, "There were two soldiers went into this house, and we must have them. You must give them up."

"There *were* two that came in, but went out again. They are not here now."

She spoke in a low but perfectly clear and steady voice, that compelled attention, and the crowd hushed its ravings to catch her words. . . .

The leader returned to the charge. "We know the men are here, and if you give them up to us you shall not be harmed. But if you do not, and we find them, you know what a mob is. I can not control them; your house will be burned over your heads, and I will not guarantee your lives for five minutes."

"You will not do that," was the reply. "We are not the kind of people whose houses you wish to burn. My only son works as you do, and perhaps in the same shop with some of you, for seventy cents a day."

She did not tell them that her amateur apprentice boy had left his place to go to Pennsylvania and fight their friends the rebels. A young man, whom she had noticed as one of the few of decent appearance, stepped to her side and whispered to her, advising her compliance with the demand, assuring her that the men could not be controlled. The tone more than the words indicated to her that she had made one friend; and she found another, in the same way, a moment later. . . .

The main party, having ransacked the basement rooms, now turned to the cellar. In a moment a loud shout announced that they had found a victim. The surgeon was dragged up, forced out at the lower door, and delivered over to the crowd outside. A blow from a bludgeon or musket felled him to the earth, inflicting a terrible wound on the head. "Hang him, hang him!" "To the post at the Twenty-second Street corner!" were the cries as they hurried him off. The search within proceeded; a moment more and they had found the Colonel. A new and fiercer shout was sent up. An order from a leader thrilled through the hall, "Come down here some of yees wid yer muskets!"

At the first cry from the cellar Mrs. P—sprung for the basement, intending to make her way at any hazard. A sentinel stood at the head of the stairway; a stalwart brute, reeking with filth and whisky. He seized her, with both arms about her waist, with a purpose of violence quite too evident. She struggled to free herself without raising an alarm, but in vain; then a sudden and piercing shriek, which rung through the house, made him for an instant relax his hold, and, wrenching herself away, she hurried back and sought the protection of the friendly sentinel.

"He will not let me pass; I must go down."

"You must not," he replied; "it is no place for you." And then he added, looking sternly at her, "You have deceived us. You said there was no one here, and there is."

"I would have done the same thing for you if you had been wounded. Look at me; do you not believe me?"

He did look, full in her eye, for an instant; then said: "Yes, I do believe it. You have done right, and I admire your spirit."

"But I must go down. Go with me."

"No; it is no place for you."

"Then go yourself, and save his life."

And turning over his charge to the sentinel at the door, he did go. Meantime the searching party, having found the Colonel, proceeded to question him. He said he was a citizen, accidentally wounded, and had been obliged to seek refuge there.

"Why did you hide, if you are a citizen?"

Because, he said, he was afraid he should be taken for a soldier. They would not believe, but still he insisted on his statement. Then the muskets were sent for, and four pieces leveled at his head, as he lay prostrate and helpless.

"Fire, then, if you will, on a wounded man and a citizen. I shall die, any how, for my wound is a mortal one. But before you fire I wish you would send for a priest."

"What, are you a Catholic?"

"Yes."

This staggered them; and while they were hesitating the sentinel joined the group, and as soon as he looked on the Colonel exclaimed: "I know that man. I used to go to school with him. He is no soldier."

This turned the scale. The leaders were satisfied, and decided to let him go. . . .

The surgeon in the mean time had been no less fortunate. In the crowd which hurried him off to death there happened to be one or two returned soldiers who had served in the same regiment with him, and when he came where it was light recognized him. They insisted on saving him, and, raising a party in their favor, finally prevailed, and having rescued him escorted him in safety to his home. . . .

It was now, we thought, past midnight. We had no hope of relief, no thought or expectation but of struggling on alone hour after hour of distress and darkness; but as I was listening in my window to some unusually threatening demonstrations from the mob, I heard the distant clank of a horse's hoof on the pavement. Again and again it sounded, more and more distinctly; and then a measured tread reached my ears, the steady, resolute tramp of a trained and disciplined body. No music was ever half so beautiful! It might, it must be, our soldiers! Off I flew to spread the good news through the household, and back again to the window to hear the tramp nearer and fuller and stronger, and see a long line of muskets gleam out from the darkness, and a stalwart body of men stop at our door. "Halt!" was cried; and I rushed down stairs headlong, unlocked the door without waiting for orders, and with tears of joy and gratitude which every one can imagine and nobody describe, welcomed a band of radiant soldiers and policemen, and in the midst of them all who should appear but my brother, pale and exhausted, who had gotten off the house-top in some mysterious way and brought this gallant company to our rescue!

There was no time for inquiries or felicitations. The wounded men were our first care. Our young soldier in his delight had hobbled to the stairway, and was borne down in triumph by his sympathizing comrades, while a larger company brought the Colonel from the cellar. A pitiful sight he was, all bleeding and ghastly, shivering with cold and suffering great pain. Both soldiers were placed carefully in the carriage brought for their conveyance, and then we ladies were requested to accompany them immediately. It was unsafe to remain in the house, soldiers could not be spared to protect it, and it was best for us to go at once to the Central Police Station. . . .

All now was life and animation. Well-dressed citizens were hurrying to and fro. Stalwart soldiers lined the street and guarded the steps and entrance, through which we were conducted to an inner apartment, and with much state and ceremony presented to the chieftains of civic power. Three days' experience of anarchy had made us feel the blessedness of lawful restraint, and surely no body of men ever looked so beautiful as these executives of law and government. Such fresh, radiant, energetic, clear-headed, and strong-hearted leaders looked able to conquer all the rioters in the land. Every body was wide-awake, dispatches coming and going, messengers flying about in all directions. . . .

Sleep was of course still impossible. The exciting scenes of the night, and the incessant roar and rumble of Broadway, kept all awake; and at four o'clock loud cheers brought us to the window to see the glorious returning "Seventh" marshaled before us, and with all our hearts and voices we joined in the welcome which greeted them. A brighter morning dawned upon the city; other regiments had arrived in the night, and we knew that it was now safe. Broadway was busy and noisy. Business was resumed, and the mob much subdued, though still rampant in our old neighborhood. A reconnaissance showed that it was still unsafe to venture there. We passed the morning comparing notes and considering what to do with ourselves. My only desire was to quit the city—to beat a retreat as soon as possible. Our quiet tour had been rudely interrupted, our plans and purposes brought to naught; we had suffered great fatigue and anxiety, and we were unwilling to stay a moment longer. It was humiliating to leave our luggage in the enemy's country; but what were clothes to rest and quiet? A place for our heads was of more consequence than *bonnets!* Our friends were compelled to stay, but we could go; and most happy were we, now that we were sure of their safety, to improve that privilege. And so at three o'clock on Thursday afternoon, just three days from our first glimpse of the rioters, we shook the dust of New York from our slippers, and, trunkless and bonnetless, sped up North River.

Introduction to Document 3

George Templeton Strong confirmed Ellen Leonard's description of the terror of mid-July 1863. Nevertheless, there are important differences between their accounts. Leonard published her narrative after the Civil War was over, whereas Strong kept his diary on a daily basis. A wealthy New York socialite, a prominent attorney, and a man devoted to service (he served as a director for Trinity Church, Columbia College, and the federal Sanitary Commission, which was responsible for dealing with the health problems caused by the Civil War), Strong revealed his utter contempt for the lower class, and for the Irish in particular. While Leonard's narrative derives its tension from the personal drama of danger and redemption, Strong's is much more attuned to the social schisms beneath the rioting. In Leonard's narrative, we do not hear much about the racism of the crowds, but Strong's gives us a very good sense of those hatreds.

DOCUMENT 3 *From* The Diary of George Templeton Strong

July 12. . . . Draft has begun here and was in progress in Boston last week. *Demos* [the people] takes it good-naturedly thus far, but we shall have trouble before we are through. . . .

July 13, Monday. . . . The crowd seemed just what one commonly sees at any fire, but its nucleus of riot was concealed by an outside layer of ordinary peaceable lookers-on. . . . At last, it opened and out streamed a posse of perhaps five hundred, certainly less than one thousand, of the lowest Irish day laborers. The rabble was perfectly homogeneous. Every brute in the drove was pure Celtic—hod-carrier or loafer. . . . The mob was in no hurry; they had no need to be; there was no one to molest them or make them afraid. The beastly ruffians were masters of the situation and of the city. After a while sporadic paving-stones began to fly at the windows, ladies and children emerged from the rear and had a rather hard scramble over a high board fence, and then scudded off across the open, Heaven knows whither. Then men and small boys appeared at rear windows and began smashing the sashes and the blinds and shied out light articles, such as books and crockery, and dropped chairs and mirrors into the back yard; the rear fence was demolished and loafers were seen marching off with portable articles of furniture. And at last a light smoke began to float out of the windows and I came away. I could endure the disgraceful, sickening sight no longer, and what could I *do?*

The fury of the low Irish women in that region was noteworthy. Stalwart young vixens and withered old hags were swarming everywhere, all cursing the "bloody draft" and egging on their men to mischief.

Omnibussed down to No. 823, where is news that the Colored Half Orphan Asylum on Fifth Avenue, just above the reservoir, is burned. "*Tribune* office to be burned tonight." Railroad rails torn up, telegraph wires cut, and so on. If a quarter one hears be true, this is an organized insurrection in the interest of the rebellion and Jefferson Davis [President of the Confederacy] rules New York today. . . .

July 14. Eleven P.M. Fire bells clanking, as they have clanked at intervals through the evening. Plenty of rumors throughout the day and evening, but nothing very precise or authentic. There have been sundry collisions between the rabble and the authorities, civil and military. Mob fired upon. It generally runs, but on one occasion appears to have rallied, charged the police and militia, and forced them back in disorder. The people are waking up, and by tomorrow there will be adequate organization to protect property and life. Many details come in of yesterday's brutal, cowardly ruffianism and plunder. Shops were cleaned out and a black man hanged in Carmine Street, for no offence but that of Nigritude. . . .

July 16. . . . The rioters of yesterday were better armed and organized than those of Monday, and their inaction today may possibly be meant to throw us off our guard, or their time may be employed perfecting plans for a campaign of plundering and brutality in yet greater force. They are in full possession of the western and the eastern sides of the city, from Tenth Street upward, and of a good many districts beside. I could not walk four blocks eastward from this house this minute without peril. The outbreak is spreading by concerted action in many quarters. Albany, Troy, Yonkers, Hartford, Boston, and other cities have each their Irish anti-conscription Nigger-murdering mob, of the same type with ours. It is a grave business, a *jacquerie* that must be put down by heroic doses of lead and steel. . . .

Charge of the police on the rioters at the Tribune office. (Harper's Weekly, August 1, 1863)

July 19, Sunday. . . . Not half the history of this memorable week has been written. I could put down pages of incidents that the newspapers have omitted, any one of which would in ordinary times be the town's talk. Men and ladies attacked and plundered by daylight in the streets; private houses suddenly invaded by gangs of a dozen ruffians and sacked, while the women and children run off for their lives. Then there is the unspeakable infamy of the nigger persecution. They are the most peaceable, sober, and inoffensive of our poor, and the outrages they have suffered during this last week are less excusable— are founded on worse pretext and less provocation—than St. Bartholomew's or the Jew-hunting of the Middle Ages. This is a nice town to call itself a centre of civilization! Life and personal property less safe than in Tipperary, and the "people" (as the *Herald* calls them) burning orphan asylums and conducting a massacre. How this infernal slavery system has corrupted our blood, North as well as South! . . . The disgrace will rest upon us without atonement.

I am sorry to find that England is right about the lower class of Irish. They are brutal, base, cruel, cowards, and as insolent as base. Choate (at the Union League Club) tells me he heard this proposition put forth by one of their political philosophers in conversation with a knot of his brethren last Monday: "Sure and if them dam Dutch would jine us we'd drive the dam Yankees out of New York entirely!" These caitiffs have a trick, I hear, of posting themselves at the window of a tenement house with a musket, while a woman with a baby in her arms squats at their feet. Paddy fires on the police and instantly squats to reload, while Mrs. Paddy rises and looks out. Of course, one can't fire at a window where there is a woman with a child!! But how is one to deal with women who assemble around the lamp-post to which a Negro had been hanged and cut off certain parts of his body to keep as souvenirs? Have they any womanly privilege, immunity, or sanctity?

No wonder St. Patrick drove all the venomous vermin out of Ireland! Its biped mammalia supply that island its full average share of creatures that crawl and eat dirt and poison every community they infest. Vipers were superfluous. But my own theory is that St. Patrick's campaign against the snakes is a Popish delusion. They perished of biting the Irish people.

Introduction to Documents 4 and 5

The following broadsides were posted on New York streets in the immediate after-math of the riots. Although intended to calm the crowds, the publications created mixed reactions among the rioters. Some supported these efforts at amelioration, while others condemned them. How do you explain these responses?

DOCUMENT 4   *To the Laboring Men of New York*

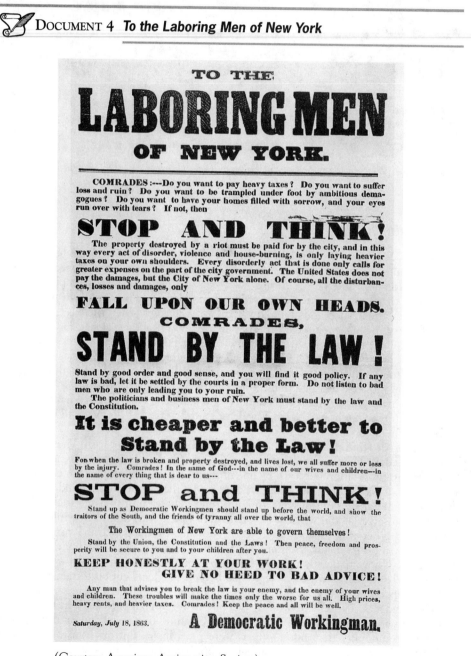

(*Courtesy American Antiquarian Society*)

 DOCUMENT 5 *Dearly Beloved!*

By the Grace of God, and the authority of the Holy See,

BISHOP OF BUFFALO.

To the Dearly Beloved Faithful Laity of the Diocese, Health and Benediction.

DEARLY BELOVED!---In the name of the God of Charity, and through that charity which He, who called us to be your Bishop, has given us for you; through that charity of Christ, in us, however unworthy, through which we would cheerfully give our life, if necessary, for each and every one of you; we beg of you, for Christ's sake, and for the sake of all that you love in heaven and on earth, to abstain from all resistance to law, from all riot, from all tumultuous gatherings, from all violence

In New York, many misguided men, yet very few we believe, of practical Catholics, have shed blood in the late riot; "and the voice of their brother's blood *cried to the Lord* from the earth." Some of the rioters have fallen, many more will, we fear, suffer much, many will, perhaps, be ruined; *all* will feel the painful sting of a guilty conscience, during the rest of life, and on their deathbed, (if indeed rioters who aid in murder could die otherwise than as it is written; "He that shall kill by the sword, must be killed by the sword." Apoc. XIII, 10;) they will either through God's mercy, sincerely repent for their participation in the riot; or be lost forever! Dearly beloved listen to the advice of a father who dearly loves you; submit to law and God will protect you. Should there be a draft, fewer will be drafted, than would, probably, be killed in an unholy struggle against law. And if any of you be drafted, we will try to protect and aid; friends will protect and aid; God will protect, aid, and bless, in more ways than we know or dare name.

Withdraw yourselves, then, we beg and exhort, from all who would excite to associations against the law of the land, or to violence, and mob-law. For God's sake; for the sake of your dear families; for the sake of your fathers and mothers, whether still pilgrims on earth, or mingling with the "blessed crowd of witnesses," who, from heaven, watch over your conduct on earth; we exhort you to *trust in God*, and not to lend yourselves to any exciter to mob or violence, which leads so often to murder. If you follow this advice of your Father in Christ, we confidently assure you that "Whosoever shall follow this rule, *peace will be unto him, and mercy;* and upon the Israel of God.---Gal, VI.

We require that this letter be read in every church on the Sunday after its reception.

Given at St. Joseph's Cathedral, Buffalo, on the Feast of Our Lady of Mount Carmel, A. D., MDCCCLXIII.

+ JOHN, Bishop of Buffalo.

(Courtesy American Antiquarian Society)

Introduction to Document 6

The *New York Times* printed the following editorial on Wednesday, July 15, as the rioting reached its height. Note not only what the editors said, but how they said it. Do you think that the *Times* believed the rioters had any legitimate grievances, or did the editors see the eruption as one of pure violence? What motives did they ascribe to the rioters? Why did they consider the draft law essential? Note the use of literary devices: "tribe of savages," "wild beast," "monster grows more dangerous," "mob for robbery, plunder and arson," "un-American, anti-American." By using such characterizations, the editors implied that the rioters were beyond the pale of respectability, that the conscription act was in the true national interest, and that riot represented selfish lusts being asserted against the Union cause.

DOCUMENT 6   ***"The Raging Riot—Its Character, and the True Attitude Toward It"***

The mob in our City is still rampant. Though the increasing display of armed force has done something to check its more flagrant outrages, it is yet wild with fury, and panting for fresh havoc. The very fact of its being withstood seems only to give it, for the time, new malignity; just as the wild beast never heaves with darker rage than when he begins to see that his way is barred. The monster grows more dangerous as he grows desperate. . . .

It is too true that there are public journals who try to dignify this mob by some respectable appellation. The *Herald* characterizes it as the people, and the *World* as the laboring men of the City. These are libels that ought to have paralyzed the fingers that penned them. It is ineffably infamous to attribute to the people, or to the laboring men of this metropolis, such hideous barbarism as this horde has been displaying. The people of New-York and the laboring men of New-York are not incendiaries, nor robbers, nor assassins. They do not hunt down men whose only offence is the color God gave them; they do not chase, and insult, and beat women; they do not pillage an asylum for orphan children, and burn the very roof over those orphans' heads. They are civilized beings, valuing law and respecting decency; and they regard with unqualified abhorrence the doings of the tribe of savages that have sought to bear rule in their midst.

This mob is not the people, nor does it belong to the people. It is for the most part made up of the very vilest elements of the City. It has not even the poor merit of being what mobs usually are—the product of mere ignorance and passion. They talk, or rather did talk at first, of the oppressiveness of the Conscription law; but three-fourths of those who have been actively engaged in violence have been boys and young men under twenty years of age, and not at all subject to the Conscription. Were the Conscription law to be abrogated to-morrow, the controlling inspiration of the mob would remain all the same. It comes from sources quite independent of that law, or any other—from malignant hate toward those in better circumstances, from a craving for plunder, from a love of commotion, from a barbarous spite against a different race, from a disposition to bolster up the failing fortunes of the Southern rebels. All of these influences operate in greater or less measure upon any person engaged in this general defiance of law; and all concerned have generated a composite monster more hellish than the triple-headed Cerberus. . . .

You may as well reason with the wolves of the forest as with these men in their present mood. It is quixotic and suicidal to attempt it. The duties of the executive officers of this State and City are not to debate, or negotiate, or supplicate, but to *execute the laws*. To execute means to enforce *by authority*. This is their *only* official business. Let it be promptly and sternly entered upon with all the means now available, and it cannot fail of being carried through to an overwhelming triumph of public order. It may cost blood—much of it perhaps; but it will be a lesson to the public enemies, whom we always have and must have in our midst, that will last for a generation. Justice and mercy, this time, unite in the same behest—*Give them grape [cannon fire], and a plenty of it.* . . .

. . . If this mob was originated in a passionate spirit of resistance to the Conscription law, it very soon changed its purpose, and assumed the character merely of a mob for robbery, plunder and arson. This is shown in the rifling of houses, hotels and stores, and the assaults and felonies upon the persons of unoffending citizens. Some of the ringleaders are noted thieves, who have served out several terms in Sing Sing and other penitentiaries and prisons. Hundreds of the workmen who joined with the crowd on Monday were, of course, as honest as the average of us, but they were at once joined by all the knaves of the City, who saw in the occasion an opportunity for plunder such as had never before presented itself. They made good use of their opportunity, as hundreds of unfortunate citizens can testify. The whole thing, if it continues, bids fair to become a gigantic mob of plunderers, with no more reference to the Conscription than to the Koran. It is remarkable, and almost incredible, how infectious this spirit becomes. A man who joins in such a mob as this may never have stolen a pin's worth in his life before, but when a jewelry store like that up town, or a mansion like those in Fifth-avenue, is broken into, the temptation is almost irresistible to rush in, and obtain a share of things. If this affair is allowed to go on, if it be not promptly put down, it will quickly result in a state of things such as was never before known in a civilized city. It is now a question of the protection of firesides, property and persons against general plunder. It has nothing to do with the conscription.

. . . It has heretofore been the boast of this country that liberty regulated by law was the principle which governed its citizens. The most perfect freedom to every man in every relation of life—freedom of person, of speech and in the pursuit of happiness, has been our glory, while the universally upheld governance of law has been the safety both of ourselves and of our liberty. The dominance of the mob strikes at the root of this great and special American principle. It reverts us back to semi-barbarism, and throws us forward into despotism. A mob is un-American, anti-American. Every grievance can here be remedied, every wrong can here be righted by *law*, which has its power in the will of the people and "its fountain in the bosom of God." It will be a dark day for the liberties of America, for its honor, its greatness, its power, its glory, when this excrescence of European despotism fastens itself upon our free institutions and society. Every man who prides himself in the name of American must use his determined efforts to drive back this black and deadly tide of human depravity.

Introduction to Documents 7 and 8

In the same issue as the editorial condemning the rioting, the *New York Times* printed two brief letters to the editor. The first was written by one of the rioters, and the other by an opponent of the draft. Note how these two individuals identified themselves as poor men who opposed the Conscription Act as class legislation that discriminated against poor people. While these letters were short and not terribly literate, they are very important for the historian because they give us clues to why individuals rioted in opposition to the draft. The first one in particular is filled with key beliefs concerning the purpose of the war, the importance of family, class relationships, and other ideas. What were the arguments presented by opponents of the draft? How do you think they would have responded to the *Times* editorial reprinted above? Why is the last sentence important in the letter signed "A Poor Man, but a Man for All That"?

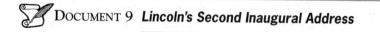

DOCUMENT 7 *A Letter from One of the Rioters*

Monday Night—Up Town.

To the Editor of the New-York Times:

You will, no doubt, be hard on us rioters tomorrow morning, but that 300-dollar law has made us nobodies, vagabonds and cast-outs of society, for whom nobody cares when we must go to war and be shot down. We are the poor rabble, and the rich rabble is our enemy by this law. Therefore we will give our enemy battle right here, and ask no quarter. Although we got hard fists, and are dirty without, we have soft hearts, and have clean consciences within, and that's the reason we love our wives and children more than the rich, because we got not much besides them; and we will not go and leave them at home for to starve. . . . Why don't they let the nigger kill the slave-driving race and take possession of the South, as it belongs to them.

A Poor Man, but a Man for All That.

DOCUMENT 8 *The $300 Exemption*

To the Editor of the New York Times:

You have been trying to vindicate the Draft from the charge that it throws the whole burden of the war upon the poor. You must know that when one hundred men are drawn, if fifty of them can pay their $300 they are released, and then their places must be filled by another draft from among the poor. If this is not releasing the rich and placing the burdens of the war, exclusively, on the poor, I should like to know what would be.

Yours,
A POOR MAN.

Introduction to Document 9

On March 4, 1865, about one month before his death, President Lincoln delivered his second inaugural address. Note the tone and the themes expressed in this speech. According to Lincoln, what was the great cause of the war?

DOCUMENT 9 *Lincoln's Second Inaugural Address*

Fellow-Countrymen:

At this second appearing to take the oath of the Presidential office there is less occasion for an extended address than there was at the first. Then a statement somewhat in detail of a course to be pursued seemed fitting and proper. Now, at the expiration of four years, during which public declarations have been constantly called forth on every point and phase of the great contest which still absorbs the attention and engrosses the energies of the nation, little that is new could be presented. The progress of our arms, upon which all else chiefly depends, is as well known to the public as to myself, and it is, I trust, reasonably satisfactory and encouraging to all. With high hope for the future, no prediction in regard to it is ventured.

On the occasion corresponding to this four years ago all thoughts were anxiously directed to an impending civil war. All dreaded it, all sought to avert it. While the inaugural address was being delivered from this place, devoted altogether to saving the Union without war, urgent agents were in the city seeking to destroy it without war—seeking to dissolve the Union and divide effects by negotiation. Both parties deprecated war, but one of them would make war rather than let the nation survive, and the other would accept war rather than let it perish, and the war came.

One-eighth of the whole population were colored slaves, not distributed generally over the Union, but localized in the southern part of it. These slaves constituted a peculiar and powerful interest. All knew that this interest was somehow the cause of the war. To strengthen, perpetuate, and extend this interest was the object for which the insurgents would rend the Union even by war, while the Government claimed no right to do more than to restrict the territorial enlargement of it. Neither party expected for the war the magnitude or the duration which it has already attained. Neither anticipated that the cause of the conflict might cease with or even before the conflict itself should cease. Each looked for an easier triumph, and a result less fundamental and astounding. Both read the same Bible and pray to the same God, and each invokes His aid against the other. It may seem strange that any men should dare to ask a just God's assistance in wringing their bread from the sweat of other men's faces, but let us judge not, that we be not judged. The prayers of both could not be answered. That of neither has been answered fully. The Almighty has His own purposes. "Woe unto the world because of offenses; for it must needs be that offenses come, but woe to that man by whom the offense cometh." If we shall suppose that American slavery is one of those offenses which, in the providence of God, must needs come, but which, having continued through His appointed time, He now wills to remove, and that He gives to both North and South this terrible war as the woe due to those by whom the offense came, shall we discern therein any departure from those divine attributes which the believers in a living God always ascribe to Him? Fondly do we hope, fervently do we pray, that this mighty scourge of war may speedily pass away. Yet, if God wills that it continue until all the wealth piled by the bondsman's two hundred and fifty years of unrequited toil shall be sunk, and until every drop of blood drawn with the lash shall be paid by another drawn with the sword, as was said three thousand years ago, so still it must be said "the judgments of the Lord are true and righteous altogether."

With malice toward none, with charity for all, with firmness in the right as God gives us to see the right, let us strive on to finish the work we are in, to bind up the nation's wounds, to care for him who shall have borne the battle and for his widow and his orphan, to do all which may achieve and cherish a just and lasting peace among ourselves and with all nations.

QUESTIONS

Defining Terms

Identify in the context of the chapter each of the following:

Copperheads	Butternuts
the Great Famine	Irish Catholics
Enrollment Act of 1863	Ellen Leonard
George Templeton Strong	The $300 Exemption
Colored Orphan Asylum	"a mob is un-American, anti-American"

Probing the Sources

$300

1. What types of exemptions were allowed in the Union conscription act of 1863? Why do you think these exclusions were allowed? Were the exemptions justified?

2. What attitudes about gender, class, and race are expressed in the accounts of the draft riots? DIRECTED TOWARDS MALE, UPPER-CLASS, + BLACKS. + SOLDIERS

3. Who and what were the targets of the rioting? Was there a pattern to the violence? BLACKS/SOLDIERS

4. What biases do you find in Ellen Leonard's account of the riots? RICH WOMEN PERSONAL DRAMA OF DANGER + REDEMPTION. SASSY

Interpreting the Sources

1. Who was responsible for the violence that hit New York in July of 1863? Why?

2. What do the documents tell us about the roles of race and class in the riots?

3. In what ways were the riots of July 1863 similar to and different from contemporary manifestations of violence in Northern Ireland, in South Africa, in the Middle East, or in American inner cities?

4. How does the history of the draft riots make us see the Civil War in a new light?

ADDITIONAL READING

The best scholarly treatment of the riots of 1863 is Iver Bernstein, *The New York City Draft Riots: Their Significance for American Society and Politics in the Age of the Civil War* (1990). Adrian Cook, *The Armies of the Streets: The New York City Draft Riots of 1863* (1974), is another meticulously researched volume that includes lists of those killed, arrested, and suspected of participation in the riots. For a discussion of New York society before the Civil War, see Sean Wilentz, *Chants Democratic: New York City and the Rise of the American Working Class, 1788–1850* (1984). Also of interest is Christine Stansell, *City of Women: Sex and Class in New York, 1789–1869* (1986), an intriguing overview of the nineteenth-century urban immigrant experience and the central place women held within it; and Richard B. Stott, *Workers in the Metropolis* (1990). Among the countless works on the war itself, James McPherson's *Battle Cry of Freedom* (1988) stands out. For blacks during the war, see C. Peter Ripley, ed., *Witness for Freedom: African American Voices on Race, Slavery, and Emancipation* (1993).

13

Reconstruction and the Rise of the Ku Klux Klan

HISTORICAL CONTEXT

In a letter to the House of Representatives dated April 19, 1872, President Ulysses S. Grant described a "grand system of criminal associations pervading most of the Southern States." Investigations by the attorney general, by the Joint Committee of Congress upon Southern Outrages, and by local officials all revealed that a terroristic organization known as the Ku Klux Klan, or KKK, exercised enormous influence in the South and worked in defiance of federal Reconstruction. Grant alleged that members swore oaths of obedience and secrecy that they considered more binding than their allegiance to the United States. "They are organized and armed," the president declared. "They effect their objects by personal violence, often extending to murder. They terrify witnesses, they control juries in the State courts, and sometimes in the courts of the United States." Klansmen spied on, murdered, and intimidated their enemies and thereby destroyed the rule of law. Their goals, according to Grant, were

> by force and terror, to prevent all political action not in accord with the views of the members, to deprive colored citizens of the right to bear arms, and of the right of a free ballot, and to suppress the schools in which colored children were taught, and to reduce the colored people to a condition closely allied to that of slavery.

The Ku Klux Klan, in other words, threatened to seize by terror what the South had lost on the battlefield. Voting, bearing arms, education, free thought—all were integral to democracy, and all were menaced by the Klan.

The KKK originated in informal organizations that Confederate men joined immediately after the Civil War. The agenda of these organizations became increasingly political as Andrew Johnson's Reconstruction policies were replaced by the more stringent ones of the so-called radical Republicans in Congress. The South was now occupied by enemy troops, its cities burned, farms barren, elected officials disgraced, and population decimated. Those who had been slaves, black men and women stigmatized as ineradicably inferior, were now to be treated as equal citizens of a democracy. There was even talk of confiscating southern agricultural land and redistributing it so that blacks and poor whites could become independent farmers, a plan, as it turned out, too radical for most radical Republicans, whose devotion to private property—even that of former rebels—brooked no exceptions.

253

For African Americans, the era of Reconstruction was a time of relative freedom. Many took the opportunity to leave the land they had been bound to and sought opportunity in southern cities and in the North. Certainly some whites feared the possible loss of their labor force. Equally threatening, the former slaves were more free to worship, work, learn, and acquire power and money than ever before. Many whites alleged that blacks were incapable of handling freedom, that black politicians were corrupt; black workers, slothful; and black masses, ignorant. But the unspoken and perhaps deeper fear was that African Americans were indeed capable of good citizenship and would compete with their former masters. In other words, the comforting idea that any white, no matter how degraded, was "better than a nigger" no longer held. If radical Reconstruction failed to secure real economic opportunity for the former slaves, it did insist that African Americans be treated as equal citizens under the law, an idea antithetical to the old southern economic and social structure, indeed to white southern identity.

But it was not just the new position of blacks that threatened white southerners. Republican rule included policies for changing the region to conform more with the tone of northern society. The "carpetbaggers" and "scalawags" generally were not corrupt individuals but people who genuinely believed that the South's salvation would come through railroads, new industries, and public schools—in short, institutions associated with economic progress in the free-labor North. Radical Reconstruction not only proposed to change racial mores but aimed to make a premodern social and economic system modern. Such drastic changes, imposed, as it appeared to many white southerners, by upstart blacks and alien Yankees, were terrifying.

The Ku Klux Klan was a response to the social, cultural, and economic changes that many white southerners found so disturbing. It might best be seen as the extreme wing of the "redeemers," those whites who sought political redemption from Reconstruction. African Americans and southern Unionists, with the aid of the federal government and the Republican party, were able to govern several states for a few years after the Civil War, but eventually the political experience, popularity, and just plain brutality of the redeemers won the day. The Klan specialized in the latter.

Klansmen typically dressed in white robes and hoods, and they tried to convince their black victims that they were the ghosts of the Confederate dead. Blacks were intimidated, not so much by the transparent ghostly ruse, but by the violence the Klansmen dealt out. By the 1860s, their pattern was clear: several Klansmen would surround a victim's house at night, shoot into the windows, set fire to the structure, poison livestock, or simply drag the inhabitants out and shoot, whip, or hang them. Usually the victims were individuals who had stood up for their rights, blacks who voted, ran for office, or refused to take whites' insults. Occasionally there was open warfare between Klansmen and black militias. White citizens, too, who dared support blacks or who expressed Unionist sympathies were terrorized by the night riders.

It is impossible to know how many southern men ever joined the Klan—it was, after all, a secret organization—but through the late 1860s and into the early 1870s, the Klan was very successful in intimidating both blacks and whites. When the federal government outlawed the organization and began prosecuting its members, the Klan lost some of its effectiveness, but by then violence, along with social ostracism and economic coercion, had become part of the arsenal of redeemer politics. Redemption came to state and local government but succeeded only because the federal government lost its resolve to make sure that all citizens were treated, as promised in the Constitution, with equality. Slowly, African Americans' rights to vote, to speak out freely, and to participate equally in social life were stripped away.

Perhaps even more important than the political disenfranchisement of African Americans that followed Reconstruction was their reduction to economic peonage. Slavery died at Appomattox, but new forms of economic and political servitude soon took its place, and they lasted for a century. In the years following the Civil War, most blacks became tenant farmers with no land of their own, and most of these sharecropped, work that offered little more freedom or material comfort than slavery. As a sharecropper, a former slave might farm a white man's land; buy tools, supplies, and food from him; and rent a shack for the family from him. Owner and renter would split the proceeds of the harvest, but the black farmer's debt for the goods that the white man had furnished would almost certainly exceed any profit. Indebted to the white planter, former slaves would be unable to leave; year after year they would have to stay on the land, trying to pay off a debt that grew ever larger.

THE DOCUMENTS

The following documents reveal the Ku Klux Klan from various points of view. The initiation oath of the Knights of the White Camelia (a part of the Klan) reveals the style, tone, and purposes of this organization. Despite the Klan's high rhetoric of defending southern honor, the passages from the narratives of former slaves and from congressional hearings give testimony to how the Klan used violence to accomplish its goals. Note here the reasons for which the victims felt they were being attacked. Congressman Stevenson's speech summarizes the federal findings on the scope of Klan activities and reveals the conflict over values and ideology between southern redeemers and northern Reconstructionists. Finally, *Experience of a Northern Man Among the Ku-Klux* gives a good sense of how northerners viewed the South and how some of them even visualized colonizing it and remaking its society to conform to northern norms. As you read these selections, ask yourself how and why the problem of race relations spilled over into issues related to ideology, economics, and labor.

Introduction to Document 1

The initiation oath of the Knights of the White Camelia reveals the attraction of such organizations. The Knights originated during the early days of the Klan in the late 1860s. Note the claims to religious faith and patriotism and the chivalric mandate: to protect the weak and defenseless against the outrages of "lawless" blacks. Aside from the reassertion of crude white supremacy, the KKK must have been very popular for its sense of mystery, pageantry, and special rituals; individuals were made to feel that they belonged to something splendid and grand. To whom would such appeals be most compelling?

DOCUMENT 1 *Initiation Oath of the Knights of the White Camelia*

I do solemnly swear, in the presence of these witnesses, never to reveal, without authority, the existence of this Order, its objects, its acts, and signs of recognition; never to reveal or publish, in any manner whatsoever, what I shall see or hear in this Council; never to divulge the names of the members of the Order, or their acts done in connection therewith; I swear to maintain and defend the social and political superiority of the White Race on this Continent; always and in all places to observe a marked distinction between the White and African races; to vote for none but white men for any office of honor, profit or trust; to devote my intelligence, energy and influence to instil these principles in the minds and hearts of others; and to protect and defend persons of the White Race, in their lives, rights and property, against the encroachments and aggressions of an inferior race.

I swear, moreover, to unite myself in heart, soul and body with those who compose this Order; to aid, protect and defend them in all places; to obey the orders of those, who, by our statutes, will have the right of giving those orders. . . .

The oath having been taken by the candidate, the C[ommander] shall now say:

Brother, by virtue of the authority to me delegated, I now pronounce you a Knight of the [White Camelia]. . . .

Brothers: You have been initiated into one of the most important Orders, which have ever been established on this continent: an Order, which, if its principles are faithfully observed and its objects diligently carried out, is destined to regenerate our unfortunate country and to relieve the White Race from the humiliating condition to which it has lately been reduced in this Republic. It is necessary, therefore, that before taking part in the labors of this Association, you should understand fully its principles and objects and the duties which devolve upon you as one of its members.

As you may have already gathered from the questions which were propounded to you, and which you have answered so satisfactorily, and from the clauses of the Oath which you have taken, our main and fundamental object is the *maintenance of the supremacy of the white race* in this Republic. History and physiology teach us that we belong to a race which nature has endowed with an evident superiority over all other races, and that the Maker, in thus elevating us above the common standard of human creation, has intended to give us over inferior races, a dominion from which no human laws can permanently derogate. The experience of ages demonstrate that, from the origin of the world, this dominion has always remained in the hands of the Caucasian Race; whilst all the other races have constantly occupied a subordinate and secondary position; a fact which triumphantly confirms this great law of nature. Powerful nations have succeeded each other in the face of the world, and have marked their passage by glorious and memorable deeds; and among those who have thus left on this globe indelible traces of their splendor and greatness, we find none but descended from the Caucasian stock. We see, on the contrary, that most of the countries inhabited by the other races have remained in a state of complete barbarity; whilst the small number of those who have advanced beyond this savage existence, have, for centuries, stagnated in a semi-barbarous condition, of which there can be no progress or improvement. And it is a remarkable fact that as a race of men is more remote from the Caucasian and approaches nearer to the black African, the more fatally that stamp of inferiority is affixed to its sons, and irrevocably dooms them to eternal imperfectibility and degradation.

Convinced that we are of these elements of natural ethics, we know, besides, that the government of our Republic was established by white men, for white men alone, and that it never was in the contemplation of its founders that it should fall into the hands of an inferior and degraded race. We hold, therefore, that any attempt to wrest from the white race the management of its affairs in order to transfer it to control of the black population, is an invasion of the sacred prerogatives vouchsafed to us by the Constitution, and a violation of the laws established by God himself; that such encroachments are subversive of the established institutions of our Republic, and that no individual of the white race can submit to them without humiliation and shame.

It, then, becomes our solemn duty, as white men, to resist strenuously and persistently those attempts against our natural and constitutional rights, and to do everything in our power in order to maintain, in this Republic, the supremacy of the Caucasian race, and restrain the black or African race to that condition of social and political inferiority for which God has destined it. This is the object for which our Order was instituted; and, in carrying it out, we intend to infringe no laws, to violate no rights, and to resort to no forcible means, except for purposes of legitimate and necessary defense.

As an essential condition of success, this Order proscribes absolutely all social equality between the races. If we were to admit persons of African race on the same level with ourselves, a state of personal relations would follow which would unavoidably lead to political equality; for it would be a virtual recognition of *status*, after which we could not consistently deny them an equal share in the administration of our public affairs. The man who is good enough to be our familiar companion, is good enough also to participate in our political government; and if we were to grant the one, there could be no good reason for us not to concede the other of these two privileges.

There is another reason, Brothers, for which we condemn this social equality. Its toleration would soon be a fruitful source of intermarriages between individuals of the two races; and the result of this *misceganation* [sic] would be gradual amalgamation and the production of a degenerate and bastard offspring, which would soon populate these States with a degraded and ignoble population, incapable of moral and intellectual development and unfitted to support a great and powerful country. We must maintain the purity of the white blood, if we would preserve for it that natural superiority with which God has ennobled it.

To avoid these evils, therefore, we take the obligation *to observe a marked distinction between the two races*, not only in the relations of public affairs, but also in the more intimate dealings and intercourse of private life which, by the frequency of their occurrence, are more apt to have an influence on the attainment of the purposes of the Order.

Now that I have laid before you the objects of this Association, let me charge you specially in relation to one of your most important studies as one of its members. Our statutes make us bound to respect sedulously the rights of the colored inhabitants of this Republic, and in every instance, to give to them whatever lawfully belongs to them. It is an act of simple justice not to deny them any of the privileges to which they are legitimately entitled; and we cannot better show the inherent superiority of our race than by dealing with them in that spirit of firmness, liberality and impartiality which characterizes all superior organizations. Besides, it would be ungenerous for us to undertake to restrict them to the narrowest limits as to the exercise of certain rights, without conceding to them, at the same time, the fullest measure of those which we recognize as theirs; and a fair construction of a white man's duty towards them would be, not only to respect and observe their acknowledged rights, but also to see that these are respected and observed by others.

Introduction to Documents 2 and 3

Despite the Klan's lofty rhetoric, the following testimonies by its victims reveal the terrorism for which the organization was renowned. Ask yourself who became Klan victims and why. The three statements in Document 2 were made by former slaves looking back on their experiences from a distance of several decades; the statements are taken from oral histories collected during the 1930s by the Federal

Writers Project. The two statements in Document 3 come from testimony before a congressional committee investigating Klan activities in the early 1870s.

DOCUMENT 2 *Testimony of Victims of the Ku Klux Klan*

Pierce Harper

After de colored people was considered free an' turned loose de Klu Klux broke out. Some of de colored people commenced to farming like I tol' you an' all de ol' stock dey could pick up after de Yankees left dey took an' took care of. If you got so you made good money an' had a good farm de Klu Klux'd come an' murder you. De gov'ment built de colored people school houses an' de Klu Klux went to work an' burn 'em down. Dey'd go to de jails an' take de colored men out an' knock dere brains out an' break dere necks an' throw 'em in de river.

Dere was a man dat dey taken, his name was Jim Freeman. Dey taken him an' destroyed his stuff an' him 'cause he was making some money. Hung him on a tree in his front yard, right in front of his cabin. Dere was some young men who went to de schools de gov'ment opened for de colored folks. Some white widder woman said someone had stole something she own', so dey put these young fellers in jail 'cause dey suspicioned 'em. De Klu Kluxes went to de jail an' took 'em out an' kill 'em. Dat happen de second year after de War.

After de Klu Kluxes got so strong de colored men got together an' made a complaint before de law. De Gov'nor told de law to give 'em de ol' guns in de commissary what de Southern soldiers had use, so dey issued de colored men old muskets an' told 'em to protect theirselves.

De colored men got together an' organized the 'Malicy [Militia]. Dey had leaders like regular soldiers, men dat led 'em right on. Dey didn't meet 'cept when dey heard de Klu Kluxes was coming to get some of de colored folks. Den de one who knowed dat tol' de leader an' he went 'round an' told de others when an' where dey's meet. Den dey was ready for 'em. Dey'd hide in de cabins an' when de Klu Kluxes come dere dey was. Den's when dey found out who a lot of de Klu Kluxes was, 'cause a lot of 'em was killed. Dey wore dem long sheets an' you couldn't tell who dey was. Dey even covered dere horses up so you couldn't tell who dey belong to. Men you thought was your friend was Klu Kluxes. You deal wit' 'em in de stores in de day time an' at night dey come out to your house an' kill you.

Sue Craft

My teacher's name Dunlap—a white teacher teachin de cullud. De Ku Klux whupped him fo' teachin' us. I saw de Ku Klux ridin' a heap dem days. Dey had hoods pulled ovah dere faces. One time dey come to our house twict. Fus' time dey come quiet. It was right 'fore de 'lection o' Grant jus' after slavery. It was fus' time cullud people 'lowed t' vote. Dey ast my father was he goin' to vote for Grant. He tell 'em he don' know he goin' vote. After 'lection dey come back, whoopin' an' hollerin. Dey shoot out de winder lights. It was 'cause my father voted for Grant. Dey broke de do' open. My father was a settin' on de bed. I 'member he had a shot gun in his han'. Well, dey broke de do' down, an' then father he shoot, an' dey scattered all ovah de fence.

Morgan Ray

. . . I heard a lot about the Klu Klux, but it warn't till long afterwards dat I evan see 'em. It was one night after de work of de day was done and I was takin' a walk near where I worked. Suddenly I hear the hoof beats of horses and I natcherly wuz curious and waited

Ku Klux Klan "mode of torture." (Library of Congress)

beside de road to see what was comin'. I saw a company of men hooded and wearin' what looked like sheets. Dey had a young cullud man as dere prisoner. I wuz too skairt to say anything or ask any questions. I just went on my sweet way. Later I found out dey acclaimed de prisoner had assaulted a white woman. Dey strung him up when he wouldn't confess, and shot him full of holes and threw his body in de pond.

DOCUMENT 3 *Congressional Inquiry into Klan Activities*

Atlanta, Georgia, October 25, 1871.

Joseph Addison (White) Sworn and Examined.

BY THE CHAIRMAN:

Question: What is your age, where were you born, where do you live, and what is your present occupation?

Answer: I am about twenty-four years old; I was born in Muscogee County, and now live in Haralson County; I have been living there ever since I was a little bit of a boy; I am a farmer.

Question: During the war which side were you on?

Answer: I never fought a day in the rebel army; I was not in it at all.

Question: Which side were your feelings on?

Answer: My feelings were on the side of what you call the radical party now.

Question: What did they call it then?

Answer: I was what you call a Union man then.

Question: Were your opinions well known?

Answer: Yes, sir; I reckon I am well known.

Question: Have you seen any people, or do you know of any, in your county, called Ku-Klux?

Answer: Yes, sir.

Question: Tell us what you know about them.

Answer: Do you want me to state just about all how they did?

Question: Yes.

Answer: I will tell you how they did me. . . . My wife looked out and said, "Lord have mercy! Joe, it is the Ku-Klux." I jumped out of the door and ran. One of them was right in the back yard, and he jabbed the end of his six-shooter almost against my head, and said, "Halt! God damn you." I said, "I will give up." I asked them what they were doing that for; they said that I had been stealing. I said, "You men here know I have not." They said, "We gave you time once to get away, and, God damn you, you have not gone; now, God damn you, you shall not go, for we allow to kill you." I said, "If you do not abuse me or whip me, I will go the next morning." They said they would not abuse me or whip me, but they would kill me. I said, "Let me go and see my wife and children." They said, "No, God damn you." I turned away from the man; he jammed his pistol in my face, and said, "God damn you, go on, or I will kill you." They took me about eighty or ninety yards from there into a little thicket. The man on my right was a high, tall man; the one on my left was a low, chunky fellow. The man on my right stepped back, and said to the little fellow on my left, "Old man, we have got him here now; do as you please with him." There were some little hickories near him; he looked at them, but did not take them. They were all standing right around me with their guns pointing at me. Just as he turned around, I wheeled and run; but before I had run ten yards I heard a half a dozen caps bursted at me. Just as I made a turn to go behind some buildings and little bushes, I heard two guns fired. I must have gone seventy or eighty yards, and then I heard what I thought was a pistol fired. I heard a bullet hit a tree. I run on eight or ten steps further, and then I heard a bullet hit a tree just before me. Every one of them took after me, and run me for a hundred and fifty yards. I ran down a little bluff and ran across a branch. When I got across there, I could not run any further, for my shoes were all muddy. I cut the strings of my old shoes, and left them there. I stopped to listen, but I never saw anything more of them. I then went around and climbed up on the fence, and sat there and watched until dark. I then went to the house and got some dry clothes, and then went back where I had fixed a place in the woods to sleep in, and went to bed. That was the last I heard of them that night. They came back Sunday night before court commenced on Monday, in Haralson County. My wife would not stay there by herself, but went to her sister-in-law's, Milton Powell's wife. They came in on them on Sunday night, or about two hours and a half before day Monday morning. They abused her and cursed her powerfully, and tried to make her tell where I was. They said that if she did not tell them they would shoot her God-damned brains out. I was laying out close by there, and I stood there and heard them. They shot five or six shots in the yard; some of them said they shot into the house. They scared my wife and sister-in-law so bad that they took the children and went into the woods and staid there all night. That was the last time they were there. . . .

Question: Have they ever molested you since then?

Answer: No, sir; they have never been on me any more since then.

Question: Do you still stay there?
Answer: No, sir; I have done moved now. I moved off, and left my hogs and my crop and everything there, what little I made. I did not make much crop this year, for I was afraid to work, and now I am afraid to go back there to save anything.

Atlanta, Georgia, October 26, 1871.

Thomas M. Allen (Colored) Sworn and Examined.

BY THE CHAIRMAN:

Question: What is your age, where were you born, and where do you now live?
Answer: I am now thirty-eight years old. I was born in Charleston, South Carolina, and I am living here at present; that is, my family is here; I am pastor of the Baptist church at Marietta, Jasper County.

Question: How long have you been living in this State?
Answer: I came to this State the year that James K. Polk died, about 1849.

Question: How do you connect your coming here with his death?
Answer: I landed in Savannah at the time they were firing cannon there, and asked what was the matter.

Question: Were you a slave?
Answer: Partly so. My father was a white man and he set us free at his death. They stole us from Charleston and run me and my brother and mother into this State. He left us ten thousand dollars each to educate us, and give us trades, and for that money they stole us away.

Question: Were you kept in slavery until the time of emancipation?
Answer: Yes, sir; I was held as a slave; I hired my time.

Question: You never were able to assert your freedom before emancipation?
Answer: No, sir, I could not do it. . . .

Question: Have you been connected with political affairs in this State since the war?
Answer: Yes, sir. When the constitutional convention was called, I took an active part, and did all I could, of course. Afterwards I ran for the legislature and was elected.

Question: In what year?
Answer: I was elected in 1868; the colored members were expelled that year.

Question: From what county were you elected?
Answer: From Jasper County.

Question: Were you reinstated in your seat in the legislature?
Answer: Yes, sir.

Question: Have you witnessed any violence towards any of your race, yourself or any others?
Answer: Yes, sir. After we were expelled from the legislature, I went home to Jasper County; I was carrying on a farm there. On the 16th of October, a party of men came to my house; I cannot say how many, for I did not see them. . . .

About 2 o'clock my wife woke me up, and said that there were persons all around the house; that they had been there for half an hour, and were calling for me. I heard them call again, and I asked them what they wanted, and who they were. . . .

They asked me to come out. At this time my brother-in-law waked up and said, "Who are they, Thomas?" I said, "I do not know." . . .

He put on his shoes and vest and hat; this was all he was found with after he was killed. He opened the door and hollered, "Where are you?" He hollered twice, and then two guns were fired. He seemed to fall, and I and my wife hollered, and his wife hollered. I jumped up, and ran back to the fire-place, where I started to get a light, and then started to go over the partition to him. I threw a clock down, and then I thought of the closet there, and went through it to him, and my wife closed the door. I hollered for Joe, a third man on the place, to come up and bring his gun, for Emanuel was killed. He did not come for some time, and then I was so excited that I could not recognize his voice. After a time I let him in. We made up a light, and then I saw my brother-in-law laying on his back as he fell. I examined him; there were four or five number one buck-shot in his breast. . . .

Question: What do you know about this organization of men they call Ku-Klux?
Answer: I have never seen one in my life; I have seen a great many people who have seen them. I have a Ku-Klux letter here that I got on the day of the election for the constitution.
Question: Will you read it?
Answer: Yes, sir; this is it.

To Thomas Allen:

Tom, you are in great danger; you are going heedless with the radicals, against the interest of the conservative white population, and I tell you if you do not change your course before the election for the ratification of the infernal constitution, your days are numbered, and they will be but few. Just vote or use your influence for the radicals or for the constitution, and you go up certain. My advice to you, Tom, is to stay at home if you value your life, and not vote at all, and advise all of your race to do the same thing. You are marked and closely watched by K.K.K. (or in plain words Ku-Klux.)

Take heed; a word to the wise is sufficient.

By order of Grand Cyclops.

Question: Where did you get this?
Answer: It was dropped in the shop the morning of the election, when I was running for the legislature. I showed it to a great many men in town; I showed it to Colonel Preston, a friend of mine. He asked where I got it, and I told him. He said, "Tear it up." I said, "No, it may be of service to my children if not to me." He said, "You need not talk so slack about it; there may be heaps of Ku-Klux in the State, and they might get hold of your talk. . . ."
Question: What is the feeling of your people in regard to their personal safety?
Answer: They do not consider that they have any safety at all, only in the cities; that is the truth. In a great many places the colored people call the white people master and mistress, just as they ever did; if they do not do it they are whipped. They have no safety at all except in a large place like this. If I could have stayed at home I would not have been here. I left all my crops and never got anything for them. My wife had no education, and when I came away everything went wrong. There are thousands in my condition.
Question: Is that the reason so many of your people come to the large cities?
Answer: Yes, sir, that is the reason. Mr. Abram Turner, a member of the legislature, from Putnam County, the county adjoining mine, was shot down in the

street in open day. He was a colored man. They have elected another in his place, a democrat.

Question: When was he elected?

Answer: Last fall.

Question: He has been killed since?

Answer: Yes, sir, shot down in broad open day. . . .

Question: Was he a republican?

Answer: Yes sir, I knew him very well; he was a good man, a harmless man; I married him to his wife.

Question: Do the people of your race feel that they have the protection of the laws?

Answer: By no means.

Question: What is their hope and expectation for the future?

Answer: They expect to get protection from the Federal Government at Washington; that is all. You ask any one of my people out there, even the most ignorant of them, and they will tell you so. . . . I believe that many of the jurymen, and lawyers too, are members of the Ku-Klux; I believe it positively; I would say so on my deathbed.

Question: How much have you been over the State?

Answer: I have traveled all over the State.

Question: Have you communicated pretty freely with the people of your own race?

Answer: Yes, sir.

Question: Have you received information from them about the Ku-Klux?

Answer: Yes, sir, occasionally.

Question: In how large a portion of the State do you find reports of Ku-Klux operations?

Answer: I find it in the counties of what is known among us as the Black Belt. Wherever the negroes are in the majority, there the Ku-Klux range more than in any other places. Up in Cobb County they are very peaceable. The democrats are always elected there to the general assembly. The whites have about seven hundred majority. The colored people get along splendidly there. In those counties where the whites are largely in the majority, the colored people get along very well; but go into the counties where the negroes are in the majority, and there is always trouble; for instance, in Monroe County, or Warren County, or anywhere in the Black Belt, there is always trouble between the whites and the colored people.

Question: Are the colored people riotous in disposition? Are they inclined to make trouble?

Answer: I suppose the colored people are as peaceable as any people in the world. The colored people of Madison, when the white people went to the jail and murdered a man there, could have burned up the town and killed all the white people there.

Introduction to Document 4

Congressman Job E. Stevenson from Ohio delivered the following address in the House of Representatives on May 30, 1872. He argued that the Klan was not merely a brutal organization devoted to terror, but part of a political conspiracy to overthrow Reconstruction and reenslave African Americans. As you read the excerpts from this speech, note Stevenson's characterization of the newly conquered South. Why did he believe that the North must stop the Klan? What were his political motivations for opposing the Klan?

DOCUMENT 4 *Speech to the House of Representatives*

Hon. Job E. Stevenson of Ohio

Mr. Speaker: The gravest question before Congress is the Kuklux Conspiracy, its origin and extent, character and actions, plans and purposes, condition and prospects.

Origin

It originated in hostility to the Government, in enmity against the Union. It is the successor of the southern confederacy, rebellion in disguise, war at midnight. It rose like an exhalation from the unsodden grave of the "lost cause." . . .

A Political Conspiracy

Such being the origin . . . of this great conspiracy, we may well inquire against whom its terrors are aimed. It strikes exclusively at the Unionists of the South, principally at the freedmen. No man can deny that it is political. The oath swears the member to oppose Radicalism, to oppose the Radical party, to oppose the political equality of the races.

General Forrest said: "It is a protective political military organization. Its objects originally were protection against Loyal Leagues and the Grand Army of the Republic; but after it became general, it was found that political matters and interests could best be promoted within it, and it was then made a political organization, giving its support, of course, to the Democratic party." . . .

It appears that in the States of Georgia, Louisiana, Tennessee, and South Carolina from the spring election in 1868 to the election for President in 1868, the Republican vote was reduced eighty-five thousand by intimidation and violence.

Commanders

The forces of the conspiracy are controlled by such men as Generals Gordon, Hampton, and Forrest, and under them by inferior officers, running down from grade to grade, to captains of companies, or chiefs of klans or cyclops of dens. The organization begins at the den and extends to the precinct, the county, the congressional district, the State, the South. It is compact, connected, consistent, moving as a perfect body from the head to the humblest member, as an army in the field, with sterner discipline than that of an army. . . .

Authority

These commands bind the members by an oath enforced by fear; administered with strange ceremonies, emphasized by penalty of death. At midnight the member is led blindfold to the den, and there, on his knees, hears the ritual and takes the oath. And as the bandage drops from his eyes he sees circles of men in frightful disguises armed with revolvers leveled on his head, and the Grand Cyclops says: "And this you do under penalty of a traitor's doom, which is death! death! death!" In some dens there are symbols of horror. In one in North Carolina, two skulls, one of a white man, a Union soldier, whose grave was rifled and his skull taken for the den; and the other the skull of a freedman, who had been murdered; and a vial of blood of the colored victim; the member is sworn "by these skulls and this blood."

Thus members are sworn to obey their superior officers on penalty of death, and under that oath they are compelled to take the field at the command and to do any deed he may order, even to murder. Scores of members have confessed and testified that they have committed outrages and murders at the command of their officers.

Outrages

The outrages vary from threats and intimidations to scourging, wounding, maiming, and killing by shooting, drowning, hanging, and burning. If we could know the whole truth it would appear that since the war this conspiracy has outraged more than thirty thousand men, women, and children—peaceful, innocent, defenseless citizens of the Republic. . . .

Excuses

Among the excuses made by those who control and defend this organization is that they feared the negroes; yet all Southern men of intelligence testify that the negroes of the South have behaved better than any other people ever did under similar circumstances. . . . They pretend that the Government of the United States has oppressed them, yet that Government, to which they had forfeited property, liberty, and life, spared their lives, allowed them their liberty, and returned them their property. No confiscated estates are withheld from their owners; although some abandoned property was taken, the only rebel estate remaining in the hands of the Government is Arlington [Robert E. Lee's estate], and gentlemen in both Houses of Congress propose to remove the remains of our soldiers and give that cemetery back to its rebel owners. No life has been taken for treason. Jefferson Davis is as free as the air, a citizen of the Republic. Few political privileges are denied, few leaders are unamnestied. The only issue that can be made on amnesty is whether the remnant should be forthwith relieved. The difference between parties on this question is whether the Republican party has been derelict in not restoring to political power even Jefferson Davis. . . .

Financial Results of Reconstruction

What has been the financial result of reconstruction? The Government and the peoples of the North forgave to the people of the South and caused them to repudiate debts amounting to more than twenty-five hundred million dollars. We relieved them by constitutional amendments, and by the generosity of our people, of debts nearly double the property their own crimes had left. If the Government and the people of the North had merely withheld their hands from the South, and left the conquered rebels to their own financial devices, the South would have sunk in bankruptcy and ruin as a man thrown into the sea with a millstone at his neck. The Government and people of the North rescued them, fed them, advanced money and property, restored peace and order, and gave them the opportunity to revive their fortunes.

The white people of the South continually upbraid the colored people, saying, "The negro will not work." Yet wherever you go you see scores of white men lounging on the piazzas of the hotels, shifting their chairs to keep out of the sun, moving only to get "refreshments," while freedmen are laboring in the fields earning money to enable the whites to lounge. The laborers of the South have produced in cotton and other agricultural products since the war nearly $4,000,000,000, more than double the value of property in 1865. And the people have saved so much of these gains, that they had in 1870 $2,700,000,000 against $1,600,000,000 at the end of the war, having increased their property since the war over $1,000,000,000. And they had in 1870, $6,000,000 more than their State assessments in 1860, excluding slaves. That is the financial result of reconstruction.

Financial Effects of Kuklux

They have not yet ceased reckless destruction of their own property. The Kuklux conspiracy is fatal to values. It disturbs business, disorganizes labor, paralyzes industry and commerce. The documents show the fall of property in those States where the conspiracy has been acting by the millions. . . . The Kuklux conspiracy has cost the South more than all the carpet-baggers of all the States (including the Louisiana leader of the new movement), have been able to misappropriate.

Depopulation

The conspiracy is driving away the people. Here is a copy of the *Freedmen's Repository*, giving an account of the emigration from this country to Liberia, showing that last fall a ship took out of the country from Virginia one passenger; from Florida, five; from North Carolina, five; from Georgia, sixty-six; and from Clay Hill, York county, South Carolina, one hundred and sixty-six. And at the head of this South Carolina party was Rev. Elias Hill, a description of whom is given here, a Baptist preacher, a cripple, whom the Kuklux scourged because he preached the gospel, taught school, and belonged to the Republican party. He was driven with a colony of one hundred and sixty-six souls out of South Carolina, out of the United States of America, even to Liberia.

Here were two hundred and thirty-eight industrious people driven at once from the United States to Africa.

Before the war these colored people—men, women, and children—were valued by their owners at $500 each. Now they are driven out of the country by outrage, scourging, and murder; and we are told that the United States Government must not interfere to protect them. Imagine Elias Hill in the wilds of Africa, telling the bushmen how the great American Republic protects its citizens.

Present Condition of the Conspiracy

But, Mr. Speaker, what is the present condition of this organization? . . .

Those who imagine that because the conspirators are now still, they will remain so, do not understand them. In South Carolina the members of this organization raided in 1868, outraged and murdered Union people, and changed votes by scores of thousands. From that time until 1870 they were quiet, and then they raided again until more than three thousand outrages were committed in less than six months. The conspiracy is so organized that it may remain quiescent for a year or for two years, ready to be called into the field by the blast of the bugle, or by the click of the telegraph. Within one week this "military political" organization could throw into action a quarter of a million men, armed with the revolver, the bowie-knife, . . . with bayonets captured from State militia, and revolving rifles furnished from New York city.

Its Power

Shall we trust them? Are we blind—blind to the red rivers of blood they have shed; deaf to the cries of their thousands of victims? Are we mad to forget our own interests and safety? These conspirators have power, if they dare—and they are men who have dared death at the cannon's mouth—to sweep the whole South at the next presidential election; and if the result depends on the South, they can seat their candidate in the presidential chair . . . *Whoever shall be the Democratic candidate will be the candidate of the Kuklux conspiracy. If the Democrats elect the next President it will be by Kuklux votes and violence; and the man thus elected will be the Kuklux President.*

Introduction to Document 5

Benjamin Bryant's *Experience of a Northern Man Among the Ku-Klux* argues that, while the South had been defeated, the region's way of life remained stubbornly unchanged. Bryant began with the problem of education, stating that the southern aristocracy kept both African Americans and poor whites in ignorance. The Klan had arisen to maintain this situation. Keeping the masses poor and ignorant, according to Bryant, was the Klan's main goal. Document 5 contains excerpts from Bryant's preface and book.

DOCUMENT 5   *From* Experience of a Northern Man Among the Ku-Klux

---

Benjamin Bryant

In order to better inform my readers of my intention for writing a book, I will say before entering into the main body of the work, that I have just returned from a long visit in the South, and have witnessed things which have occurred in the States late in Rebellion, and have kept a record of all, for the interest of the Northern people, and also, to give in detail the present situation of the people who are living there. . . .

As education is the great aim of every true American citizen, I will first inform you of its progress. The South has not had the advantages to aid in the development of education like the people of the North; but it has always been discouraged by the aristocracy of the South; and in so doing they have deprived the poor white people of education and other intelligences, as well as the black man. . . .

A great many freedmen are working on shares with their former masters, and are generally doing well, but are working for one-half, one-third, or one-fourth of their former pay, and are working under their master's hand, calling their former masters, "master," and denouncing the Proclamation of Emancipation. They hate that "old Northern woman" who is teaching the "nigger school," and resist all aid to free schools, and say, "I can live without education; I don't want it and will not have it."

"You are a good negro, and you may live on my land all your life-time."

That black man will work there for some time, and make one or two bales of cotton and give it to his master, as he calls him, to sell; and he will sell it and bring Tom, the good and smart negro, what he has a mind to.

Well, some day Tom will walk by the school-house and have a word or two with the teacher. Tom will tell him about his cotton. The teacher will say, "How much cotton did you have?"

"So much."

"How much money did you get?"

Tom says, "I got fifty dollars."

The school teacher will say, "Is that all? You should have more than that."

"How much more?"

"You should have twenty-five dollars more."

Tom says, "I am going to see him." . . .

[Tom's former master asked who told him he deserved more money.]

"The school teacher told me so."

"Who, that damn'd Yankee?"

"Yes sir."

"He told you that you could get more pay if you should go North, did he?"

"Yes sir. He told John, that black boy that lives with Mr. Brown, that he was free and should go to school. Yes, master, he told all the colored people to send their children and let them learn something." . . .

"Where is he from?"

"Massachusetts."

"We will fix him," says Tom's master. "Hitch up my horse; I am going away."

He will then go to the fork of the roads and tell everybody about what the damn'd Yankee school teacher told his niggers. If he stays here long he will have every nigger in the place think that he is as good as a white man. Well, we must run him away. Send him word to leave by Monday. If not, we will fix him.

Monday has come—Tuesday has come. The nigger-school teacher has not gone yet. We must get together. (This is not talked in the presence of Tom, but Tom is in the next room and hears it all.)

"Tom, you go and tell Mr. Brown and Mr. Bond to come here, and on your way back go round by the Pugh Place and tell Mr. Pollock to come, too, and bring every one that he can."

They will all meet and talk the matter over, and agree to meet on Wednesday night at 10 o'clock, all dressed in uniform, ready to commence their secret midnight demonstration. They went to his house and took him out, and tied a large rope round his neck, and he was seen down on his knees praying. But the party who saw him was a colored man (in the woods), and he says that he could go to the spot where he was hung with his feet up, tied to the branch of an oak tree, and a log of wood round his neck, and his tongue from five to seven inches out of his mouth. This punishment will be applied to that class of Northern people who will go South and settle, and have not received full information how to act. You know it is an old saying, and a good one too, when you are in Rome, act as a Roman, and when you are in the South, you must act as a Southern man. What are these actions? First, I will say, you must act with the majority, let their actions be good or bad. You must denounce all free schools for white or black children. You must not come South and pay more for labor than the established price, which is all the way from five to ten dollars per month, but an extra good hand, who has always been farming, may in some cases get from fifteen to sixteen dollars per month. Never give a black man, or a poor white man who cannot read, any advice to post themselves upon matters pertaining to their own welfare. Never speak a good word for New England, because her States demand human rights before the law, for all men. Never say anything about Bunker Hill, because that is in Massachusetts. Never express your political opinion, let it be Republican or Democratic, for we know that both parties wanted to maintain the Union. And, above all, you must hate niggers. There has been many a good enterprising Northern man driven from the newly established homestead because he did not know the existing circumstances. This organization, known as the "Invisible Empire," or Ku-Klux, does exist in the Southern States. There is a number of Northern people in both of the political parties that have manifested a strong unbelief in regard to the Ku-Klux Klans, but I will say a word on a verified fact, and truth, which is today being witnessed by every peace-loving and upright citizen.

Introduction to Document 6

In *The Grand Army of the Republic Versus the Ku Klux Klan*, W. H. Gannon proposed that 100,000 former soldiers be allowed to colonize the South. These men would be given land and money, and, presumably, their example would show southerners the value of Northern industriousness and the free-labor system. Such a plan would also help alleviate the unemployment caused by swings of the business cycle. The following excerpts are taken from the chapter "How to Extirpate Ku-Kluxism from the South" in Gannon's book.

📜 DOCUMENT 6 *"How to Extirpate Ku-Kluxism From the South"*

W. H. Gannon

. . . In view of the fact, that the present phase of the difficulty between the North and the South has already continued for eight long and dreary years, whereas half that time sufficed in which to annihilate the whole of rebel armies, the conclusion is inevitable that the Northern People are making some very serious mistake in conducting their case in its present form; and consequently, that they must make some radical change in their Southern policy, before they can hope to gain their cause at the South. . . .

(1.) That the fatal mistake of the Northern People in their Southern policy since the dispersion of the rebel armies, has been their reliance upon United States Marshals and United States soldiers, almost exclusively, to represent them at the South; (2.) that their true course to pursue towards the South is to colonize it with at least One Hundred Thousand (100,000) intelligent, respectable, and industrious Northern Working Men; (3.) that, inasmuch as the Federal Government found no very great difficulty, any time during the late war, in inducing a million of Northern men to exchange the security, peace, and enjoyment of their homes for the dangers and privations of prolonged active warfare in the face of a determined and powerful enemy at the South and to remain there year after year, until the overthrow of their antagonists left them free to return to their homes,—there are 100,000 of those same men who would gladly return South now with the implements of peace in their hands, to make their homes there, provided they had the means to enable them to do so; (4.) that One Thousand (1000) Dollars per man would be all sufficient to establish them comfortably there; (5.) that the required funds would readily enough be forthcoming, were the proper parties to ask the public for them; and (6.) that the proper parties to collect the required funds, and to select the proposed colonists, and superintend the suggested undertaking, generally, are the GRAND ARMY OF THE REPUBLIC, and the various WORKING MEN'S SOCIETIES throughout the North. . . .

All purely patriotic considerations aside, the success of this plan would, in a mere speculative and economic point of view, prove highly beneficial to the industrial and business interests of the North. Its operations, if extended to anything like National proportions, would necessarily open a vast field for utilizing the immense mass of well disposed and intelligent, but adventurous young energy now wandering aimless about the North; they would provide acceptable and remunerative employment, at the South, for multitudes of Northern working people who find it impossible to secure the means of a decent support for themselves and their families in their present abodes. For, while individual Northern enterprise in that direction is not just now advisable, yet throughout the whole civilized world, there is not another so favorable an opening for co-operative Northern enterprise, if it be united, systematic, and of a legitimate character, as the South, in its present condition, offers to it. Every associated enterprise, such as this plan suggests, if judiciously located and properly managed for developing the natural resources of the South, instead of (as some have done) plunging into mad attempts at competition with great Northern industries, would handsomely compensate the laborer for his work, besides, after the first year, paying cent-per-cent, per annum on every dollar of capital invested in it. Once settled at the South, the colonist, amidst congenial social surroundings that this plan would secure to him, could not, with a tithe of the industry, fail to secure an ample competency for themselves and their dependents, without that incessant toil which, for even a scanty and precarious support, the North exacts from every person who depends solely upon manual labor, for their livelihood within its great centers of population. Thus they would materially benefit themselves in all the relations of life, and, at the same time, leave a freer field to, and open a new market for, the industry of those of their fraternity who are established at the North. It would, also, give a new and lasting impetus to legitimate business of all kinds throughout the whole country. Therefore, leaving Southern interests and political considerations out of the question altogether, this plan deserves the serious attention of the Working men and the Business men of the North.

QUESTIONS

Defining Terms

Identify in the context of the chapter each of the following:

racism

redeemers

sharecroppers

Job Stevenson

miscegenation

Reconstruction

carpetbaggers and scalawags

Knights of the White Camelia

Benjamin Bryant

Liberia

Probing the Sources

1. Who were the victims of Klan violence? Why were whites sometimes attacked by the Klan in addition to African Americans?

2. Under what political circumstances did the Klan arise?

3. What were its stated goals? What were its goals as you can infer them by its members' actions?

4. How did northerners characterize southerners? How did southerners characterize northerners?

Intrepreting the Sources

1. Who opposed the Klan and why? Was the Ku Klux Klan a political organization? A terrorist organization?

2. Did the Klan's racist ideology fulfill goals beyond the simple expression of irrational hatred?

3. Did opponents of the Klan want to stop racism, or did they have an additional agenda?

4. Was the Klan successful? Why or why not?

ADDITIONAL READING

On the Ku Klux Klan, see Allen Trelease, *White Terror: The Ku Klux Klan Conspiracy and Southern Reconstruction* (1971), and David Mark Chalmers, *Hooded Americanism: The History of the Ku Klux Klan* (1981). For various interpretations of Reconstruction, see John Hope Franklin, *Reconstruction After the Civil War* (1961); Kenneth M. Stampp, *The Era of Reconstruction, 1865–1877* (1965); and Eric Foner, *Reconstruction: America's Unfinished Revolution, 1863–1877* (1988). On

African Americans during Emancipation, see W. E. B. DuBois, *Black Reconstruction* (1935); and Leon F. Litwack, *Been in the Storm So Long: The Aftermath of Slavery* (1979). For the era's legacy, see Jay R. Mandle, *Not Slave, Not Free: The African American Economic Experience Since the Civil War* (1992). On the reborn Klan of the 1920s, see Leonard Moore, *Citizen Klansmen* (1992) and Nancy MacLain, *Behind the Mask of Chivalry; The Making of the Second Ku Klux Klan* (1994).

Credits

Page xv: Poem originally published in the *Troy* (New York) *Sentinel*, December 23, 1823.

Page xx: All of the documents about the duel are reprinted from Harold Coffin Syrett and Jean G. Cooke, eds., *Interview in Weehawken: The Burr-Hamilton Duel As Told in the Original Documents.* © Wesleyan University Press, 1960. Reprinted by permission of Wesleyan University Press.

Page 6: Abridged from *The Diario of Christopher Columbus's First Voyage to America, 1492–1493,* trans. by Oliver Dunn and James E. Kelley, Jr., copyright © 1989 by Oliver Dunn and James E. Kelley, Jr. Published by The University of Oklahoma Press.

Page 11: Excerpted from *The Destruction of the Indies: A Brief Account,* by Bartolomé de Las Casas, trans. by Herma Briffault, Johns Hopkins University Press, 1992, pp. 27–43. English translation copyright © 1976.

Page 15: From Miguel Leon-Portilla, ed., *The Broken Spears: The Aztec Account of the Conquest of Mexico,* Beacon Press, 1962, pp. 63–68, 71–76, and 137–138. Reprinted by permission of the publisher. Copyright © 1962, 1990 by Beacon Press.

Page 26: Modernized from the original reprinted in *The First Colonists,* ed. by David B. Quinn and Alison M. Quinn, North Carolina Department of Cultural Resources, 1982, pp. 1–12.

Page 28: Modernized from the original reprinted in *The First Colonists,* ed. by David B. Quinn and Alison M. Quinn, North Carolina Department of Cultural Resources, 1982, pp. 46–76.

Page 29: Modernized from the original reprinted in *The First Colonists,* ed. by David B. Quinn and Alison M. Quinn, North Carolina Department of Cultural Resources, 1982, pp. 119–130.

Page 30: Modernized from the original reprinted in Philip L. Barbour, ed., *The Jamestown Voyages Under the First Charter, 1606–1609,* Vol. 1 (New York: Cambridge University Press, 1969), pp. 129–146.

Page 32: Modernized from the original reprinted in Philip L. Barbour, ed., *The Complete Works of Captain John Smith,* Vol. II (Chapel Hill: University of North Carolina Press, 1986), pp. 231–234.

Page 33: Modernized from the original reprinted in Philip L. Barbour, ed., *The Complete Works of Captain John Smith,* Vol. II (Chapel Hill: University of North Carolina Press, 1986).

Page 34: Caption John Smith, *A Map of Virginia with a Description of the Country.* Oxford, England: Joseph Barnes, 1612.

Page 34: Reprinted from Peter Force, ed., *Tracts and Other Papers Relating Principally to the Colonies in North America,* Vol. 1 (Washington, D.C., 1836–1844), pp. 11–17.

Page 103: John Wesley, A Serman Preached at St. Matthew's, Bethnal Green, on Sunday, November 12, 1775.

Page 105: Lord Dunmore's proclamation.

Page 107: Reprinted with permission of the publisher from L. H. Butterfield (ed.), *The Adams Papers: Adams Family Correspondence, Volumes I and II,* (Cambridge, MA: The Belknap Press of Harvard University Press, 1963). Copyright © 1963 by the Massachusetts Historical Society.

Page 112: Reprinted from Thomas Jefferson, *Notes on the State of Virginia (1787),* edited with an introduction and notes by William Peden. Copyright © 1955 by the University of North Carolina Press, renewed 1982 by William Peden. Used by permission of the publisher.

Page 113: Reprinted from Silvio A. Bedini, ed., *The Life of Benjamin Banneker* (New York, 1984), pp. 152–159.

Page 137: From *Extracts of Letters Containing Some Account of the Work of God Since 1800* (New York, 1805).

Page 138: From *Extracts of Letters Containing Some Account of the Work of God Since 1800* (New York, 1805).

Page 139: From "A Short History of Barton W. Stone Written by Himself." In Rhodes Thompson, ed., *Voices from Cane Ridge* (St. Louis: Bethany Press, 1954), p. 68.

Page 140: From Martin J. Spalding, *Sketches of the Early Catholic Missions of Kentucky* (1844).

Page 141: From the *Wesleyan Repository* (Philadelphia: William Smith Stockton, 1820), pp. 138–143.

Page 143: From *An Apology for Camp Meetings* (1820).

Page 151: Excerpted from *The Trial Record of Denmark Vesey* (Boston: Beacon Press, 1970), pp. 41–79, 135–137.

Page 156: Reprinted from Robert S. Starobin, ed., *Denmark Vesey, The Slave Conspiracy of 1822* (Englewood Cliffs, NJ: Prentice-Hall, 1970), pp. 72–74.

Page 158: Reprinted from Robert S. Starobin, ed., *Denmark Vesey, The Slave Conspiracy of 1822* (Englewood Cliffs, NJ: Prentice-Hall, 1970), pp. 74–79.

Page 159: Robert S. Starobin, ed., *Denmark Vesey, The Slave Conspiracy of 1822* (Englewood Cliffs, NJ: Prentice-Hall, 1970), pp. 87–89.

Page 162: "An Appeal to the Colored People of the World" by David Walker, anti-slavery pamphlet, published 1829.

Page 171: Excerpted from José María Sánchez, "A Trip to Texas in 1828," trans. Carlos E. Castañeda, *Southwestern Historical Quarterly,* Vol. 29, no. 4 (April 1926), pp. 270–271, 273–274, 281. Reprinted by permission of the Texas State Historical Association.

Page 172: Excerpted from "Mier y Terán to Guadeloupe Victoria, Nacogdoches, June 30, 1828." In Alaine Howren, "Causes and Origins of the Decree of April 6, 1830," *Southwestern Historical Quarterly,* Vol. 16, no. 4 (April 1913), pp. 395–398. Also from "Mier y Terán to Minister of War, Pueblo Viejo, November 13, 1829." In Ohland Morton, *Terán and Texas: A Chapter in Texas-Mexican Relations* (Austin, 1948), pp. 99–101. Reprinted by permission of the Texas State Historical Association.

Page 173: From *The Telegraph and Texas Register* (San Felipe de Austin), January 23, 1836, pp. 102–103.

Page 174: Reprinted from John H. Jenkins, ed., *Papers of the Texas Revolution* (Austin, TX: Presidal Press, 1973), Vol. 4, pp. 29–30.

Page 175: Reprinted from John H. Jenkins, ed., *Papers of the Texas Revolution* (Austin, TX: Presidal Press, 1973), Vol. 4, pp. 75–76.

Page 176: Reprinted from John H. Jenkins, ed., *Papers of the Texas Revolution* (Austin, TX: Presidal Press, 1973), Vol. 4, pp. 327–328.

Page 176: Reprinted from John H. Jenkins, ed., *Papers of the Texas Revolution* (Austin, TX: Presidal Press, 1973), Vol. 4, pp. 373–374.

Page 177: Reprinted from John H. Jenkins, ed., *Papers of the Texas Revolution* (Austin, TX: Presidal Press, 1973), Vol. 4, p. 423.

Page 177: Reprinted from John H. Jenkins, ed., *Papers of the Texas Revolution* (Austin, TX: Presidal Press, 1973), Vol. 4, pp. 433–434.

Page 178: Reprinted from John H. Jenkins, ed., *Papers of the Texas Revolution* (Austin, TX: Presidal Press, 1973), Vol. 4, pp. 494–496.

Page 179: Reprinted from John H. Jenkins, ed., *Papers of the Texas Revolution* (Austin, TX: Presidal Press, 1973), Vol. 4, p. 501.

Page 179: Reprinted from John H. Jenkins, ed., *Papers of the Texas Revolution* (Austin, TX: Presidal Press, 1973), Vol. 4, p. 501.

Page 179: Reprinted from John H. Jenkins, ed., *Papers of the Texas Revolution* (Austin, TX: Presidal Press, 1973), Vol. 4, pp. 504–505.

Page 180: Reprinted from John H. Jenkins, ed., *Papers of the Texas Revolution* (Austin, TX: Presidal Press, 1973), Vol. 4, pp. 518–519.

Page 180: Reprinted from John H. Jenkins, ed., *Papers of the Texas Revolution* (Austin, TX: Presidal Press, 1973), Vol. 5, pp. 11–12.

Page 180: Reprinted from John H. Jenkins, ed., *Papers of the Texas Revolution* (Austin, TX: Presidal Press, 1973), Vol. 5, pp. 20–21.

Page 181: Reprinted from John H. Jenkins, ed., *Papers of the Texas Revolution* (Austin, TX: Presidal Press, 1973), Vol. 5, pp. 71–72.

Page 181: Reprinted from John H. Jenkins, ed., *Papers of the Texas Revolution* (Austin, TX: Presidal Press, 1973), Vol. 5, pp. 80–82.

Page 182: From José Enrique de la Peña, *With Santa Anna in Texas,* trans. by Carmen Perry (College Station, TX, 1975), pp. 44–57.

Page 184: Reprinted from John H. Jenkins, ed., *Papers of the Texas Revolution* (Austin, TX: Presidal Press, 1973), Vol. 5, pp. 226–228.

Page 185: Translation by Timothy Gilfoyle and E. Gorn, from John H. Jenkins, ed., *Papers of the Texas Revolution* (Austin, TX: Presidal Press, 1973), Vol. 6, p. 173.

Page 185: Reprinted from John H. Jenkins, ed., *Papers of the Texas Revolution* (Austin, TX: Presidal Press, 1973), Vol. 6, pp. 10–14.

Page 186: Reprinted from John H. Jenkins, ed., *Papers of the Texas Revolution* (Austin, TX: Presidal Press, 1973), Vol. 6, pp. 213–220.

Page 187: Excerpted from David J. Weber, ed., *Foreigners in Their Native Land* (Albuquerque, NM: University of NM Press, 1973), pp. 114–116.

Page 188: Reprinted from Jesus F. de la Teja, ed., *A Revolution Remembered: The Memoirs and Selected Correspondence of Juan N. Seguin* (Austin, TX: State House Press, 1991), p. 156.

Page 195: Excerpted from A. J. Graves, *Women in America: Being an Examination into the Moral and Intellectual Condition of American Female Society* (New York: Harper and Brothers, 1843), pp. 155–164.

Page 196: Excerpted from Catharine Beecher, *Treatise on Domestic Economy for Young Ladies at Home and at School* (New York: Harper and Brothers, 1847), pp. 25–43.

Page 198: Excerpted from Sarah M. Grimké, *Letters on the Equality of the Sexes and the Condition of Women* (Boston: Isaac Knapp, 1838), pp. 46–55.

Page 201: Excerpted from Harriet Jacobs, *Incidents in the Life of a Slave Girl* (Boston, 1861), pp. 44–87.

Page 204: From E. C. Stanton, S. B. Anthony, and M. J. Gage, *The History of Woman Suffrage* (Salem, NH: Ayer, 1969), Vol. 1; reprint of 1922 edition.

Page 206: Excerpted from Lucy Larcom, *A New England Girlhood* (New York: Corinth Books, 1961), pp. 145–156.

Page 209: Reprinted from Thomas Dublin, ed., *Farm to Factory: Women's Letters, 1830–1860* (New York: Columbia University Press, 1981), pp. 74–108. Copyright © 1993 by Columbia University Press. Reprinted by permission of the publisher.

Page 216: From George Fitzhugh, *Cannibals All! or Slaves Without Masters* (Richmond, VA, 1857).

Page 219: From Hinton Rowan Helper, *The Impending Crisis of the South* (New York, 1857).

Page 222: From John G. Nicolay and John Hay, ed., *Complete Works of Abraham Lincoln* (New York: The Tandy-Thomas Company, 1894), Vol. III, pp. 215–216, 229–230, 304–306; Vol. IV, pp. 89–91, 254–257; Vol. V, pp. 60–65.

Page 225: From Harriet Beecher Stowe, *Uncle Tom's Cabin; or Life Among the Lowly* (Cleveland, 1852), pp. 494–500.

Page 227: From *The Liberator*, September 22, 1848.

Page 236: From U.S. *Statutes at Large*, XII, pp. 731–737.

Page 237: From *Harper's Magazine*, January 1867.

Page 244: From Allan Nevins and Milton Halsey, ed., *The Diary of George Templeton Strong* (New York: Macmillan, 1952), Vol. 3, pp. 332–343.

Page 248: From the *New York Times*, July 15, 1863.

Page 250: From the *New York Times*, July 15, 1863.

Page 256: Reprinted from Walter L. Fleming, ed., *The Constitution and the Ritual of the Knights of the White Camelia* (Morgantown: West Virginia University, 1904), pp. 21–29.

Page 258: Excerpted from George Rawick, ed., *The American Slave: A Composite Autobiography* (Westport, CT: The Greenwood Press, 1977, 1979), Supp. I, Vol. 5, p. 426; Supp. 2, Vol. 4, Part 3, p. 957; Supp. 2, Vol. 5, Part 4, pp. 1648–1649. Reprinted with the permission of the publisher.

Page 259: *Testimony Taken by the Joint Select Committee to Inquire into the Condition of Affairs in the Late Insurrectionary States* (Washington, DC: U.S. Government Printing Office, 1872), Vol. 6, pp. 545–546; Vol. 7, pp. 607–611.

Page 264: Excerpted from the *Congressional Record*, May 30, 1872, pp. 1–7.

Page 267: From Benjamin Bryant, *Experience of a Northern Man Among the Ku-Klux, or The Condition of the South* (Hartford, CT, 1872).

Page 269: From W. H. Gannon, *The Grand Army of the Republic Versus the Ku Klux Klan* (Boston: W. F. Brown & Company, 1872).

Index